Yale Historical Publications

The Rise of the Penitentiary

Prisons and Punishment in Early America

Adam Jay Hirsch

Yale University Press   New Haven and London

Published under the direction of the
Department of History of Yale University with
assistance from the income of the Frederick
John Kingsbury Memorial Fund.

Designed by Sonia Scanlon.
Set in Cheltenham type by Tseng
Information Systems, Inc., Durham, North Carolina.
Printed in the United States of America by
BookCrafters, Inc., Chelsea, Michigan.

Library of Congress
Cataloging-in-Publication Data
Hirsch, Adam Jay.
The rise of the penitentiary : prisons and
punishment in early America /
Adam Jay Hirsch.
p.   cm. — (Yale historical publications)
Includes bibliographical references
(p.   ) and index.
ISBN 0-300-04297-3 (alk. paper)
1. Corrections—United States—History.
2. Corrections—Massachusetts—History.
3. Prisons—United States—History.
4. Prisons—Massachusetts—History.
I. Title.   II. Series.
HV9304.H57   1992
365'.974—dc20   91-37294
CIP

The paper in this book meets the guidelines
for permanence and durability of the Committee
on Production Guidelines for Book Longevity
of the Council on Library Resources.

10 9 8 7 6 5 4 3 2 1

For My Parents

God dwells in the details.
Mies van der Rohe

Contents

Acknowledgments

Many institutions and colleagues offered assistance in the course of this project, and it is a pleasure (at long last) to express properly my gratitude. Stanton Wheeler did nothing less than propose the study and, once begun, generously arranged for research support out of an LEAA grant to the Yale Law School. Summer research leaves awarded by Florida State University College of Law provided the priceless free time necessary to complete the project.

I wish also to thank the staffs of a number of research libraries for their quiet competence and unfailing good humor. Without the help of the librarians of the Massachusetts State Archives, this project would not have been possible in its present form. Valuable assistance was also offered by librarians at the Massachusetts State Library, the Massachusetts Historical Society, the University Library of Cambridge University, the British Library, the University of Texas Law Library, and the Max Planck Institute for Criminal Law and Criminology. I wish in particular to thank the staffs of the Yale Law School Library and the Florida State University College of Law Library for their efforts to track down and make available even the most obscure sources. Their labors on my behalf are amply documented in the notes.

This book has benefited much from the criticism of others. Drafts of several chapters have been read at meetings of the American Society for Legal History, the American Culture Association, and at Legal History Workshops held at the Yale Law School and the Stanford Law School. I am grateful to the auditors at each of these symposia for their many thoughtful comments. A number of friends also took the trouble to review portions of the manuscript and to suggest source materials. I wish in particular to thank Edward Ayers, John Baker, John Beattie, David Brion Davis, David Flaherty, Eric Freedman, Douglas Hay, Michael Ignatieff, Joanna Innes, Linda Keeley, William E. Nelson, and Jeff Powell for the gift of their knowledge and insight. Three other scholars offered a different sort of gift. Jonathan Clark, Robert Cover, and Arthur Leff were the kind of teachers whose lessons last a lifetime. They possessed that rare and precious talent, the capacity to inspire.

Others assisted in a variety of ways. Trish Billard kept after me to complete the project (in a helpful way) when I had begun to weary of it. Jennifer Beckett made the task easier by helping to re-edit the notes. Beverly Perkins and James Wangle typed up the final manuscript. My editors at Yale University Press, Laura Jones Dooley and Charles Grench, offered the sort of wisdom and support that one can only wish for in a publisher.

My greatest scholarly debt is owed to my mentors, Barbara A. Black and Edmund S. Morgan. I do believe they will see themselves reflected in this work. If any portion of it is creditable, full credit belongs to them. The discreditable remainder is, alas, my responsibility entirely.

Introduction

Today most Americans accept the penitentiary as a given. Imprisonment is the routine sanction for serious crime in our system of justice— seemingly as elemental and inevitable a part of criminal process as police arrest, state prosecution, and judgment by one's peers. Punishments by their nature are meted out in years and months (when not dollars and cents). To be a "convict" is to be a person "serving time" in a prison cell for the commission of a crime.

Yet the frozen landscape of the criminal justice system, when glimpsed in the light of history, melts quickly; conceptual continents drift, oceans of doctrine ebb and flow. The wholesale incarceration of criminals is in truth a comparatively recent episode in the history of Anglo-American jurisprudence. Before the nineteenth century, offenders faced a variety of sanctions, including the pillory, the lash, the gallows, and exile. Though not unknown, "the sentence of confinement" was a rarity.[1] Thieves in early Massachusetts served their victims, not time. "Convicts" literally were persons found guilty of any offense, not persons serving prison sentences.[2]

To be sure, state action to confine citizens did not originate in modern times. Prisons have always played a role in Anglo-American jurisprudence. But before the American Revolution, prisons served principally a congeries of non-sanctional functions, some of which remain familiar, others of which have fled the scene.

This book explores the rise of the penitentiary in America. It is a complicated and confusing story, not least because the principal actors in the drama were themselves complicated and confused individuals. It is also a richly textured story that can be fruitfully examined from a variety of angles. Although the problem of punishment is plainly an aspect of legal history, it is no less plainly an aspect of intellectual, social, economic, and institutional history. Historians in recent years have tended increasingly to specialize, offering in-depth studies of their subjects from a single analytical frame of reference. To be sure, such an approach is not without its virtues, for the more we narrow our gaze, the sharper is our view of the details. Yet the risk remains that by so focusing an inquiry, one will miss broader connections between, say, social and intellectual conditions or will oversimplify those parts of the story that lie beyond one's principal paradigm of inquiry. My conscious aim throughout this book has been to apply the tools of several historical subdisciplines to the rise of the penitentiary and thereby to present a rounded picture of its origin and development. When faced with a phenomenon as tangled as criminal incarceration, it may be useful not only to comb but to braid.

A study of this sort poses methodological problems. The attempt to marry diverse lines of investigation does not lend itself to simple linear narrative. Instead, I have arranged this book topically, addressing in turn different substantive aspects of the background and early history of the penitentiary. If a bit untidy, the resulting organizational package functions to pull together diffuse elements of the story.

The more fundamental problem of shaping the research proved equally troublesome. The turn to the penitentiary was a geographically widespread phenomenon, spanning two continents, and sources for study are everywhere copious. Some limitations were necessary, lest the project swell beyond manageable bounds. While I have cast a wide net for published sources, I chose to concentrate my primary investigation on one American state: Massachusetts. In part, this decision reflected the convenience (and sheer pleasure) of archival research in a region long mindful of its place in history. The settlers of Massachusetts and their descendants dutifully squirreled away every scrap of paper. Their relics endure to this day, beautifully preserved.[3]

In part, my emphasis on Massachusetts was also dictated by the contours of prior scholarship. Although the early penitentiaries in New York and Pennsylvania have received book-length coverage, developments in Massachusetts remain relatively obscure.[4] It is often forgotten that Massachusetts stood in the vanguard of the penitentiary movement in America, establishing the first statewide program for criminal incarceration following independence.[5] Though rapidly eclipsed by developments in Pennsylvania and New York, the Massachusetts prison on Castle Island was the first American carceral institution to achieve international celebrity.[6] Of course, no book purporting to investigate American carceral developments can rest its case on evidence drawn from one state alone. But Massachusetts does seem a good place to begin.

A word about terminology may be in order here. It has appeared to me that certain bits of nomenclature used repeatedly in historical discourse about punishment lack the precision necessary to isolate and define relevant ideas. When needed, I have developed my own jargon to clarify sense. At the same time, in at least one instance I have cast aside precision for the sake of convenience. Throughout, I use the term *criminologist* (and *criminology*) to indicate persons who thought and wrote about the problem of crime. The label is anachronistic in the period under discussion, criminology having crystallized into a specialized discipline only late in the nineteenth century. Herein, the term is applied simply as a shorthand for an area of advocacy or involvement, not concentration, and one for which no ready substitute was apparent.

Those who would explore the history of incarceration in America are fortunate to have been preceded by a number of intrepid scholars. For his trailblazing efforts, Professor David J. Rothman in particular deserves a tip of the hat. Rothman's treatise, *The Discovery of the Asylum,* asked the right questions, even if it did not supply all the answers, and his interpretation of events has since spread through much of the literature of American penology. It seems appropriate, therefore, to begin this book by summarizing Rothman's conclusions, as a point of departure for the present study.

Rothman traces the inauguration of criminal incarceration preeminently to a series of intellectual waves that swept across America in the wake of the war for independence. During the colonial era, Rothman maintains, the Calvinist doctrine of original sin forestalled efforts to reduce crime by reforming or even deterring the criminal. Before the Revolution, punishment remained in principle retributive and expiatory—purposes that simply did not call for incarceration on a large scale.[7]

Rothman asserts that independence brought a new ideology and fresh programs. The social optimism of European Enlightenment thought found a receptive audience in the new American republic, steeped as it was in revolutionary activism. Concepts of human perfectibility overpowered the "grim determinism" of Calvinist thought and inspired in Americans an unprecedented resolve to eradicate crime. Criminal incarceration was born not of an effort to maintain crime control but of an intellectually stimulated effort to *enhance* it.[8]

The program American criminologists adopted to accomplish this feat derived from the renowned Italian theorist Cesare Beccaria. Beccaria postulated that the proliferation of crime could be traced to the viciousness and thoughtlessness of criminal codes. If the statutes were reformulated to deter criminals rather than to take revenge against them, Beccaria taught, then galling offenses would not occur in the first place. According to Rothman, Americans first seized upon incarceration as a punishment because it constituted an eminently variable mechanism of deterrence.[9]

By the 1820s, Americans had become disillusioned with the deterrent approach.[10] Beccaria's vaccine had failed to immunize American society against crime. Meanwhile, population growth, urbanization, and nascent industrialization had provoked a general fear for the stability of American society. Still, criminologists had lost none of their determination to put an end to crime. Spurred on by a mix of anxiety and ambition, the Jacksonians tackled the problem anew.[11]

The solution they lighted upon, Rothman contends, was novel—and distinctly American.[12] Taking a hint from the propounders of human perfectibility, the Jacksonians set out to *rehabilitate* criminals, to treat them and then return them to the community as reformed citizens. Distressed by social deterioration, criminologists now identified the root cause of crime to lie in the social environment, rather than in misconceived criminal codes. This identification in turn offered hope, for if the natural environment could lead persons astray, it stood to reason that an artificial environment, set off from the world, could reclaim them. Under the Jacksonians, the prison embarked on a new career as an institutional forum for the isolation and rehabilitation of criminals. Americans' faith in the institution knew no bounds: not only would the penitentiary rid the country of crime, but its carefully structured internal regime would serve as a prototype for the reformulation of American society in its entirety.[13]

Rothman deserves due credit for linking the rise of the penitentiary to happenings in society. Whereas most prior scholars had depicted the development as essentially an adventure in intellectual history, Rothman recognized that the problem also merited study from the perspective of social history.[14] Nonetheless, his account requires significant revision. Weakened, perhaps, by a tendency toward idiosyncrasy, Rothman's analysis is more seriously compromised by a curious compass of research that sweeps in all of the United States yet never strays beyond its bounds. By contrast, a close study of the evidence from Massachusetts, coupled with a survey of other American and European sources, presents a different picture. Specifically, (1) the ideology of incarceration did not go through two distinct stages, the first emphasizing deterrence and the second rehabilitation; (2) the core of that ideology derived neither from eighteenth-century Italy nor from nineteenth-century America but from sixteenth-century England; (3) social forces influenced the first adoption of criminal incarceration, which occurred well before the Jacksonian era; and (4) the Jacksonians were themselves far less starry-eyed, and far more practical-minded, than Rothman allows.

Some scholars have faulted Rothman's attribution of an ideological perspective to "Americans" generally as a more fundamental, analytical distortion. They accuse Rothman of papering over the divergent class interests that surrounded the rise of the penitentiary. *Who* were these American ideologists, one critic has demanded, and *who* stood to benefit from the institutions they promoted with such zeal?[15] Such questions—and the language of class interest in general—find little place in Rothman's work, which refers to the Jacksonians, in the conservative historical tradition, as a basic intellectual unit. Critical historians, addressing the evolution of criminal justice in both North America and Europe, have split the political atom. Trails of subatomic classes and special interest groups scatter across the pages of their scholarship. Critical scholars view the early modern Western states (and, some would add, the regimes that have succeeded them) as subservient to minority interests bent on dominating and oppressing the majority. In critical accounts, the penitentiary arose to advance the fortunes of the ruling elite, helping to entrench their political power, even as the institution served to exploit the labor power of its inmates.[16]

Critical analyses of the motives behind the penitentiary are nothing if not provocative, and they certainly need looking at. I shall explore critical conjectures at various points in this study.[17] Suffice it to say for now that, for all their boldness and vitality, critical historians have failed to make a convincing case that the individuals who advocated and built penitentiaries did so out of narrow class interest. Although all of the institution's active promoters wore the raiments of privilege, they claimed in their writings—including private correspondence, never intended for publication—to represent broader ideals. Ostensibly, the penitentiary aimed at crime control, an outcome that would adhere to the benefit all segments of society, including, incidentally, the criminals themselves.

To reach conclusions to the contrary, critical scholars perforce view the mass of contemporary literary evidence with a skeptical eye. They have tended, implicitly or explicitly, to dismiss much of the pamphlet literature as cant or self-deception; thus unburdened, they are free to postulate motives that never found expression in the historical sources.[18] Yet this modus operandi presents a number of heuristic difficulties. To the extent that critical scholars interpret events by reading between the lines of contemporary tracts, their analyses defy refutation, a quality that divorces them from traditional social science. But even accepted on their own terms, critical theses about the rise of the penitentiary are undermined by the very axiom of their submerged ideological foundation. The power of articulated ideas to win adherents and move persons to act is undoubted. But the impact of unstated, much less subconscious, ambitions on the thoughts and actions of large bodies of theorists and lawmakers is (along with being speculative) bound to be more remote. If not quite oxymoronic, the notion of a "hidden agenda" does seem a precarious means of historical interpretation.[19]

To lend plausibility to their analyses, critical historians often point to the persistence of the penitentiary, in spite of its persistent failure to control crime effectively. This (sinister) inertia suggests to critical historians that the penitentiary must have served interests other than those that had been openly avowed.[20] But this conclusion is hardly inescapable: legal institutions have always tended to outlive their usefulness, sometimes by centuries. In their own day, opponents of the older public punishments complained volubly about the difficulties they encountered when attempting to shake off settled practices. Having succeeded in initiating carceral punishment, advocates did not grow silent when faced with its inadequacies. They betrayed no hint of satisfaction with the status quo. On the contrary, advocates conceded institutional setbacks, and they strove mightily to cure systemic defects as best they could. If their efforts failed, it was not for want of trying. That the institution continued to hobble along speaks more to the advocates' hopefulness (or helplessness) than to their duplicity, for they gave every indication of seeking to make the penitentiary function precisely as they claimed it was intended to do. A fundamental premise of this book is that the writings of the advocates should be taken seriously, as an accurate reflection of their ideas and ideals. I shall devote many pages to the presentation and analysis of carceral ideology.

Legal historians have long been wont to preface their works by remarking that the history of American law has yet to be written. In light of the avalanche of scholarship that has descended on the field in the last two decades, this ritual lamentation is rapidly evolving into a cliché. Yet there remains to this day a coarse grain of truth to the old saying. The scope of our vincible ignorance is driven home to the student who plucks early tracts on prisons off the library shelf, only to discover that their pages have never been severed. Despite growing interest, the rise of the penitentiary continues to want adequate examination, much less explanation. This study offers no definitive answers. It does, I hope, attest to the complexity of a subject whose operative agents were, after all, human and which consequently reflects all of the muddle, enigma, and tragedy that are so intimately connected to that condition.

part 1

Transition

Patterns of Punishment

T he English colonists who ventured to North America in the late sixteenth and seventeenth centuries were determined to maintain order
among themselves. Whether lured by economic ambition, as in Virginia, or propelled by religious idealism, as in New England, each immigrant
group required social discipline in order to realize its respective aims. However supportive it was of those aims, the Crown certainly sympathized with
the settlers' thirst for discipline. No monarch could hope to build an empire
out of overseas anarchies. With the Home Government's blessing, criminal
justice figured prominently—and promptly—in each of the settlements in the
American wilderness.

In this the Puritan colony at Massachusetts Bay was typical. The Puritans
had taken leave of England to build a "city on a hill," a model society for the
edification of fellow Christians everywhere. Without forsaking their heritage,
the settlers hoped to erase or amend those English institutions that offended
their vision of a godly community. Though convinced that criminal justice
needed amendment, no Puritan leader for a moment considered doing without
it. As devout Calvinists, the Puritans took for granted the natural depravity of
all mankind. In spite of efforts to screen potential settlers, there would always
be "some libertines" among them who would fall into sin. Sin threatened not
only the social tranquility of the colony but also divine wrath, for the Puritans
conceived that they had covenanted with God to live according to His spiritual commands. Deviation from those commands had to be punished strictly
"if ever you expect comfort or blessing from God upon our plantation."[1] The
Puritans, then, placed a premium on social control, and they immediately set
about establishing a local apparatus of criminal justice.[2]

The colonial charter of Massachusetts Bay, granted by King Charles I in
1629, authorized the stockholders of the company to establish laws for their
settlement "not contrarie to the lawes of our realme of England" and to administer "lawfull correction" on the spot to those who violated them.[3] In keeping
with the charter, the settlers drew upon traditional categories of crime and
a more or less conventional repertoire of punishments as raw material for
their local system of criminal justice. But whereas the Crown had contemplated only marginal deviation from the specifics of English legal practice,[4]
the Puritans stretched their license under the charter to the limits of royal

tolerance (and even beyond it),[5] mixing and matching the pairings of crime and punishment to fit their religious beliefs as well as local conditions. To a degree, such modifications occurred in every American colony.[6] In the process, some English penalties receded from common use, while others vaulted into prominence.[7]

By far the most prevalent forms of criminal sanction in early Massachusetts involved monetary penalties. Fining was the punishment of choice for a variety of petty offenses, such as drunkenness, that dominated the criminal docket. The sums demanded ranged from the nominal (as when Eliphal Streeton forfeited ten shillings for doing needlework on the sabbath) to the ruinous (as when John Stone provoked a hundred-pound fine for needling a magistrate).[8] The magnitude of fines generally lay in the court's discretion, and once levied they could be remitted to the offender as the court saw fit. Remission subject to future good behavior was quite common in the seventeenth century, a practice doubtless encouraged by the scarcity of specie in the colony but also precedented by legal custom in England.[9] In a variant of this procedure that predominated in the eighteenth century, authorities ordered offenders to post a bond for their good behavior in lieu of a fine. Though structurally similar to the remitted fine, this usage had a harsher flavor, insofar as it required offenders to part with the sums that secured their future conduct.[10]

Monetary forfeitures were not mandated solely for the benefit of the colony. By statute, persons convicted of theft in Massachusetts were liable to pay treble damages to the aggrieved as restitution.[11] Those without means could instead be pressed into service for a term of years to work off the judgment. This provision had no direct counterpart in England, where theft of a shilling or more was a capital felony. The punishment probably traced to biblical proscriptions, although precedents of a sort were provided by a number of English statutes, authorizing restitution for the victims of certain specialized property offenses.[12]

Another response to crime, not strictly speaking a punishment, was the admonition. Magistrates or clergyman often lectured offenders privately in order to elicit repentance and a promise of reform. Penitent offenders then appeared in open court for a formal admonition by the magistrate, a public confession of wrongdoing, and a pronouncement of sentence, wholly or partially suspended to symbolize forgiveness.[13] Like restitution, the admonition had no precise analogue in English criminal practice. Its adoption followed from the dictates of Puritan theology, which emphasized the effectiveness of "gentle correction" to retard sin. But again, the Puritans did not develop the admonition out of whole cloth. They had only to look to the discipline imposed by English ecclesiastical courts, where the custom was entrenched. In England, though, admonitions were frequently confined to a pro forma exhortation.[14] In colonial Massachusetts, authorities took the admonition seriously, and they made use of it in all sorts of criminal cases.

Offenders subject to admonition had publicly to confess their sins. Other punishments carried out in public exposed offenders to an array of corporal chastisements. Sentences to the lash, to the stocks (which restrained the convict's hands and feet between wooden boards), and to the pillory (holding the convict's head as well) fell into this category. Authorities always administered these penalties openly, on lecture days, training days, or market days, before the assembled community. Criminal courts in England had also administered such sanctions, mainly in cases of fraud and petty larceny.[15] In Massachusetts, public punishments (sometimes in combination with a fine) became the standard response to most property offenses, as well as to moral offenses that had been widely tolerated in England.[16] But even as the Puritans took up the use of public punishments, they took care to limit their severity. Contrary to English practice, whippings were restricted to forty stripes, again in deference to biblical injunctions.[17]

Still another battery of penalties, reserved for the most serious crimes, functioned to expel or to disable offenders. In England, the sentence of transportation out of the realm was imposed incidentally in the seventeenth century; in the eighteenth century it became the principal means of ridding the country of undesirables.[18] In colonial Massachusetts, where labor was relatively scarce, transportation on a large scale would have seemed impractical. But authorities did banish convicts intermittently, mainly in cases of heresy and political misconduct.[19] In addition, chronic property offenders were sometimes branded on the cheek or forehead, or otherwise mutilated, thereby fixing on them an indelible "mark of infamy" to warn the community of their criminal propensities.[20]

Capital punishment likewise functioned to disable criminal offenders.[21] This sanction was, of course, perfectly familiar to the Massachusetts settlers. In seventeenth-century England, the capital list included not only crimes of violence but also such routine crimes against property as theft and burglary. Over the course of the eighteenth century, Parliament added to the list literally scores of capital statutes, covering a myriad of closely defined categories of takings.[22] Still, authorities palliated the rigor of England's "bloody code" by leaving open a number of safety valves. Many capital statutes allowed pleas for benefit of clergy, whereby first offenders could escape the gallows.[23] In those cases where clergy was denied, offenders often eluded the hangman through the intercession of the jury, which retained the power to convict capital defendants of lesser charges. Even condemned criminals stood a reasonable chance of receiving royal pardons. All told, only a fraction of those persons potentially subject to the death penalty were ultimately executed.[24]

Colonial Massachusetts also imposed capital punishment for a number of crimes. But the settlers assembled a capital list consistent with their religious convictions. Because "mans life is onely at God's disposing," Puritan theologians insisted that no sentence of death could pass without a "warrant from God's word." Common property offenses (such as theft) for which no divine death warrant had been issued accordingly disappeared from the capital code. At the same time, blasphemy, adultery, and several other moral offenses became capital in conformity with Mosaic law, though contrary to English criminal practice.[25] With the establishment of the provincial government in 1691, most moral offenses were decapitalized (though not decriminalized), and a growing roster of property offenses replaced them on the capital list as the eighteenth century drew forward.[26] Even so, the capital code of provincial Massachusetts never approached the length or severity of England's bloody code.

Capital punishment in Massachusetts was not rigorously enforced. Just as their English brethren hesitated to condemn common property criminals, both judges and juries in the Bay Colony demonstrated an extreme reluctance to execute moral offenders, often downgrading their convictions from capital to noncapital crimes.[27] Along with tradition, this policy reflected theology and circumstance. Puritans maintained that it lay within the judge's God-given "calling" to exercise discretion over punishment, ameliorating statutory penalties as justice required. They viewed biblical precedents as authorizations of the death penalty, not as dogmatic commands.[28] And on top of this theory stood a demographic fact: the shortage of population in the colony weighed against extensive recourse to the gallows. Thus in Massachusetts, as in England, the law's bark was worse than its bite. Widespread evasion of capital statutes held the carnage to a minimum.[29]

In sum, the criminal justice system of Puritan Massachusetts by and large duplicated Old World sanctions[30] but applied them in novel ways, treating property offenses with relative lenience and moral offenses with relative severity.[31] Blessed with abundant food and a scarcity of specie, the early settlers were little troubled by common theft; but as stern moralists, they agonized over other sins that their compatriots were content to shrug off in England. In other American colonies, different patterns emerged; each settlement developed its own criminological nuances.[32] Nonetheless, all of England's plantations featured traditional English penalties. Though the edifice of justice that the settlers pieced together in the New World departed from the configuration of the one they left behind, its building blocks remained familiar: fining, public chastisement, and capital punishment were everywhere the order of the day.

Settlers also hastened to build prisons. Although a number of Puritans had languished in jail at the invitation of Bishop Laud,[33] the leaders of the Bay Colony quickly decided to build one of their own.[34] Opened in 1635, the Boston jail served as the sole prison in Massachusetts for eighteen years. But as settlers fanned out into the wilderness, organizing new townships as they went, local facilities for incarceration sprang up elsewhere. By 1776, Massachusetts was divided into twelve counties, and each was required by law to maintain its own jail.[35]

The jail in early Massachusetts performed a fairly typical variety of functions.[36] These spanned the civil and criminal sides of the docket. Among the jail's civil roles, imprisonment for debt was the most notable. The judgment creditor of a debtor who would not pay had the legal right (by writ of capias ad satisfaciendum) to order that debtor's incarceration in the jail.[37] Similarly, any colonist adjudged delinquent in his obligations to the realm—for taxes, fines, or costs of court—could incur the same treatment as "a Debtor to the Publick."[38] Imprisonment for debt must be sharply distinguished from latter-day notions of criminal punishment. The practice was at bottom an instrument of coercion rather than sanction, intended to pry open the purse rather than to chastise debtors. The form of the writ makes this plain: delinquent debtors were to receive their freedom whenever they paid their debts in full. Insolvent debtors could avoid imprisonment by attesting under oath that they had concealed no part of their estate.[39]

In the colonial tradition of institutional austerity, Massachusetts jails performed some services beyond the scope of the legal system, civil or criminal. It was standard procedure, for example, to house prisoners of war in the county jails, which thereby doubled as military internment camps. In the seventeenth century, the principal victims of this policy were Indians, but as the eighteenth century drew on French and eventually British soldiers joined them.[40] Like the Tower of London in England, Massachusetts jails also occasionally held political prisoners. Indian sachems, Quakers, Jesuits, and Loyalists took their turns in colonial cells.[41] In all such cases, the purpose of incarceration was segregative. It prevented persons from causing political or moral harm to the community rather than punishing them for doing so.[42]

The central function of the jail in early Massachusetts was to facilitate pretrial and presentence detention. When indicted on a criminal charge, the defendant who could not raise bail was routinely imprisoned until trial and, if convicted, until the execution of sentence. The court or a single magistrate submitted a mittimus to the sheriff, ordering him to hand the defendant over to the keeper, who in turn was responsible for holding the defendant securely until further directed by due process of law.[43] Upon the return of a guilty verdict, the court routinely directed that the defendant, now a convict, "stand committed till sentence be performed."[44] Even after the punishment had been meted out, convicts might remain in custody for a time. Since courts in the eighteenth-century frequently demanded that offenders provide monetary sureties for future good behavior, convicts stayed put until they scraped together the requisite funds.[45]

Although it was in theory a status pro tempore,[46] pretrial incarceration might in practice go on and on. Not untypical was the procedural history of *Commonwealth v. Frye,* heard before the Massachusetts Supreme Judicial

Court shortly after Independence. Cato Frye allegedly committed a theft in April 1784, for which he was indicted at the June session of the court. Frye pleaded not guilty, "and from thence said Indictment was Continued from Term to Term to this Term and now the said Cato . . . is Set to the Bar"— on November 1, 1785, some seventeen months later. Frye was convicted that same day.[47] In 1765, a woman accused of infanticide lay in jail a full year before being acquitted of the crime.[48] Yet in spite of its potential harshness, pretrial incarceration bore no abstract resemblance to a criminal sanction. Cato Frye might have had difficulty distinguishing such niceties,[49] but his lawyer would not.[50] Pretrial incarceration served a custodial function: it merely ensured that the prisoner appeared for trial and, if convicted, received just deserts. Under the circumstances, the state was perfectly willing to hold the accused hostage financially instead of physically. Requests for bail were rarely denied, and only the chronic inability of criminals to raise funds necessitated resort to a more extreme safeguard.

The routine application of incarceration to defendants rather than convicts colored contemporary perceptions of the jail and spawned a kind of jurisprudential about-face not unfamiliar to historians. In 1902, Edward Jenks stunned constitutional lawyers with his "most embarrassing discovery" that the writ of habeas corpus was originally used "not to get people out of prison, but to put them in it."[51] Similarly, modern law enforcement officers would surely grimace to discover their eighteenth-century counterparts petitioning courts to expedite the trials of criminals—not so that they could lock the criminals up, but so that they could free the criminals from jail.[52] Then as now imprisonment was expensive, and in the eighteenth century prisoners stood to be released after trial whether convicted or no. Under those circumstances, it made perfect sense for sheriffs to do everything in their power to accelerate a criminal's liberation—holding criminals was not what a jail was for.

Not often, at least. On occasion, however, jails did perform a penal function in colonial Massachusetts, and the sanction of incarceration appeared with increasing frequency in the criminal statutes of the provincial period.[53] Still, a large proportion of these prison sentences were handed down to reprimand various shades of contempt,[54] and once again seemed more coercive than sanctional. Such sentences always stipulated indefinite terms, "during the Pleasure of the Court."[55] Release hinged on a display of deference to the offended authority.[56]

Criminal incarceration imposed in a strictly penal sense, for a definite span of time, was plainly a second choice: it served either as a substitute for some conventional means of punishment that proved infeasible[57] or as a supplemental penalty, tacked on to buttress the primary sanction.[58] In either event, jail terms rarely exceeded three months and often proved as fleeting as twenty-four hours.[59] Before 1750, those few criminal statutes that imposed long-term incarceration fairly shouted their eccentricity. Forgers convicted after 1692, for example, faced the loss of an ear and "imprisonment by the space of one *whole* year *without* bail or main prise."[60] Surely no modern lawmaker would emphasize the longevity of a one-year sentence with an extra adjective nor bother to add a caveat ruling out bail. Bail was allowed, of course, in cases of pretrial incarceration, not by coincidence the most familiar function of the jail. Colonial judges apparently granted bail so reflexively that a bail-less form of incarceration required careful elaboration.

Not only did the colonial jail perform functions different from the modern penitentiary, but it was itself a very different institution, both structurally and administratively. Most early jails were singularly unimpressive buildings, holding up to thirty prisoners or so. Upkeep was haphazard at best, and the thin wooden planks that stood between the inmate and freedom often rotted through, permitting easy escape.[61]

Indeed, the jail in early Massachusetts was no place to be. If negligence characterized the jail's upkeep, then its administration must be elevated to the plane of recklessness. Not even casual measures were taken to guard the inmates' physical health, and a mittimus of incarceration became an invitation to an early grave.[62] Authorities could hardly plead ignorance of the problem. Although few officials ever toured a colonial jail (and invariably denounced the conditions as "shocking [and] loathsome" whenever they did),[63] each change of season brought the legislature a fresh stack of petitions from inmates all over the colony begging alternatively for supplies of firewood or access to fresh air.[64] Even more copious than requests for relief were requests for release, and it does seem plausible that the early jail's notoriously high rate of escape owed as much to inmate desperation as to any laxness of security.[65]

The mistreatment of inmates may be traced in large measure to the constitution of prison government. Prison administration in colonial times has sometimes been described as familial.[66] Despotic seems an apter term. As in English practice, Massachusetts jails were managed by keepers, yet authorities made scarcely any effort to find reputable persons to fill the positions.[67] What was worse, in all the years preceding independence, no statute or regulation ever ventured beyond the most cursory guidelines to delineate the keeper's responsibilities or to define his duty of care.[68] Inmates could, of course, lodge protests against ill use with the legislature, and they often did so. But in practice, few strings were attached to the keeper's office. The realm that he ruled was a small one, but within its walls his word was law.

Given such license, abuse was inevitable. Keepers alternately neglected and exploited their charges.[69] Illustrative of the problem—and of the legislature's indifference toward it—was the notorious career of Zechariah Trescott, keeper of the Suffolk County jail in Boston for a decade (1727–37). A housewright by trade, Trescott had no special qualifications to speak of. And no sooner had he been installed in his post than prisoners began to issue reams of complaints against him. In 1731, the legislature ordered an investigation into Trescott's affairs and received its first taste of the keeper's audacity. Although the legislators amassed enough evidence to dismiss him, Trescott responded with a humble prayer to "overlook . . . his Faults and Misdemeanors" and reverse the decision. "[A]fter a considerable Debate," Trescott's prayer was denied. Yet the keeper managed somehow to worm his way back into office— as one learns from the fresh batch of complaints of "many grievous hardships and abuses," at his hands that turn up in the legislative minutes of the following year.[70]

On receipt of these new charges, the legislature ordered Trescott to explain himself in person. But when the appointed day arrived, the keeper was nowhere to be found. Aroused, the legislators ordered Trescott locked behind his own bars, "there to remain till further order." Once again, he begged the legislature's forgiveness and once again—incomprehensibly—was restored to favor.[71]

Although petitions continued to pour out of Suffolk jail,[72] the ax did not fall until 1736. In that year, as the inmates were about to be transferred from the old "Wooden Prison" into a new stone structure, they rebelled and took over the building. Authorities were forced to call up the militia to surround the jail, "with their Musquets charged," until the prisoners submitted.[73] Here was an event too serious to ignore or treat with another tap on the wrist. In January 1737, after a full investigation, a formal hearing was held to inquire into the management of the Suffolk jail. This time Trescott did appear to answer his accusers (his wife at his side, in the best tradition of investigative hearings), but to no avail. The legislature determined that the keeper had "extorted excessive Fees," "unreasonably prevented the Prisoners receiving Victuals and Drink when sent to them by their Friends," and "kept some of the Prisoners in close Confinement without Water, to their great Suffering."[74]

When the hearing concluded, Trescott was stripped of his office for good.[75] Still, the legislators' response to the keeper's excesses was shortsighted at best. By replacing the bureaucrat instead of taking steps to define and monitor his duties, the legislature was clipping a branch rather than grubbing up the root of the problem. The predictable sequel: a renewed stream of petitions assailing Trescott's successor.[76]

The story of the jail in Massachusetts was typical—all too typical of jails in England and other American colonies.[77] That jails everywhere offered frightful conditions was common knowledge long before John Howard began his celebrated campaign to reform them.[78] From at least the sixteenth century, commentators likened prisons to tombs.[79] William Eden, the English rationalist, condemned keepers as "a merciless race of men."[80] The jail, then, stood at the periphery of the criminal justice system, little cared for and only gradually cared about. But late in the eighteenth century another institution, upon which great care was lavished, catapulted to the forefront.

Historians usually remark on 1785 as a year when financial crisis sent Massachusetts reeling toward Shays's Rebellion. But 1785 was also a year of some criminological significance. In March the Massachusetts legislature appointed Castle Island, a fortress guarding Boston harbor, to be a repository for *convicted* criminals—and only convicted criminals—from all over the state.[81] Simultaneously, the legislature revised the criminal code to permit judges to impose long-term incarceration as an alternative to public punishments. Castle Island operated only briefly as a prison. In 1789 it was sold to the federal government and its convicts were dispersed among local facilities.[82] But in 1805, Massachusetts opened a new state prison at Charlestown and revised its criminal code anew, not simply to make room for incarceration but to supplant the old sanctions entirely.[83]

Structurally, the Massachusetts State Prison left a strong impression. Designed by one of the foremost architects in the state, its massive stone frame and looming walls consumed six years of labor and $170,000 in costs. It held not thirty but three hundred inmates, all criminal offenders sentenced to carceral punishment. They began their terms in dark isolation and then moved into congregate quarters and workshops where from dawn to dusk they labored at manufacturing shoes and nails or hammering stone.[84]

Equally striking were the facility's administrative arrangements, now elaborated as the science of "prison discipline." Here the inmates' basic needs did not go unattended. A hospital staffed by a full-time physician had been constructed on the premises. A major effort had been undertaken to ensure prison hygiene and a proper diet. In combination, these efforts dramatically reduced prison mortality. And as for our friendly jail keeper, his responsibilities were parceled out to a whole network of officials, selected with care and working under a detailed code of regulations with periodic inspection by the state government.[85] The prison's best known warden, Gamaliel Bradford, was a far cry from the likes of Zechariah Trescott. A direct descendant of the founder of New Plymouth, Bradford produced a number of influential works on carceral management and ideology.[86]

The emergence of the penitentiary, together with its complex administration, was not an isolated phenomenon. Although Massachusetts was the first American state to establish such a facility after independence, it was joined within a year by a pilot project in the city of New York and by a statewide program in Pennsylvania. By the turn of the century, eight of the sixteen American states had instituted some sort of program for criminal incarceration.[87] Southern states lagged behind, but not by far: Virginia opened a penitentiary in 1796;

Kentucky followed suit in 1798. One by one, American codes of law were re-written to prescribe prison sentences as the predominant means of punishing crime. In the process, older public punishments were gradually forgotten.[88]

The penitentiary was coming of age. But where had it come from? The roots of criminal incarceration presumably cannot be found in prior sanctions like whipping and the pillory. No natural progression from the one to the other is apparent. But neither can its roots be found in the jail, for beyond the most superficial coincidences the two institutions were as different as night and day. To discover the penitentiary's true beginnings, we must explore other ideas and institutions buried deep in England's precolonial past. And we must also take a closer look at traditional sanctions—at the social concerns and ideologies that shaped them, and at the social realities that put teeth into them.

The Ideology of Sanction

One of the most embarrassing circumstances attending the government of the [Massachusetts State] Prison," its directors observed in 1823, "is the vacillating and contradictory opinions, which prevail with respect to it. The subject of punishment for crime is one, on which most people have thought something and very few profoundly. Each man has his own theory, and each successive Committee of the Legislature its own favorite plan. . . . Opposite and conflicting expectations are entertained by different individuals, and often by the same individual."[1] The observation was as cogent as it was timeless. Like most social issues that stir emotion and defy solution, the problem of crime control provoked, if nothing else, a jumble of words. Within that jumble lie the origins of the penitentiary, for the institution had to begin as a concept before it could exist on the ground. But to speak of criminal incarceration as a singular concept (as the Massachusetts directors intimated) is deceptive. Carceral ideology encompassed a number of related strains of thought; these need to be isolated and examined independently.

The idea of incarceration as a form of sanction traced in England to the reign of the Tudors, if not earlier. In the sixteenth century, when criminology in England remained an avocation of magistrates and pamphleteers, the common wisdom attributed the realm's abundance of property crime to idleness. "[T]heir sinews . . . benumbed and stiff through idleness," some Englishmen had abandoned all thought of earning a living, and so "of necessity live[d] by spoil" while drifting about the countryside. Such tendencies were often likened to a degenerative disease. Once contracted, the illness progressed in stages: "Of sloth comes pleasure, of pleasure comes riot, of riot comes whoring, of whoring comes spending, of spending comes want, of want comes theft, [and] of theft comes hanging."[2] Idlers, then, were bound to become thieves, sooner or later. They thereby posed a threat, be it immediate or prospective, to the peace of the English realm.

Since the Statutes of Laborers in 1349 and 1351, Parliament had sought to discourage able-bodied idleness by making it a status crime. Persons convicted of leading a "Rogishe or Vagabonds Trade of Lyef" were subject to an array of criminal sanctions that by 1530 included whipping, mutilation, and even capital punishment for a subsequent "offense."[3] But with vagrancy perceived to be on the rise (possibly as a result of agricultural enclosures),[4] the municipal government of London decided to hazard a new approach to the problem. In 1557, after four years of planning, the city reopened the old royal palace at Bridewell as a repository for all vagrants apprehended within the municipality.[5] By order of any two of its governors, vagrants were committed for terms ranging from several weeks to several years.[6] In the following decades, "houses of correction" or "workhouses," as the institutions came to be known,[7] sprouted up in other major towns. In 1576, Parliament enjoined every county in the realm to build one, and they remained a fixture in England throughout the seventeenth and eighteenth centuries.[8]

The workhouse was not intended simply as a place of detention. Its inventors hoped that the experience of incarceration would operate to rehabilitate its inmates, to restore them to the community shorn of their propensities for deviant behavior. Whereas most of the residents of the common jail "come out worse than they went in," as Lord Coke observed, vagrants committed to the workhouses were expected to "come out better."[9] Yet merely to remark this general aim is to say little about the ideology that moved workhouse advocates. The concept of rehabilitation is inherently plastic: it has meant different things to different persons. To understand more fully what the builders of the workhouse had in mind, one must inquire further into the precise therapy they prescribed and the precise changes that therapy was intended to bring about.

The inventors of the workhouse operated under the assumption that idleness was a vice (or habit) that could be broken only through a regimen of enforced abstinence. The challenge of rehabilitation lay in destroying the inmate's "habit of idleness" and replacing it with a "habit of industry" more conducive to an honest livelihood. The therapy, at once depriving the idler of old habits and instilling the new, was hard labor. Formerly indolent vagrants were obliged in the workhouse to toil without surcease while receiving instruction in practical crafts (such as weaving and nail making) from which they could earn a living upon their release. Thus would the institution "alter the whole state of this Disorder," bringing "People and their Children after them into a Regular, Orderly, and Industrious course of life, which will be as natural to them as now Idleness, and Begging, and Thieving is."[10]

Not everyone was convinced that the goal was feasible. Skeptics regarded idleness as incurable, the crime that it bred inevitable.[11] Though workhouse advocates disclaimed this gloomy appraisal,[12] they did not reject it out of hand. Workhouse advocates conceded that, as the victims of a progressive illness, those persons who had become fully habituated to idleness "will hardly leave" it. Proponents of the workhouse placed their greatest hopes in the training of youths, whose habits were believed to be less ingrained, thus more amenable to reformation, than those of their elders.[13]

The workhouse embodied one paradigm of rehabilitation, one I call *rehabituation*. Rehabituation was an inherently superficial form of rehabilitation. It addressed outward routines and abilities rather than inner moral values.

Once freed, the rehabituated inmate would "have [no] need to Beg or Steal, because he may gain his living better by Working," and removing that need marked the limit of the institution's mission.[14] Rehabituation was also inherently coercive, acting quite against the inmate's will. As Coke noted, some of his contemporaries were "of opinion, that in particular townes a discrete and expert workman may set the young and idle people as *voluntaries* on work." But he concluded that these derelicts were so wedded to their vices "as they will be never brought to worke, unless they be thereunto *compelled*."[15] Incarceration facilitated this coercion.

As they developed a theory of carceral rehabilitation, the builders of the workhouse wrestled with the host of problems that have forever surrounded its implementation. One difficulty was the need to reconcile the goal of reforming inmates with the goal of deterring them. A rehabilitative regime with too small a component of deterrence might fail to discourage vagrancy or even *encourage* persons toward idleness for the very purpose of gaining admission.[16] Yet a rehabilitative regime with too large a deterrent component might occasion such "rankling enmity" against the authority inflicting it that any concurrent hope of rehabilitation would be dashed.[17]

Advocates of the workhouse navigated this Scylla and Charybdis by making hard labor the institution's hallmark. According to the prevailing doctrine, hard labor could rehabilitate idlers, but it could *also* deter them because idlers were supposed to be scared to death of work and "will rather hazard their lives" than submit to it.[18] Indeed, the beauty of hard labor was its capacity to serve simultaneously as threat and therapy. Through this one agency "their froward natures may be bridled, their evil minds bettered and others by their example terrified."[19]

A second, more practical, stumbling block lay in designing a suitable system of institutional administration. Local jails in England (as in the colonies) had been left to rot, precisely because they served only to hold their inmates. But from the moment those inmates were to be treated within walls, conscientious management of the institution became essential.[20] To protect the integrity of the workhouse's rehabilitative routine, authorities provided codes of regulations for its orderly government, which was monitored by the local justice of the peace. Unlike jail keepers, all workhouse officers were to be "fitly qualified" for their posts. And to ensure that the rehabilitative routine was not threatened by disease, authorities mandated the first rudimentary hygienic precautions against the afflictions endemic to other carceral facilities.[21]

Last, there remained the problem of funding the new establishment. Institutional treatment has never come cheap, and the builders of the workhouse hoped that proceeds from the inmates' labor would suffice to foot the bill.[22] Hard labor thus took on still another role: as threat, as therapy, and as a fountain of support for both.

The workhouse served initially as a repository for vagrants rather than for active criminals. But the idea of widening its net was in the air almost from the day the workhouse was founded. As an ideological matter, such an expansion followed naturally from the advocates' premises. If hard labor constituted an effective therapy for vagrants, it promised to be equally therapeutic for convicts, whose penchant for idleness (in the ancient equation) had simply manifested itself in a more pronounced way.[23] To extend rehabituative treatment from vagrants to convicts was roughly analogous to prescribing curative surgery along with preventive medication.[24]

Nor did the need for deterrence militate against the expansion of the workhouse—on the contrary. When Edward Hext, a Somersetshire justice of the peace, submitted in 1596 that vagrants "will rather hazard their lives than work," he illustrated the point with a startling anecdote. "And this I know to be true: for at such time as our houses of correction were put up . . . I sent divers wandering suspicious persons to the house of correction; and all in general would beseech me with bitter tears to send them rather to the gaol. And denying it [to] them, some confessed felony unto me, by which they hazarded their lives, to the end that they would not be sent to the house of correction, where they should be forced to work."[25] The moral of the story fairly leapt from the page: the workhouse, for mere idlers, was more terrifying unto *felons* than the traditional criminal law.[26] Hext did not follow his analysis to its logical conclusion and propose to substitute the workhouse for the gallows. But he did recommend that criminals convicted of noncapital crimes be committed to the workhouse *after* suffering traditional punishments.[27]

Edward Hext's critique in 1596 may have been the first to suggest an enlarged role for the workhouse. It was not, however, the first to call for some form of hard labor as a punishment for crime. At least two such proposals dated to the reign of Henry VIII, decades before the first workhouse was founded. In his classic work *Utopia* (1516), Sir Thomas More described how the ideal polity punished felons with slavery instead of death: "They say it's . . . more useful to society than getting rid of them right away, since live workers are more valuable than dead ones." More explicitly recommended a trial of this practice in England.[28] Some twenty years later, Thomas Starkey, a chaplain to Henry VIII, similarly advised that felons be "put in some commyn work . . . so by theyr lyfe yet the commyn welth schold take some profyt."[29] These early critiques betrayed a desire to preserve and exploit the labor power of felons, as well as to deter them. But even then, the ideal of rehabilitation was taking form. More would have pardoned penal slaves who "after being tamed by years of hardship . . . show signs of feeling really sorry." Starkey saw his proposal as "a way . . . whereby [criminals] myght be brough[t] to some better ordur." Neither dwelled on the philosophy of rehabituation, and neither attempted to tackle its administrative impediments, but the ideal was faintly audible nonetheless.[30]

There followed in the seventeenth and eighteenth centuries a procession of advocates for the punishment of hard labor too lengthy to detail. Some of these made no reference to the goal of rehabilitation.[31] Some, following in the footsteps of Starkey, called for hard labor in public works. But many others sought to introduce carceral labor, in the workhouse or a separate institution, expressly to rehabilitate criminals.[32]

These proposals were not mere straws in the wind. They received serious consideration and prompted a number of short-lived programs. As early as 1622,[33] a commission appointed by King James I to reprieve felons for transportation was empowered to direct them in the alternative "to toyle in some such heavie and painful manuall workes and labors here at home and be kept in chaines in the house of correction or other places." The order specified that prisoners were to remain in that condition "save only such as upon certificate of good demeanor and penitence for their former faults . . . his majestie shalbe pleased to release and pardon."[34] This commission does not appear to have exercised authority on a large scale.[35] Less than a decade later, a royal order mandated that all jail inmates "committed for final causes"—that is, sentenced to imprisonment as a punishment—should thenceforth labor in the workhouse by day "so they may learn honesty by labour, and not live idly and miserable long in prison."[36] Following the English Civil War, the Hale Commission drafted a bill that (had it passed) would have introduced criminal incarceration comprehensively in the new Commonwealth. As part of its "System of the Law," the Commission called on Parliament to abolish benefit of clergy and replace it with a term in the workhouse at hard labor. Oliver Cromwell disbanded the Barebones Parliament (which published the bill) before any action was taken.[37] Meanwhile, beginning in 1625, a growing corpus of acts authorizing incarceration in the workhouse on conviction for specifically defined petty offenses began to appear in the parliamentary statute books. This trend continued into the eighteenth century, even as the bloody code took shape.[38]

Apart from the appearance of law in books, the workhouse in action seems to have held petty criminals, probably committed under vagrancy statutes, almost from the beginning. Although many workhouses had been founded on former hospital sites, emphasizing their role within the system of poor relief, they gravitated after the Restoration toward county jails, often forming an annex to those facilities.[39] Simultaneously on the Continent, the Netherlands and many German states began sentencing convicts to hard labor in workgangs or in a specialized institution called the Zuchthaus—a development that did not go unnoticed in England.[40]

The eighteenth century brought additional legislative initiatives. Under a parliamentary act of 1706 sponsored by Sir Robert Clayton, governor of the London corporation of the poor, clergied offenders convicted of theft or larceny could be sentenced to hard labor in the workhouse for up to two years at the judge's discretion.[41] Courts of assizes put the punishment into practice until 1718, when the new Whig government decided to expand the use of trans-portation.[42] In 1751, the Fielding Committee introduced legislation to impose hard labor in the royal dockyards as punishment for conditionally pardoned or clergied felons. The bill passed in the Commons but was rejected by the House of Lords.[43] Early in the 1770s assizes judges again began to sentence clergied felons to the workhouse under the act of 1706, which had never been formally repealed.[44] In 1776, still another statute temporarily rerouted trans-portees to the Thames River, where they were to be "reclaimed from their evil courses" as they dredged the riverbed to aid navigation.[45] Finally, the Peni-tentiary Act of 1779 provided once again for therapeutic hard labor in lieu of transportation.[46] The goal "not only of deterring others from the Commission of the like Crimes, but also of reforming the Individuals, and inuring them to Habits of Industry" appeared explicitly in the bill.[47] Due to a series of ill co-incidences, the "Penitentiary Houses" mandated by the act of 1779 were never constructed, but judges still retained the option of hard labor under a provi-sion of the act designating workhouses as receptacles for convicts until the new institutions opened.[48] This legislation completed a sequence of carceral initiatives that, viewed in toto, disclosed the remarkable antiquity, continuity, and durability of rehabituative ideology.

A second school of thought on criminal incarceration traced to the eigh-teenth century and another group of English advocates. These were the "phi-lanthropists,"[49] a mélange of clerics and lay pietists of various denominations who sought to alleviate the harsher features of English criminal law not so much for reasons of secular expediency as for the sake of Christian charity.[50] And of all the features of criminal justice that cried out for amelioration in the eighteenth century, jail conditions cried the loudest.[51]

Philanthropic advocates focused initially on curing the destructive aspects of pretrial incarceration. John Howard, the most famous and influential rep-resentative of philanthropy, devoted his life to the study of prison conditions and published detailed accounts of the inmates' torments. Most suggestions offered by philanthropists in the areas of hygiene and administration either borrowed from or built on prior workhouse practices.[52] But philanthropists concerned themselves with more than the inmates' physical ordeal; they also stressed the moral degradation inherent in pretrial imprisonment. In this re-gard, philanthropists sought increased attention to inmates' spiritual needs and an end to the random commingling of prisoners that resulted in "old criminals corrupting new comers."[53]

Having set out to maintain the inmate's moral condition, philanthropists drifted easily toward proposals to improve that condition.[54] By the mid-eighteenth century, some spoke of reforming jail inmates awaiting trial.[55] With the appearance of Samuel Denne's *Letter to Lord Ladbroke* in 1771 and Jonas Hanway's *Solitude in Imprisonment* in 1776, philanthropic literature began to concentrate on postconviction rehabilitation of criminals in the carceral setting.[56]

The philanthropists thus came upon carceral rehabilitation by way of institutional benevolence rather than sanctional effectiveness—both roads led to the same destination. Or did they? The philanthropists urged carceral rehabilitation, to be sure, but theirs was a novel brand, distinct from the workhouse model.

Philanthropists tended to view crime as an outgrowth of the offender's estrangement from God. Once such a break had occurred, no punishment inflicted by mere mortals could deter the offender from sinning.[57] The challenge of rehabilitation lay in restoring the criminal's faith in, and fear of, the Lord, thereby to "to qualify [him] for happiness in both worlds."[58] Jonas Hanway went so far as to liken the function of a rehabilitative prison to that of a church.[59]

Though they did not speak with one voice,[60] many philanthropists endorsed a radical antidote to the criminal's affliction. "Solitude," Hanway proclaimed, "[is] the most humane and effectual means of bringing malefactors . . . to a right sense of their condition."[61] Since at least 1740, philanthropists had touted solitary confinement, not only to isolate prison inmates from moral contagion, but also to precipitate their spiritual recovery.[62] As John Brewster explained, "It has been recommended, both by the practice and precept of holy men, in all ages, sometimes to retire from scenes of public concourse, for the purpose of communing with our own hearts, and meditating on heaven."[63] Cloistered from the buzz of social interaction, forced to converse only with a guilty conscience, the solitary inmate would rediscover God, tearfully repent all sins, and be pledged ever after to a devout and honest life. A Bible and a minister's proselytizing could smooth the process, but the operative agent was not to be found in this world. As Hanway concluded, "Let us pursue a consistent plan, and leave the event to Heaven!"[64]

The philanthropic paradigm of carceral rehabilitation, which I call *reclamation,* intended a deeper change in the offender's character than that envisioned by rehabituation.[65] Equipping criminals for work was not enough; worldly habits and abilities would make no difference unless the offenders *wanted* to live rightly, unless their souls (under threat of *divine* sanction) demanded moral rectitude. Thus conceived, reclamation, unlike rehabituation, was inherently noncoercive, for "to compel people to be virtuous, is a contradiction in terms."[66] Incarceration only induced criminals to listen without distraction to the voice of their own consciences. Once reclaimed, former offenders would abstain from crime as a matter of choice, and would work "gladly," habit or no habit, for the sake of virtue. Some philanthropists even expected, under the dubious assumption that too much of a bad thing would do some good, that the relentless *idleness* of solitary confinement would spark a craving for employment; others, however, were prepared to countenance

voluntary labor within solitary cells, thereby blending, to some degree, reclamatory ideology with its predecessor.[67]

Though their chosen therapy was noncoercive, philanthropists remained
confident of its effectiveness: like volunteering in the army, volunteering one's
submission to God was a foregone conclusion.[68] Still, philanthropists did not
carry their faith to extremes. Like workhouse advocates, they singled out
youths as the most likely candidates for reform, and they anticipated that God
would turn His back on some of the more inveterate offenders.[69] Nonetheless, Samuel Denne prophesied that solitary confinement "would contribute
more to the reformation of manners than all the Workhouses and Bridewells
in Europe." [70] Given their belief that only deep reform could overcome propensities for crime, philanthropists reckoned their therapy a vast improvement
over hard labor.

Philanthropists also addressed the timeless obstacles to carceral rehabilitation that the builders of the workhouse had already faced. In reconciling
reclamation with deterrence, philanthropists emphasized that the fate of subjection to one's guilty conscience was painful indeed and that the ascetic
existence of a solitary cell would never tempt persons to seek entrée.[71] At the
same time, philanthropists promised that solitary confinement would not be
so unbearable as to harden inmates' attitudes. Many advocates stressed the
importance of convincing prisoners that the punishment meted out to them
was just and for their own benefit, both as part of the process of instilling
remorse and as a means of preventing any "seeds of malice or ill-will" from
infecting the rehabilitative process.[72]

The problem of financing solitary confinement left philanthropists in a
bind. Unlike advocates of hard labor, proponents of solitude could not blithely
assign prison costs to inmates. Instead, they finessed the problem by belittling
it, reciting the kingdom's ample resources for such a project, together with
its nobility and practical value.[73] The rhetoric succeeded: local facilities for
the solitary confinement of criminals appeared in Gloucestershire and several
other counties by the 1790s.[74]

A final strand of ideology, known as "rationalism" or "utilitarianism," also
took root in the eighteenth century. A product of the larger European intellectual movement known as the Enlightenment, rational criminology offered
a sharp contrast to the theologically inspired criminology of the philanthropists and other traditional thinkers. In the seventeenth century, Englishmen
had routinely equated crime with sin. Many English Puritans were biblical
literalists, and orthodox Anglicans agreed that criminal law was at least
derived from God's word. In common, they traced the commission to suppress
crime only immediately to secular authority. "Ye shall not feare the face of
man," Michael Dalton advised justices of the peace in 1619, "for the judgement
is Gods." [75] In the eighteenth century, rational theorists rejected scripture in
favor of human logic and reason as the only valid guide to the construction

of social institutions. The aim of secular government, rationalists taught, was not to do God's bidding but to maximize secular utility (in an oft-repeated phrase, to provide "the greatest happiness shared by the greatest number").[76] Considered in the abstract, the shift was as profound as any that could be imagined, and it obliged the rationalists to reconsider a vast constellation of the most venerable dogmas. They plunged into the task gleefully.

Rational philosophers argued that what made an action a crime subject to human sanction was the harm it did to other members of society. Sins that were not also socially harmful should be answered for at a different tribunal.[77] Furthermore, once a crime had been committed, the only rational purpose of punishment was the *prevention* of future harm; retribution had no place in a theory of secular utility, for "what is done can never be undone."[78] Viewed in the cold light of reason, punishment became "an evil to which the magistrate resorts only from its being necessary to prevention of a greater."[79] Any gratuitous severity (or "prodigality") of punishment constituted "abuse and not justice."[80]

Having set out a novel theory of crime, rationalists proceeded to address the problems of its cause and control. Rational notions of criminal motivation rested largely on the "sensational psychology" first developed by John Locke late in the seventeenth century.[81] Locke maintained that human behavior derived entirely from environmental stimuli, not innate proclivities or moral principles stamped on the conscience. The human mind began as a tabula rasa and formed a code of conduct by reference to continual hedonistic calculation. Given this premise, the key to controlling crime had to lie somewhere in the criminal's environment—but where exactly was a matter over which rational criminologists differed. Their ideology was sufficiently flexible to bear a variety of glosses.

Some rationalists, most notably the Italian theorist Cesare Beccaria, placed primary blame on the environmental impact of ill-considered methods of criminal justice. Because all "sensible beings" steered their actions toward maximum pleasure and minimum pain, Beccaria believed that a better crafted scheme of sanctions could prevent criminal acts by draining their utility.[82] The core notion of deterrence was, of course, ages old,[83] but Beccaria took the concept in a new direction. Whereas criminologists had traditionally assumed that deterrence hinged on the severity of punishment,[84] Beccaria postulated that the *certainty* of punishment contributed far more to the inhibition of crime. Were apprehension, conviction, and sentencing all made rapid and infallible, the punishments established for crimes could remain moderate, for it was preeminently that reed of optimism, "the hope of impunity," that sustained offenders in their moments of temptation. Punishment should always be proportioned to the magnitude of the offense, Beccaria insisted, but capital punishment should be abolished entirely because of its prodigality and "uncertainty" of enforcement.[85]

These ideas (which were influential, but by no means universally accepted by English rationalists)[86] did not lead Beccaria to advocate incarceration as a general mode of punishment. Although he suggested "perpetual servitude" as a replacement for the death penalty that "has in it what suffices to deter any determined spirit," the Italian theorist took no exception to the staple punishments of whipping and the pillory. His concern was with the structure of the code, not its substance. It was enough, Beccaria concluded, that punishment be made "public, prompt, necessary, the least possible in the given circumstances, [and] proportionate to the crimes."[87]

Other rationalists such as Jeremy Bentham deemed efforts to deter offenders as insufficient to stem the tide of crime. Whereas Beccaria had sought to make crime unattractive to "sensible beings," Bentham and others surmised that some persons would not react "sensibly" to the threat of sanction, no matter how well contrived. Ordinarily, individuals behaved in ways that advanced their self-interest. But malignant social stimuli could impair their abilities to calculate utility, leading some individuals to engage in "senseless" conduct—such as choosing the momentary gratification of crime without heed to the subsequent misery of punishment.[88] Whereas Beccaria blamed the legal environment, Bentham fixed upon the *social* environment as a fountainhead of crime.

Such ideas once again led rationalists toward the goal of rehabilitation. Nothing less would suffice to dissuade criminals from deviant behavior.[89] For rationalists, though, the challenge of rehabilitation lay simply in restoring the offender's ability to appreciate the inexpedience of crime.[90] As in workhouse ideology, the depth of the change contemplated by rationalism was shallow: the first sought to overcome people's need to steal, and the second sought to grant them the good sense not to. Incarceration became the key to rational rehabilitation because it removed criminals from their corrupting environment long enough to administer corrective therapy.[91]

The rationalists' connection of crime to the social environment, though in its own way revolutionary, was not entirely original. Other publicists had been sniffing around the edges of this concept for centuries. Workhouse advocates had sometimes traced idleness (the immediate cause of crime) more fundamentally to such extrinsic sources as improper upbringing and evil companionship, in addition to innate propensities.[92] Philanthropists also rang the changes on this theme; like the rationalists, they premised their rehabilitative program on a temporary separation from wordly corruption.[93] It was the rationalists' achievement to pull together these scattered ideas and enlarge them into a complex criminology that denied *any* role to natural depravity.[94]

But, apart from separating criminals from their surroundings, what *sort* of therapy could cure "insensible" minds? Given the novelty of sensational psychology, it is surprising to discover that the rational philosophers had few new programmatic suggestions to offer. Imagination had carried the rationalists far, but here it seems to have failed them. Instead of developing their own therapeutic designs, most rational advocates simply pirated the ones already published by their irrational predecessors.

A few rationalists, notably Jeremy Bentham, initially joined the appeal for solitary confinement, notwithstanding the spiritual imagery in which the philanthropists had steeped it. Bentham translated solitary reclamation into a secular version, based on sensational psychology.[95] (This led to the curious spectacle of a rational philosopher endorsing the philanthropists' platform, even as he heaped scorn on its ideological foundation.)[96] Most rationalists, however, remained skeptical of the therapeutic value of solitude, although they did accept and even stress the cognate principle that convict separation prevented mutual corruption.[97] As a therapy, rationalists generally preferred hard labor, in the mold of the workhouse. They conjectured that hard labor could restore the sensibility of offenders by correcting their hedonistic responses to work and thereby their responses to crime.[98] Bentham himself ultimately came round to this position, and his famous plan for the Panopticon (which, try as he might, was never constructed) called for solitary labor within cells.[99] Another rationalist, William Eden, collaborated with John Howard and Justice William Blackstone to draft the Penitentiary Act of 1779, which prescribed congregate hard labor by day but separate celling at night.[100]

In espousing such therapy, English rationalists did not lose sight of deterrence. If it was to have the desired effect, rehabilitative punishment had also to include an element of pain that persons would respect once they had been properly socialized. Lest the carceral institution's therapeutic aspects blunt its capacity to intimidate offenders, rationalists counseled that the inmate's lot should always remain less attractive than that of the most poorly paid honest laborer.[101] Thus, like earlier advocates, English rationalists found ways to reconcile ideologically the goals of deterrence and rehabilitation. Even so, the rationalists, again like earlier advocates, expected no miracles. They anticipated that only some offenders, in particular youths, would respond favorably to carceral therapy.[102]

It was against this ideological background that legislators in Massachusetts and other American colonies enacted statutes introducing carceral punishment in the 1780s. A look at those statutes and the literature of advocacy that surrounded them reveals that the postrevolutionary initiatives for criminal incarceration in America owed their inspiration primarily to the rehabituative tradition of the ancient workhouse. The more current intellectual contributions of the philanthropists and of the rationalists had only a secondary impact on carceral developments in the new republic.[103]

The Massachusetts experience may serve as illustration. Shortly before the state's first legislative initiative in 1785, a string of newspaper columns called upon the legislature to impose hard labor as a punishment for property crime. These essays recited ideological themes that had long nested in the writings of

English workhouse advocates. One Massachusetts author, who signed himself "A Friend of Industry," favored collaboration with New Hampshire on building a "nailing house" for convicted thieves. "As theft generally proceeds from idleness, labor will be the severest and most effectual punishment," the Friend promised. "A house established on this plan would I believe turn out many an *industrious member with an occupation,* who was taken in, an *idle thief* without one." As under rehabituative (and rational) theory, the change envisioned remained superficial: "To eradicate bad habits, and teach the vicious that 'HON-ESTY IS THE BEST POLICY,' " an aphorism that emphasized the sort of compliance to law that sprang from calculation rather than conscience.[104] Massachusetts commentators simultaneously emphasized the deterrent potential of hard labor. Like Edward Hext two centuries earlier, "Lucius" believed that this punishment "would be more horrid to many [offenders] then death itself." [105] Again following workhouse ideology, the two aims were alleged to be fully compatible. Hard labor would be "effectual for reclaiming Offenders, by its tendency to establish habits of Industry . . . and [for] the apparent dread which that mode of punishment excites in the more dissolute part of the Community." [106]

The act establishing Castle Island as a state prison in 1785 followed on the heels of these various missives. Although the act failed to elaborate its ideological underpinnings, these were insinuated throughout the document. Most telling was the statutory requirement that imprisoned convicts perform "hard labour," the sine qua non of the rehabituative program.[107] That lawmakers distinguished such discipline from the pretrial carceral regime is indicated by the statutory restriction of Castle Island to *convicted* offenders.[108] Subsequent statutes and a gust of gubernatorial addresses reiterated traditional rehabituative themes. Another act in 1785: "Whereas idleness is often the parent of fraud and cheating, . . . confinement to hard labour may be a means of reclaiming such offenders." [109] Governor John Hancock in 1793: "[C]rimes have generally idleness for their source, and where offenses are not prevented by education, a sentence to hard labour will perhaps have a more salutary effect." [110] Governor Caleb Strong in 1801: "A great proportion of crimes are the effects of idleness, and it seems peculiarly proper therefore to punish them by confinement to hard labour; that offenders . . . may be compelled to acquire new habits and contribute something to the good of society." [111] And so on.[112] Expectations nonetheless remained modest. As in England, advocates in Massachusetts believed that youths stood the best chance of responding to carceral therapy.[113]

In order to entertain serious hopes of rehabilitating any offenders, the architects of Castle Island had to institute administrative safeguards far more extensive than the minimal precautions taken to protect the common jails. Though only partly successful,[114] their efforts indicated that the architects' apostrophes to the ideal of rehabilitation were more than empty rhetoric.[115] Convicts confined to Castle Island served under the military discipline of the garrison "as if under voluntary enlistment," rather than under a keeper's whim.[116] The convicts' dietary and sanitary well-being were provided for, and basic efforts were undertaken to employ a competent staff, to which a full-time physician and chaplain were added.[117] Equally notable were the steps taken to ensure the physical security of the facility.[118] Finally, the legislature closely monitored affairs at Castle Island by dispatching committees to inspect it periodically.[119] Although unprecedented for a jail, these measures adhered to the tradition of the workhouse, which had featured many of the same administrative safeguards.

In the other states that launched carceral ventures in the 1780s, similar views prevailed. In New York, the first statute mandating incarceration as an alternative to corporal punishment, passed just days after the Castle Island Act, called for hard labor in the existing workhouse, though in practice the labor was performed out of doors "at the public works of this city."[120] Thomas Eddy, a Quaker merchant who became the state's foremost penitentiary advocate and principal author of the statute that brought hard labor indoors to Newgate prison a decade later, remained faithful to the premises of workhouse ideology. Eddy rated "the amendment of the offender" as "without doubt . . . of the highest importance," and he identified as "the most efficacious means of reformation," a "system of regular labor and exact temperance by which habits of industry and sobriety are formed."[121] In Pennsylvania, the first act prescribing carceral punishment in 1786 also called for hard labor, here expressly beyond walls "in the streets of cities and towns, and upon the highways of the open country and other public works." Again, as the preamble made clear, hard labor was intended "to correct and reform the offenders, and to produce such strong impression upon the minds of others as to deter them from committing the like offenses."[122] As in New York, the punishment soon moved indoors, mainly to the prison at Walnut Street, which became an early model of institutional organization.[123] Once again, hopes were tempered by common sense. Advocates in both New York and Pennsylvania deemed youths the likeliest candidates for rehabilitation, and they acknowledged that some offenders "grown old in habits of profligacy . . . yield little hope of amendment."[124] But, as in Massachusetts, authorities strove to give the therapy a chance, by carefully regulating the carceral environment.[125]

The extent to which the newer ideology of philanthropy influenced these initiatives is problematic. Many American advocates who pushed for criminal incarceration, such as Thomas Eddy, were deeply religious individuals. But the vision of solitary reclamation developed by English philanthropists was nowhere in evidence in 1785, when the first moves toward carceral punishment occurred in the new republic; reclamation took the intellectual stage only later in the story.[126] The cognate idea of separating inmates to prevent their mutual corruption appeared initially only in Pennsylvania.[127] It had no influence on the program established at Castle Island.

The role played by rationalism is still more difficult to assess. To be sure, this current of thought flowed vigorously through revolutionary America. As early as 1765, public documents in Massachusetts paraphrased rational tracts by styling prevention the "great end" of punishment.[128] The impact of the ideology is apparent in such developments as the growing tolerance of moral offenses following the Revolution.[129] Yet in the realm of carceral advocacy, most English rationalists embraced a rehabituative program that did not originate with them. They merely joined an existing chorus, though perhaps in the process drawing greater attention to its intonations.

The rational postulates associated with Cesare Beccaria also won many adherents in revolutionary America.[130] But the extent to which those postulates contributed ideological ammunition to carceral advocates is again problematic. Though perfectly compatible with a carceral program, Beccaria's structural proposals could have been implemented without recourse to any novel penalties.[131]

Beccaria's insistence that the degree of punishment be proportioned to the crime cannot be directly connected to the rise of the penitentiary. Given its divisibility, incarceration was certainly well suited to the elaboration of a proportional code. Yet this was no less true of the older public punishments, which were also divisible: one could suffer so many years in prison or so many lashes at the whipping post.[132] Beccaria himself did not assert the superiority of carceral punishment for this purpose; he merely affirmed the principle in the abstract.[133] Although several American statutes introducing criminal incarceration specified proportionality as a goal,[134] its utility for this purpose relative to lashing remained a matter of controversy.[135] Beccaria's principle was more clearly reflected in the splintering of legal categories that occurred under postrevolutionary statutory schemes than in the development of carceral programs.[136]

Beccaria's plainest contribution to the movement toward criminal incarceration was his theoretical criticism of capital punishment. Though his was hardly the first treatise to take aim at the gallows,[137] Beccaria added considerable intellectual power to the movement, and his original theorem that the uncertainty of capital punishment rendered it an ineffective deterrent influenced many American criminologists.[138] While uncertain capital statutes could have been repealed without resort to anything new,[139] Beccaria did suggest public (albeit perpetual) servitude as a suitable replacement.[140] In the 1790s, both Pennsylvania and New York sharply cut their capital lists, imposing carceral punishment in their place, and it seems more than likely that Beccarian ideology prompted, or at least added impetus to, these developments.[141] Yet this was only one (indeed, per capita, far the lesser)[142] aspect of the sanctional transition: for hard labor replaced routine public punishments as well, a change that formed no part of Beccaria's program but that had long been contemplated, along with reductions of capital punishment, by advocates of the workhouse. In fact, the initial statutory movements toward incarceration in the 1780s had all emphasized the lower end of the sanctional spectrum,[143] and they went beyond Beccaria's structural formulas by enjoining rehabilitative therapy. Once again Beccaria's rational voice—though unusually crisp and resonant—swelled an existing chorus.

That chorus had been singing in America for some time. The idea of rehabituative therapy, and its potential application to criminals, was no less deeply rooted in the British colonies than in the British Isles. Workhouses were a fixture in England when the first emigrants set sail. They carried the ideology with them to the New World, where the settlers had, if anything, more compelling inducements to combat idleness. As a matter of economics, the scarcity of labor in the colonies underscored the need for all inhabitants to do their share. As a matter of social tradition, the easy availability of employment in the colonies likewise deprived able-bodied idlers of their proverbial excuse— to wit, their inability to find a job. Those who avoided work in spite of its abundance could expect no outpouring of sympathy.[144] And as a matter of theology, at least in the New England colonies, idleness clashed directly with the Calvinist work ethic, which summoned the Lord's children to labor assiduously at their callings.[145] To be sure, idleness (except among troublesome monarchs) had never been a virtue in Old England either,[146] but in America it was more offensive still.

Central to American concerns remained, however, the venerable notion that idleness could induce criminal propensities. Old Light minister Charles Chauncy might easily have traded scripts with an Elizabethan magistrate when in 1752 he queried: "Who are so much noted for the moral Disorder of *Lying* and *Stealing,* as those who have settled into the Habits of Laziness? Their Laziness," Chauncy continued, "reduces them to Straits and Difficulties; and these, as the readiest and easiest Way to supply their wants put them upon . . . robbing [persons] of their Money, and their Goods."[147] In Massachusetts, the first recorded order for the construction of a workhouse to battle such tendencies dated to 1629, before the main body of the settlement had even arrived. From England the Massachusetts Bay Company instructed the vanguard at Salem to erect the institution "for the better governing and ordering of our people, especially such as shalbe negligent and remiss in performance of their dutyes, or otherwise exorbitant."[148] In 1656, the General Court instructed each county in the colony to construct its own workhouse and to gather a stock of raw materials to occupy its inmates at their "dayly stint."[149] Once again, the ostensible purpose of the regime was to bring delinquents "to some meet order."[150] Like their English counterparts, workhouses in colonial Massachusetts operated under detailed ameliorative regulation and regular inspection.[151] One such institution, constructed in Boston in 1739, almost rivaled later penitentiaries in scale.[152] Workhouses intended to rehabituate their inmates also appeared in Pennsylvania and New York by the early eighteenth century.[153]

The possibility of extending hard labor to criminals was as obvious to American colonists as it was to other Englishmen.[154] The settlers saw fit to experiment with such programs at various times. By far the most ambitious hard labor program conducted in the colonies dated to 1682, when the Great Law of Pennsylvania was promulgated. This code is best known for its restrictions on capital punishment (having abolished the death penalty in all cases save murder), but it also mandated hard labor in the workhouse as a punishment for most crimes.[155] Though the Great Law was repealed and capital punishment reinstated in 1718, the repealing statute retained the sanction of hard labor for certain offenses, and the number of crimes subject to hard labor in Pennsylvania grew as the century progressed.[156]

The punishment of hard labor also appeared in the criminal codes of other American colonies, though never to the extent laid down in the Great Law.[157] Developments in Massachusetts are again instructive. Under the first statute establishing county workhouses in 1656, the categories of activities made punishable by commitment already betrayed some blending of "status" crimes with the lower grades of active offenses. The list included idleness, drunkenness, pilfering, night walking, eloping from indentured service, and "uncleanness in speeches or action."[158] The provincial legislature subsequently added begging, vagabondage, juggling, brawling, harassment of women, and fortune telling.[159] From the other end of the spectrum, a number of persons convicted of serious crimes in the seventeenth century were also sentenced to the workhouse on an ad hoc basis,[160] and in 1713 the Reverend Cotton Mather proposed hard labor in the workhouse as a regular punishment for felonies.[161] Statutes appearing in 1749 and 1750 did expressly prescribe this penalty for the offenses of extortion and counterfeiting, respectively.[162] Several unsuccessful efforts to extend hard labor to additional crimes followed in the decades leading up to independence, including one bill proposed in 1765 that would have introduced the punishment comprehensively.[163]

It has sometimes been assumed that the precepts of Calvinism, stipulating the natural depravity of all mankind, precluded rehabilitative ideology in America before the emergence of rationalism. Under this theory, the penitentiary could not and did not arise during the colonial period because its criminological mission was inconsistent with contemporary theology.[164] The objective fact that workhouses sprang up in several American colonies belies this conclusion, but it is contradicted also by substantive commentaries on crime dating to colonial times. These commentaries reveal no disharmony between early American religious ideology and traditional English criminological axioms.

Of course, criminology and theology were interconnected in the New World settlements. As the principal forces of intellect in colonial society, it was the ministers who wrote and sermonized about crime, and it was the ministers who, in a number of colonies, drafted or helped to draft the early criminal codes.[165] Yet the salience of Calvinism in this criminological milieu should not be overemphasized: in early (as in modern) America, beliefs varied far more than they predominated. Settled in substantial part by those in search of spiritual freedom, the colonies fairly teemed with sectarian faiths. No single religious persuasion had a pervasive influence.

A glance at some of the more prominent patterns in America's doctrinal crazy-quilt reveals the limited reach of Calvinist thought. Baptists and orthodox Anglicans (found in increasing numbers throughout the colonies in the eighteenth century) accepted what was for Calvinists the Arminian heresy that persons could achieve redemption by dint of human effort—this contrary to the Calvinist dogma of divine omnipotence and human helplessness. Quakers (concentrated in Pennsylvania and New Jersey) also rejected this Calvinist principle, adopting in its place the belief that all human beings were imbued with the "inner light" that could lead them to salvation. Such structures of religious thought were perfectly compatible with the ideal of criminal rehabilitation, and English Quakers were active advocates of the workhouse.[166] But even in early Massachusetts—home to Calvin's most devout American disciples—rehabilitative ideology was a clear component of the Puritan creed.

Calvin taught that every human being since Adam's fall suffered from a natural depravity of the soul and deserved damnation. This innate corruption led persons inevitably to sin and "prepared [them] for the commission of atrocious and innumerable crimes." [167] The Puritans adhered to Calvin's vision; indeed, their determination to do so had led them to Massachusetts. Still, on closer inspection, one finds that while Puritan theologians professed faith in Calvinist principles, they nonetheless filtered out from those principles some of their more pessimistic and deterministic implications.

As ever brilliantly, Perry Miller identified one screen to determinism in the idea of the social covenant. Under the cognate theory of the national covenant, Puritans conceived that they had bound themselves to obey the Lord's commands; sins accordingly represented an affront to God, and their punishment constituted an expiatory obligation to His authority.[168] The social covenant provided an alternate framework of analysis, based on the secular institution of government.[169] From this vantage point, sin assumed the form of a secular compact broken, an affirmative act of will, rather than "a disease contained in the protoplasm" of mankind. The social covenant tended to "externalize" sin, Miller concluded, for "[b]y reducing original sin to legal imputations and by turning redemption into a rational transaction, the doctrine was bound to enhance the value of natural capacities . . . [and vitiate] literal application of the dogma of innate depravity." [170] What is more, even when Puritan theologians spoke of sin in its unadulterated Calvinist sense, they remained equally adamant in admonishing their listeners to *try* to overcome it—an encouragement whose hopeful phrases carried Puritanism time and again to the brink of Arminianism.[171]

In the process of softening the concept of innate and inevitable depravity,

Puritan theologians pursued additional explanations for criminal behavior. Often they found them in the social environment. Bad company, improper upbringing, poor education, and access to alcohol all were seen to beget idleness and hence were associated with criminal proclivities.[172] Such diagnoses stood alongside visions of human depravity: as interpreted by the ministers, adverse environmental conditions furnished external stimuli to the corrupt nature that lay within.[173] These ideas in turn provided an ideological bridge to Locke's sensational psychology, the intellectual foundation for rationalist criminology.[174]

Long before the arrival of rationalism, however, Puritan theologians had developed their own distinctive theory of criminal rehabilitation. Theologians posited that the soul of every person, though corrupted by original sin, possessed a "natural conscience" that could in the ideal distinguish right from wrong. Original sin clouded the conscience, but theologians maintained that secular instruction, in combination with saving grace, could restore it to near perfect clarity. Once afforded a "True Sight of Sin," the offender would sin again only by overt act of will, "against his conscience."[175] Notions of rehabituation, which were too shallow too reach the conscience, were even easier to reconcile with Calvinism; the prevalence of such notions in colonial Massachusetts has already been remarked. In England, too, Puritan writers frequently advocated rehabituative workhouses.[176]

The Great Awakening of the eighteenth century added to the complexity (and confusion) of the theological landscape of Massachusetts. But none of the faiths that evolved in the provincial period precluded concepts of criminal rehabilitation. Even Jonathan Edwards's New Divinity, while returning strongly to Calvinist first principles, nevertheless accepted sensational psychology.[177]

In short, Calvinist theology did not compel the people of Massachusetts or other colonies to view punishment as an exercise in futility. They could and did attempt to use punishment to control crime. The goals of spiritual redemption and secular prevention stood side by side. Cotton Mather typically combined the two when he explained the function of criminal sanction: "tis partly to Reclame the Offenders, and by a costly Instruction, to teach them that Sin is an *Evil and a Bitter Thing,* & make them afraid of Offending any more: Tis partly to Defend the *Beholders,* and affright others from the Sin that will bring such *Penalties* upon them. . . . Yea, Tis also to Divert the Wrath of God, which will burn and break forth against the Land, where sin is Countenanced."[178] Like all Puritan theologians, Mather held bearish views of human nature, but he still believed it possible to "Reclame" some offenders. In common with other thinkers, Mather likened criminal tendencies to an infectious and progressive disease.[179] If discovered before offenders had slid too far and become "harden[ed] . . . in their evil courses," there was hope for them. But if the infection could not be arrested, as demonstrated by relapses into crime, then an offender would be deemed "incorrigible" and dealt with accordingly.[180]

As usual, commentators singled out youths as both particularly vulnerable to, and particularly salvable from, the disorder.[181] Such ideas, of course, would not have raised an eyebrow among English theorists. American sources once again suggest the striking resilience of criminological themes dating at least to Elizabethan times.

In sum, the postrevolutionary carceral ventures signaled no fundamental departure from the colonies' intellectual past. Not only were the ideals of re-habilitation and deterrence well known to the postrevolutionary builders, but the prospect of realizing those ideals through institutional means was equally familiar to them. American programs like the one begun on Castle Island es-sentially parroted the ancient workhouse. The one coincided with the other in its therapeutic design, administrative precautions, and even institutional nomenclature.[182] Contemporaries who advocated or toured early penitentia-ries acknowledged the resemblance. One legislative report in Massachusetts referred to the proposed facility as "a Provincial [that is, province-wide] Work-house or House of correction." [183] In Philadelphia, a visitor remarked of the penitentiary at Walnut Street, "This prison is a kind of house of correction." [184] Under the circumstances, advocates of criminal incarceration did not flatter themselves into believing that they had imagined something new. In England, proponents of hard labor as a punishment traced the idea back to the ancient workhouses or to Continental institutions or to Thomas More,[185] while propo-nents of solitary confinement looked back to proposals made by the middle of the eighteenth century.[186] In America, advocates were equally aware of the longevity of these concepts, though often unwilling to admit their English roots. Whether out of revolutionary Anglophobia or pride in their priority of construction, American commentators preferred to credit the idea of criminal incarceration to William Penn or (again) to trace it to Continental institu-tions.[187] Exactly where the ideology had originated remained in dispute.[188] But, however they resolved this question, all advocates agreed that "some idea of such a plan has been entertained, even from a remote period." [189] An estab-lishment along the lines of Castle Island might easily have been conceived at a much earlier date.

The Sociology of Sanction

T he penitentiary, then, did not spring out of nowhere in the 1780s. It existed in people's minds long before it took shape as a physical construct of stone and mortar. Nor was the concept of criminal incarceration somehow lost and then "rediscovered" late in the eighteenth century.[1] As we have seen, the carceral schemes of the mid-1780s followed a steady stream of advocacy and initiatives stretching back in England to the earliest workhouses. It was the design for that venerable institution that guided American lawmakers when the initial leap to carceral punishment occurred. All of which raises a question: Why did Americans choose *this occasion* to blow the dust off a long-standing idea? Although the intellectual blueprint was prerequisite to the advent of the institution, it is not alone sufficient to explain it. For some reason, criminal incarceration became in the 1780s and 1790s an idea whose time had come.

To understand more fully the rise of the penitentiary in America, we must move beyond ideology to the social reality of criminal justice in early America. That reality was one of change—significant change over the course of the eighteenth century, which set the scene for the abandonment of traditional sanctions in a particular place and time. The place was a large one, encompassing several American states as well as Great Britain. We begin the story in Massachusetts, where the evidence is plentiful and possibly instructive.

Throughout the seventeenth century, Massachusetts remained a conglomerate of small, tightly knit communities. The first generation of Puritans settled into a string of embryonic townships. After the initial exodus from England, immigration tapered off rapidly, and even within the colony intermigration between settlements became uncommon. Massachusetts communities grew slowly but steadily over the course of the century, almost entirely by natural increase. The demographic history of Dedham was typical. Following its incorporation in 1636, Dedham grew to contain some 400 inhabitants in 1648; by 1700, the total had climbed to 750. Over these years, migration into and out of town stood at less than 1 percent per annum, and the number of family names actually declined. Kenneth Lockridge has described Dedham as "a self-contained social unit, almost hermetically sealed off from the rest of the world." As late as 1690, no town in Massachusetts, save Boston and Salem, held more than 2,000 persons.[2]

Criminal justice in Massachusetts reflected the social intimacy of its communities.[3] Because towns experienced little turnover in population, most criminal offenders were life-long residents, well known to everyone, rather than outsiders. The first impulse of all concerned was to heal the wounds as best they could. The preferred sanctions accordingly operated to draw resident offenders back into the community. Sanctions of the last resort, designed to expel offenders, were reserved for nonresidents or residents who had tried the community's patience once too often.

Fining practices afford one illustration of the settlers' communal approach to punishment. Fines, of course, depended on deterrence to hold potential offenders in check. In early colonial times, however, fines were frequently remitted subject to good behavior. Authorities may have had little choice in this decision, given the scarcity of specie, yet the process of remission, with its probationary overtones, suited close communities. By forgiving fines, residents signaled their willingness to accept offenders back into the fold. Strangers would never have had access to such a procedure.

Other punishments, such as the admonition, sought to make a deeper impression on the offender's character. We catch a rare glimpse of the admonition in action in John Winthrop's account of a case from 1639. Nathaniel Eaton, the first president of Harvard College, was presented before the General Court for assaulting one of his students. The court convicted Eaton in open session, Winthrop reported, "yet [he] continued to justify himself." Thereupon proceedings were suspended until morning, while in the interim, "for divers hours," the elder ministers "[took] pains with him, to convince him of his faults . . . [and] in the end, he was convinced, and had freely and fully acknowledged his sin, and that with tears; so as they did hope he had truly repented, and therefore desired of the court that he might be pardoned." The judges then heard Eaton's confession, were satisfied of its sincerity, and sentenced him to pay a fine, which the court remitted in part, again presumably to symbolize community forgiveness.[4]

Though built on different premises, the Puritans' noncarceral process of admonition displayed striking similarities to the later philanthropists' carceral process of reclamation: both sought to alter the offender's inner sense of right and wrong; both were voluntary processes designed to elicit tears, shame, confession, and a promise of reform. The Puritans' version depended on their own peculiar belief that a conscience clouded by original sin could be clarified through *secular* persuasion.[5] But the admonition also depended on the insular nature of society for its success. The Puritans accepted a repentance only when it was sincere, and this could not be judged unless the examiners were familiar with the culprits who came before them.[6]

Public punishments such as whipping and the pillory also sought to produce in offenders feelings of shame and remorse, though through the manifest collective disapproval of the community rather than through private instruction.[7] Again, a communal pattern of life nourished the process: feelings of shame were likely to arise only when offenders knew and respected their onlookers. Informal efforts to drive home the lesson might also follow the official act of punishment. Puritan ministers urged their congregations to participate by offering offenders "necessary advise and reproofs with most pathetical exortations . . . to reform their evil ways." These efforts complemented ceremonies of public humiliation, for the trauma of that experience left offenders "more capable of an instruction or reproof for their Emendation, than they are at other times."[8] But, of course, the practice presupposed that the offenders *had* neighbors who were willing to involve themselves, face to face, in their personal affairs.

Public punishments did not depend on rehabilitation alone. They also sought to deter offenders (together with the onlookers) by administering physical and psychic pain.[9] The sting of the lash and the contortions of the stocks were surely no balm, but even worse for community members were the piercing stares of neighbors who witnessed their disgrace and with whom they would continue to live and work. Esteem has always meant much in intimate communities, and in the world of the visible saints it had spiritual as well as secular implications.[10] Under the circumstances, authorities often felt free to dispense with the punishment's physical component entirely: some offenders were required simply to stand in public with signs cataloging their crimes, a punishment that relied solely on mental anguish for its deterrent effect.[11] At the same time, an audience was essential to the effectiveness of public punishment within a close community. Hence one sometimes finds judges in early Massachusetts attaching to their sentences a delightful caveat: "to sit in the stocks one hour next lecture day, if the weather be moderate."[12]

Other punishments evoked the English rehabituative equation, already entrenched when the colony of Massachusetts came into being. Though the workhouse was generally reserved for status criminals and other petty offenders, a sentence to *noncarceral* hard labor for serious crimes could also result, though in a more roundabout fashion. As we have seen, thieves in early Massachusetts were required to pay treble damages to their victims. Impecunious offenders were sold into servitude on behalf of the aggrieved. The expedient of service was doubtless contrived principally to ensure adequate victim compensation,[13] but it also served as a means of rehabituation, conducted under the auspices of private masters rather than a carceral facility.[14] That the two were considered functionally equivalent is suggested by the authorities' willingness to substitute a term of indenture for commitment to the workhouse, even when there was no judgment to pay.[15] Rehabilitation on a private level was once again particularly well suited to an insular community. So long as the master had an existing relationship with the offender or the offender's family, his commitment to the offender's welfare was assured.[16] Nor would masters have otherwise gladly undertaken such a responsibility.

Of course, if reintegration failed, there were other punishments waiting in reserve to cast out the deviant once and for all. But communities hesitated to resort to branding—and more so to the gallows—particularly when the offender was one of their own.[17] Such reluctance was a natural outgrowth of underpopulation but also of communal living, where anger over criminal behavior was likely to be mixed with sympathy toward the individual committing the offense.

The initial repertoire of punishments in Massachusetts appears to have held crime to an acceptable level throughout the seventeenth century. While the early settlers voiced plenty of concern about moral declension, they left no surviving record of dissatisfaction with the prevailing scheme of punishments on the ground of its inefficacy.[18] Though he had a few ideas of his own, Cotton Mather was satisfied enough to commend "these Excellent LAWES" in 1704.[19] "Happy it is for Mankind, that there is law . . . in the World," the Reverend Samuel Checkley agreed in 1733. "By These [laws], Sinners are often awed and restrained, and kept from many Villanies which otherwise their Lusts and Passions would hurry them on unto." [20] A study of Middlesex County between 1650 and 1686 indicates that most offenders subjected to public punishment were successfully reintegrated into their communities.[21] Such criticisms of punishment as arose in the seventeenth century were *political* in character: the deputies objected to the imposition of discretionary punishment, as part of their campaign to rein in the power of the magistrates,[22] while the dissident settlers led by Dr. Robert Child remonstrated against Puritan deviations from English law and criminal practice.[23] None of these critics were concerned about the substantive effectiveness of law enforcement.[24]

During the eighteenth century, Massachusetts was buffeted by demographic and social forces that distorted prior patterns of criminal activity. Having previously sustained moderate but steady population growth, the province entered upon a period of rapid growth. By 1765, some thirty towns contained over two thousand residents apiece, while Boston's population swelled above fifteen thousand.[25] What is more, the mobility of the Massachusetts population increased significantly over the same period. More than half the sons born in Andover in the eighteenth century, for example, moved out of town at some point in their lives. Such trends were most pronounced in the larger urban centers. After 1765, more than 10 percent of the residents of Boston had lived in town for five years or less.[26]

To some extent the flood of migration emanated from outside the province. A small but growing proportion of Boston's immigrants arrived from foreign ports. The remainder, Massachusetts-born, streamed out of agricultural communities whose limited arable land could no longer sustain the burgeoning population.[27] The result was not merely motion but perpetual motion, the emergence by mid-century of "a small, but significant, floating population of men and women at the bottom of society who moved from seaport to seaport and town to town in search of work." These luckless vagrants had not only broken the bonds with their native communities but had failed to tie themselves to new ones.[28]

As these demographic trends gathered momentum, changes in the configuration of crime began to develop. Literary evidence from a variety of sources—the newspapers, the pulpit, the bench, and the legislature—indicate a widespread impression, and apprehension, that property crime rates were climbing after 1700, particularly in Boston and other maritime towns.[29] And along with distress over worsening currents of lawlessness went a growing perception that responsibility for property crime rested in large measure on persons unattached to the communities they afflicted. Chief Justice Thomas Hutchinson believed that "bad People frequently come into this Province from other Governments . . . merely for the sake of committing [larceny] here." Justice Nathaniel Sargeant described the recipients of punishment as "vicious persons . . . roving about the country disturbing peoples rest and preying upon their property."[30] Evolving anxieties about the proliferation of property crime were matched by an evolving composite of the typical criminal.

Impressionistic allegations of the growing incidence of crime have an eternal ring. One thoughtful English critic remarked the tendency of his countrymen "to avow that the times, in which they are unhappily cast, are infinitely worse than the preceding. . . . [T]here never was a period free from the same complaint. To avoid, therefore, a censure of this kind, I will not venture to determine positively, that there are now more criminals than there were some years ago."[31] Yet there is some reason to believe that the testimony of observers in provincial Massachusetts had a basis in fact. Statistical evidence tracking the rate of prosecutions and convictions for offenses against property in the Massachusetts Superior Court during the eighteenth century provides a rough barometer of change in the overall rate of criminal activity. These statistics point to a gradual increase in the number of offenses over the second half of the century, sharpening into a rapid increase after the 1770s, especially in urban areas.[32] Contemporary impressions of criminal alienage probably also had a basis in fact. No systematic tabulations of the backgrounds of property criminals are extant, but the many life histories of condemned criminals published during the provincial period attest to widespread transiency.[33] In part, however, the sense that criminals were extraneous to their communities may also have followed from a psychological redefinition of the community itself. As urban centers grew to contain more than one parish, more than one quarter, more than one character, it became natural to think of one's community as encompassing something less than the sum of all the town's inhabitants.[34] By the late eighteenth century, commentators throughout America were beginning to view offenders as forming a separate and distinct "criminal class."[35]

To what did contemporaries attribute the escalation of criminal activity in Massachusetts? In part, commentators of the late eighteenth century continued to blame property crime on idleness and human depravity while also pointing to social developments that had transformed the province: rising poverty coupled with rising commercial wealth, coupled with population growth.[36] Ideologically, such a mix of organic and environmental conjectures, however astute, added only marginally to the ferment of contemporary criminology. But publicists in this period also began to attribute property crime to the deteriorating effectiveness of traditional sanctions. "It must give every man of feeling the most sensible pain, when he observes how insufficient our penal laws are to answer the end they were designed to," complained one critic in 1784. "Scarce a morning arrives, but we hear of some house or store having been broke open the past night."[37] Featured prominently in proposals for hard labor in the 1780s, this thought changed the tenor of the debate over carceral punishment. Whereas earlier advocates had presented hard labor as a "more effectual" punishment than traditional ones, their analyses had focused on its affirmative merits. By the 1780s in Massachusetts, tracts proposing hard labor had taken on an alarmist tone, and the emphasis had shifted to a delineation of the *demerits* of the prevailing body of sanctions.[38] For "A Friend of Industry," typically, it had become "the want of some effectual punishment [that] will I hope apologize for my proposing a new mode."[39] And that want was probably a tangible one, for the growing anonymity of urban offenders in Massachusetts could only have weakened old sanctional processes.[40]

One traditional sanction that seems to have broken down was the sale into servitude. Throughout the provincial period, thieves unable to raise treble damages had routinely been bound out to a term of service; the proceeds passed to the aggrieved as compensation for the loss. This practice depended on the availability of a willing buyer, however, and finding one may never have been a simple matter. As early as 1702, Massachusetts legislators felt compelled to make provisions for unsalable convicts. "Inasmuch as it often happens, that persons convicted of theft, and sentenced to make restitution to the party injured . . . are held long in prison" for want of buyers, the legislators ordered the convicts' release if not disposed of within thirty days.[41] By the late eighteenth century, the market appears to have folded up altogether. "If [thieves] are not able to pay damages, they must be sold for a term of time sufficient to discharge costs," observed a commentator in 1784. "But where are the purchasers? It is as difficult to find such persons, as for a thief to become an honest man."[42]

Just what caused the collapse of the convict-servant market can only be guessed at; the employers did not say. Economic trends do not appear to have been pivotal, for demand did not revive in the 1790s, when the state enjoyed booming prosperity.[43] It seems more likely that demand slackened over the years because the status of the available convicts had changed. It was one thing for community members to admit into their households wayward individuals whom they had known, or known of, since birth; it was quite another to take charge of wandering paupers whose sole connections to the town were born of misconduct.[44] Lawrence Towner has argued that changes in the composition of the servant population rendered the family increasingly unfit to perform its traditional function as a "socializing agency" in eighteenth-century Massachusetts. One consequence was an increase in the volume of disputation between master and servant,[45] and another may have been simple unwillingness to purchase bonded servants in the first place. With the emergence of the transient criminal, rehabilitation at the private level probably became impractical.[46]

The admonition proved equally vulnerable to social change. In the seventeenth century, John Winthrop had confidently endorsed this practice. Experience had taught him that "A Reproofe entereth more into a wise man, then 100 stripes into a foole."[47] But Puritan authorities hesitated to employ the admonition when dealing with a newcomer or a stranger, for in such cases they could not easily determine whether the offender's repentance was genuine. As crime became increasingly the province of strangers, the utility of the admonition accordingly diminished. On top of that, even community members eventually grew reluctant to bare their souls before admonishers and before the public in the subsequent confession. A culture of privacy, less dominant in Winthrop's day, tended to undermine the admonition even in its traditional, communal context.[48]

Social change also impeded other public punishments. A sentence to the lash or to the pillory had worked primarily through the media of psychic pain and shame. Criminal anonymity diluted both elements of the sanction. Certainly, the threat of a session on the pillory was less daunting when performed before persons with whom offenders were unacquainted, and with whom they need have no further personal contact. "Could your Honours but be spectators of the ease, the negligence, and unconcernedness, with which these people are led to the whipping post," a critic lectured legislators in 1784, "your blood would chill in your veins, at the depravity of human nature."[49] Its aura of psychic trauma gone, the lash had disintegrated into a "slight corporal punishment" hardly sufficient to deter offenses.[50]

As for the rehabilitative element of public punishment, this appears not merely to have dwindled but to have positively backfired. Puritan ministers had always been sensitive to the difficulty of awakening in offenders a sense of shame. "If it be needful that any Sinner be laid under punishment of the Civil Law," the Reverend Samuel Danforth reminded his congregation, "tenderness and meekness, grief and pity, . . . are most likely to affect him with remorse for his sins committed, and resolution to avoid them in the future; while (*e contra*) Scoffs and Divitions do but tend to harden Sinners, and render them the more desperately wicked."[51] Danforth's call for "tenderness and meekness," delivered in 1708, made sense in a close community where offenders were well known. Onlookers might then be inclined to compassion, while offenders could be expected to respond to the paternal rebukes of their lifelong neighbors. By the late eighteenth century, when public punishment was more commonly administered to strangers, the practice appears to have engendered little more than the mutual antipathy that Danforth had feared. "[T]he punishment [whipping] they have received has *destroyed* the fear of shame, and produces a desire of revenge, which serves to *stimulate* their vicious inclination," a commentator lamented in 1784. "They improve the next opportunity to repeat the crime, and by practice make themselves masters of the trade." [52] Another author described public punishment as a vicious circle: "A man shall be tried, sentenced, whipped and set at liberty; his character, if tolerable before, is now ruined; nothing is to be done but for him to go to the old trade of stealing, when he is again taken and goes through the same process, which instead of answering the least good purpose, serves only to harden him the more; and so he goes on stealing and being whipped, until death rids the community of him." [53] In late eighteenth-century Massachusetts, public punishment had become worse than useless.[54]

Still other traditional penalties functioned poorly in the eighteenth century. At a glance, the fine (and its analogue, the bond for good behavior) would seem the most timeless of all sanctions: a blow to the pocketbook is painful no matter how many onlookers witness the event. Yet, there remains one instance in which a fine can impart no pain—namely, when the offender's pocketbook is already empty. One of the few freedoms indigents have always enjoyed is the freedom from fear of large fines or judgments. Early colonial fines had often been remitted, doubtless in part because of the scarcity of specie. Responsibility for the upsurge of property crime in more prosperous provincial Massachusetts still fell largely on vagrants and transients. Threatening to fine them would have been tantamount to suggesting that they eat cake.[55]

Social evolution hampered even punishments aimed at isolating criminals from the community. In the seventeenth century, banishment had effectively incapacitated offenders because they were known and could not return;[56] indigent strangers, likewise, were instantly recognizable and could be "warned out," in the contemporary phrase, before they could commit crimes.[57] But as urban communities swelled, recognition of strangers and persons under sentence of banishment became increasingly difficult.[58] Even branding might not be a sufficient stigma in some quarters. Capital punishment remained the only sure way to hand offenders a one-way ticket out of town—and as it happened, even that punishment was not quite so reliable as it might seem.

Disquiet over rampant crime, and the association of crime with the ineffectiveness of traditional penalties, forged crucial links in the chain that led to the penitentiary. Crime waves invariably generate pressure for state action, and the degradation of criminal sanctions must have seemed especially threatening in a society like early Massachusetts, which lacked a professional police force;[59] for little stood between offender and victim besides the specter of punishment. Under a cloud of anxiety, the landscape of criminal justice in Massachusetts began to change.

Some time-worn punishments simply disappeared. One of the first to go was public confession, which quietly bowed out of the records after 1700.[60] Banishment and "warning out" hung on a while longer, expiring shortly after independence.[61]

Other punishments remained in effect, but took on different functions. The lash and other public punishments had served initially to instill psychic pain and shame, as a prelude to communal reintegration. But when the offender lacked community ties, this formula no longer applied. In such cases, the purpose of these sanctions shifted to expulsion, by alerting townspeople to the culprits' infamy.[62] It thus became common in the eighteenth century to sentence offenders to several sessions of public punishment, so that all the more citizens could take notice of them.[63] Such sessions also became increasingly tumultuous affairs, in which offenders were liable to be pelted with refuse or worse. Onlookers appear to have seized the occasions of public punishment to vent their frustration over crime, in the process creating scenes of chaos that would have been unheard of when they shared with offenders a sense of belonging to the same community.[64]

Still other punishments that remained viable were extended to cover a broader range of crimes. Provincial statutes increasingly prescribed short-term imprisonment in the common jail as a deterrent, though this sanction's utility was limited by the unfeasibility of longer sentences.[65] More auspicious were the first few statutes mandating long-term hard labor in the workhouse; these appeared on the statute books by mid-century.[66]

The most notable legislative response, however, was a wider recourse to capital punishment for major property offenses. In 1692, when the new provincial government passed its first set of criminal laws, the only property crimes punishable by death were third offenses of burglary and robbery.[67] But in 1711, citing to the growing insecurity of the highways, the house prescribed capital punishment for second-time robbery offenders.[68] Four years later, again pointing to rising crime, the house added first-time burglaries to the capital list.[69] In 1737, the gallows was mandated for theft, on the third offense—the first time that category of crime had ever been punishable by death in Massachusetts.[70] In 1761, the robbery statute was revised yet again to send first offenders to the gallows.[71] Finally, in 1770, still finding the old provisions "ineffectual," the house expanded the definition of burglary (subject to capital punishment) to include entry into a dwelling in the day or night, with or without a breaking, so long as the offender broke out at night.[72]

In retrospect, the legislators' reaction seems to have been a natural one.[73] When criminal penalties become ineffective, the ordinary reflex surely is to move down the *prevailing* spectrum of sanctions to more severe alternatives. But in this ointment there lay a familiar fly. Whatever the legislators' abstract views, the people of Massachusetts, when faced with individual offenders, had never had much stomach for the gallows, even when the offenders were outsiders, and the thought of extending the penalty into the range of common property crimes was more than most citizens could swallow. So they set about thwarting the new capital statutes, just as previous generations of Puritans had thwarted earlier ones. And in a contest between the people and the rule of law in Massachusetts, law had rarely stood a chance.[74]

Juries frustrated the new capital statutes in several ways. At the indictment stage, grand juries often refused to charge persons with capital crimes. They simply downgraded indictments to noncapital charges of their own devising: thus burglary could be transmuted into "theft in the night time."[75] Even when an indictment for burglary was sealed, its harsh consequences might still be avoided by the petit jury. Of course, jurors could always acquit the defendant outright, but on many occasions they instead returned a conviction on a lesser charge.[76] (This version of jury nullification, known as "pious perjury," was also used in England to avoid the rigors of the bloody code.) And if the box failed to mitigate the penalty, the bench sometimes did so, in blatant disregard of statutory prescriptions.[77]

It is possible even that legislators never intended capital statutes to be strictly enforced. In England, William Paley defended the bloody code as an effective deterrent irrespective of the rate of execution. For Paley, the *threat* of severity was key: "Few actually suffer death, whilst the dread and danger of it hang over the crimes of many." But this was hardly the universal opinion: Martin Madan, another apologist for the bloody code, expressed outrage at its evasion, accusing the judges who sat at capital trials of being "little better than accessories" to the felons who came before them.[78]

How Massachusetts legislators felt about all this will never be known,[79] but if they did initially envisage a system of sporadic severity, its efficacy was exploded by Beccaria, who powerfully denied the deterrent capacity of uncertain punishment, however severe.[80] Empirical evidence of continued epidemic crime despite movement toward capital punishment further substantiated Beccaria's theorem,[81] and Massachusetts legislators ultimately balked at proposals to continue lengthening the capital list.[82]

Here, then, were the horns of a dilemma: Although "[a]t present, our laws are no more a check to simple robbery [than] they are to getting money honestly," the alternative of "tak[ing] a man's life for every trifling theft, as is done in England, is a disgrace to a civilized nation; humanity recoils from the idea."[83] Only after the slide toward harsher traditional sanctions, the path of least resistance, proved to be a cul de sac did Massachusetts lawmakers turn sideways to explore alternative solutions to the problem of crime.

The Massachusetts experience was not atypical. Equivalent pressures preceded the construction of penitentiaries in other parts of the new republic. In Philadelphia, shortly before the legislative decision to introduce hard labor in 1786, "passing references [to social disorder] gave way to an anguished out-pouring that decried the degree of vice and crime flourishing in the area."[84] As in Massachusetts, commentators in Pennsylvania attributed the growing incidence of property crime to an influx of outsiders who were undeterred by the threat of public punishment.[85] The act of 1786 cited as its rationale the need to restore crime control, "it having been found by experience that the punishments directed by the laws now in force as well for capital as other in-ferior offenses do not answer the . . . ends of . . . reform [and] deter[rence] . . . which is conceived may be better effected by continued hard labor."[86]

In New York, the decision to construct penitentiaries is often credited to the lobbying efforts of one determined man, Thomas Eddy, who shepherded the hard labor statute of 1796 through the state assembly.[87] The importance of such individual efforts cannot be underestimated: ultimately it is human persons who do (or do not) act to accomplish social change. But Eddy's in-volvement in the movement was not immediate: New York took its first step toward criminal incarceration in the 1780s, years before he became active as an advocate. A bill passed in 1785, restricted in scope to the municipality of New York, authorized city officials to substitute up to six months' hard labor in the workhouse for corporal punishment in all cases where corporal punish-ment was mandated by prior law.[88] This provision was renewed in subsequent acts, one of which included an explanatory preamble alluding to the familiar social pressures: "Whereas not only several disorderly persons inhabiting in the city and county of New-York but many other vagrants and idle persons, passing the same from neighboring Counties and States, or elsewhere, have often committed diverse misdemeanors, breaches of the peace, and other criminal offenses. . . ."[89] Other sources also advert to an outburst of property offenses in the city at around this time.[90] Eddy's subsequent efforts to enact a statewide bill expanded on this initial program and succeeded within its social context.

In England the story appears to have been similar, insofar as the rise of criminal incarceration corresponded with the declining effectiveness of tra-ditional sanctions. There, however, transportation to the American colonies had served in the eighteenth century as the staple punishment for property crime, and the impairment of this punishment traced to a different set of social (and political) circumstances. The parliamentary act of 1706 introduc-ing hard labor in England for some twelve years dated to the War of Spanish Succession, when interruptions in merchant shipping hindered the passage of transportees to America.[91] Thereafter, as the American colonies prospered economically, English commentators came increasingly to regard transporta-tion as an inadequate deterrent.[92] But the process collapsed at the outset of the American war for independence, when the rebel colonies closed their ports to further shipments of convicts.[93] The parliamentary act of 1776 establishing the prison hulks and the Penitentiary Act of 1779 date from this period. That these acts followed from the obstruction of transportation is indicated by their charmingly understated preambles: "Whereas the Transportation of Convicts to his Majesty's Colonies . . . is found to be attended with various Inconveniencies . . . ."[94] Meanwhile, Beccarian theory and manifest ineffectiveness combined to destroy confidence in capital punishment as an alternative of first resort.[95]

As American states and England began hard labor programs, the movement gradually gathered momentum. The earliest initiatives served as models for other regions.[96] In 1785, commentators in Philadelphia cited approvingly to the pilot project that had introduced hard labor to New York.[97] Shortly thereafter, Pennsylvania embarked on its own, very similar, carceral project.[98] Virginians in turn pointed to Pennsylvania's experience with incarceration to justify sanctional revision in their own state.[99] The debate over construction of penitentiaries in the South revolved in part around the political question of whether to follow the Northerners' lead.[100] The penitentiary thus spread not merely by virtue of social pressures but also by the gradual development of a carceral tradition. Initially, however, the decision to move to criminal incarceration appears to have been prompted more by a process of elimination— that is, by the elimination of older sanctions as viable means of crime control.

The mere failure of traditional sanctions to control crime did not in and of itself point the way to criminal incarceration in America. Hard labor was only one of several alternatives offered for discussion, and there was nothing inevitable about its selection. The American colonies had long been on the receiving end of the English punishment of transportation; some American advocates now proposed to follow suit and transport criminals out of the republic. Whereas banishment by way of escort to the town limits could no longer guarantee an offender's permanent removal, advocates of transportation hoped that a more distant exile would effectively prevent the offender's return. This idea retained a following as late as the 1830s, but it was always rejected because of its cost and the suspicion that no expanse of ocean would suffice to keep offenders from finding their way home.[101]

Hard labor, by contrast, held a number of attractions for American lawmakers. The problem faced by authorities was not crime in general but *property* crime, committed in the main by indigent transients. Considered as a therapy, hard labor appeared "peculiarly proper"[102] for such offenders, for it could be administered effectively by persons with whom offenders had no communal ties, and it attacked idleness, the reputed impetus for property crime. (Ideologically, hard labor had never been a panacea, and it would not have been suggested to control an outbreak of moral offenses, for example.)[103] Considered as a deterrent, hard labor combined the rationalist virtue of certainty with the traditional virtue of severity, still emphasized by most commentators.[104] Advocates also observed that if all else failed, hard labor at least incapacitated property criminals for a time. By comparison, public punishments disabled criminals only momentarily, and the frequent repetition of offenses impressed on publicists the importance of extended physical restraint as an additional bulwark against crime.[105] By the late eighteenth century, incarceration constituted a more reliable means of incapacitation than either banishment or (when filtered through the jury process) capital punishment. In addition, advocates promised that the prisoners' labor would defray the expenses of the otherwise costly punishment.[106]

Apart from practical concerns, some advocates also commended criminal incarceration on moral grounds. Because carceral punishment sought to rehabilitate offenders, advocates viewed it as a more "benevolent" solution to crime than "sanguinary" alternatives, such as capital punishment (and, as then functioning, the old corporal punishments), that relied solely on deterrence and incapacitation.[107] Such moral comparisons, which persisted into the Jacksonian era,[108] underscored the religious idealism of many American penitentiary advocates who, like many of their English counterparts, were deeply concerned with the charity of human institutions. Still, even the benevolently inclined kept an eye on the effectiveness of punishment, and they rarely suggested that utility be sacrificed to higher principles. On the contrary, advocates generally merged the two ideals: carceral punishment would be "effectual, and at the same time consistent with the principles of justice, reason and humanity." Capital punishment was "derogatory to the principles of humanity as well as impolitick." [109] Such linkages were natural, for what could have been more inhumane than punishment that caused suffering to no good purpose? Was it not in substantial part the very ineffectiveness of the old punishments that had made them appear inhumane? Notions of charity mingled easily with notions of utility in America, for the two concepts were closely connected.[110]

The possibility of substituting hard labor for public punishments was also relatively easy to contemplate, for it required no great leap of imagination. As we have seen, carceral punishment had been frequently proposed and occasionally put to use in colonial America. It was also a conventional response to crime's close relative, vagrancy. Because "the idle and poor [have] much increased among [us]," Bostonians had built a new workhouse in 1739; Philadelphians and New Yorkers pointed to the same concern when they followed suit.[111] Americans thus had social precedents for incarceration, and they could call on at least a modicum of experience with the problems of institutional administration.

The turn to Castle Island, and to the penitentiaries that followed it in Massachusetts and other states, transformed the geography as well as the therapy of criminal punishment. Instead of receiving their correction locally and publicly in the community, offenders were now ferried across water or hauled within walls to centralized pockets of the legal system removed from public view. This movement has sometimes been interpreted as a ploy to enhance state power: authorities thereby wrested control over punishment out of the hands of the popular mobs that had clustered around the old public ceremonies.[112] Inferences of ulterior political motives are, however, quite unnecessary here. The geographical transition followed naturally from practical considerations.[113] Centralization suited carceral punishment because it provided economies of scale, convenience of oversight, and ready access to the municipal marketplace.[114] As for seclusion, this, too, made sense in a mobile and urban social environment. Once criminals were perceived as outsiders, devoid of allegiance to the community, punishment in the community's presence no longer appeared to have a salutary impact on them. For their part, community members were perfectly content to see the backs of offenders. One of the first convicts sentenced to a term on Castle Island in 1785 reported from the prison ferry a ritual exchange with the local townspeople that proclaimed as eloquently as any pamphlet the new social verities: "As we put off from the wharf, the people, standing on this, and the neighboring wharves, gave three cheers, declarative of their satisfaction in our leaving them for a state of confinement. We returned three cheers immediately after; endeavoring to retort their insult, by letting them understand that we were also glad to leave them." [115] Such antagonisms did not lead publicists in Massachusetts to jettison rehabilitative ideology. But the social context of rehabilitation was altered subtly: instead of seeking to draw the offender back into the community, as had the old public punishments, carceral punishment wrenched the offender *out* of a subculture that commentators perceived as inimical to honest society.[116] The situs of punishment shifted to the fringe because it was now intended not to integrate but to extricate offenders from their surroundings.

The old punishments had also weighed on the public, in addition to the offender, by providing general, as well as specific, deterrence. By tradition, general deterrence was believed to derive from the spectacle of punishment. As Cotton Mather put it, "[N]otorious Sinners were put to open penance in this World, that their Souls might be saved . . . and that others admonished by their Example, might be more afraid to offend." [117] Subsequent rationalist literature held to this notion; Bentham referred to "exemplarity" as a quality to be sought after in choosing a punishment.[118]

Examined from the standpoint of exemplarity, geographically remote forms of punishment could well appear to be defective. William Eden, the English rationalist, warned that a prison sentence could not "communicate the benefit of example, being in its nature secluded from the eye of the people." [119] For this reason, some English and American commentators preferred *public* hard labor to labor within walls [120] (as was tried, briefly, in New York and Pennsylvania).[121] Such had long been recommended as an improvement over the *old* public punishments, which were "too transitory to leave any long impression on the mind." By contrast, hard labor in the open air afforded "a much longer and more dreadful example to deter others," by creating "a living, visible law." [122] Yet, at a time when public punishment was seen to degrade offenders, and thereby to undermine the process of rehabilitation, penitentiary advocates opposed the idea. Public hard labor of long duration would "only . . . increase the evils" associated with whipping and the pillory.[123] Further, even from the standpoint of general deterrence, the virtues of public hard labor could be called into question. In sprawling and bustling cities, spectacles intended to edify the community appeared increasingly futile and out of place. "[S]uch exhibitions," Gamaliel Bradford commented in 1821, "are very limited in their extent. If a person is to be hanged, not one in a thousand in the community sees the tragedy performed." [124]

Rather than make this point directly, late eighteenth-century advocates of incarceration found a way to steal their critics' thunder. Proponents of public hard labor had sung the praises of extended exemplarity; penitentiary advocates now chimed in that *carceral* hard labor could similarly enhance the spectacle of punishment—certainly one of their more artful strokes. Since "all persons at proper times shall be admitted to see the prisoners at their labor," the drafters of the Pennsylvania Constitution reasoned that the penitentiary would "deter more effectually" than prior sanctions, by creating "visible punishments of long duration." [125] And as other advocates observed, "even if the prisoners are not seen, the prison is visible. The appearance of this habitation of penitence may strike the imagination and awaken salutary terror." [126] Penitentiary advocates thus disarmed their critics without challenging their anachronistic premises.[127] Eventually, criminologists took the final step and denied the value of spectacle entirely.[128] But the striking architecture of the Massachusetts State Prison and other early penitentiaries was inspired by this traditional conception; their looming walls were not a herald of the new, as some have supposed,[129] but a last intellectual vestige of the old.

In sum, the penitentiary ended community involvement in punishment because such involvement no longer seemed constructive: neither humiliation nor terror could be instilled through the old media of public participation. Still, public punishment did not disappear completely with the turn to incarceration. In Massachusetts, it lived on for a time within the walls of the state prison itself. By statute, violations of prison discipline were punishable by up to thirty lashes, and a platform was constructed in the prison yard on which offending prisoners were forced to stand, holding signs or wearing dunce caps.[130] Thus, even as society at large discarded public sanctions, they were retained by the very institution that was to serve as a substitute. Of course! The penitentiary was itself a "little community" still isolated enough for the old formulas to remain effective.[131]

The Relevance of Revolution

C hanging patterns of crime and community developed gradually, over decades. But the late eighteenth century also witnessed one of the great upheavals in American history: the movement for independence. The birth of the American penitentiary coincided roughly with the birth of the Republic, and one is drawn naturally to inquire into the possibility of a connection between those two events.[1] Of course, one should not read too much into the fact of historical concurrence. Coincidences of events may be nothing more. Still, an event so full of moment as the American Revolution must have had some impact on American criminological developments.[2]

The criminological repercussions of America's break from the British Empire can be examined at several levels. Considered as a political process, the very act of revolution produced a climate conducive to legal change of all sorts, including the move to criminal incarceration. If only by virtue of having altered substantially their form of government, Americans were led to review the efficacy of colonial laws that might otherwise have persisted for want of such attention. This phenomenon was not unique to the American Revolution. The same forces arose out of earlier rebellions. After the fall of Charles I in England, the Rump Parliament appointed the Hale Commission to consider comprehensively the reform of English law. That commission had proposed hard labor as a standard punishment for crime.[3] Now, following the fall of George III in America, revolutionary assemblies in several states established commissions to inspect and to suggest revisions of the law.[4] The Castle Island Act emerged (with some prodding) out of such a commission. In 1780, the Massachusetts legislature appointed a body of prominent lawyers and judges to "select, abridge, alter, digest, and Methodize" law for the newly independent state.[5] A section of the code was assigned to each member, and it happened that Robert Treat Paine, the attorney general, took responsibility for criminal justice.[6] The commission was still at work in November 1784 when it received fresh instructions from the assembly "to consider the expediency of adopting other punishment than already provided by law for the crimes of theft & housebreaking & report."[7] Paine responded by drafting the carceral legislation passed by the assembly four months later.

Not only did the Revolution prompt Americans to reflect on their prior laws, it also emboldened them to think creatively about ways to improve criminal justice. The radical nature of their answer to British colonial rule had sparked in Americans a readiness to innovate in all areas of public policy. Many advocates promoted the penitentiary as a criminological "experiment,"[8] just as they pronounced their republic a grand experiment in politics.[9] The long struggle for independence further contributed to the American appetite for innovation by instilling in many patriots an animus against England and English ways. Once again, penitentiary advocates reflected the national mood. They urged the abandonment of older punishments inherited "from a nation, who steadily copied from the Goth and the Vandal."[10] Other commentators went so far as to propose a thorough purge of English common law from the American system of justice.[11]

The postwar years were exciting times, when Americans were receptive to new ideas and new programs.[12] Still, the limits of the Revolution as an engine for change must be recognized. Some postrevolutionary advocates claimed that independence had freed Americans to pursue carceral initiatives that had been *suppressed* while they remained a part of the British Empire; they thanked the day when rebellion "burst the fetters of colonial law."[13] However powerful the advocates' prospective longing for change, those retrospective fetters were more imagined than real. Though the Privy Council had asserted its authority to disallow acts passed by colonial legislatures on many occasions,[14] the Home Government expressed no hostility to American undertakings in the area of criminal incarceration. If anything, the Privy Council had encouraged such ventures by issuing repeated instructions for the construction of workhouses in Massachusetts and other colonies.[15] Though several of its capital statutes were vetoed, the legislature of provincial Massachusetts mandated hard labor as a punishment for extortion and counterfeiting without challenge in 1749 and 1750.[16] In Pennsylvania, the Great Law that had instituted hard labor comprehensively in 1682 was partially disallowed in 1705, following a legislative review by the attorney general.[17] Looking back, some postrevolutionary commentators portrayed this move as conservative reaction against the Great Law.[18] In point of fact, what the Home Government acted on in 1705 was not the initial version of the Great Law (which the Crown had allowed), but a set of amendments to that code, passed in 1700, that substantially increased the Great Law's harshness.[19] The attorney general's objections to those amendments signaled, if anything, a liberal reaction, for they focused primarily on instances of unwarranted severity (in addition to vagueness, overbreadth, and various other technical errors).[20] Significantly, the attorney general raised no per se objection to hard labor as a penalty, and with minor modifications the Great Law was reenacted and ratified. Its legislative repeal in 1718 came at the suggestion of the governor, not at the insistence of the Privy Council.[21]

Smoky memories to the contrary, the Americans who rebelled against

England had not counted the criminal law among their political grievances. Within the many bills of indictment solemnly drawn up against Parliament and the Crown in the years leading to independence, no reference was ever made to the imposition of unwanted criminal penalties.[22] This silence, which prevailed despite growing concern over the effectiveness of criminal punishment, reflected the substantial elbow room that the Home Government had granted the colonies to craft criminal codes.[23] In many instances, those codes had diverged markedly from England's bloody code.[24] In short, whatever its other effects on the law, the American Revolution did *not* release pent-up pressures for sanctional change: the valve had been open from the beginning.

That the Crown registered no objection to colonial statutes prescribing carceral penalties is perhaps a testament to England's abiding interest in such solutions to the problem of crime. Rehabituative ideology was deeply rooted in English legal thought.[25] Over many of the years that the Great Law was in force, the parliamentary Act of 1706 was directing clergied felons to English workhouses, and the Penitentiary Act of 1779 preceded postrevolutionary initiatives in Massachusetts (1785), Pennsylvania (1786), and New York (1785 and 1796). Had American penitentiary advocates truly abhorred English criminal justice in all its aspects, they would have had to reject hard labor instead of embracing it. In the event, however, their Anglophobic diatribes were aimed at capital statutes and at public punishments that they also regarded as inexpedient.[26] Those diatribes notwithstanding, American criminologists remained eager to learn about English *carceral* initiatives, and they maintained an active correspondence with their English counterparts, including John Howard (the jail reformer and coauthor of the Penitentiary Act).[27] American advocates reprinted a number of England's early tracts on criminal incarceration. These contributed both ideological and administrative blueprints, and in one instance the name, for America's postrevolutionary penitentiaries.[28] Meanwhile, more radical proposals to follow a truly independent course and discard the common law in its entirety never received a serious hearing.[29]

It should also be noticed that if the political process of the Revolution in some respects facilitated legal innovation, in others it tended to sustain the status quo. Against the currents of change ran cross-currents of continuity. For even as Americans swept away much of the colonial (and all of the imperial) framework of political authority, they chose to leave the *structure* of the existing legal system largely in place. Closed for varying periods during the years of military strife, state courts reopened after the war, sometimes with new names and new faces, but institutionally indistinguishable from their predecessors.[30] As for the substance of the law, every state elected to continue in force the statutes and precedents laid down during colonial times.[31] Though they established numerous commissions to review their laws, the revolutionary assemblies declined to wipe the slate clean and make a fresh start. This

decision was inauspicious for the cause of legal change: if independence encouraged Americans to take another look at the problem of law, it did not
obliterate their legal past. By receiving colonial codes across the political
chasm of the Revolution, states ensured that the structural inertia of those
codes—including criminal justice—would be maintained.

The American Revolution was also significant as an ideological event.
Having dethroned their king, Americans installed in his place a republic, and
they embraced as their creed a theory of republican government that they
themselves had done much to refine.[32] Some advocates of the penitentiary
justified their proposals in part by citing to this intellectual transition. They
coupled their criticisms of colonial criminal laws with pleas for new laws
"more suited to the genius of a republic."[33] Nonetheless, the relevance of
political ideology to this *criminological* development is open to serious question. Calls for new criminal punishments based on "republican principles"
rarely delved into the details of those principles; the same broad general-
ization was offered by commentators who sought to replace the entire corpus of common law.[34] Such arguments may have flowed more from visceral
Anglophobia than from reasoned ideological deduction. To the extent that republican political theory did bear substantively on the debate over criminal
penalties, its applications were equivocal and derived largely from schools of
thought that long predated the Revolution.

The central axiom of republicanism was the traditional commonwealth
ideal: government should function to serve the common good. "The word *republic,*" Tom Paine declared in a typical passage, "means the *public good* or
the good of the whole, in contradistinction to the despotic form, which makes
the good of the sovereign, or of one man, the only object of government."[35]
Given this concern, *liberty* in the lexicon of republicanism was no synonym for
anarchy; it did not imply "permission to distress fellow citizens." The proper
measure of republican liberty equaled "natural liberty, restrained in such a
manner as to render society one large family; where every one must consult
his neighbor's happiness as well as his own."[36] Whenever citizens moder-
ated their conduct to fall within these constraints, they behaved "virtuously,"
and their actions deserved public sufferance. But when citizens engaged in
activities that impinged on the greater happiness of the community, their
behavior constituted "selfishness" or "licentiousness" and merited proscrip-
tion. Republicanism, then, provided a framework for criminal justice,[37] one
that advocates of the penitentiary took to heart. They often spoke of the carceral institution as an instrument of the common good.[38] Yet so long as the
prohibitions of the criminal law had been adjusted to fit the interests of the
community at large, the same could be said of any other effective punishment. This aspect of republican ideology related not so much to the means of
enforcement as to the law's substantive metes and bounds.

On the matter of establishing criminal *penalties,* republicanism tugged advocates in opposite directions. Many publicists distinguished a republic from a monarchy not only by its liberal political objectives but also by its lack of a strong state coercive apparatus. Unlike a monarchy, a republic was supposed to rely on the virtue of its citizens for survival and would have to do without, among other things, a "multitude of criminal laws, with severe penalties."[39] Notions of such political constraints appear to have contributed to the postrevolutionary movement against capital punishment and may thereby have added to the pressure for alternative forms of criminal sanction.[40] Still, there was no telling how far such anti-coercive rhetoric might be extended. A few radicals went so far as to espouse the abolition of *all* punishments (if not of the moral proscriptions for which they were mandated), a viewpoint that, had it prevailed, would not have led Americans toward the penitentiary.[41]

Political theorists' sense of the fragility of republican government simultaneously pulled commentators the other way. Like rational criminologists, republicans recognized the propensity of every person "to do just as he pleases"—that is, to provide for individual utility without a thought to fellow citizens.[42] More than most rationalists, however, republicans emphasized the political consequences of such behavior. In a republic, based on nothing more than a common agreement to establish authority for the good of the whole, acts of licentiousness, in violation of that agreement, threatened not only other individuals but also the viability of the entire social contract. "Reigning vice," the Reverend William Symmes advised, "[is no] less productive of infelicity to national communities, than to individuals. . . . It naturally tends to create dissentions, and disband society." The Reverend Moses Hemmenway agreed: "When subjects abuse their privileges, and become disorderly, ungovernable, undutiful, and irreligious, their social union is greatly weakened. . . . It is true virtue, and religion, and subjection to the laws and ordinances of GOD, that can only preserve the liberty of any people." Commentators linked this threat to the special nature of republican government. Observed the Reverend Samuel West, "In a Republic the people are not only the source of authority, but the exercise of it, is, in a great measure, lodged in their hands. Corruption therefore among the people at large, must be immediately felt, and if not seasonably prevented, proves fatal in the end."[43] Only by resisting individual advantage could citizens preserve the republic and thereby reap the rewards of cooperative behavior.

For republicans, this political hazard was no mere abstraction. No sooner had they claimed victory over the English monarchy than American citizens appeared to surrender to an orgy of luxury and license. "Could any one have conceived that a people who had given such signal displays of fortitude and patriotism, under circumstances the most distressing—who for eight long years had supported a war of virtue, should soon, very soon, so far forget their own dignity and interest, as to abuse their liberty, and prostitute it to the vile purposes of licentiousness?"[44] For Governor John Brooks of Massachusetts, the danger was clear and present, as it was for half a hundred other commentators; expressions of alarm pealed through the political discourse of the 1780s.[45] Commentators identified the proliferation of crime as one manifestation of this "political pathology."[46] The activities of criminals consequently posed an immediate threat to both "the good order of government [and] the security of the people."[47]

Authorities hoped to meet the danger of political instability in classic republican fashion, by calling the people back from the brink and convincing them to return to the path of virtue, both for their own sakes and for the sake of society.[48] But if individuals failed to reform of their own volition, what else was there to do but use the sanction of law to nudge them along? For "the man that will do presumptuously and will not hearken" to appeals for reform, the Reverend Joseph Lyman insisted, "the State must employ punishments adequate to the suppression of vice, and rewards commensurate to the encouragement of virtue and fidelity. . . . Of the legislators of our republican government, we might have expected effectual laws to discourage excesses, by which the citizens are so certainly degraded to a state of servility and dependence." The Reverend Samuel West concurred: "Without [punishment] government cannot subsist; but society must be dissolved."[49]

Republican political ideologists were thus torn over the prospect of levying severe criminal sanctions. A republic was supposed to depend on public virtue; yet, when virtue proved ephemeral, authorities felt driven to establish effective sanctions to save the republic. Postrevolutionary advocates of the penitentiary cited directly to neither of these political postulates, though fear of anarchy may have added urgency to their pleadings. While some spoke vaguely of the need to protect "public utility," others simply noted the "alarming" proliferation of crime and left the radiations of that core fact to the reader's imagination.[50] Against the background of republican political commentary, those radiations would have been plain enough.

Still, if republican political theory fed postrevolutionary anxieties over the ineffectiveness of traditional public punishments, it is scarcely clear that prerevolutionary Americans took a more complaisant attitude toward crime control. Though couched in the language of republicanism, postrevolutionary alarums of crime's threat to authority were hardly novel, at least in Massachusetts and other New England colonies. This theme had been a tangible, if tangential, element of Puritan criminology from the beginning. The Puritans also traced the authority of the state to a social covenant. Violation of that covenant constituted no less of a political affront than in the new republic. In the prerevolutionary (and distinctly unrepublican) view of Thomas Hutchinson, crime "tends to the Dissolution of all the Ties of Government, and saps the very Foundation of Society." By the same token, crime control secured "the Safety of the Community and good Order of Government."[51] The same thought informed execution sermons in Massachusetts throughout the eighteenth century.[52] Indeed, the theme reached back at least to the earliest Puritan theologians in England, among them William Perkins, who deemed the "Lawes of men, made by lawful authority according to Gods Law" to be "bones and sinewes to hold together, props, and pillars, to uphold the common wealth, and all societies."[53] The Puritans added to this political motive an additional theological imperative for the control of crime. Crime, as sin, defied God's will as set down in scripture. Under the terms of the national covenant, the people promised to do their utmost to minimize sin in exchange for God's promise to bless them with prosperity. But failure to control sin threatened to provoke demonstrations of the Lord's displeasure far more menacing to the nation than mere political chaos.[54] In short, (some) Americans had powerful motives for the prevention of crime, over and above the protection of individual citizens, from the outset. In New England, at least, the Revolution did not inaugurate a new era of criminological hypersensitivity.[55]

In determining the proper *means* of achieving crime control, republican ideology may again have weighed upon postrevolutionary criminology. Republicans exalted the ideal of individual liberty, and that exaltation may have drawn attention, by contrast, to imprisonment as a suitable deterrent to crime. A number of postrevolutionary commentators identified the loss of liberty, along with enforced laboriousness, as a powerful discouragement to criminal activity.[56] But, of course, Englishmen had long prided themselves on their rights and liberties, and English carceral advocates could be found making the same observations on deterrence earlier in the century.[57] The contribution of revolutionary republicanism to carceral rhetoric, moreover, had two edges. Liberty sanctified could make its forfeiture seem a more potent threat, but also a threat less lightly executed. As we shall see, some persons were prepared to argue that liberty was too precious a treasure to confiscate for minor (or even major) criminal infractions.[58]

Another pillar of republicanism was the ideal of individual meritocratic opportunity, and this ideal could in turn have prompted criminologists to emphasize rehabilitative therapy, as also incorporated into carceral punishment.[59] At least one advocate explicitly drew this connection, recommending the penitentiary as a means of giving convicts a chance for prosperity.[60] Yet, again, the decision to build penitentiaries cannot be traced to the novelty of this idea. The vision of America as a land of economic opportunity had its genesis at the outset of the colonial period.[61] American republicans simply codified as a political maxim that which had long been a tenet of popular culture.[62] Whether or not encouraged by such culture, colonial ancestors of the revolutionaries had also administered rehabilitative therapy within workhouses and by way of other noncarceral forms of punishment. Notions of the advisability of criminal rehabilitation did not begin with republicanism.

At the end of the day, it seems doubtful that republican political rhetoric

was central to the advent of the penitentiary. Political themes remained incidental to the advocates' arguments, which focused primarily on the relative
effectiveness of alternative modes of punishment to control crime—which is
to say, on traditional criminological concerns. That penitentiaries also grew
in the soil of England's "mixed government" as well as France's Restoration
monarchy at least indicates that the institution was not rooted narrowly in a
single political ideology.

Finally, and perhaps most significantly, the American Revolution had social
and economic ramifications that may well have influenced the move to new
forms of punishment. If the abandonment of the pillory and other public punishments was tied to the growth of criminal activity and mobility, the revolutionary struggle must be accounted a contributing factor in that growth.
Wars seldom fail to disrupt society, and the six-year fight for independence
dwarfed in scale all previous conflicts in North America. The raising and dis-
banding of the Continental Army, coupled with the flight of the Loyalists,
entailed unprecedented movements of population. Even after peace was restored, patterns of heightened migration persisted. The war had opened vast
new lands for settlement, and, as John Shy has speculated, persons "uprooted
once by the war . . . were ready to move again when conditions at home
disappointed them."[63] This motion could only have diminished the level of
community insularity that had historically given public punishment its bite.

More important in the short term were the social disruptions caused by
rapid demobilization and economic adversity. The men released from military
service could not be reabsorbed into the economy overnight. In England, discharged soldiers had often engaged in criminal activity,[64] and this pattern now
appeared in the American republic. In the decade after Yorktown, a number of
itinerant gangs of veterans plundered the Eastern seaboard.[65] To make matters
worse, the 1780s were years of commercial dislocation. Independence freed
the republic from British taxes and regulations under the Navigation Acts but
simultaneously deprived it of access to former English markets. As a result,
depression settled over the entire nation and gave veterans further cause to
move and steal.[66] It was during this critical period that the first of the new
carceral programs arose in Massachusetts, New York, and Pennsylvania.

In short, the American Revolution may well have helped to create the social
and economic conditions that underlay the search for more effective means
of crime control late in the eighteenth century. But those conditions did not
arise spontaneously after 1770. The demographic trends of the postwar era
were, as one scholar has put it, more "evolutionary" than revolutionary: they
represented culminations and accelerations of existing patterns of growth and
mobility.[67] This was also true of criminological anxieties. Dissatisfaction with
traditional sanctions peaked in the 1780s, but it began earlier in the century.[68]

Again, the Revolution was not pivotal (although it may have been catalytic) to the legal transition.

Perhaps the most unequivocal evidence of the prerevolutionary prospect for criminal incarceration in America is the fact that several American colonies considered or passed prison programs in the decade *before* independence. In Massachusetts, such a program came under serious discussion as early as 1765. In that year the legislature appointed a committee "to prepare a Bill to make the Punishments of Criminals more subservient to the public Interest, by altering the punishment of certain Felonies, and by providing a Method for a public Work-House, to which criminals of every Part of the Province may be committed."[69] The list of public servants recruited for this work reads like a Who's Who of the late provincial Massachusetts political aristocracy. Among them were Peter Oliver, justice of the Superior Court (who became chief justice in 1772), Edward Trowbridge, attorney general of the province (who also rose to the bench in 1767), Thomas Hutchinson, chief justice and lieutenant-governor of Massachusetts, Samuel Dexter, a respected merchant who served on the Supreme Executive Council of State during the Revolution, and James Otis, former advocate general and, since 1761, the leading representative from Boston.[70]

As a preliminary step, the committee prepared a report formally recommending the replacement of capital and corporal punishments with "long confinement to hard labor in a House of correction," built "in one of the maritime towns of the province where work of various kinds may be procured."[71] The plan apparently suited the genius of a province as well as a republic, for the legislature instructed the committee to draft the bill.[72] Crown officials did not disagree: when the report went up to the royal governor and council it was read and concurred.[73] But the final bill (which has not been preserved) got nowhere. Though no further entries appear in the legislative minutes, it reportedly failed after two readings.[74]

The bits and threads of this curious episode are too scant to provide much more than food for speculation. In its brief report, the committee did stress the weakening of old sanctions. Were their program adopted, the members commented, "the great end of punishment *viz* the deterring [of] the criminals and others from committing the like crimes would be better answered that it is at present."[75] That the plan emerged during a crime wave that swept through Boston and neighboring towns in 1764 and 1765 further suggests its connection to social desperation.[76] Yet, looking back some twenty years later, Samuel Dexter recalled in a letter to Justice William Cushing that the *want* of crime had derailed the committee's efforts: "A bill [to introduce hard labor] was, by order, prepared . . . in the year 1764, if I remember right; but the charge of building and supporting a workhouse, or workhouses, when neither felonies nor smaller crimes were so common as at this day, discouraged the members of the House."[77] Crime, it seems, had progressed far enough to prompt proposals for change but not quite so far as to goad the legislators into expensive action.

In tipping the political scales, the timing of this proposal is also suggestive: for the committee's labors over the spring of 1765 were rapidly eclipsed by the Stamp Act crisis. James Otis soon became immersed in leading the fight against parliamentary taxation of the American colonies; while for Thomas Hutchinson, a suspected supporter of the tax, the problem of protecting the people from crime became subordinate to the problem of protecting himself from the crimes of the people.[78] Given these distractions, committee members may not have pushed their program with all the weight that such a prestigious group could otherwise have summoned to the task.[79]

The contemplation of criminal incarceration in prerevolutionary Massachusetts was not an anomaly. At least two other colonies did the same. In Connecticut, the legislature ventured beyond proposals to pass an act in 1773 authorizing the construction of a "Public Gaol or Work-House," and prescribing hard labor therein as the sole penalty for six property crimes, including burglary and robbery.[80] This act took effect during the period of relative calm that preceded the Boston Tea Party; the war for independence followed, and soon the Connecticut prison was given over to housing political prisoners. Following a fire in 1782 the prison was abandoned, just as the war was ending, and it was not rebuilt as a state prison for criminals until 1790.[81] In Pennsylvania as well there were some late provincial stirrings, though they got no further than the planning stage. A number of Philadelphians became interested in the subject of the penal code "a few years before the revolution," and in February 1776 they formed themselves into the Society for Assisting Distressed Prisoners. Their efforts contributed to the insertion of a resolution to establish carceral punishment in the state constitution of 1776, but General Howe and his redcoats soon occupied Philadelphia and the society ceased to operate.[82] In all three colonies—Massachusetts, Connecticut, and Pennsylvania—efforts to amend the criminal law appear to have been overtaken by political events. The temporal proximity between independence and the advent of the penitentiary may therefore be deceptive. Far from precipitating its rise, the Revolution may actually have delayed the penitentiary for a generation.[83]

The Fledgling Institution

Once begun, the move from pillory to penitentiary was not over in a day. Like most legal transitions, it took time—time to put the new institutions in place, of course, but also time for legislators to convince themselves to take the plunge. Old punishments might seem to be failing, but the alternative of a full-scale carceral program, whatever its promise, remained untested. In most instances, the experimental zeal of the new state governments did not extend to an immediate and total break with traditional means of crime control.

In Massachusetts, the bills establishing carceral punishment reflected legislative caution in several ways. The choice of Castle Island as site for the new sanction was in itself a sign of hesitancy. With its existing barracks, the facility could be rendered minimally suitable for convicts without a substantial capital outlay.[1] Equally half-hearted was the composition of the accompanying criminal code. Under the new statutes of 1785, some twenty-four categories of crime were made punishable by hard labor,[2] yet with two minor exceptions,[3] carceral punishment became an alternative to, not a replacement for, the old public sanctions. Under the revised larceny statute, hard labor was not even a primary option: along with a fine or whipping, convicts were required to pay treble damages to their victims and could be sold into bonded servitude to satisfy this judgment. Only in those cases where victims failed to sell convicts were they to serve up to three years on Castle Island[4] (although courts do not appear always to have followed the strict letter of this limitation).[5] In other instances, however, the code simply added hard labor to the judge's menu of options. At the same time, many of the new provisions widened the latitude of judges to choose among *traditional* penalties. Whereas arson against a building other than a dwelling was previously punishable by whipping only, the revised statute of 1785, with typical inclusiveness, authorized sentences to hard labor "for life or years," the pillory, whipping, imprisonment in the jail (again, any term), binding to good behavior, fining, "or to any or all of these punishments, according to the nature and aggravation of the offense."[6]

What are we to make of such a statute? Does it signify a structural preference for wide judicial discretion or simply an abdication of authority, a decision by baffled lawmakers to relegate to judges the problem of arresting rampant crime?[7] Whatever the answer, judges retained their broad powers to choose among sanctions for some twenty years, and they hardly availed themselves of every opportunity to impose hard labor.[8] The Massachusetts legal system eased its way from pillory to penitentiary.

It arrived there in due course. Castle Island initiated Massachusetts to the practice of criminal incarceration. Over its fourteen-year history, the prison held an average of fifty convicts at a time, "criminals of almost every species, and from every part of the Commonwealth."[9] By 1797, the sanction of hard labor had become sufficiently familiar as to enter the vocabulary of banal humor.[10] But it had also won the confidence of persons in high places. "I believe it will not be doubted," Governor Increase Sumner lectured the legislature, "that the Commonwealth, since the Institution of that mode of punishment, has been abundantly more free from high-handed offenses, than at any former period."[11] The state's attachment to carceral punishment was tested in 1798, when the federal government prevailed on the state to convert Castle Island into a federal military fortification. Legislators reacted initially by ordering the dispersion of Castle Island inmates to local workhouses, but these proved so insufficient that within a year judges ceased pronouncing sentences to hard labor.[12] By allocating funds to build a new, larger prison at Charlestown from the ground up, the legislature in 1800 renewed and deepened its commitment to the sanction of incarceration.[13]

The criminal statutes of the Massachusetts were revised for the second time in twenty years to reflect this commitment. The legislature appointed Judge Nathan Dane and Justice Samuel Sewall to draft a code "applicable . . . to the spirit and nature of the proposed establishment."[14] Adopted to coincide with the opening of the state prison in 1805, the new code at last abandoned the public sanctions that had been a part of life in the state for close to two centuries. Bonded servitude for single (not treble) damages remained an option at the judge's discretion for those convicts who failed to compensate their victims out of prison earnings; but servitude in this connection merely supplemented the carceral sanction and, in any event, appears to have been disused.[15] After 1805, all crimes in Massachusetts were punishable by fine, incarceration, or the death penalty, in the pattern of all modern American statutory schemes.[16]

There remains one curiosity in this legislative transition: the lag in efforts to formalize the shift. A catch-all statute making hard labor the alternative sanction for *every* crime meriting corporal punishment was passed by the House in 1785 but rejected by the Senate.[17] This statute did not become law until 1813, years after corporal punishment had been effectively interred.[18] Meanwhile, a law to formally abolish the old punishments was drafted by Dane and Sewall as part of their code of 1805, but it too died in the Senate, even as the rest of their statutes were passed.[19] Corporal punishment was not abolished de jure until 1826, nor was bonded servitude until 1836.[20] Just what caused the legislature to delay these enactments is difficult to say. Perhaps it was less jarring to turn the pages of the old laws than to close the book on them entirely.

Massachusetts was not alone in its gradualism. In other jurisdictions as well, the pillory and penitentiary stood side by side for a time. But patterns of evolution varied. In New York, the legislature established a pilot project in New York City in 1785 and expanded it into a statewide program after a decade of operation, a deliberate approach to legal change that (in a different context) the state's leading penitentiary advocate, Thomas Eddy, endorsed.[21] In Connecticut, carceral legislation applied from the first to the entire state but was passed in driblets, eventually covering the spectrum of criminal law. Though the first provisions for centralized hard labor, aimed at six crimes, dated to 1773, corporal punishment did not disappear from Connecticut until 1830.[22] Among the states spearheading criminal incarceration in the 1780s, only Pennsylvania replaced corporal with carceral punishment in a single step. Reassured, perhaps, by its historical recollection of the Great Law, the legislature in 1786 abolished all traditional public punishments under the first postrevolutionary statute that mandated hard labor.[23] If not quite at the head of the carceral procession, Pennsylvania did take the lead in finalizing the transition.

Having received the imprimatur of their state legislatures, American penitentiaries began to take shape. Postrevolutionary carceral institutions conformed to the rehabituative tradition. Congregate hard labor by day and congregate confinement by night became the institutional routine. But before long, the ideological innovations then blossoming in England began to infiltrate the American states. Harmonious in 1785, American carceral rhetoric soon fragmented, leaving advocates at loggerheads over how best to chart their state prison programs.

The new ideological element that caused all the commotion was solitary confinement and the theory of reclamation. Not a whisper of this approach was audible in 1785; but philanthropic prison literature from England was rapidly becoming available in America.[24] And one state was soon prepared to act upon it.

Pennsylvania initially instituted hard labor out of doors, and for three years the wheelbarrowmen (as these convicts were known) formed a part of the landscape, cleaning and repairing the roads of Philadelphia and its suburbs.[25] This program worked out badly—traffic and confrontations between the convicts and passersby ensued—and in 1790 the legislature moved hard labor indoors, simultaneously authorizing construction of an inner block of solitary cells at Philadelphia's Walnut Street prison. Whereas some prisoners would continue to suffer hard labor, "the more hardened and atrocious offenders" could now be sentenced to serve part or all of their terms under a solitary regime.[26] Caleb Lownes, a Walnut Street inspector, published a pamphlet in

1793 extolling the facility and its system of solitary confinement.[27] When law-makers in New York embarked on a full-scale carceral program at Newgate Prison in 1796, they mimicked this approach, giving judges discretion to sentence felons and petty larcenists to spend any portion of their terms in solitary confinement or alternatively at hard labor.[28] Thomas Eddy, principal author of the legislation of 1796, had consulted the Pennsylvania code and met with Caleb Lownes before drafting the bill.[29]

These developments did not go unnoticed in Massachusetts. An anonymous newspaper column presently appeared praising Walnut Street and proposing to divide the Castle Island prison into "small apartments, where convicts may be placed, either alone or in classes."[30] This appeal had no immediate impact, but when the Massachusetts assembly began to plan a replacement for Castle Island in 1799, it ordered three hundred copies of Lownes's pamphlet.[31]

Still, legislators proceeded cautiously. A committee appointed to study the Walnut Street plan was duly impressed,[32] but the representatives voted only to construct the state prison in such a manner as to accommodate solitary confinement, were they subsequently minded to introduce it, "without any alteration in said buildings."[33] An inroad had nonetheless been made, and when Dane and Sewall drafted the new code in 1805, they provided for a combination of the two schemes. On conviction under any criminal statute mandating incarceration in the state prison, the judge was to set two successive terms: an initial term of solitary confinement and a subsequent term of hard labor, each to be served within the Charlestown facility.[34] As elsewhere, this dual sentencing structure seems to have been fashioned in order to combine or balance the two ideologies.[35]

If this was a compromise, it did not endure. By the beginning of the 1820s, different ideological circles were vying for influence over the internal management of various American penitentiaries.[36] In Massachusetts, the battle lines were clear. At the one extreme stood the board of directors of the state prison at Charlestown. Thoroughgoing advocates of solitary confinement, the directors insisted that the only way to rehabilitate a convict was "to turn the mind in upon itself [and] awaken remorse"—in other words, to bring about a "change of heart."[37] From the directors' perspective, hard labor had no therapeutic value. On the contrary, labor obstructed the process of arousing remorse, by offering "relief . . . [from] the painful monotony of self-contemplation."[38] Hard labor did, however, generate revenue to support the facility. On this basis, the directors concluded that "economy and reformation are adverse objects in the establishment of the Massachusetts State Prison. They are antagonistic principles. . . . [S]training the one relaxes the other." The problem was to bring the two into some reasonable balance, so that neither goal was sacrificed.[39]

At the other extreme stood Gamaliel Bradford, warden of the state prison from 1812 to 1824. His was the voice of the rehabituative tradition, under which hard labor remained the be-all and end-all of the rehabilitative process: "Industry is the nurse of virtue, and the enemy of vice. . . . [T]o overcome habits of idleness, and beget a custom and taste for labour, would be the most acceptable offering which could be laid on the altars of religion and morality." [40] From this perspective, economy *and* reformation flowed from the same source; they were not antagonistic principles at all. [41]

Though well acquainted with the theory of solitary confinement, Bradford remained skeptical of its rehabilitative powers. This skepticism emanated, perhaps, from the lingering influence in Massachusetts of Puritan convictions. [42] One of the most essential of those convictions was that men must live within their sinful world, and not seek to escape it. [43] Bradford echoed that

> Man was made for society, and although some men, for pious purposes, have withdrawn themselves from the world and to avoid the corruptions which abound in it, have shut themselves up in monasteries or caves, yet it is not allowed that the cause of religion and virtue is promoted by such retirement. . . . [A] long confinement in total solitude, might destroy [the convict's] social feelings, and produce a sort of stupid apathy which would render him very unfit for an useful or happy member of any society. [44]

In addition, Calvinist perceptions of human frailty suggested that attempts to influence fundamental moral values held less promise than rehabituation. [45] Finally, a term of idle solitary confinement ran counter to the work ethic. [46] Bradford conceded that solitary confinement for short periods could promote reflection, and he favored separate celling at night, but Bradford registered unequivocally his opposition to any further extension of solitude: "*I am very sure this will not do,*" he wrote to an English correspondent, underscoring his words for emphasis, "on experiment, the advocates for it, and the community, *will be disappointed.*" [47]

In short, both camps in Massachusetts were prepared to accept some mixing of solitary confinement and hard labor, but for different reasons and with different ends in view. For advocates of rehabituation, hard labor meant therapy as well as economy, and solitary confinement served (if at all) in a subordinate capacity; the primary object of the exercise was to break bad habits. For advocates of reclamation, hard labor meant economy and (at best) a secondary therapy; solitary confinement served as the principal medium for rehabilitation, the object being to reach the offender's heart. This conceptual disagreement ultimately bred conflict within the prison administration. The directors made "repeated representations" to the legislature for funds to further the use of solitary confinement; the warden preferred to expand the workshops. [48] Overlapping administrative responsibilities of the contending factions added fuel to the fire. [49] By 1823, the two sides were trading insults in the public press, while the directors petitioned the legislature to abolish the office of the warden.[50]

Even as rival advocates locked horns, they also locked arms in a rear-guard action to preserve the penitentiary system. For, ideology aside, the new prisons were rapidly beset by administrative difficulties that in time aroused a storm of criticism. Carceral advocates were thrown on the defensive, and before long the future of the institution lay in question.

A generation after the penitentiary's debut, Governor Levi Lincoln of Massachusetts looked back and pondered, "Whence it arises, that disappointment in results so often follows the best promises of success, in the affairs of that establishment."[51] The disappointment had not been long in coming. In spite of extensive precautions,[52] the Massachusetts State Prison was plagued almost from the outset by violence, escapes, overcrowding, and expenses far in excess of earnings. In 1813, the inmates contrived to burn their workshops, and three years later they staged a full-scale insurrection that resulted in one death. Meanwhile, the frequency of recommitments began to cast doubt on the rehabilitative capability of the facility.[53]

By 1816, a reaction had set in. Newspapers ran commentaries questioning the utility of the penitentiary, and objections were soon "in the mouths of so many of the community, as to become a sort of popular clamor against the whole system."[54] Official concern was no less intense. Disheartened legislators contemplated abandoning "the beautiful and brilliant theory of reclaiming the unprincipled," as "vain and illusory," and substituting a harsher carceral policy intended "to deter and restrain the atrocity of offenders."[55] Some refugees from the seventeenth century even advocated restoring traditional public punishments and scrapping criminal incarceration entirely.[56] This possibility also received legislative consideration.[57] In other states, the story was similar. Throughout the nation in the late 1810s and early 1820s, the penitentiary encountered a crisis of confidence that threw its survival into jeopardy.[58]

In Massachusetts, public criticism of the penitentiary drew rival advocates toward common ground. All advocates in unison defended the institution's potential for rehabilitation by emphasizing the number of inmates who never returned instead of the recommitment rate.[59] All advocates in unison underscored the value of the penitentiary as a means of incapacitation.[60] And all advocates, though not quite in unison, disputed the adequacy of a system of criminal law that relied entirely on deterrence, as some legislators had proposed.[61]

Defenders of the penitentiary in Massachusetts also wrestled with the age-old problem of reconciling rehabilitation and deterrence. A charge repeatedly leveled by armchair criminologists ("men who sit quietly over a fire or round a luxurious table on a cold winter day") was that the facility lacked sufficient hardship to terrify prospective offenders.[62] Some even believed that inmates had become gluttons for punishment, preferring the quality of life in the penitentiary to what they had known outside it.[63] Such claims tested the patience of carceral advocates, who, though prepared to engage in rational debate, could only dismiss as outlandish the notion that convicts entered the state prison with a song on their lips.[64] Advocates responded by detailing the dreadful severity of life within prison walls and by recounting the long record of escape attempts—no gilded cage, this. What few amenities the institution offered were essential to the rehabilitative process, advocates explained; any further harshness could tip the precarious balance.[65]

All penitentiary advocates also defended the fiscal responsibility of the state prison, in spite of its persistent deficits. Like English philanthropists, many advocates portrayed the institution as a humane enterprise. The costs represented "a beneficent gratuity . . . which humanity and heaven required," and were alleged to be fewer per capita than those of other social projects borne by the state.[66] To satisfy persons unmoved by such appeals, the advocates also insisted that what appeared to be red ink on the state prison's balance sheet was in reality black. As Warden Bradford explained, a system of incarceration and hard labor ensured that each convicted offender at least "produces something." Without it convicts produced nothing, "and probably would have been twice as much damage to society as the amount of all the expenses of the Prison establishment." According to this logic, any gross earnings "ought to be considered as clear gain to the State."[67] But even as advocates argued the sufficiency of prison labor, they were whipsawed by the converse accusation that convicts "work too much," undercutting the market for goods produced by free labor. So, from the other corner of their mouths, advocates depicted the economic impact of prison production as minimal.[68]

The problem of maintaining the rehabilitative integrity of the penitentiary system could not be as easily dismissed. Critics charged that the state prison had become "a sink of corruption," a collection point where novices in crime learned the state of the art from older, more accomplished offenders. Contact between prisoners, so the argument ran, counteracted whatever therapeutic benefits the penitentiary offered, and compounded disciplinary problems by facilitating organized disruptions and escape attempts.[69] Such criticism had been heard before. As early as 1796, a commentator identified prisoner congregation as a flaw in the Castle Island facility, and three years later the legislative committee appointed to plan its replacement repeated the point.[70] But these warnings fell upon deaf ears. As constructed, the state prison of Massachusetts featured supervised, congregate workshops for hard labor in the daytime and unsupervised, congregate cells for the night hours—cells that eventually lodged anywhere from four to sixteen prisoners each. The block of cells provided for solitary confinement during the first phase of a convict's sentence was far too small to be put to more general use.[71] Having neglected the problem once, the legislature had now to grapple with it again.[72]

Rather than deny that inmate congregation was causing mischief, defenders of the penitentiary responded with a call for prison renovation.[73] Proponents of reclamation seized on the criticism as another ground for imposing solitary imprisonment throughout the inmate's course of confinement.[74] Proponents of rehabituation were caught in a bind. Although they felt compelled to agree (if somewhat less enthusiastically) that congregation could corrupt,[75] they still considered it essential to the process of learning a practical skill. *Solitary* labor, as suggested by many advocates of reclamation, would not do, for it reduced productivity, precluded instruction, and tended to "render labor irksome and disgusting" instead of making it "habitual and easy."[76] Warden Bradford thus proposed to continue supervised, congregate hard labor during the day, but to introduce separate celling at night, when supervision was impractical. This plan had first appeared in the English Penitentiary Act of 1779 and was pressed by Thomas Eddy along with a number of English rationalists.[77]

Penitentiary advocates ultimately weathered the storm; in Massachusetts and virtually every other state the institution hung on, if only by a thread.[78] In the end, however, lawmakers were reluctant to abandon without further trial a program to which they had already committed a considerable capital investment; nor had any credible alternative presented itself.[79] Instead, state legislatures made their first attempts to correct the correctional facility in America. In Massachusetts, an act passed in 1818 for "the better regulation of the State Prison" set sterner guidelines for enforcing discipline and provided for progressively harsher sentences for second and third offenders.[80] And while legislators hesitated to authorize expensive structural renovations to separate convicts,[81] they did take a less costly step in that direction: henceforth, the prison population was to be split into three classes according to deportment, each class lodged and employed separately from the others.[82] Another statute granted judges discretion to divert offenders sentenced to three years or less to local jails, thereby preserving them from contact with more hardened state prison inmates.[83]

At first, Massachusetts authorities felt confident of these reforms. Governor John Brooks and the legislators congratulated one another for setting matters right at the state prison, and they reacclaimed the principle of carceral rehabilitation as abruptly as each had repudiated it the year before.[84] But these jubilations proved premature.[85] Escapes and disruptions continued as before, and the closefisted measures to ensure separation of convicts quickly disintegrated.[86] In 1826, Governor Levi Lincoln reported that prison industries were turning a profit but added "a melancholy reverse to the picture"— namely, "the system is utterly ineffectual, to purposes of reform or amendment." Structural alterations to accommodate separate confinement were still "imperiously required," and legislators at last resigned themselves to this expense.[87]

By this time the two competing rehabilitative ideologies had matured, *pari pasu,* into full-fledged administrative systems in other states. In Pennsylvania, the Walnut Street prison of Philadelphia with its block of solitary cells was replaced by two new penitentiaries featuring solitary confinement of all inmates throughout their course of confinement. The Western State penitentiary, opened in Pittsburgh in 1826, was designed to accommodate idle solitude. The Eastern State penitentiary, under construction in Philadelphia since 1823, was fitted for individual labor within solitary cells—a system that the legislature ordered extended to Pittsburgh after its eastern counterpart opened in 1829.[88] These institutions, featuring what came to be known as the Pennsylvania plan, realized the ideal of reclamation as it had long been advocated by English philanthropists.[89] Meanwhile in New York, the Auburn Prison (successor to Newgate) thoroughly overhauled its system of discipline around 1823. The new Auburn plan contemplated separate confinement at night and congregate hard labor by day, supplemented by a cluster of disciplinary innovations: a strict rule of silence, orderly marching to and from the cells, and constant oversight by prison authorities while the inmates were at labor.[90] For advocates of rehabituation, these administrative devices fully reconciled the dual imperatives of congregate therapy and inmate separation. Though prisoners labored in a team, each inmate under the Auburn system of order and silence "form[ed] a class by himself."[91]

In 1826 the Massachusetts legislature elected to renovate its state prison according to the Auburn model, rather than either of the solitary models.[92] This decision accorded with the preference of Governor Lincoln,[93] as well as the counsels of the Reverend Louis Dwight, founder of the influential Prison Discipline Society of Boston.[94] In 1829, the "New Prison" opened, administered under a code of regulations which ordained the Auburn discipline.[95]

The underlying philosophy of incarceration in Massachusetts thus remained decidedly rehabituative. Relying "on the presumption that habit will have some influence," prison authorities assigned each convict to "that [prison] occupation . . . for which he seems best qualified, and by which therefore he may be most likely to earn a subsistence after his release." Once his sentence expired, the convict was launched back into the world, prepared to "obtain an honest livelihood with less exertion and risk than a dishonest one [whereby he] may perhaps pay some regard to [his] own interest."[96] Retained as an internal sanction, solitary confinement all but disappeared as the preliminary stage of a convict's sentence.[97] As if to crown the victory of the rehabituation advocates, the board of directors of the state prison, having previously sought to eliminate the warden's office, was instead itself dissolved.[98]

In other states where penitentiaries remained to be constructed, carceral debates during the Jacksonian period centered on the relative merits of the Auburn and Pennsylvania plans.[99] Advocates competed furiously,[100] the champions of the Auburn system emerging triumphant in almost every state.[101] And because nothing succeeds like the appearance of success, Auburn advocates happily trumpeted each new adoption of their carceral program as another endorsement of its superiority.[102]

Substantive carceral analyses in the Jacksonian period devoted somewhat greater attention than in the past to regulatory and architectural details.[103] Advocates of the contending systems produced elaborate arguments to demonstrate the administrative expediency and cost efficiency of their preferred designs.[104] As to carceral therapy, some supporters of the Auburn and Pennsylvania plans sought to merge rehabituative and reclamatory ideology, asserting that their system could serve both to accustom offenders to labor *and* to promote moral reflection.[105] For most, however, the issue came down to the relative urgency of those two purposes—the same argument that had divided prior generations of criminologists.[106] Expectations of the proponents of both plans remained moderate. Like earlier thinkers, most Jacksonians drew the sober conclusion that some (in particular, youthful) offenders could be reformed, while others could not. As a consequence, they anticipated that the penitentiary would prevent some, but not all, crime. If anything, Jacksonians tended to be less sanguine than their predecessors. Having learned through bitter experience the limitations of the penitentiary, many Jacksonians faulted the postrevolutionary builders for promising "[m]ore benefit . . . than it was prudent to propose."[107] The new schemes of prison discipline, then, reflected no ideological break with previous strains of carceral theory. On the main points of rehabilitative process and prospects, Jacksonians reiterated the conventional wisdom (and dissension) of carceral advocates who had preceded them.

Of course, whenever a social or institutional transition occurs, there will be those whose views of the event run to extremes. So it was with carceral punishment. Some commentators clung to their past, resisting the movement doggedly; while several others looked to the future with visions that lured them into enthusiasm. For advocates of the first sort, mere political defeat lay in store.[108] Advocates of the second sort awaited the deeper embarrassment of derision and disregard.

Carceral enthusiasm took several forms. A few publicists indulged the hope that the penitentiary might suppress crime so thoroughly as to remake society; one early Maryland advocate predicted that carceral therapy could become "a grand instrument of future reformation and happiness among mankind."[109] Others were so charmed by their carceral designs that they fancied prison architecture a suitable model for other social institutions.[110] In England, Jeremy Bentham conceived that his Panopticon was "capable of applications of the most extensive nature." The blueprint was equally well suited for "workhouses, or manufactures, or mad-houses, or hospitals, or schools."[111] Two generations later, the American advocate Louis Dwight returned to this theme. "If there are principles in architecture, by the observance of which great moral changes can be more easily produced among the most abandoned of our race," Dwight speculated, "are not these same principles, with certain modifications, applicable to persons who are not yet lost in virtue but prone to evil?" Such principles "would greatly promote order, seriousness, and purity in large families, male and female boarding schools, and colleges." [112] Although Dwight's list of institutions eligible for a dose of carceral discipline ran past Bentham's to include even families, the Bostonian publicist did at least have sense enough to float his ideas tentatively: "It is the object of these questions to put the friends of improvement to thinking. . . . How far this principle ought to be extended we do not pretend to decide." [113] Visions of the penitentiary's utility as an institutional template, even among advocates as visionary as these, did have limits. [114]

That commentators as prominent as Bentham and Dwight could seriously entertain the notion of fashioning schools or family homes after carceral prototypes speaks volumes about early attitudes toward the penitentiary. Plainly, it was for many a symbol of pride, not (as in aftertimes) an object of shame or obscurity. But even so, pride led few contemporaries to join in such "philosophical reveries." [115] Occasional suggestions that the penitentiary could beget a crime-free society were repudiated time and again as unrealistic. [116] And when the directors of the Massachusetts State Prison hinted in a pamphlet that the institution could serve in some vague exemplary capacity, operating "both in respect to the criminal and society, by endeavoring to reform the one, and elevate the moral condition of the other," Warden Bradford fired off a response that refused even to take the statement as a literal expression of the directors' ideology. "[T]his is the first time we ever heard that the State Prison was intended to 'elevate the moral condition of society,'" Bradford scoffed. "This florid, but perplexing exordium . . . is no doubt the effect of a too abundant flow of ideas from the prolific imagination of the writer." [117] Another publicist stated emphatically that the penitentiary "has no relation to society at large, further than the knowledge of . . . seclusion, to remove criminal propensities, may deter those [citizens] whom the fear of the penalty . . . keep to the path of virtue. . . . The prisoner in his cell is lost sight of by the world, and the whole operation of the system relates to himself." [118] Apart from producing a few red faces, exaggerated assertions of the penitentiary's significance met mainly with audible silence. Bradford curtly dismissed the Panopticon as "castles in the air," [119] and Bentham's musings generated no perceptible debate in England. [120] Likewise in the United States, Dwight's large view of the institution as a model worthy of emulation received not so much as a passing nod, and it had no apparent impact on public policy. The vast majority of Jacksonian advocates looked narrowly upon the penitentiary as an instrument of crime control. [121] The tone of the discussion remained for the most part level-headed and practical-minded; those who wandered off into the clouds were liable to be yanked sharply back to earth.[122] While all advocates wished to plant the institution in plain view,[123] only a handful of eccentrics thought to follow John Winthrop's lead and build a "prison on a hill."

Still, the early years of the penitentiary in the United States were not un-eventful. For even if advocates of incarceration embraced no novel or gran-diose ideologies, they did ultimately score a more mundane administrative success.[124] By all accounts, the Massachusetts State Prison turned a corner with the reforms of 1829. The internal disruptions that had plagued the insti-tution since its inception rapidly subsided, and legislators who h'ad previously wrung their hands now sang its praises.[125] Throughout America this pattern was repeated; criticism of carceral punishment by and large collapsed in the northern states by 1830.[126] For better and for worse, criminologists of the Jack-sonian era could at least claim credit for establishing the administrative via-bility of the penitentiary. And with that much proved, the institution became fixed upon the nation's criminological landscape.

part 2

Context

Penitentiary and Slavery: Form

O nce on the scene, the penitentiary did not subsist in an intellectual vacuum. It stood beside a host of social entities and was seen in conjunction with those entities. In the foregoing pages, we have examined the penitentiary as a problem in *transition*. The evolution of carceral punishment was charted and analyzed along the plane of time. But the early penitentiary can also be investigated from another perspective—that of institutional *context*. Publicists contemplating criminal incarceration often drew contrasts and connections between the penitentiary and its ideological neighbors. Those contrasts and connections add depth to our understanding of the carceral institution, its place in society, and what its builders were up to.

Among the institutions that hovered about the penitentiary, one stood out, for it had not only to be seen but also affirmatively to be reckoned with if advocates of incarceration were to construct a logical foundation for their program. As a consequence, that other institution figured repeatedly—and provocatively—in carceral advocacy.

The penitentiary arose in an age of slavery. When the first of the new carceral institutions went up, the peculiar institution had been a fact of life in Britain's American colonies (though not in Britain itself) for close to two centuries.[1] In the decade following independence slavery disappeared from northern states. But Southerners clung tenaciously to their traditional mode of labor discipline until its abolition at gunpoint after the Civil War.

One may perceive in the penitentiary many reflections of chattel slavery as it was practiced in the South.[2] Both institutions subordinated their subjects to the will of others. Like Southern slaves, prison inmates followed a daily routine specified by their superiors. Both institutions reduced their subjects to dependence on others for the supply of basic human services such as food and shelter. Both isolated their subjects from the general population by confining them to a fixed habitat. And both frequently coerced their subjects to work, often for longer hours and for less compensation than free laborers. Inmates in the Massachusetts State Prison toiled at assigned tasks from dawn to dusk. No conscientious objection to hard labor was tolerated.[3]

Given these common denominators, it comes as no surprise that the penitentiary and slavery generated many of the same cultural sequelae. As a matter of form, the two institutions shared some of their nomenclature and customs.

The "overseer" resided in the penitentiary as well as the plantation, and he supervised the performance of "hard labor" by inmates as well as slaves.[4] Inmates and slaves were both distinguished from the free community by a conspicuous insignia: the color and quality of their garb.[5] And the most resonant symbol of the slave plantation—the clanking of chains—echoed just as loudly from within prison walls.[6]

The penitentiary and the plantation also evoked some of the same emotional responses from their respective residents. Foremost among these was the mutual hostility that darkened the relationship between master and slave, as between keeper and inmate. No one has ever enjoyed being forced to act against one's will; by the same token, persons have always found it easier to oppress others once they have convinced themselves that those others deserve to be despised. John Locke described slavery as "nothing else but the State of War,"[7] and Massachusetts inmates such as Stephen Burroughs endorsed this view by declaring "open war" against their jailers.[8] Just as slaveholders expressed intense, even paranoid, fear of insurrection from within the plantations they had created, so too did prison officials dread prison uprisings.[9] In the event, slave uprisings were rare, though individual slaves often attempted to escape captivity. Penitentiary inmates did the same.[10]

Much of the animosity generated by incarceration and slavery centered on aspects of the institutions that involved coercion, especially forced labor. Observers noted that inmates, like slaves, frequently exhibited a sullen attitude toward their work, a result of their perception that authorities were exploiting them. Feeling badly used by prison officials, convicts paid them back in the same coin. Stephen Burroughs resolved to thwart "every effort which my overseers should make, to render me profitable in my situation" and added that in this respect prison authorities "found me possessing what the West India Planter would call sullenness, or incorrigible obstinacy, in one of his slaves."[11] The records of the Massachusetts State Prison are replete with references to inmates disciplined for refusing to work and for threatening their overseers.[12] Acts of violence perpetrated by inmates also frequently centered around their work. Just as slaves occasionally committed acts of sabotage, penitentiary inmates sometimes endeavored to spoil their materials and tools.[13] In 1813 Massachusetts inmates set their workshops on fire, a scene replayed on many subsequent occasions.[14] Inmates also went to heroic lengths to avoid work. Like sullen slaves, convicts grew adept at feigning illness, and some were driven to self-mutilation and even suicide in their efforts to end (as one suicide note in Massachusetts declared) "seven years of slavery."[15] In the face of such resistance, authorities recognized that inmates, like slaves, constituted a less productive pool of labor than free workers.[16] Evidence to the contrary was cause for wonder, as when the directors of the Massachusetts State Prison identified inmates who had "extended themselves with as much apparent alacrity as if they were in pursuit of their own emolument."[17]

To enforce alacrity among unwilling inmates and slaves, supervising authorities resorted to harsher measures than those applied to discipline the free population. Because they lacked many of the rights of free citizens, slaves and inmates responded only to the menace of more drastic deprivations. Thus were born the slave codes in the South, authorizing corporal chastisement of slaves to the point of death;[18] prison regulations prescribing corporal punishments that had disappeared outside prison walls mirrored these codes.[19] A ritualization of hierarchical relationships also reinforced order in both institutions. Just as masters demanded that slaves address them in submissive tones, "whenever it is necessary for [a convict] to speak to a Keeper, [he must] do it with a humble sense of his degraded condition."[20] Such ritual submission had an underside: quite apart from its influence on the subject,[21] Thomas Jefferson believed that the master-slave relationship corrupted *owners* by turning them into tyrants.[22] A French visitor to the Walnut Street Prison made the same observation: "In putting a man in prison, you subject him to the power of the gaoler. . . . This state of humiliation . . . renders his *masters* imperious, unjust, vexatious, and wicked."[23]

Outsiders who considered the economic implications of slavery and incarceration had additional, often analogous, concerns. In the South, craftworkers occasionally protested that slave labor led to unfair competition.[24] In the North, craftworkers looked on prison labor as a major grievance.[25] More generally, in a society that glorified hard work, many commentators feared that forcing work upon a despised class would degrade the dignity of labor. Benjamin Franklin, among others, believed that slavery rendered owners "disgusted with labor, and . . . educated in idleness."[26] Such suggestions were of a piece with the frequent criticism that penitentiaries might discredit the crafts practiced within them.[27]

Even some obvious contrasts between slavery and the penitentiary appear less salient on closer inspection. The qualifications for enslavement and imprisonment certainly differed. Not even the most vicious white person in the South was eligible for slavery; and no black person in the North qualified for incarceration until he or she had committed an offense. The one status had a categorical and the other a transactional basis in law. Despite this juristic distinction, as a practical matter both institutions collected into their net groups of persons alleged to have similar characteristics. Black slaves, like penitentiary inmates, were perceived to be prone to criminality; their enslavement ostensibly prevented dreams of dispossession from coming to fruition.[28] And though they were incarcerated for specific offenses, northern penitentiary inmates were commonly labeled members of a criminal class that included blacks.[29] By the 1820s, anatomical explanations for crime began to appear, culminating in the 1870s in Lombrosianism.[30] In short, both slavery and criminal incarceration were explicitly intended, in part, to disable prospective criminal offenders.[31] At times the connection was direct as well as parallel: northern penitentiaries contained a disproportionate number of blacks, many of them manumitted slaves.[32] These persons must have found northern freedom, at best, a mixed blessing.

Of course, most convicts served finite terms of imprisonment. They did not have to resign themselves, like chattel slaves, to perpetual captivity. Still, because of the high rate of recidivism, many more convicts became, in effect, permanent residents of the penitentiary than the sentencing rolls would suggest. One observer referred to this group as "state prison characters," inmates who seemed incapable of readjusting to the outside world. For state prison characters, the penitentiary no less than the plantation became a way of life—though not, to be sure, a hereditary condition.[33]

Yet another distinction that blurs on closer scrutiny involved the nature of institutional authority. Prison inmates labored under the supervision of the state and never became the private property of an individual master. But the significance of this refinement was diminished by the policy, rapidly adopted at most penitentiaries, of leasing convict labor to private contractors.[34] Although inmates did not suffer the indignity of public sale on the auction block,[35] public advertisements inviting bids for their services appeared in Massachusetts newspapers.[36] In several states, authorities even leased entire penitentiaries to a single entrepreneur who thereby came close to becoming the lord of a private plantation.[37] Meanwhile, the administrative safeguards associated with state supervision sometimes appear in practice to have availed convicts little. Despite strict codes of regulations, treatment no less arbitrary than on the plantation could still ensue.[38]

All told, the penitentiary and slavery were alike in many ways—a fact acknowledged, implicitly or explicitly, by many contemporary commentators. In one genre of analysis, commentators applied the lessons of one institution to the other, under the unspoken assumption that they pertained to both. Given "the productive value of barbarous and unskillful African slaves," one critic concluded that "such expenses as are now incurred for the support of convicts, are chiefly owing to defective managements."[39] More directly, publicists sometimes *compared* penitentiary inmates to slaves. The inmates themselves were quick to draw such comparisons. Stephen Burroughs repeatedly likened his condition to a state of slavery—indeed, not to slavery in the United States but to "abject slavery, as the Negroes in the West Indies."[40] Burroughs spiced his narrative of escape attempts with allusions to another struggle: "These were the outlines of my plan. . . . Either to lose my life in the course of liberty, or else gain a glorious freedom."[41] One can only wonder whether Patrick Henry would have been impressed. A number of publicists also explicitly termed their proposals for workhouses and hard labor by criminals as "slavery" programs, and some advocates continued to describe inmates as slaves after the penitentiaries went up.[42] The equation could help to mold carceral policy. When Thomas Jefferson proposed to punish convicts in Virginia "by working on high roads, rivers, gallies, etc., a certain time proportioned to the offence," he added a caveat: "But this would be no change of condition to slaves (me miserum!) let them be sent to other countries." [43] To punish slaves with hard labor seemed to Jefferson a contradiction in terms. Other observers spied more fundamental contradictions in the very implementation of criminal incarceration. Just as commentators had remarked the disharmony of the South's marriage of freedom to chattel slavery, [44] Tocqueville marveled that "while society in the United States gives the example of the most extended liberty, the prisons of the same country offer the spectacle of the most complete despotism." [45]

Given the fraternity between slavery and incarceration, one might expect that at least some persons who objected to the one would also have found fault with the other. This was indeed the case, at least in England. From the seventeenth century on, advocates who sought to build workhouses and to extend the use of hard labor to criminals had to contend with the accusation that such programs would contravene the principles of liberty enshrined in the English constitution. "I shall be told by some of my readers," Bernard Mandeville anticipated in his criminological tract, that "free-born subjects ought never to be made slaves for any reason, or at any rate whatever. But this is a singularity peculiar to *Englishmen,* more built on an excess of good-nature, than any sound reason." [46] Whether sound or no, good-natured Englishmen continued to dog advocates of the penitentiary with this criticism throughout the eighteenth century. Jeremy Bentham reported that "Enthusiasts . . . are not wanting, who, . . . condemn . . . imprisonment accompanied with penal labor as a violation of the natural rights of man. In a free country like this, say they, it ought not to be tolerated, that even malefactors should be reduced to a state of slavery. . . . When the establishment of the penitentiary system was proposed, this objection was echoed and insisted on, in a variety of publications." [47] English advocates of hard labor throughout the century devoted much ink to answering the objection, which Bentham attributed to "impatient spirits too easily kindled with the fire of independence." [48]

It is a striking fact, and something of a mystery, that in another land, where the people were noted even less for their patience and where the flame of independence burned brighter still, scarcely anyone seems to have been troubled by the resemblance of the penitentiary to slavery. In America, advocates of the postrevolutionary generation rarely acknowledged that their schemes might face moral or constitutional challenge. The plan of forcing offenders "to forfeit their liberty to the Commonwealth for three, five, ten or twenty years" [49] appears to have given no one pause. On the contrary, advocates touted hard labor as *more* suitable to a republic than the punishments that had preceded it. [50] As we shall see, subsequent American advocates did challenge certain forms of criminal incarceration and some elements of prison discipline as inappropriate to "this republican, christian land," [51] but (in the North at least) [52] they never challenged the *concept* of the penitentiary on this ground. Its constitutionality was sufficiently uncontroversial as to be glanced over. In 1827 the Prison Discipline Society felt free to assert that hard labor was "consonant with republican principles" without any analysis at all.[53]

It is difficult to account for the asymmetry of English and American concerns about the penitentiary.[54] Contemporary rhetoric provides only a few hints and reflections. One English commentator viewed the problem as essentially cosmetic: "I find, where the shoe pinches; change the word slavery into a term that has not so harsh a sound to a *British* ear, and all is easy."[55] But other advocates detected more substantial concerns. In 1735, Thomas Robe, an English advocate of hard labor, met with the objection that "ill Consequences will happen, (from inflicting any kind of Slavery on freeborn Subjects) which in Time may affect our Liberties."[56] Half a century later, when the virtues of the Penitentiary Act were debated, Jeremy Bentham again encountered the fear that "the precedent is dangerous and pernicious."[57] In England, where a number of proposals to enslave the working poor appeared in the seventeenth and eighteenth centuries,[58] citizens apparently felt threatened by any institution that Parliament might cite as a precedent for their further degradation. In America, where the liberty of the poor was more secure, citizens possibly had greater confidence that an institution establishing slavery under limited circumstances would not subsequently be enlarged. Edmund S. Morgan has argued that the existence of slavery in southern colonies made inhabitants (paradoxically) more receptive to the philosophy of republican liberty.[59] Perhaps the paradox can be reversed: in northern colonies, the firm establishment of liberty made Americans less suspicious of, and eased the way for, a special form of slavery.[60]

Even more intriguing than the absence of opposition to the penitentiary in America on libertarian grounds is the discovery that many of the same persons who lobbied for the construction of penitentiaries—in England *and* America—also stood at the forefront of the antislavery movement. The impulse to break down plantations, it seems, was often accompanied by a longing to build up prison walls. William Blackstone, who helped to draft England's Penitentiary Act in 1779, could also declare in the 1765 edition of his *Commentaries* that "this spirit of liberty is so deeply implanted in our constitution and rooted even in our very soil, that a slave . . . the moment he lands in England . . . becomes *eo instanti* a freeman."[61] Jeremy Bentham, whose proposal for a Panopticon prison would have made "solitary confinement, in the darkest dungeon," appear by comparison "a place of liberty," according to his critic William Roscoe, nonetheless pronounced himself "an anti-slavist."[62] Roscoe, himself a proponent of congregate hard labor and an active promoter of penitentiaries, doubled as president of the Liverpool Society for Promoting the Abolition of Slavery.[63] The list goes on and on[64]—and extends to America, where this pattern was repeated.[65] In Pennsylvania, according to one contemporary visitor, "almost all the inspectors [of Walnut Street Prison] belong to a society which pleads for the freedom of the blacks."[66] Benjamin Rush, perhaps the leading penitentiary activist in the state and a charter member of the Philadelphia Society for Alleviating the Miseries of Public Prisons, also served as president of the Pennsylvania Abolition Society. He wrote extensively in both arenas.[67] New York's foremost penitentiary advocate, Thomas Eddy, was active in the state's Manumission Society.[68] In Massachusetts, Louis Dwight, founder of the Prison Discipline Society, also took part in antislavery advocacy.[69] And in Virginia, one of the state's few proponents of abolition, Thomas Jefferson, also played a part in planning the state's first penitentiary.[70] Nor did advocates in any sense dissociate the two movements; on the contrary, they frequently mingled their campaigns. Robert Turnbull, a South Carolinian pamphleteer, interrupted his tract advocating criminal incarceration with a diatribe against slavery.[71] In Philadelphia, "the Society for the gradual abolition of slavery . . . have free access to the prison, at all times."[72] At least one defender of the old public punishments pointed out the anomaly. The Reverend Robert Annon, author of a series of articles criticizing Benjamin Rush's criminological proposals, reminded his readers of Rush's antislavery stance. "But on his plan we should have slavery in abundance," Annon continued, "because a slight punishment would multiply murders, and according to his plan all the murderers must be forever slaves."[73]

Annon's observation may be rephrased as a question: How did Benjamin Rush and other advocates in England and America reconcile their adherence to the penitentiary with opposition to chattel slavery? How could they plead simultaneously for the construction of the one and the destruction of the other with such evident complacency? An analysis of contemporary rhetoric suggests a vast tree of answers branching from two theoretical trunks: answers that acknowledged the fraternity of the two institutions but distinguished the circumstances under which persons were condemned to them, and answers that drew theoretical distinctions between the two institutions per se. For some, the penitentiary imposed a *justified* form of slavery; for others, the resemblance was superficial, and the penitentiary imposed something completely different from slavery.

Those commentators who identified hard labor as a form of justified slavery distinguished between the enslavement of criminals and the enslavement of others. Penal slavery, they insisted, differed from chattel slavery because it served legitimate criminological ends. "Slavery is often mentioned with detestation by a freeman, as a scandal to his country," one English advocate observed, "but it is because he does not understand the effect intended by it, as a consequence of some crime committed."[74] Having alerted their readers to this distinction, advocates had still to justify slavery within the specified bounds. To do so, they dipped into several wells of political theory. One argument frequently advanced to defend penal slavery was that, by violating the law, criminals had forfeited their own right to enjoy the law's protection. John Locke was the most influential philosopher to put forward such an argument. Under Locke's political philosophy, all men had a natural right to life and liberty, guaranteed in the civil state by the social contract. In Locke's view no man who placed himself under the protection of civil government could ever be enslaved so long as he abided by the natural laws it was created to uphold. But once a man under the protection of government violated natural law, he took himself *outside* the social contract and lost his natural rights, having "declare[d] himself to quit the Principles of Human Nature." Thus, captives taken in a just war as well as criminals (who had also "declared war against all mankind") might with justice suffer the pains of death; and they might with equal justice suffer enslavement, for this constituted a mitigation (or, in Locke's terminology, a "delay") of the capital penalty they deserved.[75]

Locke's "contractual" justification for punishment, and his analysis approving slavery *only* when imposed as a punishment, had roots in prior political theory.[76] Puritan theologians had similarly conceived of the state as founded upon a social covenant, the violation of which could result in sanctions up to and including death. In early Massachusetts, chattel slavery was proscribed and "the haynos & crying sinn of man stealing" was a capital crime. Nevertheless, the Body of Liberties of 1641 made exception for "lawfull Captives taken in just warres . . . [and persons] who shall be Judged thereto by Authoritie."[77] The early Puritans enforced this distinction, freeing slaves whom they judged to have been "unlawfully taken" on entering the colony.[78] But authorities did not hesitate (in their own words) to enslave Indians captured in the Pequot War of 1637 and in King Philip's War of 1671. On a number of occasions the Court of Assistants also ordered the enslavement of Massachusetts citizens brought up on criminal charges (including simple theft).[79] Subsequent generations of Puritans had no qualms about selling into servitude convicts unable to pay treble damages.[80] Such punishment, according to the Reverend Samuel Willard, resulted from the convicts' "self alienation," a contractual turn of phrase rooted in the conceptions of John Winthrop as well as John Locke.[81]

English advocates of criminal incarceration in the eighteenth century returned to this line of argument. "A Student of Politics," who explicitly identified hard labor as slavery and sought to impose it (for varying periods) as punishment for all noncapital crimes, bristled at the criticism that "Britons will . . . forfeit their lives sooner than permit their liberty to be wrested from them. This would be a most noble and laudable declaration from a virtuous citizen, but coming from the lips of a subject that has been convicted by the laws of his country, it denigrates into a mere idle empty Gasconade: for no man can properly be said to lose, that which he has already lost."[82] Other advocates focused on Locke's equation of slavery and capital punishment. Under

England's bloody code, criminals could be condemned to death for a wide range of property crimes. Given acceptance of the constitutionality of *this* punishment, some commentators concluded that hard labor must, a fortiori, also have been constitutional. That Englishmen might approve of hanging but reject hard labor seemed to these advocates the height of absurdity. "Such a Plan of punishing the Delinquents [as in Denmark, with hard labor] . . . has been rejected as inconsistent with the Constitution of a free Country," one eighteenth-century commentator complained,

> But why it should be any Objection amongst a free People to deprive those of their Liberty who by the Laws have forfeited their Lives, is what I never could comprehend. . . . As we are distinguished by the respectable Name of Britons, and are stationed in a Land of Liberty, we cannot act so far out of character as to doom those of our Countrymen who are guilty of Sheep-stealing, &c. to an ignominious Servitude. No: For the Honour of our Country we will order them not to be made *Slaves,* but to be *hanged*: And that they may not be deprived of their Liberty, we will deprive them of Life; and generously keep them out of the Hands of severe Task-masters by sending them out of the World. Such a Conduct is quite constitutional, and suitable to the genius of a *free* people.[83]

In England, transportation, as an early variant of enforced servitude,[84] took the form of a reprieve from the gallows,[85] and English advocates sometimes urged that a sentence to hard labor be conceived in the same way.[86] In North America, this conception enjoyed little statutory authority, given the limited scope of capital punishment to begin with, though advocates occasionally repeated the idea.[87] At the same time, Locke's overall perspective on slavery under the social contract was widely accepted and ultimately enshrined in the Thirteenth Amendment, which begins: "Neither slavery nor involuntary servitude except as a punishment for crime whereof the party shall have been duly convicted, shall exist within the United States."[88]

Thus within Lockean theory there lurked an analysis that appeared sufficient to distinguish penal slavery from chattel slavery. Penitentiary advocates were always careful to confine their proposed institutions to *convicted* offenders; debtors and persons awaiting trial were to be kept out or (under some English plans) to be given the *option* of entry.[89] Alert to the potential of this argument, some southern advocates also sought refuge between the covers of *Two Treatises of Government*. American slavetraders protested that they purchased only captives taken in African wars or criminals condemned by their own tribal law and refused all others who were offered to them.[90] Locke evidently conceded the point, for he approved of slavery as practiced in the colonial South.[91] Yet, even granting that southern blacks had been "justly" enslaved, the peculiar institution fit Lockean theory less snugly than the penitentiary: under the plantation system, condemned slaves were retained by *private* masters, and they passed their status on to their *innocent* off-spring. These incidents of southern servitude were inconsistent with, or at least anomalous under, Lockean theory. At any rate, most Northerners dismissed the slavetraders' pleadings of "just" enslavement as a fraud. On the contrary, answered antislavery advocates, it was southern *masters* who were criminals and who deserved punishment.[92]

Publicists who looked to social contract theory to defend hard labor also faced more direct challenges. Whereas some theorists assumed that any violations of natural law would suffice to deprive offenders of their own civil rights, others sought to qualify this notion. Francis Hutcheson, the moral philosopher, argued that an intent test should be applied to breaches of the social contract. On this basis Hutcheson concluded that the enslavement of captives, even in a just war, would generally be unjust, for most enemy citizens probably had not concurred in the decision to commence hostilities or had been misled by their own rulers. But because criminals were culpable (by definition) for their crimes, Hutcheson added, they could with justice be enslaved; to hold otherwise would be to "favour liberty immoderately." On this basis, he advocated penal servitude.[93]

Hutcheson's gloss on social contract theory might have served to ameliorate the plight of captives, but it offered little solace to criminals. Other political theorists carried Locke's ideas in directions from which criminals as well as captives could take heart. Locke had equated the right to punish by enslavement with the right to punish by death. Yet, by the eighteenth century, some theorists had begun to challenge the constitutionality of capital punishment. Such challenges raised new questions about the justice of penal slavery.

In one line of analysis tracing to Beccaria, political theorists scrutinized the unwritten terms of the social contract more closely. Under the social contract, persons delegated to civil government some of their natural rights, such as the right to punish each other for violations of natural law. But, said opponents of capital punishment, because no man had the natural right to kill *himself* (as Locke had stated),[94] he could not concede this right to government: the right to life was *inalienable,* belonging only unto God, and any social contract to the contrary was ipso facto null and void. That capital punishment was *convenient,* they added, did not make it *constitutional*: only rights legitimately delegated to civil government could be exercised by government.[95] Now, this was an argument pregnant with potential for opponents of hard labor. For Locke had *also* denied the right of individuals to sell themselves into slavery,[96] and if other theorists accepted this dictum, it could follow by analogy that government never acquired the right to enslave citizens either.

This very thought had been highlighted in connection with American political rhetoric of the revolutionary era. James Otis, among others, had insisted that because the American colonists did not themselves possess "a power of surrendering their own liberty," Parliament in turn could not possibly have the right to make "slaves" of them by taxing them without their consent.[97] From this point, an argument denying government the right to enslave criminals lay only a small step away—but a step that no one at the time thought to take. Only later, and with splendid irony, did opponents of hard labor recall Otis's logic when the issue of penitentiary construction arose in the 1840s in *southern* states. "In surrendering individual rights to society," one North Carolinian remarked, "it is reasonable to suppose that the right to remain with his wife and children, and to labour for their benefit was retained; and that the very principle of Penitentiary punishment is an encroachment on individual rights." Demanded another, "What are *inalienable* rights? In the time of the Revolution it was admitted that by taking away any part of our labor, without our consent, amounted to slavery . . . but under the Penitentiary system the freeborn citizen is made to labor directly under the lash as a slave."[98] Such arguments must have lifted a few eyebrows in the South. In the North, the one advocate who appears to have anticipated this proposition was Benjamin Rush, an opponent of capital punishment who simultaneously advocated hard labor. Rush repeated Beccaria's contractual argument against the death penalty but then ducked the second edge of his ideological sword simply by asserting that every person did enjoy "an absolute power over his own liberty and property, but not his own life."[99] Rush dealt with Locke and Otis the easy way: by ignoring them.

Another branch of social contract analysis focused on the problem of breach. Although it was possible to conclude that any violation of law ended the obligation of civil government to protect the criminal, Locke held that authorities were bound to take, as it were, a *quantum meruit* approach to breaches of the social contract. Some offenses were sufficiently heinous to merit death, but others were not. "Each Transgression," said Locke, "may be *punished* to that *degree,* and with so much *Severity* as will suffice to make it an ill bargain to the Offender, give him cause to repent, and terrifie others from doing the like."[100] Such an approach, anticipating by many decades Beccaria's call for proportionality,[101] could be reconciled with the concept of penal slavery simply by assigning a different *term* of enslavement to each offense.[102] But here one could point to Locke's equation of capital punishment and slavery to denounce slavery for *any* term where capital punishment would be unduly harsh.

In North America (unlike England), authorities had *never* used capital punishment extensively, and in the wake of the American Revolution, some voices called for its complete abolition.[103] Against this background, penal slavery could appear unjust. "I know that it will be said, that for my crimes I am deprived of liberty," allowed Stephen Burroughs, yet "[i]t has been abundantly said by the leading men in this state, that life without liberty is not worth the possessing . . . ; therefore, that the same characters, upon a revision of the

criminal code, with a pretence of mollifying those laws which were sanguinary and cruel, should substitute slavery for death, is to me, conduct truly
enigmatical." [104] William Roscoe likewise argued that incarceration under the
Auburn plan would be "equally, if not more repugnant to the dictates of justice,
than the infliction of capital punishment," which Roscoe noted was "either
abolished, or greatly restricted, in every civilized country." [105]

Where to draw the line between capital and noncapital crimes, however,
remained open to debate. Stephen Allen, a New York politician and defender
of the Auburn plan, joined issue with Roscoe by insisting that all persons convicted of crimes in the United States for which they might have been punished
with death *in England* were "dead in law, and consequently without rights,
natural or political." [106] Thus, said Allen, they had no call to protest a carceral
regime that resembled slavery. Roscoe, who considered the English code to
be irrational, disagreed. To divest the convict of all political rights, even for
lower grades of offenses, seemed to him an "unreasonable retaliation for his
offense." In Roscoe's view, convicts were not "dead in law"; rather, they retained all rights not taken from them by rational decisions of law. The Auburn
regime, in Roscoe's view, did not fill this prescription, and it therefore deprived inmates of rights to which they were constitutionally entitled.[107] Still,
Roscoe believed that a penitentiary, properly conceived, could comport with
convicts' rights.[108] Advocates of hard labor thus got around quantum meruit
theory either (like Allen) by defining capital crimes broadly or (like Roscoe)
by defining them narrowly, but implicitly distinguishing the institution they
had in mind from one equivalent to the death penalty.

Roscoe, along with Locke and Beccaria, believed that the social contract
demanded *rational,* graded penalties to minimize crime. But Roscoe also believed that the social contract imposed an autonomous set of limits, which
might diverge from "convenience." [109] Other rational commentators such as
Jeremy Bentham abandoned the concept of the social contract entirely as a
source of justification for, and limits upon, criminal punishment. For Bentham,
whatever was expedient was *eo ipso* just. If slavery constituted an effectual
punishment, he declared, then let it be unabashedly imposed.[110]

Utilitarian rationalism thus provided another avenue whereby the legitimacy of penal and chattel slavery could be distinguished. Laissez-faire economists denounced chattel slavery as an inefficient labor system.[111] But advocates who identified hard labor as slavery always touted it as an efficient
system for controlling crime.[112] From the standpoint of rationalism, slavery
might be valid in the one situation, and not in the other, because its function was different. And, even at the cost of slavery, crime control might well
appear a good bargain for society; for the alternative to effective crime control, advocates asserted, was the virtual enslavement of honest citizens and

criminals alike. Had not republican political theorists protested that taxation without representation amounted to slavery?[113] How then was the case different when the power to confiscate a citizen's property lay in the hands of a criminal? Henry Fielding, a London magistrate, looked upon the two scenarios as equivalent:

> I cannot help regarding these depredations in a most serious light; nor can I help wondering that a nation so jealous of her liberties, that from the slightest cause, and often without any cause at all, we are always murmuring at our superiors, should tamely and quietly support the invasion of her properties by a few of the lowest and vilest amongst us: doth not this situation in reality level us with the most enslaved countries? . . . is not my condition almost equally bad whether a licensed or unlicensed rogue, a dragoon or a robber, be the person who assaults and plunders me? The only difference which I can perceive is, that the latter evil appears to be more easy to remove.[114]

Political theorists furthermore feared that crime, left unchecked, would undermine republican government, paving the way for political tyranny and slavery.[115] Indeed, by veering from the path of virtue, criminals had already in a sense lost their freedom, some clergymen insisted. "When a man goes beyond, or contrary to the laws of nature and reason, he becomes the slave of base passions, and vile lust," lectured the Reverend Samuel West. "This therefore cannot be called a state of freedom, but a state of the vilest slavery, the most dreadful bondage. The servants of sin and corruption are subjected to the worst kind of tyranny in the universe."[116] All of this was live ammunition for advocates of hard labor. "To say that [penal] slavery is contrary to the spirit of our free constitution, is a silly objection," William Smith observed, "for true freedom is only found where life and property are secure."[117] For utilitarian rationalists, penal slavery could well seem the lesser of two evils, whereas chattel slavery was an unnecessary, indeed costly, encumbrance.

Chattel slave owners, of course, saw the facts differently. Having sought first to turn social contract theory against its propounders, defenders of slavery now lobbed utilitarian arguments right back at their critics. Southerners disputed the dictates of laissez-faire economics, claiming that slavery *did* maximize the economic welfare of the community.[118] And, like advocates of the penitentiary, proponents of chattel slavery protested that their institution also performed a crime control function by disabling the crime-prone population of slave states. If freed, this population would produce "numerous banditti" preying on the property of others.[119]

But even if advocates of chattel slavery and of hard labor each justified their institution on the basis of utilitarian conceptions of crime control, the methods they espoused to achieve that end were not exactly in harmony.

Southerners saw fit to stem the tide of crime through the mass disablement of potential criminals. Although northern penitentiary advocates also recognized the utility of incapacitation, they placed greater emphasis on other tactics that could control crime more economically. Given their perception that crime was linked to idleness, advocates of incarceration thought hard labor a most effective *deterrent* against crime. This approach to the problem of crime control did not lead advocates away from the ideal of penal slavery. "For if the people of *Great-Britain* are so enamour'd of their liberty to a degree of enthusiasm," one early publicist noted rhetorically, "what barrier will be more likely to contain them within the boundaries of a well-regulated life . . . than the horrid dread of losing so inestimable a jewel?"[120] To the extent that hard labor resembled slavery, its effectiveness to deter crime could only be enhanced. Still, when employed for deterrence instead of disablement, penal slavery could operate on a smaller scale than chattel slavery.

Advocates of incarceration also hoped that the penitentiary would *rehabilitate* its inmates. Whereas philosophers perceived a ceaseless state of war between chattel slaves and their masters, criminologists hoped to negotiate a peace treaty of sorts within the prison's walls.[121] Yet herein lurked a paradox: If the penitentiary's internal regime resembled that of the plantation so closely that the two were often loosely equated, how could the prison possibly function to rehabilitate criminals? After all, when speaking out against slavery, penitentiary advocates asserted that the plantation environment *debased* its black residents and made them *prone* to crime! Even as Benjamin Rush strove to establish the penitentiary system in Pennsylvania, he simultaneously maintained that "[s]lavery is so foreign to the human mind, that the moral faculties, as well as those of the understanding are debased, and rendered torpid by it. All the vices which are charged upon the Negroes in the Southern colonies and the West-Indies, such as Idleness, Treachery, Theft, and the like, are the genuine offspring of slavery."[122] If chattel slavery bred theft, how could penal slavery instill virtue?

Here we reach the second trunk of theory reconciling support for the penitentiary with antislavery advocacy—namely, theory that *distinguished* the two regimes, identifying the one as beneficial and the other as detrimental to the morals of those confined. Many criminologists recognized that similarities between the penitentiary and slavery might jeopardize rehabilitation. In formulating carceral programs, advocates often sought explicitly to avoid elements of chattel slavery that, in the guise of antislavery advocates, they decried as pernicious to moral advancement. Such advocates frequently denounced competing carceral programs that failed to weed out those elements in much the same terms as they denounced chattel slavery. In response, defenders of those competing programs sometimes drew inspiration from southern proslavery rhetoric in order to vindicate their carceral designs. Thus, to a certain extent, the penitentiary debate that engaged criminologists of all regions in the early nineteenth century tracked the more momentous debate that raged simultaneously between North and South.

One variation of carceral discipline often singled out for attack was hard labor carried out in *public*. Under Pennsylvania's first postrevolutionary code, inmates left the prison each day to labor at road repair and other public works.[123] Though the state's hard labor program rapidly moved inside the prison's walls, carceral programs out of doors remained under consideration in the North as late as the 1820s.[124] Given prevailing criminological precepts, one might assume that such a policy would have received widespread ap-probation: hard labor without the prison would at least have afforded greater "exemplarity" (or general deterrence) than hard labor within. Yet advocates of the postrevolutionary era by and large opposed the idea. Such a spectacle, like the public punishments of old, was now considered degrading and thus inimical to rehabilitation.[125] But even more worrisome to some advocates was the moral threat such a punishment would pose to the general population. "The practice of employing criminals in public labour, will render labour of every kind disreputable," Benjamin Rush warned. "It is a well known fact, that white men soon decline labour in the West-Indies, and in the southern states, only because the agriculture and mechanical employments of those coun-tries, are carried on chiefly by Negro slaves." [126] Having learned his lesson from slavery, Rush proceeded to endorse hard labor so long as it was restricted to the penitentiary.[127] William Tudor went further, using Rush's distinction to assess the legitimacy of alternative forms of punishment. A warm friend of the penitentiary, Tudor condemned public hard labor with equal warmth: such a program would resurrect the "galley slave[ry] of Europe" and was "wholly unsuitable to a free country." [128]

For their part, southern apologists of slavery were quick to respond to the allegation that chattel slavery undermined the dignity of labor. On the con-trary, they said, slavery *elevated* the status of white laborers, by distinguishing them from the slaves who lay beneath them; in the North, by contrast, white laborers had no one to look down on but themselves.[129] Proponents of public hard labor drew on similar arguments to defend their programs against the same charge. "A Student of Politics" maintained that the sight of convicts "re-duc'd to a state of bondage" was bound to enhance free citizens' "happiness in the enjoyment of liberty." [130] Southerners would have nodded in agreement, yet such views did not preclude their expositors from taking an antislavery stance. John Lettsom, one of Benjamin Rush's English correspondents, used the same reasoning to counter Rush's suggestion that public hard labor would render free labor ignominious. That matter out of the way, Lettsom proceeded without pause to commend Rush's efforts against the slave trade.[131]

Advocates of incarceration also distinguished the penitentiary from the plantation by contrasting the sorts of supervision afforded by each institu-

tion. Whereas chattel slaves lived under the unbridled authority of individuals, prison inmates were held by the state, under whose auspices hard labor
could "be attended with much less difficulty, and not liable to so many grievances."[132] Opponents of slavery had long decried the moral consequences of
the master-slave relationship: it turned masters into tyrants and undermined
the ethical principles of slaves who met with capricious rewards and chastisements. Thus, "[t]he slave, in bad hands, is rendered a liar and a thief, as
a matter of course."[133] In carceral institutions established to put an end to
thievery, authorities sought to avoid this outcome through detailed regulation
and oversight. Bound (no less than inmates) to abide by strict rules of conduct, prison officials would never get the chance to tyrannize their charges.[134]
The effectiveness of such regulations remained problematic; state legislatures
troubled by the costs of carceral programs were sometimes willing to reduce
their emphasis on expensive supervision.[135] But when New York effectively
abandoned its policy of prison regulation by delegating and concentrating administrative authority in the warden's hands in the latter half of the 1820s,
critics quickly denounced the move. The new plan, William Roscoe protested,
would make the keeper-inmate relationship analogous to "no relation but
one, . . . and that is the relation of owner and slave." Such total subjection
would undermine rehabilitation and at any rate was "abhorrent to every principle of law, justice and reason."[136] An American critic agreed that the plan
"can[not] be, or ought [not] to be, endured in a free country."[137] Others attacked the practice of convict leasing on similar grounds: by placing inmates
in private hands, authorities sabotaged their prospects for effective rehabilitation. The lease, again, "holds up to view the relation which exists between
master and slave in its plainest form."[138]

Slaveholders had a ready answer for the contention that their latitude of
discretion over slaves led to mistreatment: so long as slaves constituted property, masters had every incentive to treat them well, for even "the most brutal
man will not use his beast ill only out of a humor."[139] Advocates of administrative latitude in the New York penitentiary could not parrot this reasoning, for
its officers owned no interest in the labor of their inmates. Instead, advocates
asserted that discretion was necessary to ensure discipline and that the risk
of abuse was small so long as the power was lodged in good hands.[140] This
argument again implicitly distinguished the penitentiary from chattel slavery.
In the South, government had no authority to choose masters, a fact that
plainly magnified the hazards of arbitrary power. Advocates in New York also
distinguished convict leasing, emphasizing the contractors' limited powers of
supervision.[141] In England, however, Jeremy Bentham borrowed a leaf from
proslavery pamphleteers when he suggested that administrative precautions
would never suffice to curb internal abuses against convicts unless prison
administrators were personally interested in inmates' welfare. Bentham proposed to lease his model Panopticon to contractors and give them unlimited

discretion over its government. Once they had an interest in prison labor, contractors would never harm the convicts, Bentham maintained in words that might as well have appeared in a proslavery tract, "since the contractor, of himself, knows better things than not to take care of a cow that will give milk."[142] Ironically, Bentham made a point of distinguishing public from private servitude, insisting in another tract that "public servitude is a different thing from slavery."[143] Yet in his proposal for the Panopticon, Bentham drew upon theory connected with slavery in order to make penitentiary discipline and economy more like slavery.

Apart from the problem of maintaining the integrity of the penitentiary's rehabilitative regime, questions remained about the effectiveness of that regime, even when operating as prescribed. Advocates of hard labor contended that criminals had to acquire a "habit of industry" before they could become honest. Slaves, renowned in equal measure for their dispositions to idleness and theft, were nonetheless the most overworked persons in the world. Why, then, did not *slaves* acquire a habit of industry? The answer issued out of any number of antislavery tracts: because they were coerced to labor in return for nothing above subsistence, slaves lacked an incentive for their efforts. No matter how accustomed they became to industry, slaves would continue to loathe and resist work so long as they were denied its fruits. What is more, one could hardly expect slaves to respect the property rights of others when they enjoyed no such rights themselves. "A man's moral sense must be unusually strong, if slavery does not make him a thief," Thomas Jefferson observed, for "he who is permitted by law to have no property of his own, can with difficulty conceive that property is founded in any thing but force." For this reason, manumitted slaves "chose to steal from their neighbors rather than work."[144] Abolitionists granted that before slaves gained their freedom, they had to become acquainted with *voluntary* labor and *wages*—only then would slaves gradually be "prompted to industry, and exercise the virtues of honesty and frugality" necessary to life in free society.[145]

The implications of this analysis were not lost on advocates of the penitentiary. Many opposed a policy of requiring convicts to toil under threat of punishment, insisting instead that they be stimulated to effort by the prospect of reward. Oddly enough, one of the first advocates to take stock of this aspect of antislavery theory was none other than Jeremy Bentham, whose administrative philosophy otherwise bore the imprint of proslavery thought. "To me, it would seem but so much the better, if a man could be taught to love labour, instead of being taught to loathe it," he counseled. To instill a habit of industry, "[r]eward, not punishment, is the office you must apply to. Compulsion and slavery must, in a race like this, be ever an unequal match for encouragement and liberty."[146] The "encouragement and liberty" Bentham envisioned in the Panopticon were notably limited, but they remained distinct in his mind from "compulsion and slavery." Bentham planned to confine inmates to their cells on bread and water until they agreed to work. Each inmate would then strike a bargain with the contractor of the prison, who would pay over a wage the inmate could either save or use to upgrade his diet with meat and beer. "[N]ot a stroke does he strike but he gets something, which he would not have got otherwise. . . . It is necessary that every exertion he makes should be sure of its reward." Bentham described this system of labor not as slavery but as subjection to a "monopoly"—a term that would later echo through literature condemning prison industry.[147] Because Bentham's contractor enjoyed enormous leverage over the inmates, he could strike favorable bargains for their labor; still, he could not starve them, and all earnings were on top of this guaranteed subsistence, thus producing, in Bentham's view, the proper environment for habituation to industry.[148]

Bentham's proposal to compensate convicts for their labor was not fundamentally novel. Like so many aspects of penitentiary ideology, it had roots in the ancient workhouse. Inmates in English and continental workhouses had received wages that were credited against their maintenance costs. Inmates received the surplus either immediately or on release.[149] To do otherwise, workhouse advocates understood as well as Bentham, "rather makes People hate Imployment as a hell than to Entertain it as a means of comfortable support."[150] The first American penitentiaries followed in this tradition. In Massachusetts, officers assigned each convict a "stint" of labor that ostensibly covered all expenses to the institution. Anything performed above this amount ("overstint") was compensated at a rate set by the authorities. Convicts who refused to labor were not compelled to do so by blows but were instead condemned to solitary confinement until they relented.[151]

Several considerations prompted the introduction of overstint into penitentiaries. In part, authorities turned to the practice in the hope that convicts would thereby work more diligently and provide greater net revenue to the institutions. William Roscoe, among others, recognized that a prison system based on voluntary labor was more likely to support itself than one based on enforced labor.[152] (Likewise in the South, masters sometimes offered slaves small rewards for their industry, surely without a thought to the rehabilitative consequences of such transactions.)[153] These mercenary motives blended with, but did not supplant, the didactical ends of compensation in the carceral setting. Pennsylvania's act mandating overstint in 1790 tersely summarized the duality when it stated that authorities hoped thereby "to encourage industry, as an evidence of reformation."[154]

The issue came to the fore after officials in New York developed the Auburn system of prison discipline. Under the Auburn plan, which eventually spread to Massachusetts and other states, overstint was abolished and congregate hard labor was thereafter compelled, as on the plantation, by the threat of corporal punishment. This system immediately drew the fire of other publicists (in particular, proponents of the rival Pennsylvania plan) on the ground that it would counteract rehabilitation. Advocates of the Pennsylvania plan, which featured solitary labor, generally stressed the rehabilitative power of solitude more than habituation to labor. But they also recognized how advocates of the Auburn system had undermined their own rehabilitative program. Under the Auburn plan, where the convict was "[u]rged to labor by the dread of the lash, and deprived of that which sweetens it, he will be apt to detest it," one critic observed. By contrast, the labor prescribed under the Pennsylvania plan was entirely voluntary, offered to the convict as a "favor," and was compensated with overstint. Prisoners would desire labor as a relief from idleness, advocates of the Pennsylvania plan maintained. "Under the [Pennsylvania] system, then, men have an opportunity *every day* of knowing how much more pleasant labor is than idleness, and in time will form a voluntary habit of work. . . . As far as the moral effects of labor contribute to a man's reformation, the [Pennsylvania] system, then, seems to us far superior to the [Auburn]." [155] Other advocates explicitly linked the Auburn plan with pernicious elements of the plantation regime. William Roscoe echoed Jefferson when he urged that a convict's earnings "should be *as sacred to his use,* as he should be taught to regard that of others to theirs." Roscoe continued in the vein of Bentham: "It is not perhaps too much to say, that the *greatest cruelty* that can be exercised upon an individual, is to separate his *labour* from his *hope*; to compel him to strike a certain number of strokes, but to deprive him of the sentiment that should invigorate them. Let the reader reflect upon this," he concluded, "and consider what is the curse of slavery!" [156] Again, some American advocates questioned the constitutionality of Auburn-style prison discipline. [157]

Defenders of the Auburn plan sought to justify the abolition of overstint and the compulsion of convict labor in part with arguments that again implicitly distinguished the penitentiary from slavery. Advocates pointed out that rehabilitation was not the only object of hard labor: it also aimed at deterrence, and overstint greatly weakened this aspect of carceral punishment. [158] But the same advocates also defended convict compulsion with arguments that rhymed with proslavery rhetoric. Slaveholders protested that nothing short of bondage could induce their slaves to labor; once freed, they would neglect work despite offers of wages. [159] Similarly, advocates of the Auburn plan insisted that when convicts received overstint they succumbed to *greater* idleness, for once they had performed their obligatory stint they almost invariably preferred sleep to work—better, then, to compel convicts to labor throughout the day. [160] Slaveholders also submitted that the compulsion inherent in slavery was in truth a universal aspect of labor relations. Free laborers, they said, were compelled to work, as literally as slaves, out of the need to feed themselves and their families. [161] Here was a classic move of proslavery rhetoric, an effort to justify the institution not on the merits but by assimilating it to alternatives. And it was a move that proponents of the Auburn system feared not to repeat. Stephen Allen answered William Roscoe's charge that coercive penal labor was tantamount to enslavement by contrasting such coercion with the conditions of free labor:

> Do men labour because they derive pleasure from the employment? by no means. It is from necessity, which is the same in fact as compulsion, that induces men to labour. And permit me to inquire, how many of the human beings employed in your extensive manufacturing establishments [in England] would perform the labour to which they are subjected, if they were not compelled to it by necessity? Where then is the hardship of compelling a convicted felon to earn his bread by the sweat of his brow? [162]

Like Lettsom and Bentham before him, Allen was an antislavery advocate.[163] But even for antislavery advocates, proslavery rhetoric had its uses.

In addition to analyzing the effects of coercion, commentators debated the rehabilitative implications of inmate dependence. For their part, abolitionists identified slave dependence as another debility, related to coercion, that had to be overcome before slaves could make a go of freedom. Just as the plantation deprived slaves of the material rewards of their exertions, and thereby taught them to hate labor, so it robbed slaves of the power to think for themselves, to develop the self-reliance that defined life in free society. "[T]o abandon persons whose habits have been formed in slavery is like abandoning children," Thomas Jefferson urged.[164] Such abandonment could only end in crime. As Tocqueville explained:

> The freed person commits . . . crimes . . . for a very simple reason; because, becoming emancipated, he has to provide for himself, which, during his bondage, he was not obliged to do. Brought up in ignorance and brutality, he has been accustomed to work like a machine, all the motions of which are caused by an external power. His mind has remained entirely undeveloped. His life has been passive, thoughtless, and unthinking. . . . The day when liberty is granted to him, he receives an instrument which he does not know how to use. . . . His actions, involuntary when he was a slave, now become disorderly: judgment cannot guide him; for he has not exercised it.[165]

Slaves had to acquire good judgment, as well as proper values, before their masters could safely set them free.

Critics recognized that the penitentiary, no less than the plantation, could deaden inmates' abilities to make decisions. "A long habit of restraint, disqualifies a man to act without the restraint," observed Daniel Raymond, a Maryland attorney familiar with both institutions. Once freed from incarceration, "Instead of being subject to the will of another, as he has long been accustomed to be, [the convict] is left to his own will, to which he is not accustomed. Is it rational to expect a man to preserve a proper equilibrium of mind under such a shock? . . . Is it not far more rational to expect, that such a man will immediately return to the paths of vice, and again become a tenant of a Penitentiary? We see this same principle operating," Raymond concluded, "throughout this part of the country, and producing the same effect in regard to manumitted slaves."[166] Again, proponents of the Pennsylvania system made use of this issue to denounce their Auburn rivals while implicitly distinguishing their own program from slavery. Coercive labor under the Auburn plan, its opponents emphasized, was merely the salient feature of a regimen that enforced conformity, and uniformity, in every aspect of institutional life. Under the Pennsylvania plan, by contrast, convicts chose whether or not to work, just as they chose whether to exercise and accept religious instruction. Although a dissident member of the Prison Discipline Society had to admit that "the opportunities for self-control" under the Pennsylvania plan remained "few and inadequate," nonetheless "they are far greater than under its rival," and thus better preserved the convict's ability to function as an "independent" member of society.[167]

Advocates responded to such criticism in several ways. Some sought to avoid the merits of the case by rhetorically assimilating the carceral institution to other institutions, just as slaveholders did. Though he opposed coercive labor, Bentham recommended a prison system that was coercive in other respects. His simple solution was to link such coercion with other forms of punishment: "All punishment is an infringement on liberty: no one submits to it but from compulsion."[168] Whether knowingly or not, Bentham's line of reasoning ran parallel to one used by slaveholders to justify slave dependency: "All government is restraint; and this is but one form of restraint."[169]

More forthrightly, proponents of discipline on the Auburn model responded with an analysis that confirmed their intention to impose a sort of slavery over inmates. Radical proslavery advocates such as George Fitzhugh championed dependency as a positive good, checking the tendency of citizens to do evil and of society to collapse into anarchy.[170] Similarly, admirers of the Auburn plan claimed that its dependent, obligatory regime actually benefited criminals. By "oblig[ing] him to do every thing he is ordered to do," the Auburn inmate developed "habits of obedience" to law, which would stand him in good stead when he departed.[171] That the inmate hated those laws because of the coercive nature of the learning process made no difference; the force of habit to obey them would suffice. "It may be said that this obedience is compulsory and irksome," one European visitor who toured New York prisons remarked. "Still the habit is engendered; and a man who by any means, no matter what, is compelled to obey for any length of time the consistent laws of a well-regulated prison, will leave it, I should think, better disposed to obey the general laws of society than he ever was formerly."[172]

This analysis, though original to the penitentiary, represented only a broader application of the rehabituative philosophy of hard labor developed centuries before in the Elizabethan workhouse. Advocates of hard labor had always taken a bearish view of efforts to reform the criminal conscience and had placed their hopes instead in a reformation of superficial habits.[173] If early workhouses had compensated inmates for their labor in order to appeal to their free will, the emphasis still lay on a process of coercive routinization. At Auburn, routinization remained the paramount mode of rehabilitation; some advocates even spoke of the need to *break* the convict's will.[174] What is more, Auburn advocates extended the therapy from habits of labor to habits of obedience generally; not only would convicts become accustomed to work, they would also become accustomed to obeying the law. Unlike antislavery advocates who sought to unfasten not only the bodily chains but also "the rivets that have so long held down the understanding" of the slave,[175] advocates of the Auburn plan intended to impose a sort of mental bondage upon inmates: nothing less would answer to prevent them from returning to the courses of crime.

Proponents of solitary confinement and the Pennsylvania system of prison discipline took the opposite tack. They doubted that any habit formed against the inmate's will would long survive his restoration to free society. These advocates relied primarily on a program designed to reclaim the inmate's conscience.[176] Thus, they denounced efforts to crush the free will of convicts as destructive of the only thing that could save them.[177] In a sense, then, only the advocates of criminal reclamation sought to "liberate" convicts as they would have liberated slaves. Advocates of the Auburn plan frankly admitted that "the reformation of the convicts, required that they should feel that they were in reality, the slaves of the state," as one put it.[178] Only slavery instilled the habits of obedience necessary to control crime.

But, of course, this was only the half of it. Whatever the similarities in form between the penitentiary and slavery, the economic substance of the two institutions also merited comparison. Southern planters alleged that the peculiar institution, like the carceral one, served the end of crime control. Yet planters could scarcely deny that slavery operated primarily as an economic system. Had social safety been uppermost in their minds, slaveholders would never have imported their crime control problem to begin with. And it was the economic impact of chattel slavery—namely, the diversion of slave labor profits to the master class—that northern abolitionists, steeped in the work ethic, decried as slavery's worst injustice.[179] Yet, given the element of convict labor, the prisons promoted by northern advocates also had undeniable economic ramifications. Were these distinguishable from those generated by chattel slavery? To this question, and to the problem of convict exploitation generally, we now turn.

Penitentiary and Slavery: Substance

"I can readily believe that the difference between freedom and
slavery is not so great as it seems to some ardent and biased minds."
Jeremy Bentham

In some respects, the plantation economy had a counterpart in the prison economy.[1] Both engaged in the production of commodities,[2] and both remunerated their involuntary residents, if at all, with less than a free market wage.[3] Like slave industries, the enterprises favored in prisons were labor intensive, taking maximum advantage of the captive work force.[4] In other respects, however, the economic features of the two institutions differed. Southern plantations were run for *profit*. Masters purchased slaves in the expectation that those slaves would make them rich—richer than they could hope to become by engaging the services of voluntary laborers. Northern authorities set a more modest objective for the captive labor in their prison workshops. "[I]t would be doing well if the convicts could be made to defray the expense of their *own support*," the directors of the Massachusetts State Prison opined typically in 1823. "The idea of a revenue to the State from the iniquity of these felons would be more disgracious than the indecent tax of Vespasian."[5] Although authorities expected convicts to enrich the institution by their labors, they generally aspired only to an income sufficient to maintain it without government subsidy.

Insofar as they obliged inmates to defray the expenses of the penitentiary by laboring for low (or no) compensation, authorities viewed carceral labor relations as in no wise exploitive. By yielding up the full value of their labor, inmates simply reimbursed society for the costs generated by their misdeeds. The public's "claim of indemnity" for sustaining convicts in the penitentiary appeared to commentators to be "most obvious and unobjectionable."[6] And this was hardly a novel moral outlook. Though the ancient public punishments had entailed no analogous expense, authorities had always demanded that jail inmates awaiting punishment in England and North America pay their prison fees. In early Massachusetts some indigent inmates were sold into servitude to raise the necessary funds.[7] To incorporate such servitude into the prison changed the practice somewhat, but the theory remained the same.

Advocates might have stretched this theory to cover exactions of convict labor over and above institutional costs. For "[i]f the matter is considered in

a financial point of view," one publicist observed, "the convict owes to society a far greater debt than that of his support. Does he not oblige society to
establish courts for him, to pay juries, to have a police, and to incur numerous other expenses? Has he refunded all the injury he has done?"[8] Applied
rigorously, such logic would again have led criminologists to a vision of hard
labor as justified slavery, in contradistinction to the economic exploitation
of innocent chattel slaves.[9] A few advocates, intrigued perhaps by the prospect of prison revenues, did reach this conclusion.[10] Most stopped short of the
mark. Even proponents of the Auburn plan generally set a balanced budget
as their goal and wheeled out the logic of the larger costs of crime only to
justify incidental prison profits.[11] To the extent that profits did accrue, advocates frequently urged that these be allocated to prison renovation and to
educational projects associated with crime control.[12] Accordingly, when the
Massachusetts State Prison earned a net surplus in 1824 and 1825, Governor Levi Lincoln applauded this "unlooked for result" but proposed to apply
the proceeds to internal construction.[13] Other advocates, while acknowledg-
ing the "abstract right" of the state to appropriate convict labor, feared that
even incidental profits would prove therapeutically damaging. These advocates wished to allocate all earnings above the expenses of confinement to
the inmates, lest they "distrust . . . the motives of [their] imprisonment."[14]
Still other advocates disputed as a theoretical proposition the state's right to
extract revenue from convicts above their immediate prison costs. The prospect of profit-making prisons thus could be seen not only as injudicious but—
again with allusions to slavery—as "unjust and tyrannical."[15]

However much income they sought from the penitentiary, advocates of all
rehabilitative philosophies cautioned their readers against exalting this goal
above functional efficiency. "Considering the advantage contemplated to result from the penitentiary system," Thomas Eddy observed, again in a typical
passage, "the mere expense is a matter of secondary consideration."[16] Efforts
to make penitentiaries even self-sustaining appear to have been induced more
by the threat of adverse publicity than by ideological imperatives. Advocates
feared that large deficits would sour citizens on incarceration before they
had a chance to savor the criminological benefits of the new punishment. "In
order to recommend it [the penitentiary system] to the favor of the people,
the low principle of avarice has been appealed to," a Massachusetts commentator related in 1826, thus "extraordinary efforts have been employed, and
successfully in a few instances, to make the prisoners support themselves."[17]

Public pressures notwithstanding, authorities generally abided by their priorities. They eschewed measures to increase prison income that they deemed
inimical to rehabilitative therapy. Of course, just what measures would compromise rehabilitation were in the eyes of the beholder. Analyses of prison
economics frequently reflected the competing ideological premises of the
analysts. While agreeing that financial considerations should bow to effective
crime control, rehabituation advocates viewed hard labor as the proper path

to that end. By contrast, advocates of reclamation pinned their hopes on solitary confinement. As a result, many innovations inspired by the balance sheet could appear compatible with crime control in the eyes of the former; few in the eyes of the latter. Advocates of rehabituation happily observed that the most profitable prison industries also offered convicts the best opportunities for employment upon their release;[18] advocates of reclamation rejected all congregate industries as pernicious, despite their relative profitability. Advocates of reclamation repeatedly denounced their rivals for putting aside the goal of rehabilitation in pursuit of maximum production—but advocates of rehabituation denied that they had done anything of the sort.[19]

In choosing *between* competing ideologies, authorities may well have been moved by mercenary considerations. Contemporaries noted the responsiveness of state legislatures to the perceived economy of alternative prison plans,[20] and even some theorists confessed to being swayed by such considerations.[21] Having adopted one system or another, however, authorities willingly operated within their respective ideological constraints. In states that pursued the Pennsylvania plan of solitary labor, advocates explicitly rejected the possibility of still greater remuneration via congregate crafts.[22] In certain penitentiaries at certain times, convicts received compensation for their efforts; in some instances, compensation may have been set at a level that precluded any net proceeds for the institution.[23] And even under the Auburn plan, featuring uncompensated, congregate hard labor, the authorities' devotion to economy had limits. All convict enterprises were conducted within walls, though contemporaries recognized that a system of leasing inmates out of doors (as emerged in the postbellum South) would have been more profitable.[24]

Certainly the most direct conflict between crime control and revenue, faced by advocates of all penal philosophies, arose in connection with the scale of the carceral institution. In the South, planters sought to maximize the number of slaves in their possession; the more slaves one owned, the more income one could derive from them. This logic was especially apposite to penitentiaries, where maintenance costs were inelastic.[25] From the standpoint of the balance sheet, therefore, authorities ought to have done all they could to *encourage* crime (like African tribes that "strain for Crimes very hard, in order to get the Benefit of selling the Criminal").[26] In the event, authorities sought the opposite result; they measured the success of the penitentiary by *reductions* in the convict rolls. Even proponents of the Auburn plan applauded downturns in the population of their prisons as "the pleasantest thing about this institution."[27] Authorities established prison policies in general without regard to their demographic impact. Thus, in most penitentiaries, the "manumission" of inmates (via pardon) was common.[28] Conversely, southern planters would have hesitated before purchasing an aged or infirm slave, whereas judges readily sentenced, and penitentiaries received, aged and infirm criminals.[29]

This distinction of priorities drew few direct comparisons, but it did yield one strain of rhetoric diametrically opposed to its analogue in the writings of slaveholders. Southerners defended the plantation environment by stressing its positive features, asserting that slaves lived lives without care and achieved greater happiness even than masters, who were loaded down with burdens of administration.[30] By contrast, carceral apologists defended their institution by highlighting the *negative* aspects of prison life. To suggest that incarceration was better than freedom would have confirmed their critics' worst suspicions—that free laborers committed crimes in order to get inside prisons.[31] (This last assertion, though painful to advocates of the penitentiary, could have provided opponents of slavery with a powerful line of argument: if slavery was so comfortable, why did the free poor not seek to enslave themselves?)[32] Critics of incarceration shouted from the rooftops that the penitentiary inflicted insufficient hardships to deter crime, and proponents took pains to address this concern—whence the doctrine of "less eligibility," casting into ideological stone the proposition that the prison environment must always be harsher than that of the most poorly compensated free worker.[33] When legislators in New York remarked (in a manner curiously reminiscent of proslavery rhetoric) that convicts "have no cares, incumbrances . . . or burdens of any kind," they meant to condemn, not commend, the manner in which the penitentiary was run as a "revolting injustice."[34] Contemplating the plantation primarily as an economic system, southerners naturally wished to project an image of happy slaves; but for northerners focused on crime control, the analogous image of happy convicts was anathema.

Prison accounts reflected carceral aims and priorities. Then as now, most penitentiaries operated at a consistent loss; at best, they had spotty records of earnings performance. This was true even of prisons run strictly on the Auburn plan.[35] Indeed, accounts were often bleaker than they appeared. Rather than alter policies that would have undermined criminological goals, prison authorities habitually endeavored to camouflage institutional finances. Given that solitary prison industries earned smaller sums than congregate ones, advocates for whom solitude was essential contrived ingenious arguments to show how revenue shortfalls were offset in solitary prisons by lower operating expenses.[36] Warden Bradford, who was never afraid to admit that the Massachusetts State Prison cost money to run, charged that the ingenuity of his counterparts extended beyond the merely rhetorical. "The warden is more desirous of making known [state prison expenses]," Bradford stated in a report to the governor, "as he has good reason to believe that a different practice has prevailed in other institutions of this kind in the United States; and that in the returns made by them much of the real expense is concealed, and that their fiscal concerns are given to the public in a much more flattering view than an accurate regard to the facts would justify."[37] As a capital venture, the penitentiary was a dismal failure. By contrast, profits derived from southern plantations financed a way of life.[38]

It is understandable that, even at prisons mired in deficits, convicts continued to resent hard labor as much as chattel slaves did. Many had doubtless convinced themselves that their prosecutions were unjust to begin with; they felt no obligation toward an institution in which they were unwilling occupants.[39] In explaining his resentment of forced labor, Stephen Burroughs confessed that "I know my situation did not admit of that cool and rational thinking upon these subjects which real justice required."[40] Situated differently, carceral advocates understood the difference between penitentiaries and profit-driven plantations. Northern captive labor programs were designed to sustain convicts, not to capitalize on their plight.

The matter, however, cannot be ended there. For even if the state reaped no economic harvest from criminal incarceration, the possibility remains that other parties, lurking in the wings, stood to benefit financially from the subjugated workers of the penitentiary. Unlike slave labor, prison labor was not nakedly profitable. It may nonetheless have been surreptitiously profitable. Such profitability, if demonstrated, could suggest a more sinister reconciliation between antislavery and carceral advocacy than its advocates were prepared publicly to aver. Advocates—either in their own interest or as the representatives of others—may have sought to substitute for politically unstable modes of labor discipline less conspicuous institutions whereby those on top could continue to gain from those below them. Prisons might simply have implemented or engendered slavery with a gentler face.[41]

Among those holding a more shadowy interest in convict enterprise were private manufacturers. Authorities initially had operated most prison industries directly for the benefit of the state. But as penitentiaries began to experience financial embarrassment, authorities in many states sought to lease convict labor within walls to independent contractors.[42] These entrepreneurs assumed the risks, but also the opportunities, offered by the penitentiary's workshops.

It is extremely difficult at this remove to assess the profitability of convict labor to early prison contractors. State authorities did not keep such records. Still, the opportunities for private profit out of prison enterprises would appear to have been limited. Given the state's adverse interest in protecting the taxpayer, authorities were not about to undertake annual losses in order to enable contractors to amass a fortune. On the contrary, authorities demanded for convict labor as much as the market would bear,[43] and because they controlled whole prisons authorities stood in a stronger bargaining position than individual free laborers; convict labor had, after a fashion, been "unionized" as early as the 1790s!

At the Massachusetts State Prison, the first labor contract dated to 1807, when authorities let twenty inmates to a merchant engaged in the plate and harness making business.[44] Hiring out convicts became official policy once administrators found the practice to be more remunerative than enterprises run directly on the state's account.[45] To induce merchants to take part, prison administrators let convict labor at well below the free market rate.[46] But such arrangements hardly ensured windfall gains to the contractors—as one of them learned in 1822 when his supplies were destroyed in a fire set by the inmates he employed. The directors of the Massachusetts State Prison commented on this setback: "Contractors are invariably informed that all accidents or losses incident to carrying on business with the convicts are at their own risk and the low price of their labour is the indemnity for such risk."[47] Even when the workshop remained tranquil, there were no guarantees that its unskilled labor pool would turn out salable merchandise.[48] In short, contractors took a gamble on the costs and quality of prison production—sometimes the gamble paid off, sometimes it did not.

It is suggestive that few merchants rushed forward to try their luck. In 1816, six merchants had outstanding contracts with the Massachusetts State Prison, and two of those leased labor by the day;[49] contractors came and went. In 1817, a screw manufacturer abandoned efforts to carry on his business in the penitentiary. Prison administrators continued to produce screws for the benefit of the state account until another private manufacturer agreed to take over the business five years later.[50] But contractors never employed all of the inmate labor that the institution made available, and "the low price of their time has not been a sufficient inducement to procure a demand."[51] If the business community's poor reception is any indication, the penitentiary as a source of cheap labor left much to be desired.

Contractors were not the only free citizens who prowled around prisons.[52] The institutions were also inhabited by administrators and guards. A number of carceral advocates, such as New York merchant Thomas Eddy, made personal sacrifices to devote themselves to their penitentiaries.[53] But not everyone was animated by philanthropic sentiments: though officials had hoped to staff the Board of Directors of the Massachusetts State Prison with volunteers, in the event "it was found necessary to give a compensation to induce Gentlemen to serve."[54] Salaries at American penitentiaries were set at a relatively high level, both to recompense employees for the unpleasant aspects of the working environment and to attract persons of "competent character" to fill the available positions.[55]

In the latter quest, alas, authorities were not always successful. Placed in positions of "trust and confidence,"[56] guards too often violated that trust. Prison personnel have always wielded enormous power over inmates, and authorities had long tolerated abuses of that power in the old English and colonial jails, applied to their keepers' emolument. Aware of the problem and of the threat it posed to prison discipline and rehabilitative therapy, the builders of the penitentiary set out to regulate and monitor the institution's affairs.[57] But old traditions die hard, and despite precautions some prison personnel managed to derive large sums from their positions—though without the blessings of the public officials who employed them.

In Massachusetts, abuses developed almost immediately. One problem was simple embezzlement: in 1815, a number of officers were caught converting a portion of the convicts' daily allowances to their own use.[58] The introduction of prison industries multiplied the opportunities for such practices. In 1812, the directors complained that raw materials and manufactured goods "were liable to great waste and embezzlement by their remaining in the yard, workshops, and chambers of the prison." They ordered that a storehouse be erected and a commissary appointed, to whom officers would have to make weekly accounts.[59] Resourceful officers found other ways to take advantage of convict production. In 1814, the directors discovered that a prison contractor had made payments to his workshop's overseer, who presumably undertook in return to ensure that the shop operated efficiently.[60]

The most rampant abuse in the Massachusetts State Prison was one that had plagued the old jails: illicit trading. Condemned to prison fare, convicts with money were willing to pay any price for such forbidden luxuries as tobacco and liquor, smuggled into the cells by corrupt guards. According to the prison bylaws of 1806, a convict's overstint wages not directed to the use of his dependents were to be accumulated and paid to him only upon his discharge.[61] But this rule was not enforced, and before long thousands of dollars were circulating through the prison, fueling transactions between inmates and their keepers.[62] In 1819, a turnkey was dismissed for trading, but by then the practice had become entrenched.[63] An investigation in 1828 revealed that overseers throughout the prison set the convicts' stint low in order to augment the sums available to internal exploitation.[64] The commissary, appointed sixteen years earlier to prevent embezzlement, confessed to earning half again his salary by selling goods to convicts.[65]

The prison official most successful by far in lining his pockets at the institution's expense was Samuel Johnson, overseer of the stone department from 1816 until his dismissal in disgrace in 1828. Johnson's contract of employment, renewed periodically at the behest of the directors, promised the overseer a salary plus 5 percent commission on all stone sold by the state prison; Johnson also received permission (contrary to law, as the warden insisted) to negotiate sales on the prison's behalf.[66] In 1823, Warden Bradford suspended Johnson on discovering that he was trafficking in contraband, but on appeal the directors ordered him reprimanded only.[67] Three years later, Bradford's successor found that the overseer had received payments from contractors on account of the prison that he had not, in all instances, tendered over. Charges were again preferred to the directors, and again Johnson got off with an acquittal of "bad intentions."[68] Legislative committees investigating prison affairs in 1826 and 1828 were shocked to discover that the overseer's commissions had amounted to two to three thousand dollars per annum and that he had set the daily stint in his department at no more than half that of other quarries in the state. Along with other officers, Johnson had also appropriated prison stores, stock, and manufactures and had used convict labor all at "very low prices." As a result, the committeemen concluded, Johnson "has long had the *most lucrative post in this Commonwealth.*"[69]

Abuses of the sort exposed in Massachusetts crept into penitentiaries in many states.[70] But they differed from the abuses of the old local jails in that, once discovered, they were dealt with strictly. Johnson was stripped of his office, and the board of directors that had protected him and covered up the corruption of overstint was dissolved.[71] Penitentiaries certainly were not intended to profit the state employees who worked in them. On the contrary, dereliction of duty in the penitentiary was treated as a serious offense.[72]

One charge of exploitation leveled against prisons emanated from beyond their walls. Free artisans and craftworkers railed against the state for establishing competitive industries within carceral institutions. Operating with the assistance of captive labor, these industries ostensibly constituted a "monopoly" that undercut the free market wage.[73] Artisans thus accused the state of mistreating *them,* gleaning income ultimately at their expense.

Free labor agitation against prison competition had a long history. It influenced legislation regulating production within the earliest English workhouses.[74] But with the proliferation of the penitentiary in the United States, prison manufacturing emerged as a major political controversy. In Massachusetts, the state assembly was inundated with petitions protesting convict industry.[75] In New York, political campaigns were won and lost on this issue, and free laborers on occasion resorted to violence to press their demands.[76]

Despite their vehemence, free labor complaints against prisons were limited in scope. Because prison industry aimed only at paying for institutional expenses, artisans could not protest that their foregone wages swelled the general coffers of the state. They objected only that the support of *convicts* was borne unevenly, craftworkers against whom the prison competed bearing an unfair share of the load.[77] Given the relative lightness of that load, defenders of the penitentiary could respond that any downward pressure on wages caused by prison industry was, at best, marginal, and even labor advocates had to admit as much.[78] To the extent that such pressure nonetheless fell disproportionately on craftworkers, carceral advocates reminded them that (under the rehabituative model) craftsmanship was an essential ingredient of criminal rehabilitation; were trades not conducted in prison, the "fatal alternative" would be the continued depredation of society by ex-convicts. Thus again, the penitentiary's primary focus on crime control helped to distinguish its labor policies from exploitive ones; when viewed from a criminological perspective, labor protests against prison industry suddenly appeared petty. Supporters of the institution assailed artisans for placing their narrow financial interests ahead of the common good.[79]

Still, by focusing on the *external* consequences of prisons, artisans may have been on to something. For the labor and training conducted in prisons also had implications for convicts *after* their release, implications that could be seen, in the proper light, as exploitive. To be sure, the goal of prompting convicts to labor was not autonomous: advocates typically conceived of industry and crime as opposite sides of a coin. But by transforming idle thieves into diligent workers, indoctrinated to accept their lot in life,[80] prisons arguably conferred a *double* benefit on employers, sparing them from theft and also swelling their work force with ex-convicts from whose toil they stood to profit. Advocates who beat the drums of crime control were no less emphatic about this second side of carceral rehabilitation. They frequently spoke of "reduc[ing] such a description of men to a regular course of labor" or of transforming criminals into "useful members of society."[81] Was this, was "rehabilitation" itself, an oppressive arrangement—similar in spirit to the "seasoning" of chattel slaves?[82]

The answer, of course, will depend on the respondent's economic philosophy. Marx considered the wage relation to be inherently exploitive because it robbed workers of the surplus value of their endeavors. Though penitentiaries rarely produced surplus value,[83] the industries they prepared inmates to enter certainly did. But such laissez-faire economists as Adam Smith, writing at the time when penitentiaries went up, were untroubled by profit-making enterprise per se, given the associated cost of capital and the overall objective of maximum production. For these ideologists, the revenue siphoned off by investors represented the return necessary to spur them to undertake capital ventures. Just as crime induced by idleness was perceived to disserve the common good,[84] production induced by industriousness was seen to serve the national interest, even when carried on within ventures imposing the wage relation.[85]

Ironically, it was southern planters who first suggested the oppressive character of employment relations in the North. Faced with the charge that slavery was exploitive, Southerners retorted that free northern laborers fared no better than chattel slaves. Indeed, claimed the apologists, they often fared worse: abandoned during economic recession and on infirmity or old age, "white slaves" or "wage slaves" (as the publicists termed northern workers) faced the threat of starvation, whereas southern masters remained bound by law to provide for their slaves from cradle to grave.[86] The northern contention that free enterprise was more "profitable" than enterprises run on slave labor indicated to George Fitzhugh that free enterprise was simply more exploitive: "[Slave enterprise] profits are less, because the master allows the slave to retain a larger share of the results of his own labor than do the employers of free labor."[87] Nor was it meaningful to distinguish the wage relation from the master-slave relation on the ground that wage laborers entered into employment of their own free will; free laborers were coerced to work, no less than slaves, by the need to put food on their tables.[88]

Southern observations along these lines (which trace back at least to the late eighteenth century)[89] generally took the form of *tu quoque* justifications for chattel slavery; it was left to George Fitzhugh to carry the argument to its logical conclusion and urge the extension of chattel slavery to the North.[90] Occasionally, the argument was also turned outside-in and used to convince slaves that they should gratefully accept their fate. Cotton Mather advised slaves in prerevolutionary Massachusetts that they "live[d] Comfortably, in a very easy Servitude. . . . If you were *Free* many of you would not *Live* near so well as you do." Southern slaves sometimes received similar admonishment.[91]

To complete the triangle, Southerners also asserted that the dominion implied by chattel slavery was no different in substance from the dominion implied by workhouses and penitentiaries. Recalling the characterizations that had often appeared in carceral literature, southern publicists maintained that "[a]ll our penitentiaries" institutionalized "slavery . . . of the most abject and degrading character." If the state abolished chattel slavery, consistency required that it also "abolish all restraints imposed by penal codes, prison discipline, and poor laws, upon the rest of the population."[92] In England, too, such arguments surfaced on occasion. During the celebrated *Somerset* litigation of 1772, in which Lord Mansfield declared free a slave brought into England from one of its colonies, counsel for the master answered the contention that Great Britain did not sanction involuntary servitude: "I may observe, there is an establishment, by which magistrates compel idle or dissolute persons, of various ranks and denominations, to serve [i.e., the workhouse]. In the case of apprentices bound out by the parish, neither the trade is left to the choice of those who are to serve, nor the consent of parties necessary; no contract therefore is made in the former instance, none in the latter; the duty remains the same."[93] Slave, inmate, wage earner. For defenders of slavery, they differed only in name.

Slaveholders who asserted the virtual enslavement of convicts and wage earners found agreement, if not support, from another quarter: the convicts and wage earners themselves. Penitentiary inmates frequently likened their condition to slavery, as we have seen.[94] So, too, did many free laborers, both in England and in northern American states.[95] In England, where feudal conceptions of serfdom lingered on, such analogies appeared well before the emergence of an industrial proletariat. One mid-eighteenth-century commentator reported that Irish workers "think their Labour profits themselves nothing, but that they are like Slaves," toiling for masters who "keep them in a State of Slavery and Subjection."[96] Like chattel slaves and penitentiary inmates, some free laborers in England adopted a sullen attitude toward their work, breaking machines and committing other forms of sabotage.[97] And to complete the triangle, when not comparing themselves to slaves, English laborers sometimes compared their plight to that of convicts![98] In America, free workers regularly evoked images of slavery to describe wage labor during the Jacksonian period, although isolated examples of the equation date back to early colonial times.[99] American laborers, of course, applied the slaveholders' rhetoric to a different end: not the vindication of slavery but the vilification of prevailing wage relations. Many labor activists bitterly resented the preoccupation of northern antislavery advocates with the miseries of the South while neglecting the misery that lay at their own doorsteps.[100]

Was Bentham then correct when he asserted that the difference between freedom and slavery was not so great as some minds had made it out to be?[101] Antislavery advocates did not shrink from answering southern allegations that the two social systems were synonymous. Yet a number of their counterarguments have a ring of sophistry about them. Some commentators took the position that free labor differed substantively from slave labor because free laborers received money for their efforts, a symbol of voluntary exchange.[102] But the slave also received compensation, in kind if not in cash; from the standpoint of pure economics, this distinction was too clever by far.[103] In a similar vein, antislavery advocates distinguished "forced" labor under threat of hunger from forced labor under threat of the lash—one was force "of a moral kind," the other brutalizing and demeaning.[104] But some also felt demeaned by hunger, and considered this too nice a distinction[105]—which, at any rate, again addressed the sensibilities, rather than the substance, of labor relations.

More to the point was the argument that free laborers wielded political power.[106] If slaves felt themselves to be oppressed, they could do little about it. But free laborers could vote—and vote they did, to curtail what they conceived to be oppressive competition from prison manufactures, for example.[107] Along with such political rights, antislavery advocates also distinguished the dynamics of free and slave labor. It had long been a commonplace of American social rhetoric that free citizens, by dint of individual effort and virtue, could improve their position in society. "He that gets all he can honestly, and saves all he gets . . . will certainly become RICH," proclaimed Poor Richard, and other American publicists echoed this chant throughout the antebellum years.[108] The wage relation was widely portrayed as a temporary expedient, providing free laborers with the stake they needed to fund their own capital ventures.[109] In the same breath, Northerners condemned slavery (and, often, wage labor in England) as a hopelessly static condition, from which even the most diligent exertions and painstaking frugality offered no escape.[110] Antislavery advocates thus denounced the equation of slavery and freedom as economically unsound: free employment in capitalist society was only a stepping stone from which laborers leaped to fortune, and those who never got their fortunes off the ground failed because they lacked the virtue of their more successful comrades. "I believe the terms 'wage slavery' and 'white slavery' would be utterly unintelligible to an audience of laboring people," declared one hopeful Boston abolitionist. "Does capital wrong them?—economy will make them capitalists." [111]

Advocates of the penitentiary fully shared this vision of upward mobility in the North. One argument initially offered for the turn to incarceration was the tendency of traditional punishments to halt that mobility. The point emerges most clearly from a postrevolutionary tract penned by an anonymous Massachusetts commentator, Philanthropos, whose social vision blended neatly with his Anglophobic sentiments, so common at the time. In America, Philanthropos observed, "the son of the poorest family may become rich, and the child of the servant, may become a distinguished ruler," whereas in the country from which America had newly won its independence, "the toiling hungry peasant, in tears and pains, weeps upon the wretched rising hour of his misery, and contemplates him as born to the state of slavery and vassalage." Colonial public punishments had originated in England and were suitable, Philanthropos contended, only to the social relations prevalent there: "Where the people are divided into two ranks, masters and slaves, the same modes of correction may be adopted, as are found necessary for the government of horses and mules. The idea of entailing disgrace on posterity, can have no influence on men, who know that their children can never rise from servitude. The idea of bodily pain is useful there; and lacerating the body may have a servile and temporary effect." However, "in a country where freedom is the civil object, and all have an equal title to riches, and to that kind of honor which alone is honorable, the confidence and esteem of their fellow-citizens, a quite opposite mode of punishment ought to be pursued." As usual, Philanthropos urged authorities to "correct [the] habits" of criminals in a carceral facility; this therapy would safeguard offenders from stigmatization and prepare them to reenter the march upward to success. "It is now full time that we should lay aside our leading strings, [and] contemplate our own situation and circumstances," Philanthropos concluded. "[W]e should correct our laws, and render them conformable to the ideas and feelings of a people, who must soon lose, even the historical recollection of slavery; and who will continue to view themselves as born free, equal, and independent." [112]

The philosophy explicitly laid out by Philanthropos in 1796 was implicit throughout the penitentiary programs that developed in the United States in later years. The status of the inmate under sentence to hard labor was always distinguished from the status of the inmate whose sentence was up. Convicts, like slaves, were differentiated from the general population by the distinctive clothing that they wore; the English poor, dismissed as slaves by Philanthropos, had occasionally been subject to similar restrictions.[113] But when convicts emerged from the penitentiary, they left their prison stripes behind; many states made it a practice to grant ex-convicts *new* suits of clothing, symbolic of their graduation into the ranks of free society.[114]

More significant still were the steps taken while convicts remained within walls. Education in the United States has always been conceived as a springboard to social advancement.[115] In the South, slaves rarely received any education, and in some states their instruction was a punishable offense.[116] (General education had not been much encouraged for the English poor, either.)[117] Nor were many slaves schooled in trades; most performed unskilled manual labor on the plantation. By contrast, many penitentiary programs focused not merely on inuring convicts to labor but also on *training* them, in skilled or semiskilled crafts.[118] Advocates hoped to make each convict the "master of a trade,"[119] and they explicitly distinguished such tutoring from the alternative of conducting unskilled labor in prison. The latter, Francis Lieber observed, would prepare the convict only to become "a porter, day laborer, work on a farm, etc.," which he deemed inappropriate.[120] William Roscoe was disturbed by the prospect of employing convicts at stonecutting: "[I]t is the entire ruin of his future prospects and situation in life, as it instructs him in no art or trade he may be enabled to carry on for himself, and by which he may hope to obtain a livelihood in case of his discharge."[121] But Stephen Allen had a different understanding of the economics of quarrying: "Now so far from this being the case, the business of stone cutting in the city of New York . . . is one of the most profitable that is followed." Laborers "who carry it on extensively, have generally accumulated handsome fortunes in a reasonable number of years."[122] Allen was delighted to report instances in which former inmates of Auburn Prison became industrious citizens and amassed savings.[123] In addition, convicts in many penitentiaries received general education in reading and writing, as well as religion.[124] Such basic skills, like trade skills, would be "of inestimable value in their future progress through life."[125] Of course, the prison curriculum was a far cry from that of Harvard College, and no convict left the penitentiary equipped to practice law or other exalted professions. But, then, such a radical shift in social position would have seemed impractical, whether or not it was deemed desirable.[126] Penitentiary advocates were content to raise the status of convicts one step at a time.

Many prisons were eventually given over to manufacturing and factory training. Ideals unique to the factory, such as the division of labor, repetitive production processes, and recourse to mechanical aids, gradually found their way into penitentiaries run on the Auburn plan.[127] Although in retrospect this trend could appear ominous—a regimen conditioning convicts to enter a "free" institution that for many came to symbolize the darker side of capitalism—in prospect it was anything but. When factories began to go up, commentators hailed them as vibrant new enterprises that would offer unprecedented opportunities to their employees.[128] Given the goal of readying convicts for gainful employment, it was only natural for authorities to move in that direction.[129] By contrast, the association of industrialization with upward mobility tended to *discourage* Southerners from employing slaves in factories. James Hammond, a South Carolinian publicist, urged that factory work be restricted to white laborers, so that they could soon afford to buy slaves of their own. "[E]xtensive employment [of slaves] in manufactures and mechanic arts, is [in]consistent with safe and sound policy," Hammond advised. "Whenever a slave is made a mechanic he is more than half freed." [130] Other commentators prophesied that industrialization of the South would spell the end of slavery.[131]

Here, then, was the essential difference between the penitentiary and slavery, the difference that enabled advocates to flourish their approbation of the one and their abhorrence of the other without a trace of irony or hypocrisy. Northern advocates might distinguish the two institutions on the basis of ends: the penitentiary preserved individuals and society from the evils of crime. But this distinction was not foolproof, for southern advocates could plausibly argue that chattel slavery did the same. Even the line drawn between profit-making plantations and nonprofit penitentiaries could be obscured by southern claims that the plantation economy provided amply for all its inhabitants.[132] It was rather their preferred means of accomplishing crime control (and, by the same token, prosperity), by uplifting criminals, that permitted advocates of the penitentiary to capture indisputably the intellectual high ground. From this vantage point, carceral advocates protested any suggestion that the institution as a whole could face constitutional objection. "The Penitentiary System [is] a mode of punishment very consonant with our republican institutions," one American commentator observed. "That any institution the object of which is to better the condition of our fellow men, would meet with opposition . . . is much to be regretted." [133] The same regret was registered in England, where as early as 1751 Henry Fielding distinguished between rehabilitative hard labor and penal slavery (which Fielding opposed). "There is a difference," he insisted, "between making men slaves and felons and compelling them to be subjects; in short, between throwing the reins on the neck of idleness and riding it with spurs of iron." Fielding's proposal called for the construction of "county houses" where idle vagrants and thieves would be rendered industrious. He counted among the critics of this (by then familiar) plan, those "who find Advantage in the present wretched State of the Poor." [134]

Southern republicans might speak of raising African slaves out of barbarism or even of preparing them, over generations, for freedom in some future age. Still, Southerners built their economic prosperity and individual security on the wholesale subjugation of an underclass, which might otherwise have posed a threat to them.[135] Advocates of the penitentiary based their prosperity and security on an effort to give criminals a chance to climb. If that required authorities initially to make convicts feel that they were "slaves of the state," to instill in them "habits of obedience," so be it—on that score, adherents of the Auburn plan parted company with their rivals.[136] But even Auburn supporters who incorporated elements of coercion and dependency into their penal discipline, and who sometimes grasped the forensic utility of proslavery rhetoric to defend such practices,[137] did not intend to establish a system of economic slavery. To this extent, their references to "slavery" in the penitentiary were metaphorical rather than literal:[138] under both systems, the convict returned to society economically, if not psychologically, free.[139] The "complete despotism" of the prison, which Tocqueville found such a contrast to Jacksonian democracy,[140] was only a prelude to freedom of some sort. Southern slavery was not a prelude to freedom of any sort. Abolitionists seized on this fact, and they rejected the contention that effective crime control demanded the hereditary bondage of chattel slaves. If properly prepared for freedom, manumitted slaves would pose no more of a threat to property than any other citizens.[141] Slaveholders, responding to such criticism, had only a little to gain by quoting tracts advocating criminal incarceration. Slaveholders could point to the contractual and utilitarian arguments offered by criminologists to justify their peculiar institution. But no slaveholder could have found solace in a penitentiary advocate's plea to instill in persons a habit of industry, let alone a reclaimed conscience. Such rhetoric perforce called for liberation, once the therapy was done.

Slaveholders brushed aside proposals to liberate their slaves because they rejected the proposition that slaves could *ever* be rehabilitated. Slaves, most Southerners asserted, were congenitally lazy and would work only when forced to do so.[142] Such conjectures sustained (or at least rationalized) an approach to economic organization and crime control fundamentally different from the one in the North. For if the rehabilitation of idlers was impossible, then mass subjugation could well appear the most sensible, and even ethical, means of inducing labor and preventing crime. Surely there could be no harm in holding persons down when one began with the premise that they could never rise.[143]

The notion that some persons suffered from congenital laziness was not unique to the South, nor was it restricted to African slaves. It formed part of a broader vision, of long standing in England, that attributed incorrigible idleness to all who lay at the bottom of society. The English poor in the eyes of many of their betters appeared "vicious, idle, dissolute," laboring only at the call of hunger. Were their wages raised above subsistence for a full day's work, the poor would inevitably choose to labor fewer hours and settle for subsistence.[144] To commentators of this persuasion, the possibility of *enslaving* the poor had some appeal, and proposals to do just that appeared sporadically in England in the seventeenth and eighteenth centuries.[145] And to commentators of this persuasion, the prospect of rehabilitating criminals was no less quixotic than the prospect of uplifting the poor.[146] There had always been those who viewed proposals for hard labor as effective only to deter crime or to extract the maximum amount of labor from unwilling hands. For these commentators, hard labor constituted justified slavery in a literal sense.[147]

It was this pessimistic vision that advocates of the penitentiary rejected—in all of its manifestations. Advocates insisted that criminals could be rehabilitated, just as they insisted that slaves could be emancipated.[148] Many of these same thinkers were also vocal members of the school of political economy begun by English workhouse advocates who challenged the dogma that the poor were hopelessly lazy. By offering them an opportunity to escape their condition, paupers could be persuaded to give up their idle ways.[149] One early proponent of hard labor, Bishop Berkeley, put the case succinctly: "The way to make men industrious [is] to let them taste the fruits of their industry." [150] Berkeley was referring to the laboring poor, but he might as well have been speaking of convicts or slaves. For advocates of this persuasion, the theory applied to all three groups. And just as penitentiary advocates favored education within walls as a means of preparing convicts for freedom, so they also often supported public education for the poor and for emancipated slaves. Once again, the theory pertained to all three groups.[151]

This is not to say that advocates expected rehabilitative therapy to work in every case. Like workhouse advocates before them, penitentiary advocates believed that only some convicts would respond favorably to the therapy.[152] Adherents of the Auburn plan tended toward greater skepticism than others, and several skated close to the line of unalloyed pessimism.[153] In New York, Warden Elam Lynds went so far as to oppose efforts to educate inmates,[154] and the protestations by others that overstint diminished convict output sounds suspiciously similar to the old maxim that higher wages would stimulate the poor to fewer exertions.[155] But even those who rebuked Lynds for failing to enter into the "true spirit" of the penitentiary agreed that rehabilitation was not infallible.[156] When faced with an *incorrigible* criminal (as demonstrated by repeated offenses), all concurred that the effort to rehabilitate might as well be abandoned. For criminals of this sort, some other punishment was necessary: one possibility was transportation,[157] and another was incarceration (as viewed by the pessimists) solely for the purposes of incapacitation, deterrence, and production. But promoters of rehabilitation sharply distinguished this form of incarceration from the *penitentiary*. One commentator accordingly proposed the construction of two separate institutions: a "penitentiary" for salvable convicts, and a "perpetual work-house" for the irremediable ones.[158] This attitude of guarded optimism also permeated antislavery rhetoric. Advocates hoped to prepare chattel slaves for freedom but recognized that some might never make the adjustment successfully. For such persons, again, transportation or some other form of forced labor, distinct from the treatment of freed persons, would be necessary.[159]

It thus appears that antislavery and penitentiary advocacy were not only reconciled but loosely connected in the minds of some publicists. Tocqueville linked both movements to "the cause of reform and of progress in the United States."[160] Although the penitentiary responded to a specific criminological problem, it also fit into a broader social theory for the improvement (or, more precisely, attempted improvement) of all deprived citizens.[161] This theory vied with others that ascribed immutable characteristics to, and prescribed the debasement of, criminals, paupers, and slaves.[162] And in combating such notions, publicists applied some of the same rhetorical devices to different arenas of policy. Faced with the argument that the inherent characteristics of blacks required their enslavement, opponents of slavery turned the tables on apologists by answering that slavery had itself engendered those characteristics.[163] By the same token, labor economists maintained that the laziness of the English poor was a *product* of subsistence wages rather than a reason for them.[164] And just as opponents of slavery sought to convince Southerners of the ill effects of slavery by asking them to imagine how they would behave if they were enslaved,[165] penitentiary advocates demanded of opponents of rehabilitation whether they, "if placed in the miserable condition from which these convicts were taken," would have resisted the like temptations to crime.[166] Such rhetorical parallels reflected deeper intersections of premise and purpose. Ultimately, it was the ideal of improvement that united the antislavery and penitentiary movements.

Yet how closely did the rhetoric of rehabilitation fit the reality? Did ex-convicts truly face prospects that distinguished them substantially from slaves? Or was free society for ex-convicts merely the penitentiary writ large? Many free American citizens found the dream of success credible, and more than a few lived it; during his visit to the United States, Tocqueville was struck by "the innumerable crowd of those striving to escape from their original social condition."[167] But for some American labor advocates, the rhetoric rang hollow,[168] and ex-convicts with a literary bent were inclined to agree. The training designed to propel convicts into the ranks of skilled craftworkers was often directed by incompetent instructors, charged one graduate of Newgate Prison. What was worse, authorities frequently rotated convicts from one workshop to another. As a consequence, "No man ever learnt any mechanical business in the prison, that he was capable of practicing, *with credit,* when liberated."[169] Other ex-convicts complained of the poor opportunities for employment awaiting them when they left prison; nor did authorities grant them "money to get into business" on their own. The award of new clothing to the ex-convict, ostensibly a "freedom suit," often turned out to be shabby and distinctive, marking out former inmates as clearly as prison stripes.[170]

Even the rhetoric of penitentiary advocates occasionally betrayed uncertainties about the true nature of American society. Criminologists who maintained that effective deterrence demanded prison conditions inferior to the living conditions of poor laborers appear to have presupposed that such persons could not easily escape their poverty. Had they fully accepted the dynamic model, advocates would never have feared that even the poorest of citizens would willingly trade their opportunities in free society for the convict's static way of life. Within walls, authorities often sought to propagate the dynamic vision, promising inmates that their punishment was "inflicted . . . with a view to [their] own improvement." [171] But sometimes authorities fell back on a static model, at odds with their public pronouncements. Following a convict uprising in 1816, one of the directors of the Massachusetts State Prison urged an assembly of the inmates that "here, while suffering the punishments of a free and mild government, you are better provided for, than thousands of our citizens, who have committed no crime and are subject to harder labour than is required from you for their daily support." [172] Change a word or two, and this lecture was identical to others given to mollify chattel slaves.[173]

What, then, are we to make of all the fine words about convict training and improvement spoken by proponents of the penitentiary? It is, of course, impossible to reconstruct the private thoughts of the advocates with any degree of certainty. Disentangling text from subtext (or pretext?) is truly a dismal science. But if one is prepared to grant that persons sometimes err, that their plans go awry, then one finds little reason to doubt the advocates' sincerity—as opposed to their wisdom—in implementing carceral programs. The travails faced by ex-convicts were well publicized, and advocates responded with a variety of efforts to overcome them.[174] In all the mountains of paper produced on the subject, both for public consumption and for private communication, nowhere does one encounter expressions of satisfaction with the economic stagnation of ex-convicts. Nor would stagnation, cast alongside promises of economic opportunity, necessarily have suited the interests of the social elite. Wage earners and ex-convicts might labor without surcease under the illusion that their lot would improve, but when in time they came to realize that they were treading down the garden path, then surely their employers, no less than slaveholders, would have to look out. To encourage rising expectations that employers had no intention of fulfilling might temporarily have eased the problem of labor discipline in free society, but only at the hazard of long-term political instability. Rising expectations, after all, have triggered more than one revolution.

Even the inconsistencies that occasionally crept into the advocates' rhetoric betrayed no sinister turn of mind. Rhetorical inconsistency was, and remains, a common failing in even the most idealistic of mortal beings. Criminologists in particular were perfectly aware that their field of inquiry suffered from the ills of muddled thinking.[175] To the extent that publicists tailored their arguments to different audiences—as they sometimes did to legislators, free laborers, and inmates—their verbal gymnastics most likely reflected nothing more than zeal for the carceral experiment. Faced with an uphill battle for support, both outside and inside penitentiaries, advocates did what they had to do, and made the arguments that had to be made, to keep alive their hopes for the institution. At day's end, it is those hopes that strike, and sadden, the mind: hopes expressed in pamphlet after pamphlet, in letter after letter. Hopes that survived a thousand disappointments. And hopes that were eventually doomed to crumble against an unyielding array of social and systemic obstacles.

Conclusion

T he penitentiary had its heyday in the United States in the 1830s. Facilities proliferated, the literature thrived, and visitors traveled great dis-
tances to view American prisons in action.[1] In spite of persistent difficulties, the penitentiary became for Jacksonians a symbol of achievement.
They brimmed with pride at all the foreign interest their carceral institutions
succeeded in attracting.[2]

Ballyhoo often has a way of clouding objectivity. Some Jacksonians were
eager to claim paternity of the penitentiary and to portray it as a theoretical break with older visions of punishment—assertions that have lingered
in the writings of some historians. In fact, the ideological roots of criminal
incarceration lay in Europe, where they had been deepening for centuries.
The American penitentiary was born not of new ideas but of old conceptions
that, set against a background of social change, seemed more sensible and
attractive than ever before.

In part, the sense of novelty that surrounds the American penitentiary de-
rives from an optical illusion. What we *see* before us when we view the state
prison is an institution without precedent: a facility with looming walls, holding hundreds of prisoners. Its very scale bespeaks innovation. But there is less
here than meets the eye. Once authorities resolved to initiate a general policy
of criminal incarceration, they had little choice but to design new structures
to accommodate it. As authorities in Massachusetts learned the hard way,[3] the
old ones were simply inadequate for the task.

Equally deceptive is the wealth of attention that visitors lavished on
Jacksonian penitentiaries.[4] The deluge of European delegations in the 1830s
masked a subtle shift in the intellectual center of penal advocacy. Before 1800,
European theorists dominated the field of criminology, supplying the basic
postulates and blueprints upon which American facilities were built. Even the
term *penitentiary* derived from English sources.[5] But as American efforts got
off the ground, the new builders gained increasing renown. What the Jacksonians had to offer was not fresh theories about what the penitentiary could or
should accomplish but fresh suggestions for the practical implementation of
old paradigms: primarily refinements in the realm of administration and design.[6] Europeans flocked to American penitentiaries to learn these valuable,
but secondary, lessons.[7]

The English experience illustrates this intellectual migration. Having operated workhouses since the sixteenth century, English lawmakers had toyed
with more extensive carceral programs over the years. The intricate Peni-

tentiary Act of 1779, drafted by the towering figures of Howard, Eden, and Blackstone, owed nothing to the thoughts or experience of American advocates. Though the act was stillborn, English penitentiaries did open late in the eighteenth century, based on local plans without American input.[8]

By 1834 things had changed. Before embarking on a major new prison project, the English government dispatched William Crawford to tour American prisons. When Pentonville opened in 1842, its structure and internal routine closely resembled the Eastern State Penitentiary of Pennsylvania, with which Crawford had been most favorably impressed. Yet English criminologists never lost track of the facility's lineage. As Crawford protested, the penitentiary was "British in its origin, British in its actual application, British in its legislative sanction." [9] And he was right. The Jacksonians reared the penitentiary; they did not conceive it.

What the British had conceived and the Jacksonians helped to rear was an institution founded on traditional ideas. Though built amid the intellectual upheavals of the Enlightenment, the penitentiary drew little inspiration from new ideologies. Beccaria's radical reconceptualization of deterrence was of marginal significance to advocates of the penitentiary: carceral punishment promised to provide no greater certainty than had most traditional sanctions. The Beccarian critique brought only capital punishment into disrepute, and that had accounted historically for a small fraction of criminal sentences.[10] Nor did sensational psychology significantly alter or enliven rehabilitative theory. Instead of developing a novel carceral therapy, most rational advocates endorsed hard labor—the same therapy that workhouse advocates had been promoting for close to three centuries. And while proponents of the penitentiary sometimes included references to the precept of human perfectibility in their proposals, such ideological convictions did little to lift therapeutic expectations. Like earlier generations of criminologists, most postrevolutionary and Jacksonian advocates displayed a practical turn of mind. Few viewed the program as a panacea. According to one student, perfectionism combined with environmentalism to give the Jacksonian penitentiary "a utopian flavor." [11] Jacksonian advocates would have taken offense at the suggestion. They used the term *utopian* as a pejorative, to dismiss extravagant criminological aspirations.[12]

But if carceral ideology was not utopian, it did include an element of idealism which, from the vantage point of more recent criminological values, cannot fail to impress. Like their predecessors in the workhouse movement, proponents of the penitentiary hoped to control crime by *uplifting* criminals, just as many sought to elevate the condition of other depressed social groups. Both in England and in North America, religious impulses frequently mingled with traditional criminological concerns (into which they were fully soluble). Tocqueville remarked that "the progress of the reform of [American] prisons has been of a character essentially religious. Men, prompted by religious feelings, have conceived and accomplished everything which has been under-taken."[13] Carceral ideology was conventional in that it remained focused on the goal of crime control. But carceral ideology was also socially progressive, in that it sought to reduce offenses by enabling criminals to better themselves.

That legislators eventually embraced such a program probably owed less to its ideological appeal than to the social context in which it was offered—namely, growing criminal anonymity, failing public punishments, and ram-pant property crime, particularly in urban centers and ports. Absent this context, the penitentiary would have encountered far greater resistance; for only in an atmosphere of palpable crisis could legislators be persuaded to adopt a policy as wrenching, and potentially expensive, as the replacement of ancient public sanctions.[14] The advocates themselves were first to bemoan their inability to make headway against the forces of legal inertia. "The voice of a philosopher is too weak to contend against the tumults and the cries of so many who are guided by blind custom," Cesare Beccaria lamented. "How fortunate humanity would be if laws were for the first time being decreed for it. . . . If these monarchs, I say, suffer the old laws to subsist, it is because of the infinite difficulties involved in stripping from errors the venerated rust of many centuries."[15]

How much more unyielding is that rust when reinforced with the virtues of economy? Jeremy Bentham learned the answer not once but twice. As a young critic of the first draft of the Penitentiary Act, Bentham noticed that the logistical impediments to transportation of convicts brought on by the Ameri-can Revolution "gave great weight to the inducements, if they were not the sole inducements, that led to the institution of this plan." The novice crimi-nologist was amused that it had required "the misfortunes from which those difficulties took their rise . . . [to] force us into the adoption of a plan that promises to operate one of the most signal improvements that have ever yet been made in our criminal legislation."[16] But the elaborate Penitentiary Act was never implemented, and the lesson of the episode, so perceptively recog-nized, did not sink in. Bentham's imagination had been warmed, and he spent the next twenty years beseeching Parliament to transform his own carceral scheme, the Panopticon, into reality. These efforts came to naught,[17] and Ben-tham eventually abandoned the project embittered rather than amused. "A jail," he complained to Lord Pelham, "is not quite so easily built as talked of, not even in England, as I have had occasion to know but too well."[18]

The early stages of the penitentiary movement in North America were shaped less by intellectuals such as Bentham than by a general clamor for action. The dominant theme was not moral principle but glaring necessity for change. As one Massachusetts columnist framed the issue, the decline of crime control was "truly alarming—to your august body [the legislature] we look for redress—from you we have a right to expect it—and from you we will no doubt receive it."[19] This was the sort of plea that could generate activity in the American statehouse. Criminological theories and abstractions did not drive the process. As another columnist added briskly, the need for an overhaul of the prerevolutionary system of criminal punishment required "no great stretch of philosophy to discover."[20] Only after alarmism overpowered the resistance of inertia and economy did American states begin to take stock of carceral ideology and move away from traditional sanctions.[21]

None of this is to belittle the importance of individuals in making criminal incarceration happen. In New York, Thomas Eddy played a central role in drafting carceral legislation and steering it through the state assembly. In Pennsylvania, Benjamin Rush and the Philadelphia Society for Alleviating the Miseries of Public Prisons pushed the idea with equal determination.[22] Lobbying efforts in every state encouraged the transition and continued to guide the development of the fledgling penitentiary.[23] But advocates did not act in isolation. Their success was primed, and their own efforts were in some measure prompted, by a sense of crisis in the world around them.[24]

Indeed, the years of change were numbered by this stubborn fact. Once the immediate perception of crisis had passed, criminologists who sought institutional modifications again encountered the familiar roadblocks. We have noted the reluctance of the Massachusetts legislature to authorize funds for renovation of the state prison at Charlestown.[25] On another front, the same legislature in 1819 responded to the pleas of activists by passing a sweeping reform of local houses of correction for juveniles and petty offenders.[26] But the crucial section of the statute mandating construction of individual cells and workshops was repealed within four months,[27] and the rest of the act soon stood "little more than a dead letter upon the statute book." "Why," Judge Josiah Quincy grieved, "should not the ancient houses of correction be revived? . . . There is but one reason; that mistaken reason; that abused word; economy! The expense! As if any expense was of weight when put into the scales against humanity; against the duty, incumbent on every society, to multiply the means of moral advancement."[28] Quincy's cry has a timeless quality: in political life, principles are no substitute for panic as a lever of change.

And therein lies the tragedy of the penitentiary. For it is hardly clear, whatever the advocates' administrative achievements, that carceral punishment ever truly held promise as a substantive solution to the problem of crime. Under early schemes of public punishment, the community played an integral role in the rehabilitative process, readmitting offenders or even shepherding them back into the fold of society. Demographic trends rendered these mechanisms of conciliation increasingly ineffectual, and instead of correcting them, the turn to incarceration sealed their abandonment. At one level, then, the transition sounded a retreat in the face of adversity. With the advent of the penitentiary, the rehabilitative focus shrank from the offender vis-à-vis the community to the offender alone. *His* orientation was all that process sought to correct. And once carceral methodology was wedged into place, the older, communal approach to rehabilitation was quickly forgotten.

Not everyone had been blind to the drawbacks of the penitentiary. Jacques Brissot de Warville, an astute French republican who toured the Walnut Street prison in 1788, saw virtues in carceral punishment. But he also saw risks: "By imprisonment, you snatch a man from his wife, his children, his friends; you deprive him of their succour and consolation. . . . He returns to his family, from whom he has been long sequestered; he no more meets from them, or experiences in himself, the same attachment and the same tenderness." Warville intuitively grasped the prison's potential for social alienation. Though incarceration might be "the best method of ameliorating men," still it "cut [them] off from all those connections which render [their] existence of any importance."[29] Subsequent events bore out Warville's misgivings. "[T]he system is incomplete," the directors of the Massachusetts State Prison admitted in 1823, "and therefore the evil complained of necessarily occurs. Convicts are discharged who have no friends, acquaintances or money; or who, by being known as convicts, are avoided as infectious and driven by necessity to commit new crimes. They are willing to labour, but can get no employment; and cannot consent to starve, even at the hazard of renewed imprisonment."[30]

Nor, in their haste to isolate offenders, had advocates kept sight of another shortcoming of criminal incarceration: its impact on the offender's innocent dependents. The early Puritans had not been so careless. In 1695, a Massachusetts statute mandating a fine or twenty days' imprisonment for unlicensed sale of liquor was abruptly amended to make whipping the alternative to the fine. As the revisors' preamble explained the change, "divers ill disposed and indigent persons . . . if detected and convicted of any such offense, are unable to satisfy the fine imposed by law for the same, and cannot be punished by imprisonment without wrong to their families."[31] Yet, try as they might, the effects of subsequent criminologists to combat these systemic defects had little positive impact.[32]

The irony is that even as advocates trumpeted the ideal of rehabilitation, the scheme they seized on to accomplish it merely reinforced the conception of a criminal underclass. It built a wall instead of a bridge between offenders and society. Paradoxically, this may well have been the penitentiary's foremost attraction. At a time when community involvement in punishment seemed unworkable, an institution that promised to rehabilitate offenders without the need for such involvement held great appeal. But if rehabilitation is inherently a reciprocal process, if it requires not only contrition but forgiveness as well, then the very concept of carceral rehabilitation was flawed at the source.

Advocates eventually closed the chasm between theory and practice, though in a perverse manner. Disillusioned by decades of blighted hopes, advocates ultimately ceased trying to perfect the system. They simply abandoned the rehabilitative ideal.[33] Instead of hunting on for ways to make the practice fit their "beautiful and brilliant" theory,[34] advocates lowered their sights and let theory fall back into step with practice. The upshot was that advocates sustained their faith in the rehabilitative potential of the penitentiary just long enough to overcome the initial reaction against the institution. By the time they, too, had become disillusioned, the institution was embedded in the American grain.

And so the penitentiary persists to this day: a monument to failure, hallowed only by time. In an age of spiraling costs, explosive internal conditions, and escalating crime rates despite all, the institution's grip over legislators' imagination may be weakening at long last. In recent decades, public anxiety over criminal justice has sparked a renewed interest in and testing of alternative modes of punishment—among them community service, a form of sanction similar in spirit to the communal punishments of old.[35] It would be ironic, to say the least, if history were to come full circle after a mere two centuries of failed experiment. At any rate, historians can do their part by broadening the modern criminologist's horizons. If legal history does not tell us how things ought to be, it can at least tell us that they need not be the way they are. If "the venerated rust of many centuries" can be loosened a bit, then perhaps others will step forward to strip the errors bare.

A Note on the Sources

The fundamental difficulty with a study of this sort is not the dearth of evidence but the glut. The problem of punishment has concentrated minds for centuries; proponents of criminal incarceration began committing their thoughts to paper at least as early as the sixteenth century. This Note describes a research strategy that was selective by necessity. Although I shall refer here to the sources that I found most important or helpful, the reader is encouraged to return to the notes to the text for a fuller recitation of the evidence upon which this study was grounded.

A. Primary Sources

To place American developments in perspective, it was necessary to explore the English background to criminal incarceration. I focused my primary research on the parliamentary record and the extensive pamphlet literature dating from the sixteenth through the eighteenth centuries. Perhaps the earliest work to suggest the possibility of imprisonment at hard labor was Thomas More, *Utopia* [1516], trans. Paul Turner (London, 1972). Many detailed proposals followed in the seventeenth century, among which Richard Haines, *Proposals for Building in Every County a Working-Alms-House or Hospital* (London, 1677), is typical. The eighteenth century witnessed not only the birth of "rational" criminology but also the development of new strands of thought on how the prison could rehabilitate its inmates. On rational criminology generally, see Cesare Beccaria, *On Crimes and Punishments* [1764], ed. Henry Paolucci (Indianapolis, 1964), a much celebrated essay that influenced the thinking of a generation of criminologists. On rational theories of criminal incarceration, see *The Works of Jeremy Bentham,* ed. John Bowring (Edinburgh, 1843), which contains Bentham's major tracts. In these works one can observe Bentham's ideas evolving over time. On the new theory of solitary confinement as a rehabilitative therapy, see the several works by Jonas Hanway, especially *Solitude in Imprisonment* (London, 1776). For general background on the state of prison administration at this time, the outstanding work is John Howard, *The State of the Prisons* [1777] (London, 1929). Howard's treatment of English jails had no American counterpart, but his description of pervasive neglect was apposite to American jails as well.

My research into the development of criminal incarceration in Massachusetts was intended to be comprehensive. I sought out evidence from all forums, both published and unpublished, in an effort to track changes in both theory and practice. Much of the legislative record in Massachusetts is available in print. For the eighteenth century, the *Acts and Resolves of the Province of Massachusetts Bay* (Boston, 1869–1922), together with the *Journals of the House of Representatives of Massachusetts,* ed. Mass. Hist. Soc'y (Boston, 1919–80), provide a thorough record of legislative activity. Additional legislative reports and records of unpassed bills can be found within the manuscript collections at the Massachusetts State Archives, Boston. See in particular "Senate Documents (unpassed)," "Massachusetts Archives" (microfilm series), and "Acts and Resolves (passed)." Subsequent printed (but unpublished) legislative reports can be found in the "Massachusetts Legislative Documents" series at the Massachusetts State Library Annex, Boston. Printed acts and resolves for the postrevolutionary period can be found in several published versions. I have cited to the official set, which for some years combines the acts with the resolves and for other years separates them. These volumes also contain the governor's semiannual message to the legislature and thus provide an important source for gubernatorial opinion. A number of unpublished legislative reports on the Massachusetts State Prison are conveniently collected into a series at the Harvard Law Library. Duplicates of these reports are also scattered through the "Massachusetts Legislative Documents."

Although I made no concerted effort to examine municipal records, I did find the Boston town records helpful, especially as a source of information on Boston's early workhouse. These records have been published as a series of *Reports of the Record Commissioners of the City of Boston* (Boston, 1876–1909), containing both the town records and the selectmen's records.

Judicial evidence is, of course, essential to any legal historical study that purports to be descriptive; as any student of the subject knows, the chasm between law-in-books and law-in-action is often vast. Unfortunately, few court records from the eighteenth century have yet been published. The two principal exceptions are *Plymouth Court Records, 1686–1859,* ed. David T. Konig (Wilmington, 1978–81), and "Records of the Court of General Sessions of the Peace for the County of Worcester, Massachusetts, from 1731–1737," in *Collections of the Worcester Society of Antiquity* 18 (1882), both of which contain county court records. To follow events in the Superior Court (renamed the Supreme Judicial Court following the Revolution), one must consult the manuscript minute books currently housed in the Massachusetts State Archives, Boston. Finally, a number of interesting grand jury charges are contained in Josiah Quincy, *Reports of Cases Argued and Adjudged in the Superior Court of Judicature of the Province of Massachusetts Bay, between 1761 and 1772* (Boston, 1865).

The copious administrative records of the Massachusetts State Prison, stored in the Massachusetts State Archives, Boston, became available to scholars only in 1982; they are used here for the first time. The principal sources are the "Warden's Daily Reports" and the "Minutes of the Meetings of the Board of Visitors/Directors/Inspectors," but these are supplemented by several collections of miscellaneous letters and papers. (Also of interest for administrative details is Gideon Haynes, *Pictures from Prison Life: An Historical Sketch of the Massachusetts State Prison* (Boston, 1870), by a later warden who had access to the records.) Taken as a whole, these materials surely comprise one of the most thorough surviving administrative chronicles of an early American penitentiary, which could (and should) form the basis for a detailed administrative history that this study has merely adumbrated.

Literary commentary on crime and punishment in prerevolutionary Massachusetts appeared mainly in sermons. Such sources must be read cautiously, but they do articulate the premises for criminal punishment at a time when criminology and theology were closely connected. Within this body of literature, I found most helpful the works of Charles Chauncy, in particular *The Horrid Nature and Erroneous Guilt of Murder* (Boston, 1754) and *The Idle-Poor Secluded From the Breads of Charity by the Christian Law* (Boston, 1752), together with the sundry works of Cotton Mather, who often dwelled on criminological matters, e.g., *Pillars of Salt* (Boston, 1699), *A Faithful Monitor* (Boston, 1704), *A Flying Roll, Brought Forth, to Enter into the House and Hand of the Thief* (Boston, 1713), and many others.

Commentary from the postrevolutionary period was rapidly secularized. Doubtless the best known Massachusetts advocate before 1826 was Gamaliel Bradford, warden of the Massachusetts State Prison, whose notoriety extended to England. Bradford's two published pamphlets, *Description and Historical Sketch of the Massachusetts State Prison* (Charlestown, 1816) and *State Prisons and the Penitentiary System Vindicated* (Charlestown, 1821), should be read in conjunction with the writings of his rivals within the state prison administration; see "Remarks on the Massachusetts State Prison," in *Rules and Regulations for the Government of the Massachusetts State Prison Adopted by the Board of Directors* (Boston, 1823). See also from this period *Remarks on Prisons and Prison Discipline* (Boston, 1826). These works make for a fascinating juxtaposition. Beginning in 1826, the Prison Discipline Society, founded by the Reverend Louis Dwight, assumed the mantle of the most powerful organization of advocates in Massachusetts, and its influence spread to other states. *The Annual Report[s] of the Board of Managers of the Prison Discipline Society* (published in several editions; my citations are to the first) form an invaluable source of contemporary ideology and, especially, of factual data on early penitentiaries throughout North America. For a dissenting view within the society, see Samuel Gridley Howe, *Report of the Minority of the Special Committee of the Boston Prison Discipline Society* (Boston, 1846), also published under the title *An Essay on Separate and Congregate Systems of Prison Discipline*.

Following the American Revolution, a fair number of commentaries on criminal incarceration appeared in Massachusetts newspapers. These sources contain some of the best clues for piecing together opinions in the early postrevolutionary period. My study of periodical evidence was not exhaustive, but

I did find much helpful material in the *Independent Chronicle* and the *Massachusetts Centinel* (which became the *Columbian Centinel* in 1790). Finally, a good deal of correspondence on criminal incarceration in Massachusetts can be found within the manuscript collections of the Massachusetts Historical Society, Boston. See in particular the Cushing Papers, the Rotch Family Papers, the Robert Treat Paine Papers, the James Sullivan Papers, and the Quincy Papers.

My primary research into other American states focused on legislative records, pamphlet literature, and periodical sources. Compilations of legislative acts are available for every state and are cited in the notes. Occasionally, reports on prisons or carceral theory appeared in the published legislative records. Two such sources deserve mention: Stephen Allen, Samuel Hopkins, and George Tibbits, "Report," in *Journal of the Assembly of the State of New York* (New York, 1825), and Charles Shaler, Edward King, and Thomas Wharton, "Report on Punishment and Prison Discipline," in *Journal of the Senate of the Commonwealth of Pennsylvania* (Harrisburg, 1828), vol. 2, appendix; each signaled developments in penal thinking. Nonetheless, pamphlet sources remain the most plentiful reservoir of information on early American penitentiaries and penal ideology. Before 1800, most of this literature hailed from Pennsylvania; see Society for Alleviating the Miseries of Public Prisons, *Extracts and Remarks on the Subject of Punishment and Reformation of Criminals* (Philadelphia, 1790), William Bradford, *An Enquiry How Far the Punishment of Death Is Necessary in Pennsylvania* (Philadelphia, 1793), and two important works by Benjamin Rush, *An Enquiry into the Effects of Public Punishments upon Criminals and upon Society* (Philadelphia, 1787) and *Considerations on the Injustice and Impolicy of Punishing Murder by Death* (Philadelphia, 1792). The literature mushroomed in the nineteenth century, particularly after 1820. It would have required a herculean effort to track it all down, but I did peruse the published works of the major American commentators outside Massachusetts. See especially the writings of Stephen Allen, Mathew Carey, Thomas Eddy, Francis Lieber, Edward Livingston, James Mease, Gershom Powers, and Roberts Vaux, all of whom made significant contributions to the antebellum criminological debate. Especially useful as a dragnet for contemporary opinion is the Society for the Prevention of Pauperism, *Report on the Penitentiary System in the United States* (New York, 1822), which collected responses to a series of pertinent inquiries from advocates throughout the country. Among periodicals, the *American Musium,* the *American Quarterly Review,* the *North American Review,* and the *United States Gazette* all contained relevant articles.

Several other sources provide special perspectives on the penitentiary that merit attention. A surprisingly large number of convicts published "inside accounts" of their experiences in the early penitentiaries. Of course, these works must be read with great care, but they do supply information on the gap between carceral theory and practice, and they provide a sort of balance against the accounts of penitentiary advocates, who were often inclined to gloss over shortcomings of the institution. Within this genre, I found particularly interesting Stephen Burroughs, *Memoirs of the Notorious Stephen Burroughs of New Hampshire* [1798] (New York, 1924), W. A. Coffey, *Inside Out* (New York, 1823), and John Reynolds, *Recollections of Windsor Prison* (Boston, 1834).

European visitors also published accounts of American penitentiaries. These offer many insights, often of a comparative nature. See especially Jacques Brissot de Warville, *New Travels in the United States of America Performed in 1788* (London, 1792), Duke de la Rochefoucauld-Liancourt, *On the Prisons of Philadelphia* (Philadelphia, 1796), and Gustave de Beaumont and Alexis de Tocqueville, *On the Penitentiary System in the United States and Its Application in France* (Philadelphia, 1833). Other European commentators carried on lively debates with their American counterparts. See in particular several works by the Scottish advocate William Roscoe, who was deeply distressed by American carceral developments; *Observations on Penal Jurisprudence* (London, 1819), *Additional Observations on Penal Jurisprudence* (London, 1823), *Observations on Penal Jurisprudence, Part III* (London, 1825), and *A Brief Statement of the Causes That Have Led to the Abandonment of the Celebrated System of Penitentiary Discipline in Some of the United States of America* (Liverpool, 1827).

Roscoe's works include many examples of his personal correspondence with American advocates. Other editors have also collected and reproduced the private letters of public commentators on the penitentiary that can serve both as an autonomous source of information and as a barometer of the commentators' public candor. For such collections, see the *Letters of Benjamin Rush*, ed. Lyman H. Butterfield (Princeton, 1951), and Samuel L. Knapp, *The Life of Thomas Eddy* (New York, 1834). (Many other letters are scattered throughout published sources.)

B. Secondary Sources

Secondary works on criminal incarceration are many and varied. I sought to consult all the relevant texts in order to place my account in the context of prior scholarship. By far the best treatment of the early English workhouses is Joanna Innes, "Prisons for the Poor: English Bridewells, 1550–1800," in *Labour, Law, and Crime: An Historical Perspective,* ed. Francis Snyder and Douglas Hay (London, 1987), 42. Much useful information also appears in Austin Van der Slice, "Elizabethan Houses of Correction," *J. Am. Inst. Crim. L. & Criminology* 27 (1936–37):50; in A. L. Beier, *Masterless Men: The Vagrancy Problem in England, 1560–1640* (London, 1985), ch. 9; and in Valerie Pearl, "Puritans and Poor Relief: The London Workhouse, 1649–1660," in *Puritans and Revolutionaries: Essays in Seventeenth-Century History Presented to Christopher Hill,* ed. Donald Pennington and Keith Thomas (Oxford, 1978), 206. For ideological background, see also Joyce O. Appleby, *Economic Thought and*

Ideology in Seventeenth-Century England (Princeton, 1978). For parallel developments in Holland, see J. Thorsten Sellin, *Pioneering in Penology: The Amsterdam Houses of Correction in the Sixteenth and Seventeenth Centuries* (London, 1944).

For subsequent English criminological developments, there are several excellent works to choose from: see the classic study by Sir Leon Radzinowicz, *A History of English Criminal Law and Its Administration from 1750,* vol. 1 (London, 1948), and the counter-classic, *Albion's Fatal Tree: Crime and Society in Eighteenth-Century England* (New York, 1975). A more recent work, to some extent synthesizing these two perspectives, is J. M. Beattie's tour de force, *Crime and the Courts in England, 1660–1800* (Princeton, 1986), now the leading treatise for this period. For works focusing specifically on the rise of the penitentiary in England, see Michael Ignatieff, *A Just Measure of Pain: The Penitentiary in the Industrial Revolution, 1750–1850* (London, 1978), and U. R. Q. Henriques, "The Rise and Decline of the Separate System of Prison Discipline," *Past and Present* 54 (1972):61. Also useful is John H. Langbein, "The Historical Origins of the Sanction of Imprisonment for Serious Crime," *J. Legal Stud.* 5 (1976):35, which incorporates evidence from continental Europe. For institutional histories, see also Sean McConville, *A History of English Prison Administration, 1750–1877,* vol. 1 (London, 1981), and Robin Evans, *The Fabrication of Virtue: English Prison Architecture, 1750–1840* (Cambridge, 1982).

When one moves from England to North America, the field grows somewhat sparser, though hardly barren. There are a number of general studies on the evolution of criminal law in early Massachusetts; see especially Edwin Powers, *Crime and Punishment in Early Massachusetts, 1620–1692* (Boston, 1966), David H. Flaherty, "Crime and Social Control in Provincial Massachusetts," *Hist. J.* 24 (1981):357, Eli Faber, "The Evil That Men Do: Crime and Transgression in Colonial Massachusetts" (Ph.D. diss., Columbia University, 1974), Linda Kealey, "Crime and Society in Massachusetts in the Second Half of the Eighteenth Century" (Ph.D. diss., University of Toronto, 1981), summarized in "Patterns of Punishment: Massachusetts in the Eighteenth Century," *Am. J. Legal Hist.* 30 (1986):163, and for the larger background George Lee Haskins, *Law and Authority in Early Massachusetts: A Study in Tradition and Design* (New York, 1960). For social change in the eighteenth century, Douglas L. Jones, *Village and Seaport: Migration and Society in Eighteenth-Century Massachusetts* (Hanover, 1981), is a good place to begin. For the postrevolutionary transformation of the criminal law, see William E. Nelson, "Emerging Notions of Modern Criminal Law in the Revolutionary Era: An Historical Perspective," *N.Y.U. L. Rev.* 42 (1967):459, which first suggested the possibility that traditional sanctions were failing, a line of investigation I have found most fruitful. Some of my preliminary findings are reported in Adam J. Hirsch, "From Pillory to Penitentiary: The Rise of Criminal Incarceration in Early Massachusetts," *Mich. L. Rev.* 80 (1982):1179. Finally, for a comparative study, see Michael S.

Hindus, *Prison and Plantation: Crime, Justice, and Authority in Massachusetts and South Carolina, 1767–1878* (Chapel Hill, 1980), contrasting criminal justice in Massachusetts and South Carolina during the nineteenth century. Hindus's work includes a chapter on the early administrative history of the Massachusetts penitentiary.

Other regional studies are also extant. For criminal justice in early New York, see Julius Goebel, Jr., and T. Raymond Naughton, *Law Enforcement in Colonial New York: A Study in Criminal Procedure, 1664–1776* (New York, 1944), and Douglas Greenberg, *Crime and Law Enforcement in the Colony of New York, 1691–1776* (Ithaca, 1976). On the early penitentiary in New York, see W. David Lewis, *From Newgate to Dannemora: The Rise of the Penitentiary in New York, 1796–1848* (Ithaca, 1965), by far the best local study of an American prison system to date. On the early penitentiary in New Jersey, see Harry Elmer Barnes, *A History of the Penal Reformatory and Correctional Institutions of the State of New Jersey* (Trenton, 1918). Barnes also produced a useful general treatise on criminological developments in early Pennsylvania, *The Evolution of Penology in Pennsylvania* (Indianapolis, 1927). For a modern effort, see Michael Meranze, "The Penitential Ideal in Late Eighteenth-Century Philadelphia," *Pa. Mag. Hist. & Biog.* 108 (1984):419. For institutional studies, see Negley K. Teeters, *The Cradle of the Penitentiary: The Walnut Street Jail at Philadelphia, 1773–1835* (n.p., 1955), on the first penitentiary in the state, and Negley K. Teeters and John Shearer, *The Prison at Philadelphia: Cherry Hill* (New York, 1957), on its successor. Another work by Negley K. Teeters, *They Were in Prison: A History of the Pennsylvania Prison Society, 1787–1937* (Philadelphia, 1937), follows Pennsylvania's most influential body of advocates and includes an extensive appendix, reproducing important primary documents. Also germane for social and ideological background is John K. Alexander, *Render Them Submissive: Responses to Poverty in Philadelphia, 1760–1800* (Amherst, 1980). Finally, for a thoughtful study of incarceration, and of the problem of criminal justice generally, in the southern states, see Edward L. Ayers, *Vengeance and Justice: Crime and Punishment in the Nineteenth-Century American South* (New York, 1984).

A number of general studies of the penitentiary in America also merit inspection. Orlando F. Lewis, *The Development of American Prisons and Prison Customs, 1976–1845* (Albany, 1922), Blake McKelvey, *American Prisons: A History of Good Intentions,* rev. ed. (Montclair, 1977), and Harry Elmer Barnes, "The Historical Origins of the Prison System in America," *J. Am. Inst. Crim. L. & Criminology* 12 (1921–22):35 (reprinted in Harry Elmer Barnes, *The Repression of Crime: Studies in Historical Penology* [New York, 1926]) set out traditional ideological and institutional themes. The leading modern treatment is David J. Rothman, *The Discovery of the Asylum: Social Order and Disorder in the New Republic* (Boston, 1971), which I examine in the Introduction. The instant work grew out of my doctoral dissertation, "From Pillory to Penitentiary: The

Rise of Criminal Incarceration in the New Republic" (Yale University, 1987), which contains some textual and reference material omitted here. Finally, for a recent study of a related problem, see Louis P. Masur, *Rites of Execution: Capital Punishment and the Transformation of American Culture, 1776–1865* (New York, 1989).

A distinctive corpus of scholarship has explored "critical" explanations for the rise of the penitentiary—that is, explanations having to do with class interests and divisions within the larger society. Among the many interesting works in this genre, the pathbreaking treatise of Georg Rusche and Otto Kirchheimer, *Punishment and Social Structure* (New York, 1939), is essential reading. More recent studies have developed critical themes with care and subtlety; see especially Michel Foucault, *Discipline and Punish: The Birth of the Prison* (New York, 1977), Dario Melossi and Massimo Pavarini, *The Prison and the Factory: Origins of the Penitentiary System,* trans. Glynic Cousin (London, 1981), Thomas L. Dumm, *Democracy and Punishment: Disciplinary Origins in the United States* (Madison, 1987), and Michael Ignatieff's aforementioned *Just Measure of Pain*.

Two chapters of this book deal with the relation of slavery to penitentiary ideology. I had therefore to investigate broadly the problem of slavery in the southern states. The literature on slavery is vast and need not be detailed here. But three works stand out as brilliant introductions (and much more) to the subject: Winthrop D. Jordan, *White Over Black: American Attitudes toward the Negro, 1550–1812* (Chapel Hill, 1968), David Brion Davis, *The Problem of Slavery in the Age of Revolution, 1770–1823* (Ithaca, 1975), and Edmund S. Morgan, *American Slavery, American Freedom: The Ordeal of Colonial Virginia* (New York, 1975), set a standard for scholarship that few historians can ever hope to match.

Notes

Introduction

1. [Gamaliel Bradford], *State Prisons and the Penitentiary System Vindicated* (Charlestown, 1821), 11.
2. John Howard, *The State of the Prisons* [1777] (New York, 1929), 19, 296.
3. For a fuller discussion of those relics, see A Note on the Sources.
4. Imprisonment in Massachusetts received initial treatment in Edwin Powers, *Crime and Punishment in Early Massachusetts, 1620–1692* (Boston, 1966), ch. 8; Michael S. Hindus, *Prison and Plantation: Crime, Justice, and Authority in Massachusetts and South Carolina, 1767–1878* (Chapel Hill, 1980), ch. 7.
5. Powers, *Crime and Punishment,* 240–41. Connecticut passed legislation to establish a carceral program shortly before the American Revolution, but the project was aborted and not restarted until five years after the Massachusetts initiative.
6. Samuel Stearns, *The American Oracle* (London, 1791), 258–59.
7. David J. Rothman, *The Discovery of the Asylum: Social Order and Disorder in the New Republic* (Boston, 1971), 3, 14–15, 17–18, 45–46, 52–53.
8. Rothman, *Discovery of the Asylum,* 57–62, 83.
9. Rothman, *Discovery of the Asylum,* 59–62, 89. "To reformers, the advantages of the institution were external, and they hardly imagined that life inside the prison might rehabilitate the criminal" (62).
10. Rothman, *Discovery of the Asylum,* 62, 68. For Rothman, the intellectual eras are distinct: "Almost no eighteenth-century assumption about the origins or nature of . . . deviancy survived intact into the Jacksonian era" (3). Jacksonian advocates "now looked to the life of the criminal, not to the statutes, in attempting to grasp the origins of deviancy. They presented biographical sketches, not analyses of existing codes. . . . Such questions were for the 1790s, not the 1820s and '30s" (68).
11. Rothman, *Discovery of the Asylum,* 52, 57–59, 69–71, 78.
12. Rothman, *Discovery of the Asylum,* 89, 94, 108, 330 n.20. The penitentiary was "America's discovery" (xviii).
13. Rothman, *Discovery of the Asylum,* xviii–xix, 62–78, 82–84, 107–8. Hindus, *Prison and Plantation,* 163, also traces rehabilitative ideology in Massachusetts to the Jacksonian era, specifically to the period following the prison reforms of 1829. The best review of Rothman's work, containing much useful material, is Carl E. Schneider, "Book Review," *Mich. L. Rev.* 77 (1979):707
14. On the ideological origins of the penitentiary in America, see Harry Elmer Barnes, "The Historical Origin of the Prison System in America," *J. Am. Inst. Crim. L. & Criminology* 12 (1921–22):35; Blake McKelvey, *American Prisons: A History of Good Intentions,* rev. ed. (Montclair, 1977), ch. 1; Orlando F. Lewis, *The Development of American Prisons and Prison Customs, 1776–1845* (Albany, 1922), chs. 1, 4. The best such study, which weaves in social analysis later in the story, is W. David Lewis, *From Newgate to Dannemora: The Rise of the Penitentiary in New York, 1796–1848* (Ithaca, 1965), ch. 1. For a study of the rise of the English penitentiary from the perspective of novelistic discourse, see John Bender, *Imagining the Penitentiary: Fiction and the Architecture of Mind in Eighteenth-Century England* (Chicago, 1987).

15. William Muraskin, "The Social-Control Theory in American History: A Critique," *J. Soc. Hist.* 9 (1976):559.
16. For critical accounts of the rise of the penitentiary, see esp. Georg Rusche and Otto Kirchheimer, *Punishment and Social Structure* (New York, 1939); Michel Foucault, *Discipline and Punish: The Birth of the Prison* (London, 1977); Dario Melossi and Massimo Pavarini, *The Prison and the Factory: Origins of the Penitentiary System,* trans. Glynic Cousin (London, 1981); Michael Ignatieff, *A Just Measure of Pain: The Penitentiary in the Industrial Revolution, 1750–1850* (London, 1978); and focusing on American penitentiaries, Martin Miller, "At Hard Labor: Rediscovering the Nineteenth-Century Prison," *Issues in Criminology* 9 (1974):91; Martin Miller, "Sinking Gradually into the Proletariat: The Emergence of the Penitentiary in the United States," *Crime & Soc. Just.* 14 (1980):37; Paul Takagi, "The Walnut Street Jail: A Penal Reform to Centralize the Power of the State," *Fed. Probation* 39 (1975):18; and Thomas L. Dumm, *Democracy and Punishment: Disciplinary Origins of the United States* (Madison, 1987). Some of this literature is surveyed in Robert P. Weiss, "Humanitarianism, Labor Exploitation, or Social Control? A Critical Survey of Theory and Research on the Origin and Development of Prisons," *Soc. Hist.* 12 (1987):331. For Rothman's response to critical analysis, see his "Social Control: The Uses and Abuses of the Concept in the History of Incarceration," *Rice U. Stud.* 67 (1981):9.
17. For a more systematic rejoinder to critical analysis of the rise of the penitentiary, see Adam J. Hirsch, "From Pillory to Penitentiary: The Rise of Criminal Incarceration in the New Republic" (Ph.D. diss., Yale University, 1987), chs. 6–7, 9.
18. For example, Miller, "At Hard Labor," 91–93; Michael Ignatieff, "State, Civil Society, and Total Institutions: A Critique of Recent Social Histories of Punishment," *Crime & Just.* 3 (1981):169, 173. For a classic exposition of this approach, see also Douglas Hay, "Property, Authority, and the Criminal Law," in *Albion's Fatal Tree: Crime and Society in Eighteenth-Century England,* ed. Douglas Hay et al. (New York, 1975), 17.
19. For a related discussion of the weakness of critical analysis, see Thomas Haskell, "Capitalism and the Origins of the Humanitarian Sensibility," *Am. Hist. Rev.* 90 (1985):339–61, 547–66.
20. Ignatieff, *A Just Measure of Pain,* 210; Foucault, *Discipline and Punish,* 271–72; see also Hay, "Property, Authority, and Criminal Law," 24.

Chapter 1

1. *Records of the Governor and Company of the Massachusetts Bay,* ed. Nathaniel Shurtleff (Boston, 1853–54), 1:393, 406 [hereinafter *Mass. Rec.*]. On the Puritan theory of the "national covenant," see generally Perry Miller, *The New England Mind: The Seventeenth Century* (Cambridge, Mass., 1939), 463–91.
2. The discussion that follows is highly abbreviated. For a detailed treatment of criminal justice in Massachusetts, see Edwin Powers, *Crime and Punishment in Early Massachusetts, 1620–1692* (Boston, 1966). For a description of the judicial system that administered criminal justice, see for the seventeenth century George Lee Haskins, *Law and Authority in Early Massachusetts: A Study in Tradition and Design* (New York, 1960), 32–35, 174–77, and for the eighteenth century, *Legal Papers of John Adams,* ed. L. Kinvin Wroth and Hiller Zobel (Cambridge, Mass., 1965), 1:xxxviii–xliv.
3. *Mass. Rec.,* 1:16–17. In a few instances, the early settlers shipped offenders home along with "certificate . . . of their misdemeanor" for punishment in England (1:393).

But the vast majority of criminals were punished locally, and no appeal to England was entertained in criminal cases. Joseph H. Smith, *Appeals to the Privy Council from the American Plantations* (New York, 1965), 45–49, 243.

4. The curious negative phrasing of the charter traced to the king's wish to preserve the royal prerogative, which would have been lost, under the doctrine of *Calvin's Case,* upon an affirmative grant of English law to the colony. See Joseph H. Smith, *Cases and Materials on the Development of Legal Institutions* (St. Paul, 1965), 415–18, 432.

5. The Massachusetts settlers were saved from Charles I's efforts to revoke their colonial charter by the onset of the English Civil War, but they eventually lost it following the Restoration, in 1684. The second "provincial" charter, issued in 1691, bound Massachusetts more closely to the will of the Home Government. On the Puritans' efforts to justify their deviations from English law, see Richard B. Morris, "Massachusetts and the Common Law: The Declaration of 1646," in *Essays in the History of Early American Law,* ed. David H. Flaherty (Chapel Hill, 1969), 135.

6. For general studies of criminal justice in colonial America see Bradley Chapin, *Criminal Justice in Colonial America, 1606–1660* (Athens, Ga., 1983); Douglas Greenberg, "Crime, Law Enforcement, and Social Control in Colonial America," *Am. J. Legal Hist.* 26 (1982):293; and Kathryn Preyer, "Penal Measures in the American Colonies: An Overview," *Am. J. Legal Hist.* 26 (1982):326. For regional studies see Harry Elmer Barnes, *The Evolution of Penology in Pennsylvania* (Indianapolis, 1927); Julius Goebel, Jr., and Thomas R. Naughton, *Law Enforcement in Colonial New York: A Study in Criminal Procedure, 1664–1776* (New York, 1944); Douglas Greenberg, *Crime and Law Enforcement in the Colony of New York, 1691–1776* (Ithaca, 1974); Donna J. Spindel, *Crime and Society in North Carolina, 1663–1776* (Baton Rouge, 1989); Gail Sussman Marcus, "'Due Execution of the Generall Rules of Righteousnesse': Criminal Procedure in New Haven Town and Colony, 1638–1658," in *Saints and Revolutionaries,* ed. David Hall, John Murrin, and Thad Tate (New York, 1984), 99; Richard Gaskins, "Changes in the Criminal Law in Eighteenth-Century Connecticut," *Am. J. Legal Hist.* 25 (1981):309; John O'Connor, "Legal Reform in the Early Republic: The New Jersey Experience," id. 22 (1978):95; and David T. Konig, "'Dale's Laws' and the Non–Common Law Origins of Criminal Justice in Virginia," id. 26 (1982):293.

7. For a thorough treatment of criminal justice in seventeenth- and eighteenth-century England, see J. M. Beattie, *Crime and the Courts in England, 1660–1800* (Princeton, 1986).

8. Powers, *Crime and Punishment,* 204–6, 415–16.

9. Remission of fines is discussed in Jules Zanger, "Crime and Punishment in Early Massachusetts," *Wm. & Mary Q.,* 3d ser., 22 (1965):471. Court records failed to disclose the frequency with which fines were remitted in England. Beattie, *Crime and the Courts,* 457 n.15, 456–61.

10. For example, *Plymouth Court Records, 1686–1859,* ed. David T. Konig (Wilmington, 1978–81), 1:267, 4:131, 149, 202.

11. The first statute of this kind, passed in 1646, applied only to theft from a garden or orchard, though courts often ignored this restriction. After 1692, all thieves were liable to treble damages. *The Colonial Laws of Massachusetts,* ed. William Whitmore (Boston, 1890), § 2:13 [hereinafter *Mass. Col. Laws*]; *Acts and Resolves of the Province of the Massachusetts Bay* (Boston, 1869–1922), 1:52 [hereinafter *Mass. Prov. Laws*]. For cases see, e.g., *Records of the Court of Assistants of the Colony of the*

Massachusetts Bay, 1630–1692 (Boston, 1901–28), 1:145, 189, 200, 284; 2:32, 66, 70, 79, 90, 94, 97, 99, 118, 131, 134 [hereinafter *Ct. of Assistants*].

12. Haskins, *Law and Authority,* 153–54, 178; Eli Faber, "The Evil That Men Do: Crime and Transgression in Colonial Massachusetts" (Ph.D. diss., Columbia University, 1974), 363–66.

13. Powers, *Crime and Punishment,* 206–8; Rosemary Zagarri, "Public Confession in Seventeenth-Century Massachusetts" (unpublished paper, Yale University, 1978, on file with author); for references in the court records see, e.g., *Records and Files of the Quarterly Courts of Essex County, Massachusetts, 1678–1680,* ed. George Dow (Salem, 1911–21), 1:174 [hereinafter *Essex Ct. Rec.*]; *Colonial Justice in Western Massachusetts, 1639–1702: The Pynchon Court Record,* ed. Joseph H. Smith (Cambridge, Mass., 1961), 207 [hereinafter *Pynchon Ct. Rec.*]; and *Ct. of Assistants,* 2:65, 68, 91–92, 94, 104, 109, 116–18, 131, 139. For legislative references see *Mass. Col. Laws,* § 2:13. 26, 59.

14. *Mass. Rec.,* 1:393; Haskins, *Law and Authority,* 206–10; George Lee Haskins, "Precedents in English Ecclesiastical Practices for Criminal Punishments in Early Massachusetts," in *Essays in Legal History in Honor of Felix Frankfurter,* ed. Morris P. Forkosch (Indianapolis, 1966), 321. On the religious theory underlying the admonition see chapter 2, text at note 175. Because of its Puritan overtones, the admonition was largely restricted to the New England colonies, though there are examples of its use elsewhere, see Goebel and Naughton, *Law Enforcement,* 689 n.72.

15. Beattie, *Crime and the Courts,* 461–68; J. A. Sharpe, *Crime in Seventeenth-Century England: A County Study* (Cambridge, 1983), 149.

16. Powers, *Crime and Punishment,* chs. 6, 7. Moral offenses in England ordinarily came under the jurisdiction of ecclesiastical courts, which frequently enjoined small fines or public confession in such cases. See Keith Thomas, "The Puritans and Adultery: The Act of 1650 Reconsidered," in *Puritans and Revolutionaries: Essays in Seventeenth-Centruy History Presented to Christopher Hill,* ed. Donald Pennington and Keith Thomas (Oxford, 1978), 257. The leniency of the ecclesiastical courts toward moral offenders had long been a grievance of the English Puritans. Id., 263–64; Sharpe, *Crime in Seventeenth-Century England,* 60–62.

17. Haskins, *Law and Authority,* 153.

18. Beattie, *Crime and the Courts,* 470–519. Simple banishment had roots in medieval criminal practice. A. G. L. Shaw, *Convicts and the Colonies* (Victoria, Australia, 1977), 21–22.

19. Powers, *Crime and Courts,* 14, 117, 125–29, 135–36, 152, 183, 210, 271, 332–34.

20. Powers, *Crime and Courts,* 180–84, 188–91. The most common form of mutilation was ear-cropping. Sometimes offenders were mutilated *and* banished (182–83). Mutilation also had roots in English practice. Haskins, *Law and Authority,* 175 n.57.

21. Blackstone spoke of the death penalty as serving society "by depriving the party injuring of the power to do further mischief." William Blackstone, *Commentaries on the Laws of England* (London, 1765–69), 4:*11–12. Banishment was often ordered "on pain of death" if the outcast were ever to return: the two punishments were closely linked. E.g., *Ct. of Assistants,* 2:35, 3:68–69. Likewise in England see Shaw, *Convicts and the Colonies,* 26–27.

22. Leon Radzinowicz, *A History of English Criminal Law and Its Administration from 1750* (London, 1948), 1:3–79. Questioning the functional significance of the expansion of England's capital list, see Clive Emsley, *Crime and Society in England, 1750–1900* (London, 1987), 203–14.

23. Clergied felons were branded (usually on the thumb) to identify them in the event of a repeat offense. After 1706, clergied felons could be sentenced to hard labor or transportation. Some capital statutes passed in the eighteenth century denied benefit of clergy entirely. Beattie, *Crime and the Courts,* 141–48, 490–506.

24. Beattie, *Crime and the Courts,* chs. 8–9; Sharpe, *Crime in Seventeenth-Century England,* 141–49; Frank McLynn, *Crime and Punishment in Eighteenth-Century England* (London, 1989), ch. 14; Radzinowicz, *History,* 1:83–164. The common jury practice of downgrading the value of goods stolen in order to steer clear of capital statutes was known as "pious perjury."

25. Haskins, *Law and Authority,* 145–52 (quotation at 152). Twenty-five capital statutes were passed by the colonial government of Massachusetts between 1630 and 1684. The only property crimes covered were third offenses of burglary and robbery. Powers, *Crime and Punishment,* 252–73. The changes instituted in Massachusetts were also advocated by Puritans in England and were enacted in part for a brief period following the English Civil War. Donald Veall, *The Popular Movement for Law Reform, 1640–1660* (Oxford, 1970), 127–31; Thomas, "Puritans and Adultery."

26. On the revision of the capital list under the second charter, see Powers, *Crime and Punishment,* 303–8. The evolution of the capital list in the eighteenth century is discussed in chapter 3, text at notes 67–72.

27. Thus, e.g., the capital statute against adultery was rarely enforced: juries almost invariably returned convictions of "libidinous Actions" or "acts leading to Adultery" or the like, never for adultery per se. In some cases, the court took the initiative to downgrade the penalty, and the General Court also granted pardons on occasion. Benefit of clergy, however, was denied in Massachusetts before the eighteenth century. Powers, *Crime and Punishment* 92, 275–86, 607 n. 151 (quotations at 279).

28. Powers, *Crime and Punishment,* 273–74, 446–51; Haskins, *Law and Authority,* 151–52. (Some crimes that were capital under the Mosaic code were omitted from the Puritans' capital list; see Haskins, *Law and Authority,* 126 and n.84.) These themes were first developed by English Puritans such as William Perkins, who argued against inflexible sentences and justified judicial deviation from statutory prescriptions; see William Perkins, "EPIEKEIA, or a Treatise of Christian Equity and Moderation," excerpted in *Puritan Political Ideas, 1558–1794,* ed. Edmund S. Morgan (Indianapolis, 1965), 59–73.

29. Of the twenty-five capital statutes in force in seventeenth-century Massachusetts, only nine were ever invoked to order sentences of death. Between 1630 and 1692 some sixty persons were executed (twenty-three of them for witchcraft). Powers, *Crime and Punishment,* 286–94. Between 1750 and 1796, the Massachusetts Superior Court sentenced 110 persons to death—an average of fewer than three executions per annum, accounting for 2.4 percent of the criminal penalties imposed. Linda Kealey, "Crime and Society in Massachusetts in the Second Half of the Eighteenth Century" (Ph.D. diss., University of Toronto, 1981), 328. This proportion appears to have been remarkably close to England's, despite the relatively greater length of the bloody code; see Radzinowicz, *History,* 1:160 (statistics for 1805). See also the sociological discussion in Barbara A. Black, "The Judicial Power and the General Court in Early Massachusetts" (Ph.D. diss., Yale University, 1975), 182–93.

30. There were minor exceptions. Following Mosaic law, judges in colonial Massachusetts were empowered to enjoin persons found guilty of fornication to marriage, not a "punishment" under English law. And the Puritans also proscribed punishments deemed "inhumane, Barbarous, or cruell," apparently to preclude burning at the

stake and drawing and quartering, sanctions imposed on rare occasion in England for the crime of treason. Powers, *Crime and Punishment*, 92, 172–73; cf. Beattie, *Crime and the Courts*, 75, 79n, 100, 451.

31. For a broader discussion, see David H. Flaherty, "Law and the Enforcement of Morals in Early America," in *Perspectives in American History: Law in American History*, ed. Donald Fleming and Bernard Bailyn (Cambridge, Mass., 1971), 203.

32. See above, note 6. One pattern that did appear widely was the restriction (relative to England) of colonial capital lists and limited enforcement of capital statutes; see Goebel and Naughton, *Law Enforcement*, 702–4; Greenberg, *Crime and Law Enforcement*, 130–31; Herbert Fitzroy, "The Punishment of Crime in Provincial Pennsylvania," *Pa. Mag. Hist. & Biog.* 60 (1936):253–58, 268–69.

33. Roger Lockyer, *Tudor and Stuart Britain, 1471–1714* (New York, 1964), 255–56.

34. *Mass. Rec.*, 1:74.

35. *Mass. Prov. Laws*, 1:426; Powers, *Crime and Punishment*, 212–17.

36. On the functions of the jail in other colonies, see Goebel and Naughton, *Law Enforcement*, 514–16, 709; Barnes, *Evolution of Penology*, 50–51, 54–55; in England, see Christopher Harding, Bill Hines, Richard Ireland, and Philip Rawlings, *Imprisonment in England and Wales: A Concise History* (London, 1985), 76–83.

37. Robert Feer, "Imprisonment for Debt in Massachusetts before 1800," *Miss. Valley Hist. Rev.* 48 (1961):252.

38. For example, *Mass Prov. Laws*, 12:71 (quotation); *Plymouth Ct. Rec.*, 3:308, 4:40, 42; *Journals of the House of Representatives of Massachusetts*, ed. Mass. Hist. Soc'y (Boston, 1919–80), 29:58, 61 [hereinafter *Mass. House J.*].

39. *Mass. Col. Laws*, § 2:6; *Mass. Prov. Laws*, 1:330. This conceptual distinction was recognized in England; see Harding et al., *Imprisonment in England and Wales*, 78.

40. *Winthrop Papers*, ed. Mass. Hist. Soc'y (Boston, 1929–47), 3:481; *Mass. House J.*, 22:18, 96; Resolve of Dec. 6, 1775, ch. 416, *Mass. Resolves*, 1775–76:164; Resolve of July 6, 1776, ch. 201, id., 513; Resolve of Sept. 24, 1777, ch. 329, id., 1777–78:134.

41. For example, John Winthrop, *Winthrop's Journal "History of New England," 1630–1649*, ed. James K. Hosmer (New York, 1908), 2:134–35; Resolve of June 21, 1776, ch. 72, *Mass. Resolves*, 1775–76:457; Resolve of June 29, 1776, ch. 134, id., 485; Resolve of Oct. 18, 1777, ch. 453, id., 1777–78:177; Resolve of Jan. 29, 1779, ch. 422, id., 1778–79:578.

42. See, e.g., the act of 1700 "against Jesuits and Popish priests," which automatically accounted any such person "an incendiary and disturber of the publick peace and safety," subject to banishment or "perpetual imprisonment" if he refused to depart. *Mass. Prov. Laws*, 1:423. Likewise, the danger posed by prisoners of war called for "a total & instant Separation" through confinement. *A Report of the Record Commissioners of the City of Boston Containing the Boston Town Records* (Boston, 1876–1909), 1770–77:278–79, 1742–57:104–5.

43. For example, *Records of the Suffolk County Court, 1671–1680*, ed. Zechariah Chaffee (Boston, 1933), 724, 753 [hereinafter *Suffolk Ct. Rec.*]; *Ct. of Assistants*, 1:90; *Pynchon Ct. Rec.*, 307; *Mass. Prov. Laws*, 1:424.

44. For example, "Records of the Court of General Sessions of the Peace for the County of Worcester, Massachusetts, from 1731 to 1737," in *Collections of the Worcester Soc'y of Antiquity* 18 (1882):42, 80, 143, 159, 184 [hereinafter *Worcester Ct. Rec.*].

45. See above, note 10.

46. *Mass. Col. Laws*, § 2:38.

47. Mass. Sup. Jud. Ct., Nov. 1785, fol. 323 (unpublished court records, Mass. Archives).

48. *Boston Gazette*, Mar. 25, 1765, at 3; see also, e.g., *Plymouth Ct. Rec.*, 2:31.

49. The sheriff of Suffolk County complained in 1739 of "Cursing and Swearing" by the inmates confined in his jail "who regard not the Laws already made in that Case, for they being Prisoners conclude they cannot be further punished, and so presume to commit that Sin very Frequently." *Mass. House J.,* 17:241.

50. "Our Gaol is not intended as a Punishment, it is only to keep Offenders for Trial, or after Trial till Sentence is fulfilled." Grand Jury Charge, 1765, in Josiah Quincy, *Reports of Cases Argued and Adjudged in the Superior Court of Judicature of the Province of Massachusetts Bay between 1761 and 1772* (New York, 1865), 112. In 1799 a legislative committee urged that sentencing a convicted criminal to imprisonment in the county jail would be "unequal, as a person charged with an offense would suffer before conviction as rigorously as he would after his guilt had been established by a trial." "Report Respecting Convicts," appended to "Resolves," 1802, ch. 54 (passed) (unpublished MS, Mass. Archives).

51. Edward Jenks, "The Story of the Habeas Corpus," *Law Q. Rev.* 18 (1902):64–65 (emphasis omitted).

52. *Mass. House J.,* 25:156, 38:141; "Mass. Archives," 44:487–89 (unpublished MS, Mass. Archives).

53. Incarceration as a sanction was sufficiently familiar to be included in the list of punishments expressly permitted by the Massachusetts charters of 1629 and 1691, *Mass. Rec.,* 1:17, 171; *Mass. Prov. Laws,* 1:16. Imprisonment as a sanction was also used infrequently in other colonies; see Goebel and Naughton, *Law Enforcement,* 514–16, 703 n.138, 709; Herbert Fitzroy, "The Punishment of Crime in Provincial Pennsylvania," *Pa. Mag. Hist. & Biog.* 60 (1936):258–59; Spindel, *Crime and Society,* 120–21. In England, see Beattie, *Crime and the Courts,* 492–94, 498–99, 560–64, and Harding et al., *Imprisonment in England and Wales,* 7–9, 77–83. Other aspects of the early history of imprisonment as a sanction are discussed in chapter 2.

54. Contempt of court: e.g., *Mass. Col. Laws,* § 2:36; *Suffolk Ct. Rec.,* 121, 146, 232. Contempt of the magistrate: e.g., *Pynchon Ct. Rec.,* 307. Contempt of the constable: e.g., *Suffolk Ct. Rec.,* 867. "Contemptuous Carriages" or "Reproachful speeches" in public: e.g., *Plymouth Ct. Rec.,* 1:192, 267; *Essex Ct. Rec.,* 7:406–8. More particularly, "indecent reflections cast on the proceedings of the Governor and Council and the House of Representatives," *Mass. Prov. Laws,* 13:307.

55. For example, *Plymouth Ct. Rec.,* 1:210.

56. For example, *Plymouth Ct. Rec.,* 1:266, 3:308; *Ct. of Assistants,* 2:62–63, 132; *Mass. Prov. Laws,* 13:307. Occasionally, judges ordered imprisonment "till the next court," when the prisoner's attitude would presumably be reexamined, e.g., *Suffolk Ct. Rec.,* 867.

57. *Mass. Prov. Laws,* 1:122.

58. For example, *Ct. of Assistants,* 1:285, where the court readily dispensed with the imprisonment that accompanied a fine. Hardly any prosecutions resulted in incarceration without additional public or monetary sanction. For a rare example, see *Plymouth Ct. Rec.,* 3:187 (five days for house breaking without theft).

59. For example, *Plymouth Ct. Rec.,* 1:267; *Worcester Ct. Rec.,* 153–54. The longest term of incarceration mandated by statute for a criminal act before 1749 was one year. *Mass. Prov. Laws,* 1:51, 54.

60. *Mass. Prov. Laws,* 1:51, 54 (emphasis added). The caveat against bail or mainprize (a variation of bail, now obsolete) appeared in various other statutes and court records as late as 1753, e.g., King v. Cook, Mass. Super. Ct., Jan. 1753, fol. 218 (unpublished court records, Mass. Archives). The caveat also appeared in at least one early English statute mandating criminal incarceration. 5&6 Ann. c.6 (1707).

61. Powers, *Crime and Punishment*, 212–16. On the small size of prisons, see *Mass. Prov. Laws*, 2:119. On the high rate of escape, see, e.g., *Mass. House J.*, 7:108. Special precautions were occasionally taken to prevent dangerous prisoners from escaping—and even these did not always suffice; see *Mass. Prov. Laws*, 9:33, 14:318, 324.

62. Jail keepers' petitions for reimbursement of expenses not uncommonly included burial fees, e.g., *Mass. Prov. Laws*, 11:33, 84. Thomas Hutchinson made the observation directly, Grand Jury Charge, 1765, in Quincy, *Reports*, 112; Hutchinson to Robert Treat Paine (Nov. 29, 1766), in "Robert Treat Paine Papers" (unpublished MS, Mass. Hist. Soc'y) (Hutchinson's pardon of one inmate "that he might not be [imprisoned] another winter"). Massachusetts jails were also firetraps, e.g., *A Report of the Record Commissioners of the City of Boston, Containing the Records of the Boston Selectmen* (Boston, 1884–1909), 1754–63:150, 1769–75:4.

63. Grand Jury Charge, 1765, in Quincy, *Reports*, 111 (quotation); *Plymouth Ct. Rec.*, 3:308.

64. For example, *Mass. House Journal*, 1:164, 2:103; *Mass. Prov. Laws*, 14:71–72, 171; *Essex Ct. Rec.*, 7:227, 8:335; Resolve of Apr. 18, 1777, ch. 1069, *Mass. Resolves*, 1775–76:890; Resolve of Mar. 16, 1780, ch. 811, id., 1779–80:373.

65. John Howard, who examined English jails, drew this conclusion. Howard, *The State of the Prisons* [1777] (London, 1929), 40 n.1.

66. David J. Rothman, *The Discovery of the Asylum: Social Order and Disorder in the New Republic* (Boston, 1971), 53–56.

67. Keepers were often awarded the post because of their physical proximity to the prison or because their fathers had held the position. Faber, "Evil That Men Do," 274–77.

68. Keepers were required to keep a "true List" of their inmates, to separate debtors from other inmates, and to discharge inmates from custody only on judicial warrant. *Mass Col. Laws*, § 2:6, 128; *Mass. Prov. Laws*, 1:424, 565, 2:119. For other provisions, see id., 1:95, 330, 381.

69. Keepers probably earned more from the sale of liquor to inmates than from their regular fees. *Plymouth Ct. Rec.*, 2:145; "Mass. Archives," 44:512–13; *Mass. House J.*, 22:240, 245; *Suffolk Ct. Rec.*, 912. At least one keeper made a habit of using his prisoners as personal servants, *Essex Ct. Rec.*, 5:84. At the same time, the right to exercise was routinely withheld, e.g., id., 8:335, and as late as 1833, a House committee visiting the Springfield jail on a tour of inspection "found the keeper absent, and the Prison left in charge of his two sons, one aged 13 and the other 11." *Report on Gaols and Houses of Correction in the Commonwealth of Massachusetts Made by a Committee Appointed by the House of Representatives* (Boston, 1834), 10.

70. *Mass. House J.*, 8:52, 10:327, 348, 350, 356, 11:142.

71. *Mass. House J.*, 11:142, 144, 147, 149, 153, 161.

72. *Mass. House J.*, 13:59.

73. *Mass. House J.*, 14:176–77.

74. *Mass. House J.*, 14:177, 238, 240–41, 243–44 (emphasis omitted).

75. *Mass. House J.*, 14:244.

76. *Mass. House J.*, 17:235, 247, 18:51, 98, 129, 146, 19:40, 41, 80, 82, 83, 91, 201.

77. New York: Greenberg, *Crime and Law Enforcement*, 124–27, 168; cf. Thorsten Sellin, "New Amsterdam's Jail Regulations of 1657," *Fed. Probation* 45 (1980):24. Pennsylvania: Negley Teeters, *They Were in Prison: A History of the Pennsylvania Prison Society* (Philadelphia, 1937), 448–51; Barnes, *Evolution of Penology*, 55–71. North Carolina: Spindel, *Crime and Society*, 120–21. England: W. J. Sheehan, "Finding Solace in Eighteenth-Century Newgate," in *Crime in England, 1550–1800*, ed. J. S. Cockburn

(London, 1977), 229; Beattie, *Crime and the Courts*, 288–313; Sean McConville, *A History of English Prison Administration, 1750–1877* (London, 1981), 1: chs. 1, 3; Harding et al., *Imprisonment in England and Wales*, 17–49, 83–96; see also Joanna Innes, "The King's Bench Prison in the Later Eighteenth Century: Law, Authority, and Order in a London Debtor's Prison," in *An Ungovernable People: The English and Their Law in the Seventeenth and Eighteenth Centuries*, ed. John Brewer and John Styles (New Brunswick, 1980), 250.

78. On early investigations into jail conditions and (unanswered) calls from reform, see Radzinowicz, *History*, 1:32, 235 n.11, 409 n.34; Harding et al., *Imprisonment in England and Wales*, 56, 96–102; D. L. Howard, *The English Prisons: Their Past and Their Future* (London, 1960), 8–9. For a modern reevaluation, suggesting that the horror of English jail conditions may have been exaggerated, see Margaret Delacy, *Prison Reform in Lancashire, 1700–1850: A Study in Local Administration* (Stanford, 1986), ch. 1.

79. "Art thou poor and in prison? Then art thou buried before thou art dead." Thomas Dekker, quoted in *The Elizabethan Underworld*, ed. Gamini Salgado (London, 1977), 169 and generally ch. 9; "A Prison is a grave to bury men alive. . . . It is a *Microcosmus*, a little world of woe." G[eoffrey] M[ynshal], *Essays and Characters of a Prison and Prisoners* (London, 1618), 3. "[T]hose tombs for living men." Jacques Brissot de Warville, *New Travels in the United States of America Performed in 1788* (London, 1792), 371.

80. William Eden, *Principles of Penal Law* (London, 1771), 54.

81. Act of Mar. 14, 1785, ch. 63, *Mass. Acts & Resolves*, 1784–85:163.

82. Act of June 25, 1798, ch. 13, *Mass. Acts & Resolves*, 1798–99:16; Resolve of June 26, 1798, ch. 47, id., 196; Governor's Message, Jan. 11, 1799, id., 636.

83. The legislative transition is discussed at greater length in chapter 5, text at notes 1–20.

84. On the legislative history of construction, see Resolve of Jan. 22, 1800, ch. 68, *Mass. Acts & Resolves*, 1798–99:558; Resolve of Nov. 15, 1800, ch. 64, id., 1800–1801:176; Resolve of June 23, 1802, ch. 54, id., 1802–3:380; Resolve of June 22, 1803, ch. 51, id., 861. Additional documents relevant to construction can be found appended to "Resolves," 1802, ch. 54 (passed). For a structural and industrial description, see [Gamaliel Bradford], *Description and Historical Sketch of the Massachusetts State Prison* (Charlestown, 1816).

85. For a brief administrative history of the state prison, see Michael S. Hindus, *Prison and Plantation: Crime, Justice, and Authority in Massachusetts and South Carolina, 1767–1878* (Chapel Hill, 1980), 162–81.

86. [Bradford], *Description*; [Gamaliel Bradford], *State Prisons and the Penitentiary System Vindicated* (Charlestown, 1821). Bradford's writings won international notoriety; see William Roscoe, *A Brief Statement of the Causes Which Have Led to the Abandonment of the Celebrated System of Penitentiary Discipline in Some of the United States of America* (Liverpool, 1827), 49–50. Though no biographical sketches are extant, Bradford's lineage is ascertainable from the fact that Alden Bradford, the historian, was his sibling. Alden Bradford to William Roscoe (Nov. 9, 1826) in "Roscoe Papers: Materials Relating to the United States," no. 418 (unpublished MS, Picton Library, Liverpool).

87. These were: Massachusetts (1785), New York (pilot project 1785, statewide program 1796), Pennsylvania (1786), Connecticut (preliminary legislation 1783, institution opened 1790), Virginia (1796), Rhode Island (pilot project 1796), Kentucky (1798), and New Jersey (1799).

88. Virginia might have instituted criminal incarceration as early as 1786, but the legislation proposing this change, drafted by Thomas Jefferson (and first submitted for
consideration seven years earlier) was defeated by a single vote. On the emergence
of the penitentiary in the South, see Edward L. Ayers, *Vengeance and Justice: Crime
and Punishment in the Nineteenth-Century American South* (New York, 1984), ch. 2;
Paul W. Keve, *The History of Corrections in Virginia* (Charlottesville, 1986); Kathryn
Preyer, "Crime, the Criminal Law, and Reform in Post-Revolutionary Virginia," *Law
& Hist. Rev.* 1 (1983):53. Of the twenty-four states of the Union in 1834, sixteen had
penitentiaries and eight did not. Seven out of the eight states without penitentiaries
were slave states. William Crawford, *Report on the Penitentiaries of the United States*
(n.p., 1835), 3–4 and n (see the appendix for a thorough description of American
prisons at this time). In addition, the federal government opened a national penitentiary in 1831, in Washington, D.C., but federal convicts were also contracted out
to state institutions. See generally Paul W. Keve, *Prisons and the American Conscience: A History of U.S. Federal Corrections* (Carbondale, 1991). The last state to
abandon corporal punishment was Delaware, whose judges continued to sentence
offenders to lashing, on occasion, as late as the 1960s. Corporal punishment was
finally abolished under the Delaware Revised Code of 1974, see *Del. Code Ann.,*
tit. 11, § 4205 (1974).

Chapter 2

1. "Remarks on the Massachusetts State Prison," in *Rules and Regulations for the
Government of the Massachusetts State Prison Adopted by the Board of Directors*
(Boston, 1823), 23, 27.
2. Edward Hext to Lord Treasurer [1596], in John Strype, *Annals of the Reformation and
Establishment of Religion,* rev. ed. (Oxford, 1824), *290–93; "Eastward Ho!" [1605],
quoted in Cynthia B. Herrup, *The Common Peace: Participation and the Criminal
Law in Seventeenth-Century England* (Cambridge, 1987), 4 and n.5. For other early
examples of these themes, see J. A. Sharpe, *Crime in Early Modern England, 1550–
1750* (New York, 1984), 6; Paul Slack, *Poverty and Policy in Tudor and Stuart England*
(London, 1988), 22–27, 91–107, 115–16; Thomas Starkey, "A Dialogue between Cardinal Pole and Thomas Lupset" [1538], in *England in the Reign of King Henry the
Eighth,* ed. Joseph Cowper (London, 1878), 196; "The Book of Orders" [1631], in *The
Stuart Constitution, 1603–1688,* ed. John Kenyon (Cambridge, 1966), 497; Thomas
Harman, "A Caveat or Warning for Common Cursitors, Vulgarly Called Vagabonds"
[1566], in *The Elizabethan Underworld,* ed. A. V. Judges (New York, 1930), 61. Analo-
gies to a progressive disease remained common in England at least into the eigh-
teenth century; see, e.g., J. M. Beattie, *Crime and the Courts in England, 1660–1800*
(Princeton, 1986), 421–22; Lincoln B. Faller, *Turned to Account: The Forms and
Functions of Criminal Biography in Late Seventeenth- and Early Eighteenth-Century
England* (New York, 1987), 52, 55 and n.4, 65; A. L. Beier, *Masterless Men: The
Vagrancy Problem in England, 1560–1640* (London, 1985), 55. Suggesting that the
literary sources exaggerated the criminality of vagrants, see id., ch. 8.
3. On the development of early English vagrancy law, see W. S. Holdsworth, *A History
of English Law,* rev. ed. (London, 1923), 2:459–64, 4:387–402. Capital punishment
was in fact imposed sporadically. Beier, *Masterless Men,* 160.
4. For example, John Howes, *A Ffamiliar & Frendely Discourse Dialogue Wyse* [1582],
ed. William Lemprier (London, 1904), 1–7; Beier, *Masterless Men,* ch. 2; Christopher
Hines, Richard Ireland, and Philip Rawlings, *Imprisonment in England and Wales: A
Concise History* (London, 1985), 65–68.
5. Proposals along similar lines had been floated since the early sixteenth century.

Beier, *Masterless Men*, 149–52, 161. The irony of a palace-turned-prison did not go unnoticed. The following scrap of doggerel ended an account of Bridewell in the London Spy (1703): Twas once the palace of a prince, / If we may books confide in, / But given o'er by him long since / For Vagrants to reside in / . . . . Unhappy their ignoble doom, / Where greatness once resorted; / Now hemp and labour fill each room, / Where lords and ladies sported. Quoted in A. J. Copeland, *Bridewell Royal Hospital* (London, 1888), 77.

6. The ordinances of Bridewell specified no guidelines for the term of commitment, which may well have been indeterminate. "Ordinances and Rules Drawn Out for the Good Government of the House of Bridewell" [1557], in *Parl. Papers* 19, pt. 1 (1840):399 (British Library); Sean McConville, *A History of English Prison Administration* (London, 1981), 1:33; Austin Van der Slice, "Elizabethan Houses of Correction," *J. Am. Inst. Crim. L. & Criminology* 27 (1936–37):51; Joana Innes, "Prisons for the Poor: English Bridewells, 1555–1800," in *Labour, Law, and Crime: An Historical Perspective,* ed. Francis Snyder and Douglas Hay (London, 1987), 54, 57. The institution had, in all, forty-four governors; "Order Appointed to Be Executed in the City of London, by Act of Common Council" [1579], in *Parl. Papers* 19, pt. 1 (1840):407.

7. The terms *workhouse, bridewell,* and *house of correction* had no precise definitions and were often used interchangeably. (From the last we have perhaps derived the modern term *correctional facility*.) Hereinafter, I use the term *workhouse,* even when another name appears in the contemporary reference (though not when directly quoting), for the sake of consistency.

8. 18 Eliz. c.3 (1576); Innes, "Prisons for the Poor," 62, 67, 72–80, 92–97; Beattie, *Crime and the Courts,* 492–95. The traditional assumption that English workhouses fell into decline in the eighteenth century is no longer accepted, but cf. Harding et al., *Imprisonment in England and Wales,* 71–73. For primary information on eighteenth-century workhouses, see *An Account of Several Work-Houses for Employing and Maintaining the Poor* (London, 1725). In the seventeenth century, institutions similar to the workhouse also developed on the Continent, in the Netherlands, France, and Germany; the extent to which they were influenced by English practice remains unclear; cf. J. Thorsten Sellin, *Pioneering in Penology: The Amsterdam Houses of Correction in the Sixteenth and Seventeenth Centuries* (London, 1944), 9–22, 27, 102–10; John H. Langbein, "The Historical Origins of the Sanction of Imprisonment for Serious Crime," *J. Legal Stud.* 5 (1976):48–51.

9. Edward Coke, *The Second Part of the Institutes of the Laws of England* [1642] (London, 1817), 734.

10. The rehabilitative philosophy of the workhouse advocates is spelled out in a raft of pamphlets, statutes, and other legislative records dating from the sixteenth and seventeenth centuries. Matthew Hale, *A Discourse Touching Provisions for the Poor* (London, 1683), 11–12, 19–20, 26 (quotation at 11); "A Supplication Made by the Assent of the Governors of the Poor in the Name of the Same Poor, to the King's Majesty, for Obtaining the House of Bridewell" [1552], in *Parl. Papers* 19, pt. 1 (1840):395; "Ordinances and Rules Drawn Out for the Good Government of the House of Bridewell" [1557], in id., 398–401; "Order Appointed," 402, 405; "Book of Orders," 497; 18 Eliz. c.3 (1576); *Stanleyes Remedy; or, The Way How to Reform Wandering Beggars, Thieves, High-Way Robbers, and Pick-Pockets* (London, 1646), i, 4–5; R[ichard] H[aines], *Proposals for Building in Every County a Working-Alms-House or Hospital* (London, 1677), 2; R[ichard] Haines, *Provision for the Poor; or, Reasons for the Erecting of a Working-Hospital in Every County* (London, 1678), 3–6; T[homas] F[irmin], *Some Proposals for the Imployment of the Poor* (London, 1681),

1–3, 42–44; Josiah Child, *A New Discourse of Trade* (London, 1693), 67–79; John Cary, *An Account of the Proceedings of the Corporation of Bristol in Execution of an Act of Parliament for the Better Employing and Maintaining the Poor of That City* (London, 1700), 19–20; Joyce O. Appleby, *Economic Thought and Ideology in Seventeenth-Century England* (Princeton, 1978), 139–44; Van der Slice, "Elizabethan Houses of Correction," 50–52, 60–65; Beier, *Masterless Men,* 55–56, 165; Innes, "Prisons for the Poor," 52, 67, 100–101; Stephen Macfarlane, "Social Policy and the Poor in the Later Seventeenth Century," in *London, 1500–1700: The Making of the Metropolis,* ed. A. L. Beier and Roger Finlay (London, 1986), 252; Valerie Pearl, "Puritans and Poor Relief: The London Workhouse, 1649–1660," in *Puritans and Revolutionaries: Essays in Seventeenth-Century History Presented to Christopher Hill,* ed. Donald Pennington and Keith Thomas (Oxford, 1978), 206–32. Eighteenth-century workhouse advocates held similar views, e.g., Henry Fielding, *A Proposal for Making an Effectual Provision for the Poor* (London, 1753).

11. Thus Daniel Defoe wrote somewhat later: "I humbly suggest this Distemper's so General, so Epidemick, and so deeply Rooted in the Nature and Genius of the *English,* that I must doubt it's being easily redress'd, and question whether it be possible to reach it by an Act of Parliament." [Defoe], *Giving Alms No Charity, and Employing the Poor a Grievance to the Nation* (London, 1704), 27.

12. In 1683, Matthew Hale answered the "obj[ection]" that "there are a sort of idle People that will rather beg than work" with the assertion that education in "a way of Industry" would produce "gradually a Disaccustomedness to that way, which would in time quite remove it." To the suggestion (made in his day as well as Defoe's) that Englishmen were especially susceptible to the disease of idleness, Hale answered that "if we had the same industrious Education [as other countries], we should have the same industrious Disposition." Hale, *Discourse,* 12, 20; see also Richard Dunning, *A Plain and Easie Method* (London, 1686), 3.

13. E.g., F[irmin], *Some Proposals,* 1–3. See above, note 10.

14. Hale, *Discourse,* 11, 20.

15. Coke, *Second Part of the Institutes,* 734, 728 (emphasis added); for similar statements see, e.g., F[irmin], *Some Proposals,* 11; Hale, *Discourse,* 12, 20, 24; cf. *Stanleyes Remedy,* 5.

16. It is unclear when the second fear was first voiced. Certainly it was current in the eighteenth century, when some persons imagined that the poor might find carceral facilities "more comfortable places of residence than their own houses." John Howard, *The State of the Prisons* [1777] (London, 1929), 44; see also Jonas Hanway, *Solitude in Imprisonment* (London, 1776), 30.

17. *Annual Report of the Board of Managers of the Prison Discipline Society* 1 (1826):26 [hereinafter *Prison Discipline Soc'y*].

18. Hext to Lord Treasurer, in Strype, *Annals,* *291 (quotation); *Stanleyes Remedy,* 4. This assumption continued in England into the eighteenth century, e.g., Howard, *State of the Prisons,* 44.

19. Michael Dalton, *The Countrey Justice* [1661 ed.], quoted in Beattie, *Crime and the Courts,* 492.

20. "[E]ndeavour yourselves to the good government thereof, that it may yield the worthly fruit that the same is erected for." "Ordinances and Rules," 398.

21. "Ordinances and Rules," 398–402; "Order Appointed," 402–7; Van der Slice, "Elizabethan Houses of Correction," 60–65. Emphasizing the importance of good administrators and careful regulation, see H[aines], *Proposals,* 2, 8 (quotation at 2); Haines, *Provision,* 3; Richard Haines, *A Method of Government for Such Publick Working*

Alms-Houses as May Be Erected in Every County for Bringing All Idle Hands to Industry (London, 1679), 2; Hale, *Discourse,* 25; Child, *New Discourse,* 70–71; and in the eighteenth century, Fielding, *Proposal,* 58. In an effort to enhance security, inmates at Bridewell and other workhouses were required to wear distinctive uniforms. Pendry, "Elizabethan Prisons and Prison Scenes," *Salzburg Stud. in Eng. Literature: Elizabethan and Renaissance Stud.* 17 (1974):42; Paul Slack, "Poverty and Politics in Salisbury, 1597–1666," in Peter Clark and Paul Slack, *Crisis and Order in English Towns, 1500–1700* (London, 1972), 192.

22. Hale, *Discourse,* 18–23; "Order Appointed," 406; F[irmin], *Some Proposals,* 42; Pearl, "Puritans and Poor Relief," 221–22. John Howard knew better. Howard, *State of the Prisons,* 41–42.

23. Jeremy Bentham considered the difference between "the inferior degrees of *dishonesty*" and "*idleness* as yet untainted with dishonesty" to be "microscopic." Bentham, "Panopticon; or, The Inspection-House" [1791], in *Works of Jeremy Bentham,* ed. John Bowring (Edinburgh, 1843), 4:59 (emphasis in original).

24. The notion that workhouses for idlers forestalled crime by those idlers reaches back to the inauguration of Bridewell; see "Ordinances and Rules," 399; "Book of Orders," 497; Hale, *Discourse,* 26; Haines, *Provision,* 8; S[amuel] H[artlib], *Londons Charity Inlarged, Stilling the Orphans Cry* (London, 1650), 10 (urging the incarceration of those *acquitted* of petty larceny); Joseph Massie, *A Plan for the Establishment of Charity-Houses for Exposed or Deserted Women and Girls, and for Penitent Prostitutes* (London, 1758), 119–20.

25. Hext to Lord Treasurer, in Strype, *Annals,* *291.

26. Other English criminologists also identified hard labor as a punishment more terrifying than death, e.g., Starkey, "Dialogue," 120, 197; *Acts of the Privy Council* (London, 1932), 1621–23:294; [Samuel Denne], *A Letter to Sir Robert Ladbroke . . . With an Attempt to Shew the Good Effects Which May Reasonably Be Expected from the Confinement of Criminals in Separate Apartments* (London, 1771), 76–77n (seventeenth-century proposal by Sir William Temple); Samuel Chidley, *A Cry against a Crying Sinne* (London, 1652), 17; Leon Radzinowicz, *A History of English Criminal Law and Its Administration from 1750* (London, 1948), 1:263 n.11 (quoting George Berkeley, *Querist,* 1735–37).

27. Hext to Lord Treasurer, in Strype, *Annals,* *293.

28. Thomas More, *Utopia* [1516], trans. Paul Turner (London, 1972), 53, 105.

29. Starkey, "Dialogue," 197.

30. More, *Utopia,* 105; Starkey, "Dialogue," 120.

31. Francis Hutcheson, *A System of Moral Philosophy* (London, 1755), 2:201–2; William Petty, "A Treatise of Taxes and Contributions" [1622], in *The Economic Writings of Sir William Petty,* ed. Charles Hull (New York, 1899), 1:68–69; Richard Overton, "An Appeal from the Degenerate Representative Body of the Commons of England" [1647], in Don M. Wolfe, *Leveller Manifestoes of the Puritan Revolution* (New York, 1944), 193; *Long-Parliament-Work* (London, 1659), 5–6; *The Anti-Leveller Antidote* (London, 1652), 20; *Good Work for a Good Magistrate* (London, 1651), 56; A Student of Politics, *Proposals to the Legislature for Preventing the Frequent Execution and Exportation of Convicts* (London, 1754), 26–39; [Denne], *Letter to Lord Ladbroke,* 76n (proposal by Sir William Temple); *Hanging Not Punishment Enough* [1701] (London, 1812), 20; Timothy Nourse, *Campania Foelix; or, A Discourse of the Benefits and Improvements of Husbandry* (London, 1700), 229; George Ollyffe, *An Essay Humbly Offer'd for an Act of Parliament to Prevent Capital Crimes* (London, 1731), 13–14.

32. Chidley, *Cry against a Crying Sinne,* 16 (hard labor in the workhouse or in public);

Gerrard Winstanley, "The Law of Freedom in a Platform" [1652], in *The Works of Gerrard Winstanley,* ed. G. H. Sabine (Ithaca, 1941), 591–92, 597–99 (hard labor for private citizens); William Thomlinson, "Of Hanging for Theft, So Filling the Land with Blood" [1657], in Basil Montagu, *The Rise and Progress of the Mitigation of the Punishment of Death* (London, 1822) (unspecified work); William Sheppard, *Englands Balme* (London, 1657), 23, 33 (hard labor in the Bridewell); H[aines], *Proposals,* 7–8 (hard labor in the workhouse); Haines, *Method,* 6 (hard labor in the workhouse); John Bellers, "Essays about the Poor" [1699], in *John Bellers: His Life, Times, and Writings,* ed. George Clark (London, 1987), 102–3 (hard labor in prison); Sollom Emlyn, "Preface," in *Collection of State Trials* (London, 1730), 1:xxxiii (hard labor "at home"); [Thomas Robe], "Some Considerations for Rendering the Punishment of Criminals More Effectual" [1733], in *A Collection of Political Tracts* (London, 1735), 45–47 (hard labor in the workhouse); [Thomas Robe], *A Method Whereby Criminals Liable to Transportation May Be Render'd Not Only Useful but Honest Members of the Publick* [c. 1727] (n.p., n.d.) (hard labor in "hospitals of mercy"); [William Hay], *Remarks on the Laws Relating to the Poor with Proposals for Their Better Relief and Employment* (London, 1735), 40–41 (hard labor in the workhouse); George Berkeley, "Querist," quoted in Radzinowicz, *History,* 1:263 n.11 (hard labor in public works); Fielding, *Proposal,* 24, 71–72 (hard labor "at home"); Joshua Fitzsimmons, *Free and Candid Disquisitions, On The Nature and Execution of the Laws of England* (London, 1751), 38–53 (unspecified hard labor); Massie, *Plan,* 118–19 (hard labor in the workhouse); *An Account of John Westcote* [c. 1765] (London, n.d.), 19–21; *Thoughts on Capital Punishment* (London, 1770), 2–3, 5–6, 11–13, 19–22 (hard labor in public); William Smith, *Mild Punishments Sound Policy* (London, 1777), 19–23, 29–43 (hard labor in prison).

33. There are still earlier statutes and orders of unclear relevance. In 1576, Parliament granted assize judges authority to commit clergied felons to "Prison" for up to a year for their "further correction," though there is no reference in the statute to hard labor and no indication whether "Prison" meant the workhouse. 18 Eliz. c.7 (1576). Privy Council orders that followed in the 1580s (renewed by royal commission in 1602) authorized assize judges to reprieve felons for service in the "gallies," though again there was no express rehabilitative motive (and it does not appear, at any rate, that England ever built a galley fleet); see Langbein, "Historical Origins," 55–56 and n.143; A. G. L. Shaw, *Convicts and the Colonies* (Victoria, Australia, 1966), 23–24; David T. Konig, " 'Dale's Laws' and the Non–Common Law Origins of Criminal Justice in Virginia," *Am. J. L. Hist.* 26 (1982):356–57. A tract in 1582 also referred to an order to send clergied and reprieved thieves to the "house of labour & there kept untyll they might be better provided for." Howes, "Ffamiliar and Frendely Discourse," 16–17. In 1621, Parliament rejected a proposal that petty thieves be subject on summary trial to whipping, the stocks, or a term in the workhouse. Innes, "Prisons for the Poor," 75.

34. *Acts of the Privy Council of England,* 1621–23:294. The commission had been operating since 1615. Shaw, *Convicts and the Colonies,* 23–24.

35. According to Shaw, transportation was a "desultory process" before 1640. Shaw, *Convicts and the Colonies,* 24.

36. "Book of Orders," 501.

37. "Several Drafts of Acts Heretofore Prepared by Persons Appointed to Consider the Inconvenience, Delay, Charge and Irregularity of the Proceedings of the Law" [1653], in *A Collection of Scarce and Valuable Tracts . . . Particularly That of the Late Lord*

Somers, ed. Walter Scott (London, 1811), 6:236–37. The bill was first considered by the Rump Parliament, which failed to act on it before the Rump was dissolved. On the history of the Hale Commission, see Donald Veall, *The Popular Movement for Law Reform, 1640–1660* (Oxford, 1970), 79–88. Hale was a workhouse advocate in his own right. See Hale, *Discourse.*

38. Innes, "Prisons for the Poor," 86–88.

39. Beattie, *Crime and the Courts,* 269–70, 492–93; Innes, "Prisons for the Poor," 57–58, 68, 74–75, 84–86, 94–96; Beier, *Masterless Men,* 167; J.A. Sharpe, *Crime in Seventeenth-Century England: A County Study* (Cambridge, 1983), 149–52. Workhouses were also used along with jails to hold criminals awaiting trial. (The physical transfer of workhouses to the vicinity of the jail was first mandated in 1631 to facilitate labor by *jail* inmates; see "Book of Orders," 501.)

40. Langbein, "Historical Origins," 51–53; Sellin, *Pioneering in Penology,* 41–48, 80–86, 90–93. For English references to continental practices, see, e.g., below, note 52; [Robe], "Some Considerations," 45; Radzinowicz, *History,* 1:263 n.11; Jeremy Bentham, "Principles of Penal Law" [MSS 1775–1802] in *Works,* 1:438–39. See generally on Continental developments, Pieter Spierenburg, ed., *The Emergence of Carceral Institutions: Prisons, Gallies, and Lunatic Asylums* (Rotterdam, 1984); Pieter Spierenburg, *The Prison Experience: Disciplinary Institutions and Their Inmates in Early Modern Europe* (New Brunswick, 1991).

41. 5 Ann. c.6 (1706); Innes, "Prisons for the Poor," 88–90. Sir Robert Clayton was governor of the London corporation of the poor and "was especially interested in the reformative effects of poor law discipline." Beattie, *Crime and the Courts,* 493, 497–98.

42. 4 Geo. 1 c.11 (1718). On the rate of criminal incarceration during this period, see Beattie, *Crime and the Courts,* 498–500. The act of 1718 made clergiable felons and pardoned felons subject to transportation.

43. Radzinowicz, *History,* 1:415–23; Beattie, *Crime and the Courts,* 520–25 and n.11.

44. Beattie, *Crime and the Courts,* 560–64.

45. 16 Geo. 3 c.43 (1776) (quotation in preamble). This legislation established the infamous "prison hulks"; see generally William Branch-Johnson, *The English Prison Hulks* (London, 1957).

46. 19 Geo. 3 c.74 (1779). The bill established a complex range of sentencing options and set forth administrative provisions for the new carceral institutions it mandated. The bill went through two separate drafts: the first, unsuccessful version, known as the Hard Labor Bill, circulated in 1778 and called for the construction of nineteen institutions. The second version, which passed, called for two model institutions. See Beattie, *Crime and the Courts,* 573–75.

47. 19 Geo. 3 c.74 § 5 (1779). The bill simultaneously expanded on the workhouse model, in calling for separation of convicts (§§ 5, 32–33).

48. 19 Geo. 3 c.74 § 26 (1779); Beattie, *Crime and the Courts,* 576–82.

49. Also referred to as the "humanitarians" or the "evangelicals."

50. As described by Gamaliel Bradford, "the heart of the benevolent man and philanthropist is full of compassion and sympathy for the suffering of his fellow being . . . [even] where interest is opposed to the feeling." [Bradford], *State Prisons and the Penitentiary System Vindicated* (Charlestown, 1821), 32. Among the most celebrated English philanthropist prison reformers were Thomas Bray, Jonas Hanway, and John Howard. For discussions of the movement, cf. David E. Owen, *English Philanthropy, 1660–1960* (Cambridge, Mass., 1964), 11–88; W. David Lewis, *From Newgate*

to Dannemora: The Rise of the Penitentiary in New York, 1796–1848 (Ithaca, 1965), 19–28; Michael Ignatieff, *A Just Measure of Pain: The Penitentiary in the Industrial Revolution, 1750–1850* (London, 1978), 44–65, 76, 143–53; Rod Morgan, "Divine Philanthropy: John Howard Reconsidered," *History* 62 (1977):388. Earlier workhouse advocates could also wax philosophical, e.g., Hale, *Discourse,* 25–26 ("a Work of great Humanity. . . . A Work that as well becomes a Christian"); Pearl, "Puritans and Poor Relief," 220.

51. This concern was not strictly benevolent; "gaol fever" was an occupational hazard for everyone who participated in the criminal justice system. John Howard insisted that efforts to ameliorate inmate morality had to accompany hygienic reform, for "it is obvious that if [morals] be neglected, besides the evil consequences that must result from such a source of wickedness, a suspicion will arise, that what has been already done has proceeded, chiefly, from the selfish motive of avoiding the danger to our own health, in attending courts of judicature." Howard, *State of the Prisons,* 268. On the hazard see, e.g., id., 6, 258–59, and J. S. Cockburn, *A History of English Assizes, 1558–1714* (Cambridge, 1972), 53.

52. For example, Howard, *State of the Prisons,* 11–45 (proposing regulation as well as careful selection of officers, esp. 25); George Paul, *Considerations on the Defects of Prisons and Their Present System of Regulation* (Gloucester, 1784); Thomas Bray, "An Essay towards the Reformation of Newgate and Other Prisons in and about London" [1702], in William H. Dixon, *John Howard and the Prison-World of Europe* (New York, 1850), 33–41 (in 1st ed. only); and Hanway, *Solitude in Imprisonment,* 29–36, 111–24. Howard derived many suggestions for reform from the practices of Continental workhouses; see Howard, *State of the Prisons,* 30–31 and nn, with which Hanway was also familiar (Hanway, *Solitude in Imprisonment,* 117).

53. For example, Bray, "Essay," 34, 38 (quotation at 34); [Denne], *Letter to Lord Ladbroke,* 15–21, 30–32; Hanway, *Solitude in Imprisonment,* 13, 24; Howard, *State of the Prisons,* 6, 8, 10, 37–38. This was an occasional theme in the earlier writings of workhouse advocates. See Beier, *Masterless Men,* 168; Innes, "Prisons for the Poor," 103; Petty, "Treatise of Taxes and Contributions," 1:68; John Howes, "[Second] Famyliar and Frendly Discourse Dialogue Wyse," [1587] in *Tudor Economic Documents,* ed. R. H. Tawney and Eileen Power (London, 1924), 3:421, 439.

54. Alexis de Tocqueville later noticed this phenomenon: "[I]t is natural that having preserved the prisoner from the corruption with which he was threatened, [penitentiary advocates] aspire at reforming him." Gustave de Beaumont and Alexis de Tocqueville, *On the Penitentiary System in the United States and Its Application in France* (Philadelphia, 1833), 81. The two principles soon stood side by side, e.g., Thomas Bowen, *Thoughts on the Necessity of Moral Discipline in Prisons, as a Preliminary to the Religious Instruction of Offenders* (London, 1797).

55. Joseph Butler, "A Sermon Preached before the Right Hon. the Lord Mayor, the Court of Alderman, the Sheriffs, and the Governors of the Several Hospitals of the City of London" [1740], in *Fifteen Sermons* (London, 1749), 345–71 (esp. 365–67); Roger North, *A Discourse of the Poor* (London, 1753), 25–26.

56. See also Jonas Hanway, *The Defects of Police the Cause of Immorality* (London, 1775), 210–35 (reissued in 1780 under the title *The Citizens' Monitor*). Philanthropists did not in the process forget preconviction rehabilitation; Hanway noted that in particular cases this might negate the need for a formal sanction. Hanway, *Solitude in Imprisonment,* 110.

57. "When only the fear of temporal punishments makes impressions, the world can

never be well governed: the power cannot be wrested out of the hands of the great Ruler and supreme Legislator of the world." Hanway, *Solitude in Imprisonment,* 5, 26, 72–73, 105, 117 (quotation at 5).

58. Hanway, *Solitude in Imprisonment,* 4, 18, 39, 72–73, 98–99, 109 (quotation at 4); Howard, *State of the Prisons,* 261; John Brewster, *Sermons for Prisoners* (Stockton, 1790), vi–vii.

59. He added dryly that under his program "the *repentance* and *amendment,* the *sorrow* for the past, and the *resolution* with regard to the future part of life, will be more sincere in the *prison,* than it usually is in the *church.*" Hanway, *Solitude Imprisonment,* 98–99 (emphasis in original).

60. One philanthropic advocate appears to have had noncarceral therapy in mind when he urged that to "reach the heart" of a criminal "Gospel and not law should be employed. . . . The clergy therefore should be called upon, and not the magistrate. This is under God, the peculiar business of the ministers of the gospel." William Romaine, *A Method for Preventing the Frequency of Robberies and Murders* (London, 1770), 25–26.

61. Hanway, *Solitude in Imprisonment,* 4. For other works promoting solitary confinement as a mechanism for rehabilitation, see William Dodd, *Thoughts in Prison* (London, 1777); John Brewster, "The Use of Solitude in Prisons," in *A Companion for the Prisoner,* ed. Thomas Bowen (London, 1828), 13–24 (also printed in Brewster, *Sermons for Prisoners,* 23–44); John Brewster, *On the Prevention of Crimes, and on the Advantages of Solitary Confinement* (London, 1792), 27–34; Kettlewell, "Advice to Persons in Confinement How to Bear Solitude and Want," in *A Companion for the Prisoner,* 166–73.

62. See above, note 55. Sellin traces the first use of solitary confinement as a rehabilitative punishment to the Florentine Hospice of San Filippo Neri, reorganized by Filippo Franci around 1677, although there is no evidence that the English philanthropists borrowed directly from this model. J. Thorsten Sellin, "Fillippo Franci: A Precursor of Modern Penology," *J. Am. Inst. Crim. L. & Criminology* 17 (1926–27):104.

63. Brewster, "Use of Solitude in Prisons," 16; similarly, Kettlewell, "Advise to Persons in Confinement," 167. As is evident from Brewster's statement, the notion of solitary confinement had roots in the monastic tradition and in church discipline.

64. Hanway, *Solitude in Imprisonment,* 31. Stressing the importance of religious instruction in the prison, see, e.g., John Brewster, *On the Religious Improvement of Prisons: A Sermon* (London, 1808).

65. Contemporaries who compared the two programs were perfectly aware of this difference. Hanway: "Solitude will thus accomplish the work, not in a *vague, formal,* and *unmeaning* manner, but by creating a real change in the heart, to raise them that are fallen." Hanway, *Solitude in Imprisonment,* 44 (emphasis in original). Bentham: "This kind of discipline [hard labor] does not, indeed, like the other [solitary confinement], pluck up corruption by the roots; it tends however to check the growth of it, and render the propensity to it less powerful." Bentham, "Principles of Penal Law," in *Works,* 1:440.

66. Hanway, *Solitude in Imprisonment,* 37.

67. Hanway, *Solitude in Imprisonment,* 33–34, 123 (quotation at 34); Hanway, *Defects of Police,* xii, 225–30; William Paley, *The Principles of Moral and Political Philosophy,* 7th ed. (London, 1790), 2:292. John Howard hovered somewhere between the rehabituative and reclamatory models, favoring enforced hard labor "ten hours a day; mealtimes included," but also solitary confinement at night (and, so far as

practical, during the day as well) in order to promote repentance and salvation, "a more important object than gaining the whole world." Howard, *State of the Prisons,* 21–22, 38–40, 260–63 (quotations at 39, 261). The Penitentiary Act of 1779, which Howard helped to draft, contemplated such a program. 19 Geo. 3 c.74, §§ 5, 32–33 (1779). Hanway criticized the act as "defective," however, because it failed to mandate separation of offenders at all hours. Jonas Hanway, *Distributive Justice and Mercy* (London, 1781), i–vi, 158–258 (extended discussion of the act) (quotation at i). Hanway agreed that labor could have therapeutic value, but he insisted that solitude not be made "secondary" to labor (226).

68. Hanway asserted by analogy: "The arts practiced to seduce women are often successful: in this case *gentle* treatment and *tenderness* alone will prevail . . . it does not change its name when employed in the cause of virtue." Hanway, *Solitude in Imprisonment,* 37–38 (emphasis in original).

69. [Denne], *Letter to Lord Ladbroke,* 80; Hanway, *Solitude in Imprisonment,* 31, 37.

70. [Denne], *Letter to Lord Ladbroke,* 40.

71. Hanway, *Solitude in Imprisonment,* 30–31, 103; Hanway, *Defects of Police,* 213, 223; Paley, *Principles,* 2:291.

72. Brewster, *Sermons for Prisoners,* 15; Brewster, *On the Prevention of Crimes,* 29; Hanway, *Solitude in Imprisonment,* 104–5.

73. Hanway, *Solitude in Imprisonment,* 25, 35–36, 71–72; Hanway, *Defects of Police,* xiii. See also Hanway, *Distributive Justice,* 92 (suggesting that the expense would be small because the therapy was rapid). It was this issue that prompted Jeremy Bentham to reconsider, and ultimately to abandon, his ideological commitment to solitary confinement when he drew his blueprints for the Panopticon in 1791. Bentham, "Panopticon," in *Works,* 4:71–76, 137–41 (esp. 138n).

74. Ignatieff, *A Just Measure of Pain,* 96–109; J. R. S. Whiting, *Prison Reform in Gloucestershire, 1776–1820* (London, 1975); Margaret DeLacy, *Prison Reform in Lancashire, 1700–1850: A Study in Local Administration* (Stanford, 1986), 75–80, 95–115; Robin Evans, *The Fabrication of Virtue: English Prison Architecture, 1750–1840* (Cambridge, 1982), ch. 4. (Hanway had first experimented with solitude in 1758 in a magdelan house established for prostitutes [71].) While some local penitentiaries of the late eighteenth century provided for solitary labor, others followed the model of the Penitentiary Act and implemented congregate labor by day and solitary confinement at night. Ignatieff, *A Just Measure of Pain,* 97.

75. Michael Dalton, *The Countrey Justice* (London, 1619), 1, 4–5 (quotation at 5); Herrup, *Common Peace,* 3, 186 and n.31; Faller, *Turned to Account,* 73 and n.5; Sharpe, *Crime in Early Modern England,* 5–6; George Lee Haskins, *Law and Authority in Early Massachusetts: A Study in Tradition and Design* (New York, 1960), 141–45; Harding et al., *Imprisonment in England and Wales,* 14–15. For an analysis of God's place in English criminal justice, see Randall McGowen, "The Changing Face of God's Justice: The Debates over Divine and Human Punishment in Eighteenth-Century England," *Crim. Just. Hist.* 9 (1988):63.

76. The phrase traces to Beccaria but is often misattributed to Bentham. Cesare Beccaria, *On Crimes and Punishments* [1764], ed. Henry Paolucci (Indianapolis, 1963), 8 and n.10.

77. For example, Montesquieu: "In things that prejudice the tranquility or security of the state, secret actions are subject to human jurisdiction. But in those which offend the Deity, where there is no public action, there can be no criminal matter; the whole passes betwixt man and God, who knows the measure and time of his ven-

geance. . . . [W]e must honor the Deity, and leave him to avenge his own cause." Charles de Secondat Montesquieu, *The Spirit of Laws* (London, 1752), 263–64; Beccaria, *On Crimes and Punishments*, 64–66.

78. For example, William Eden, *Principles of Penal Law* (London, 1771), 6–7 ("The prevention of crime should be the great object of the Lawgiver. . . . It is from an abuse of language, that we apply the word 'Punishment' to human institutions: Vengeance belongeth not to man"); William Blackstone, *Commentaries on the Laws of England* (London, 1765–69), 4:*11–12.

79. For example, Paley, *Principles*, 2:270; Bentham, "Principles of Penal Law," in *Works*, 1:396–97.

80. Beccaria, *On Crimes and Punishments*, 13–14, 45, 63.

81. John Locke, *An Essay Concerning Human Understanding* (London, 1690).

82. Beccaria, *On Crimes and Punishments*, 17, 47, 62–63.

83. See, e.g., above, note 19.

84. As an American follower of Beccaria later put it: "Severity was inconsiderately taken to be the main property of criminal law; and it was hastily thought, that in proportion to the severity of the sanction, would be the tranquility of society." [James Austin], "Book Review," *N. Am. Rev.* 10 (1820):236. See generally Radzinowicz, *History*, 1:231–67.

85. Beccaria, *On Crimes and Punishments*, 13–17, 42–52, 55–59, 62–64, 99.

86. On Beccaria's influence among the English rationalists, see Radzinowicz, *History*, 1:283 n.60, 303–4, 346, 377–79. In contrast to Beccaria, Paley and Madan defended England's bloody code, though they adhered otherwise to the basic premises of rationalism; see Radzinowicz, *History*, 1:239–59; cf. Blackstone, *Commentaries*, 4:*12–19.

87. Beccaria, *On Crimes and Punishments*, 19–20, 47–50, 54–55, 68, 74–76, 99 (quotations at 48, 99).

88. "Delinquents are a peculiar race of beings. . . . Their weakness consists in yielding to the seduction of the passing moment. Their minds are weak and disordered." Bentham, "Principles of Penal Law," in *Works*, 1:499; see also Ignatieff, *A Just Measure of Pain*, 66–67.

89. Bentham spelled this out, lest there be misunderstanding: "It is an excellent quality in a punishment that it is calculated to conduce to *the reformation of the delinquent*. I do not mean merely through fear of undergoing punishment a second time, but by reason of a change in his character and habits." Jeremy Bentham, *Bentham's Theory of Legislation* [MSS 1775–1802], ed. Etienne Dumont, trans. Charles M. Atkinson (London, 1914), 2:146–47 (emphasis in original).

90. Warville spoke typically of "leading back to industry and reason these deluded men." Jacques Brissot de Warville, *New Travels in the United States of America Performed in 1788* (London, 1792), 370; Ignatieff, *A Just Measure of Pain*, 66–68.

91. Romilly described the penitentiary as "a kind of asylum to that very large description of offenders, who are rendered such by the defects of education, by pernicious connexions, by indigence, or by despair." Samuel Romilly, *Observations on a Late Publication, Intitled Thoughts on Executive Justice* (London, 1786), 60; similarly, Jeremy Bentham, "Panopticon vs. New South Wales" [1802], in *Works*, 4:174–75.

92. For example, Starkey, "Dialogue," 196; Dalton, *Countrey Justice*, 275; *Stanleyes Remedy*, i; Faller, *Turned to Account*, 56–60. The theme, indeed, has biblical roots: "Be not deceived: evil Communications corrupts good Manners," 1 Cor. 15:33. Such notions also prompted suggestions by at least the mid-seventeenth century that

crime could be forestalled by curing the social environment. In 1651 an anonymous Commonwealth reformer traced crime to "base swinish drunkenness" and urged as a "cure" for crime, the prohibition of alcohol consumption. *Good Work for a Good Magistrate* (London, 1651), 56–57. In a similar vein, Daniel Defoe in 1731 traced crime to the rise of *"Night-houses* and *Bowdy-houses;* and this brings me to the very bottom of the Sore or Wound. These . . . are the Nurseries of Thieves." His solution: "If these Houses of Retreat are once demolished and blown-up, that is to say, their Licenses taken away . . . the Gangs will . . . immediately disappear." The author acknowledged that natural depravity might be "the Original of all Wickedness," but he continued, "We will not enter into that Part here; for I am not talking Divinity in this Work." [Daniel Defoe], *An Effectual Scheme for the Immediate Preventing of Street Robberies* (London, 1731), 16, 31; see also Henry Fielding, "An Enquiry into the Causes of the Late Increase of Robbers" [1751], in *The Works of Henry Fielding, Esq.* (London, 1806), 10:333–467; Radzinowicz, *History,* 2:1–25.

93. "The evil, in most instances, arising from bad company; let them by kept out of it, in prison." Hanway, *Defects of Police,* vi (n); see also John Brewster, "On the Influence of Evil Company," in *A Companion for the Prisoner,* 98–110.

94. Compare David J. Rothman, *The Discovery of the Asylum: Social Order and Disorder in the New Republic* (Boston, 1971), 68–71, 82–83 (tracing environmentalism to the Jacksonians).

95. Bentham, "Principles of Penal Law," in *Works,* 1:424–29 (Bentham, an agnostic, does speak of religion in this section, but in pragmatic terms); Paley, *Principles,* 2:291–92.

96. For Bentham's animus against "your sentimental orators," see his "Principles of Penal Law," in *Works,* 1:412–13. Bentham dismissed their analyses of the operation of solitude as "[not] very explicitly developed" and "an imperfect theory" (425). The philanthropists returned the favor, though they remained willing to participate in a wary marriage of convenience. Thus, in the pages of his journal, *The Philanthropist,* the Quaker advocate William Allen praised Bentham's early writings after determining that they contained "nothing at variance with my religious feelings." Quoted in Ignatieff, *A Just Measure of Pain,* 146–47.

97. U. R. Q. Henriques, "The Rise and Decline of the Separate System of Prison Discipline," *Past & Present* 54 (Feb. 1972):64. This notion, which also formed a part of philanthropic rhetoric, followed naturally from environmentalism.

98. Ignatieff, *A Just Measure of Pain,* 66–68.

99. Bentham, "Panopticon," 46–47; Bentham, "Panopticon vs. New South Wales," in *Works,* 4:137–53. Bentham's scheme did incorporate a therapeutic innovation, one of the few to emerge out of rational penal theory: the "inspection principle," holding that carceral therapy would operate more effectively if convicts conceived themselves be to under constant observation. Bentham, "Panopticon," in *Works,* 4:40, 44–46. This thesis had its critics; see, e.g., William Roscoe, *Observations on Penal Jurisprudence and the Reformation of Criminals, Part III* (London, 1825), 58.

100. 19 Geo. 3 c.74 §§ 5, 32–33 (1779) (convicts were also to be kept apart while at labor as much as possible). For the similar views of the rationalist Samuel Romilly, see Romilly, *Observations,* 54–61.

101. Bentham, "Panopticon," in *Works,* 4:122–23. Bentham called this the "rule of severity," but it eventually came to be known as the principle of "less eligibility," see McConville, *History of English Prison Administration,* 1:238–41.

102. For example, Bentham, "Principles of Penal Law," in *Works,* 1:500.

103. Compare Rothman, *Discovery of the Asylum,* 57–62 (tracing the postrevolutionary

movement to rational ideology and denying any concern for rehabilitation before the Jacksonian era).

104. *Mass. Centinel,* Sept. 22, 1784, at 1 (emphasis in original).

105. *Mass. Centinel,* Oct. 16, 1784, at 1. This commentary was reprinted in Pennsylvania; see *Independent Gazetteer,* Nov. 27, 1784, at 2.

106. Governor's Message, Jan. 11, 1799, *Mass. Acts & Resolves,* 1798–99:636; see also *Mass. Centinel,* Oct. 20, 1784, at 1.

107. The preamble to the statute alluded to the presumed idleness of offenders: "Whereas it has become necessary to the safety of the industrious inhabitants of the Common-wealth. . . ." Act of Mar. 14, 1785, ch. 63, *Mass. Acts & Resolves,* 1784–85:163. The general goal of rehabilitation is also mentioned in a personal letter by a member of the committee responsible for drafting the statute. Samuel Dexter to William Cushing (Jan. 15, 1785), in "Robert Treat Paine Papers" (unpublished MS, Mass. Hist. Soc'y).

108. Act of Mar. 14, 1785, ch. 63, *Mass. Acts & Resolves,* 1784–85:163.

109. Act of Nov. 1, 1785, ch. 21, *Mass. Acts & Resolves,* 1784–85:472.

110. Governor's Message, Jan. 30, 1793, *Mass. Acts & Resolves,* 1792–93:692–94.

111. Governor's Message, Jan. 15, 1802, *Mass. Acts & Resolves,* 1800–1801:583.

112. For additional discussions of hard labor in Massachusetts before 1800, see Answer of the Legislature, Feb. 15, 1793, *Mass. Acts & Resolves,* 1792–93:242; *Columbian Centinel,* June 1, 1796, at 1; *Salem Mercury,* Dec. 30, 1788, at 3; "Report Respecting Convicts" [1799], appended to "Resolves," 1802, ch. 54 (passed) (unpublished MS, Mass. Archives); John Lathrop, *God Our Protector and Refuge in Danger and Trouble* (Boston, 1797).

113. For example, Resolve of Nov. 17, 1786, ch. 134, *Mass. Acts & Resolves,* 1786–87:413; Governor's Message, Jan. 30, 1793, id., 1792–93:694 (object was to "check the progress of crime"). Cf. Rothman, *Discovery of the Asylum,* 61 ("In this first burst of enthusiasm, Americans expected that a rational system of correction . . . would dissuade all but a few offenders").

114. Over its thirteen-year history, some forty-five inmates (16 percent of the prison population) managed to escape the facility. And in 1792, smallpox broke out on Castle Island. Edwin Powers, *Crime and Punishment in Early Massachusetts, 1620–1692* (Boston, 1966), 241–42; Governor's Message, Nov. 9, 1792, *Mass. Acts & Resolves,* 1792–93:688–89.

115. Compare Rothman, *Discovery of the Asylum,* 62, 89–93 (suggesting that the post-revolutionary builders were as yet unconcerned with rehabilitation, and therefore devoted little attention to prison administration). And cf. the critical historian Martin Miller, who dismisses rehabilitative ideology as "a facade of rhetoric" that "played on words more than it affected the course of prison methods." Martin B. Miller, "At Hard Labor: Rediscovering the Nineteenth-Century Prison," *Issues in Criminology* 9 (1974):92, 94–95.

116. Act of Mar. 14, 1785, ch. 63, *Mass. Acts & Resolves,* 1784–85:163; Resolve of Mar. 11, 1791, ch. 170, id., 1790–91:244–45. Cf. Rothman, *Discovery of the Asylum,* 82–83, 106 (dating military discipline in prisons to the Jacksonian period).

117. Act of Mar. 14, 1785, ch. 63, *Mass. Acts & Resolves,* 1784–85:163; Resolve of Feb. 16, 1789, ch. 113, id., 1788–89:357; Resolve of Nov. 22, 1788, ch. 73, id., 270 (halting the practice of staffing the garrison with invalids); Resolve of June 24, 1790, ch. 81, id., 1790–91:136; Resolve of Mar. 11, 1791, ch. 170, id., 244; Resolve of Mar. 22, 1786, ch. 166, 1784–85:928; "Senate Documents," nos. 2219, 2219.2 (1797) (unpassed) (unpublished MSS, Mass. Archives).

118. As in some English workhouses, convicts on Castle Island wore special uniforms. See note 21, above. One innovation in institutional security was the construction of "lamps" around Castle Island—a precursor of the modern search light. On these measures, see Act of Mar. 14, 1785, ch. 63, *Mass. Acts & Resolves,* 1784–85:163; Resolve of June 30, 1792, ch. 76, id., 1792–93:183; see also Governor's Message, Nov. 5, 1785, ch. 39, id., 1784–85:755–56; Resolve of Mar. 22, 1786, ch. 166, id., 927–29; Resolve of July 8, 1786, ch. 123, id., 1786–87:338; Resolve of Nov. 17, 1786, ch. 126, id., 405–6.

119. Resolve of Mar. 22, 1786, ch. 166, *Mass. Acts & Resolves,* 1784–85:927–29; "Senate Documents," nos. 2219, 2219.2 (1797) (unpassed). For a rare description of confinement on Castle Island, confirming the implementation of hard labor, military discipline, divine worship, and government inspection but denying the presence of a resident physician, see Stephen Burroughs, *Memoirs of the Notorious Stephen Burroughs of New Hampshire* [1798] (New York, 1924), 136–38, 151–53, 159, 167–68, 170–71. See also Henry Tufts, *The Autobiography of a Criminal* [1807], ed. Edmund Pearson (New York, 1930), 283–97, and Linda Kealey, "Punishment at Hard Labor: Stephen Burroughs and the Castle Island Prison, 1785–98," *New Eng. Q.* 57 (1984):249. For a European account, see Samuel Stearns, *The American Oracle* (London, 1791), 258–59. Such administrative efforts were continued and expanded at the Massachusetts State Prison, opened in 1805; see chapter 5, note 52.

120. Act of Mar. 18, 1785, ch. 40, *Laws of the State of New York,* 8th sess.:31 (act restricted to the city of New York); *Independent Gazetteer,* Aug. 26, 1786, at 2. Likewise in Connecticut under legislation passed in 1783, convicts were to be confined at hard labor in "any Work-House or House of Correction." *Acts and Laws of the State of Connecticut in America* (New London, 1784), 18, 24, 244–45.

121. [Thomas Eddy], *An Account of the State Prison or Penitentiary House in the City of New-York* (New York, 1801), 20, 31–35, 50–53 (quotations at 50, 53); see also Governor's Message, Jan. 6, 1796, in *Journal of the Senate of the State of New York,* 19th sess.:6. The act of 1796 made no reference to rehabilitation, but it did provide for the training of convicts. Act of Mar. 26, 1796, in *Laws of the State of New-York* (New York, 1797), 3:291, 295–96.

122. Act of Sept. 15, 1786, ch. 1241, *Statutes at Large of Pennsylvania from 1682 to 1801* (Harrisburg, 1908), 12:280 [hereinafter *Pa. Stats. at Large*]. The statutory language originated with a report of the Judges and Grand Jury of the Court of Oyer and Terminer, issued in September 1785. Michael Meranze, "The Penitential Ideal in Late Eighteenth-Century Philadelphia," *Pa. Mag. Hist. & Biog.* 108 (1984):425–28.

123. Act of Apr. 5, 1790, ch. 1516, *Pa. Stats. at Large,* 13:511. On the Walnut Street prison, see generally Negley K. Teeters, *The Cradle of the Penitentiary: The Walnut Street Jail at Philadelphia, 1773–1835* (n.p., 1955).

124. Act of Sept. 15, 1786, ch. 1241, *Pa. Stats. at Large,* 12:286, § 10; [Eddy], *Account,* 51, 54, 58–59 (quotation at 51); William Bradford, *An Enquiry How Far the Punishment of Death Is Necessary in Pennsylvania* (Philadelphia, 1793), 23, 45–46, 70–71 n.13. Cf. Benjamin Rush, *An Enquiry into the Effects of Public Punishments upon Criminals and upon Society* (Philadelphia, 1787), 26.

125. New York: [Eddy], *Account.* Pennsylvania: "Report of the Board of Inspectors of the Prison for the City and County of Philadelphia in the Year 1791," in William Roscoe, *Observations on Penal Jurisprudence* (London, 1819), app. 1–2; Caleb Lownes, "An Account of the Alteration and Present State of the Penal Laws of Pennsylvania" [1792], in Bradford, *Enquiry,* 73ff.; Teeters, *Cradle of the Penitentiary,* ch. 3. Recog-

nizing the need for good officers, see Bradford, *Enquiry,* 70 n.13; *Am. Musium* 7 (1790):194. When a South Carolinian visitor toured Walnut Street in 1796, he was astonished at the quality of its officers and explicitly contrasted them with the low quality of traditional jailkeepers. Robert Turnbull, *A Visit to the Philadelphia Prison* (London, 1797), 23, 33 (first published in the *Charleston Gazette*). An English commentator confirmed: "As reformation is now the great object in Pennsylvania, . . . it is of the first importance that the gaoler and the different inspectors should be persons of moral character. . . . Hence it is a rule . . . that none are to be chosen . . . but such as shall be found on inquiry to have been exemplary in their lives." Thomas Clarkson, "Portraiture of Quakerism" [1807], in Basil Montague, *The Opinions of Different Authors upon the Punishment of Death* (London, 1809), 48–49; see also Negley K. Teeters, *They Were in Prison: A History of the Pennsylvania Prison Society, 1787–1937* (Philadelphia, 1937), 455, 496.

126. See chapter 5, notes 24–35 and accompanying text.

127. Act of Sept. 15, 1786, ch. 1241, *Pa. Stats. at Large,* 12:286–87, § 11.

128. "Mass. Archives," 44:538–39 [1765] (unpublished MS, Mass. Archives) (quotation); Grand Jury Charge, Mass. Super. Ct., 1767, 1768, in Josiah Quincy, *Reports of Cases Argued and Adjudged in the Superior Court of Judicature of the Province of Massachusetts Bay between 1761 and 1772* (New York, 1865), 235, 258–60 ("the Supreme Being will avenge his own wrongs"). In later years, see, e.g. [Bradford], *State Prisons,* 6–7, 10–11. Cf., e.g., Beccaria, *On Crimes and Punishments,* 93 ("ultimate end"); Eden, *Principles,* 6 ("great object").

129. In Massachusetts, prosecutions for moral offenses dropped off after the Revolution, though most of them remained on the statute book. William E. Nelson, *Americanization of the Common Law: The Impact of Legal Change on Massachusetts Society, 1760–1830* (Cambridge, Mass., 1975), 37–39, 110–11, 117–18. Biblically inspired criminal legislation appeared quaint by the Jacksonian period; see Francis Gray, *Remarks on the Early Laws of Massachusetts Bay* (Boston, 1843), 3.

130. On Beccaria's intellectual impact in America, see generally Paul M. Spurlin, "Beccaria's Essay on Crimes and Punishments in Eighteenth-Century America," *Stud. Voltaire & Eighteenth Century* 27 (1963):1489. In some respects, Beccarian ideology was explicitly rejected in America; see Hirsch, "From Pillory to Penitentiary," 45–51.

131. Compare Rothman, *Discovery of the Asylum,* 59–62 (emphasizing Beccaria's significance).

132. The notion that punishment should be proportional was older than Beccaria's essay, though he did highlight the concept. Nonetheless, the Massachusetts colonists had always modulated whippings according to the severity of the offense, see N. E. H. Hull, *Female Felons: Women and Serious Crime in Colonial Massachusetts* (Urbana, 1987), 113. For an early reference to the principle of proportionality in Massachusetts, see *Records of the Governor and Company of the Massachusetts Bay,* ed. Nathaniel Shurtleff (Boston, 1853–54), 2:93–94 [1644] [hereinafter *Mass. Rec.*], and in England, e.g., Radzinowicz, *History,* 1:261, 266; Beattie, *Crime and the Courts,* 554–59; Veall, *Popular Movement,* 127–28; [Robe], "Some Considerations," 43; Fielding, *Proposal,* 71–72; and William Webster, *A Casuistical Essay on Anger and Forgiveness* (London, 1750), 64–65.

133. Beccaria, *On Crimes and Punishments,* 62–64.

134. *Pa. Const.,* ch. 2, §§ 38–39 (1776); Act of Mar. 26, 1796, *N.Y. Laws,* 3:291; Spurlin, "Beccaria's Essay," 1501 (defeated act in Virginia).

135. Some commentators stressed the physical limitations on the number of lashes that

a judge could prescribe or asserted that lashing cast a uniform ignominy on its subjects, but others pointed out that persons reacted differently to the experience of incarceration, thereby reducing its *subjective* proportionality—an argument cited by at least one southern opponent of the penitentiary. Cf. William Tudor to William Roscoe (Apr. 24, 1819), in William Roscoe, *Additional Observations on Penal Jurisprudence and the Reformation of Criminals* (London, 1823), app. 81; Rush, *Enquiry,* 15; *Prison Discipline Soc'y* 1 (1826):26; *Messages of the Governors of Tennessee,* ed. Robert H. White (Nashville, 1952), 2:168; and in England, cf. Webster, *Casuistical Essay,* 64–65; Fielding, *Proposal,* 71–72; Emlyn, "Preface," xxxvi; and Bentham, "Principles of Penal Law," in *Works,* 1:402–3, 415, 424, 440.

136. Compare, e.g., *Acts and Resolves of the Province of the Massachusetts Bay* (Boston, 1869–1922), 1:577–78 [1705] [hereinafter *Mass. Prov. Laws*]; Act of Mar. 16, 1805, ch. 131, *Mass. Acts & Resolves,* 1804–5:202; and cf. *Mass. Prov. Laws,* 2:5 [1715]; Act of Mar. 13, 1806, ch. 101, *Mass. Acts & Resolves,* 1804–5:522.

137. On theoretical criticism of capital punishment before Beccaria, see Radzinowicz, *History,* 1:263–67; Veall, *Popular Movement,* 127–31; Robert Zaller, "The Debate on Capital Punishment during the English Revolution," *Am. J. Legal Hist.* 31 (1987):126. Beccaria was one of the few, though not the first, commentators to propose the *complete* abolition of capital punishment, but this extreme position was not accepted in any American state.

138. Massachusetts: *Mass. Centinel,* Jan. 5, 1785, at 3; *Independent Chron.,* Feb. 7, 1793, at 1, and Feb. 14, 1793, at 1–2; Answer of the Legislature, Feb. 15, 1793, *Mass. Acts & Resolves,* 1792–93:242; Governor's Message, Jan. 15, 1801, id., 1800–1801:584; Report of Committee, Jan. 26, 1802, appended to 1802 "Resolves" ch. 54 (passed). New York: e.g., [Eddy], *Account,* cover sheet, 9, 16, 64. Pennsylvania: e.g., Lownes, "Account," 92–93; Harry Elmer Barnes, *The Evolution of Penology in Pennsylvania* (Indianapolis, 1927), 108–9 and nn. On the ideology of capital punishment, see generally Philip E. Mackey, *Hanging in the Balance: The Anti-Capital Punishment Movement in New York State, 1776–1861* (New York, 1982); Louis P. Masur, *Rites of Execution: Capital Punishment and the Transformation of American Culture, 1776–1865* (New York, 1989); David Brion Davis, "The Movement to Abolish Capital Punishment in America, 1787–1862," *Am. Hist. Rev.* 63 (1957):23; and in England, *Executions and the British Experience from the Seventeenth to the Twentieth Century: A Collection of Essays,* ed. William Thesing (Jefferson, N.C., 1990).

139. Thus, in advocating a retreat from the gallows, the rationalist William Eden initially urged that "corporal pains might certainly with good effect be substituted, in some cases, in the room of capital judgements." Eden, *Principles,* 60. When Tennessee considered building a penitentiary in 1831, Governor William Carroll argued against its construction, noting that if certainty of punishment was its aim, this could be obtained without incarceration. "If any punishment can be pointed out which is too severe, it is easy to make it more mild." *Messages of the Governors of Tennessee,* 168.

140. Beccaria, *On Crimes and Punishments,* 47–50. Like English and American commentators, Beccaria remarked the severity of penal servitude (48–49). At least one American critic saw this as a contradiction: if hard labor was severe, then it was likely to encounter the same sort of jury nullification that had rendered capital punishment uncertain! *Messages of the Governors of Tennessee,* 168.

141. In 1796, New York abolished the death penalty for all crimes, save murder and treason. Thomas Eddy, who drafted the statute, cited to Beccaria on the cover of his pamphlet, see [Eddy], *Account,* cover sheet. In 1794, Pennsylvania abolished the

death penalty in all cases except murder. The preamble of the statute cited to the principle of certainty (as well as rehabilitation). Act of Apr. 22, 1794, ch. 1777, *Pa. Stats. at Large,* 15:174. Asserting the influence of "the principles of Beccaria," see also Bradford, *Enquiry,* 20. In Massachusetts, five of the fourteen capital statutes of the provincial era were left after 1805 (murder, burglary, arson, rape, and treason; robbery again became capital in 1819). The drafters of the code of 1805 planned to consider further cutbacks on capital punishment after incarceration had been tried. One drafter cited to Beccaria in a separate work. Nathan Dane and Samuel Sewell, "Report of the Committee Appointed to Revise Penal Laws and on the Subject of the State Prison," Feb. 16, 1805, "Senate Documents," no. 3232 (1805) (unpassed) (also printed in *Mass. Legislative Documents,* 1798–1809: no. 3, [State Library Annex]; Nathan Dane, *A General Abridgment and Digest of American Law* (Boston, 1824), 625, 630–32; *Salem Gazette,* Nov. 18, 1794, at 3 (reporting on a trial in which Dane and Sewell had served as the capital defendant's co-counsel). On the decision to restore the capital statute against robbery, see "Mass. Legislative Report," 1819, in Roscoe, *Additional Observations,* app. 67; Act of Feb. 19, 1819, ch. 124, *Mass. Acts,* 1818–22:201. Beccaria was also cited as the source for Virginia's hard labor proposal. *The Writings of Thomas Jefferson,* ed. Paul L. Ford (New York, 1892), 1:62–63.

142. See chapter 1, notes 25–29, 32, and accompanying text.

143. In Massachusetts, the code of 1785 downgraded three capital crimes to noncapital ones (polygamy, counterfeiting, and third offenses of theft). In New York, the provision of 1785 did not apply to capital crimes at all. In Pennsylvania, the code of 1786 downgraded four previously capital crimes (robbery, burglary, sodomy, and buggary) and retained eight others (murder, treason, malicious maiming, manslaughter, arson, rape, concealing the death of a bastard child, and counterfeiting).

144. "'Alas, Sir, I would be glad to work, but I can find none.' . . . And he spoke truth." *The Means of Effectually Preventing Theft and Robbery* (London, 1783), 39, 78 (quotation at 39). Several English publicists urged the construction of workhouses in order to "take away all such defenc[es] and usual answers." *Stanleyes Remedy,* 5 (quotation); F[irmin], *Some Proposals,* 10.

145. For example, *The Colonial Laws of Massachusetts,* ed. William Whitmore (Boston, 1890), § 2:236 [1675] [hereinafter *Mass. Col. Laws*]. On the theory of the work ethic and its centrality to Puritanism, see Michael Walzer, *The Revolution of the Saints* (Cambridge, Mass., 1965), ch. 6.

146. For a discussion of old English attitudes toward labor and labor practices, see Edmund S. Morgan, *American Slavery, American Freedom* (New York, 1975), 61–70.

147. Charles Chauncy, *The Idle-Poor Secluded from the Breads of Charity by the Christian Law* (Boston, 1752), 13, 16. For additional examples of this theme, see Benjamin Wadsworth, *Vicious Courses, Procuring Poverty Described and Condemned* (Boston, 1719), 6–11; Samuel Moodey, *Summary Account of the Life and Death of Joseph Quasson, Indian* (Boston, 1726), 3; Cotton Mather, *A Good Master Well Served* (Boston, 1696), 10; Cotton Mather, *A Flying Roll, Brought Forth, to Enter into the House and Hand of the Thief* (Boston, 1713), 33; *A Report of the Record Commissioners of the City of Boston Containing the Boston Town Records* (Boston, 1876–1909), 1758–69:274–75 [hereinafter *Boston Town Records*]; Eli Faber, "The Evil That Men Do: Crime and Transgression in Colonial Massachusetts" (Ph.D. diss., Columbia University, 1974), 60 and n; and elsewhere in the colonies, e.g., Raymond A. Mohl, *Poverty in New York, 1783–1825* (New York, 1971), 44–46; Barnes, *Evolution of Penology,* 62.

148. *Mass. Rec.,* 1:401. A workhouse was ordered built in Boston once the main body of the settlers arrived (1:100).

149. *Mass. Rec.,* 3:399–400; 4, pt. 1:222, 256–57, 305; *Mass. Col. Laws,* § 2:127 [1646].

150. *Mass. Col. Laws,* § 2:127 [1646]. Another statute referred to the institution as a "House for Correction and Reformation" (§ 2:66 [1668]), and the Boston workhouse built in 1739 operated under the slogan: "Labor improbus omnia vincit" (hard labor conquers all), *Boston Town Records, 1729–42:*234. Persons could be committed to Massachusetts workhouses under indeterminate sentences, release to follow upon "reasonable caution or assurance to the satisfaction of the justice or court, that [the inmate] will reform." *Mass. Col. Laws,* § 2:127 [1646]; *Mass. Rec.,* 1:401; *Mass. Prov. Laws,* 1:67 [1692], 538–39 [1703], 655 [1701]; 2:183 [1720], 580 [1730]; *Plymouth Court Records, 1686–1859,* ed. David T. Konig, (Wilmington, 1978–81), 2:6; Act of Mar. 26, 1788, ch. 54, *Mass. Acts & Resolves,* 1786–87:625–26.

151. *Mass. Prov. Laws,* 1:378–80 [1699], 674 [1711], 3:108–11 [1743]; *Boston Town Records, 1729–42:*104, 230–31, 234–40, 251–52, 1742–57:150–51. By statute, counties were enjoined to choose as the master of their workhouse "an honest, fit person." *Mass. Prov. Laws,* 1:378 [1699]. The workhouse and the jail were under separate government. *Boston Town Records, 1729–42:*230–31, 1700–1728:93; *Mass. Rec.,* 5:237 [1679]. Without question, the workhouse regime was superior to the jail. In 1764 we find one Mary Robinson, in jail on suspicion of theft and near the term of her pregnancy, ordered removed to the workhouse until she had given birth, and when "in a fit condition to be removed back again to the said Gaol." *A Report of the Record Commissioners of the City of Boston, Containing the Records of the Boston Selectmen,* 1764–68:2.

152. This structure took two years to build. Some fifty-five inmates were housed there in 1741, and in a nineteen-month period between 1739 and 1741 the facility produced some £1,620 worth of merchandize for sale. *Boston Town Records, 1729–42:*251, 273. See also Gary B. Nash, *The Urban Crucible: Social Change, Political Consciousness, and the Origins of the American Revolution* (Cambridge, Mass., 1979), 188–89 and nn. Carceral institutions plainly were administratively feasible from an early date. Cf. James Stephen, *A History of the Criminal Law of England* (London, 1883), 2:92.

153. Barnes, *Evolution of Penology,* 56–63, 68–70; Robert E. Cray, Jr., *Paupers and Poor Relief in New York City and Its Rural Environs, 1700–1830* (Philadelphia, 1988), 45–47, 70–78, 94–99. Cf. Rothman, *Discovery of the Asylum,* 41 (claiming that there were few workhouses in the colonies and none in New York). In New York, workhouse inmates were to perform "hard labor," and once again care was taken to find "an able and sufficient Person" to run the facility, whose purpose would be "to teach the Sloathful Industry." *Minutes of the Common Council of the City of New York, 1675–1776* (New York, 1905), 4:305–10 [1736]; *New-York Gazette,* no. 434, Feb. 11–18, 1734, at 3. In Pennsylvania, the local records included no discussion of the function or administration of workhouses, though their purposes can be gauged by examining contemporary Quaker literature in England; see below, note 155.

154. As in England, vagrancy and criminality were closely related by the colonists, e.g., Mather, *Flying Roll,* 11–12.

155. Act of Dec. 7, 1682, in *Charter to William Penn and Laws of the Province of Pennsylvania, 1682–1700,* ed. John B. Linn (Harrisburg, 1879), 107 ff.; Barnes, *Evolution of Penology,* 31–39. The statutory record was silent on the ideological underpinnings of this code, though it would appear to have been strongly influenced by

the writings of an English Quaker, John Bellers, a landowner in Pennsylvania and close friend of William Penn, who endorsed several of Bellers's pamphlets; see *John Bellers: His Life, Times, and Writings,* ed. George Clarke (London, 1987), 5–7, 79, 250, 275. All of Bellers's structural proposals—that the death penalty be curtailed, that hard labor replace it, and that all prisons be workhouses—were incorporated into the Great Law. Bellers believed that hard labor would operate "in time [to] alter [thieves'] evil habits, to a more honest one" (54–57, 102–3, 198–201, 274, 277– 78 [quotation at 103]). A subsequent Jacksonian advocate suggested that Penn was influenced by the carceral system in Holland, where he had traveled. George W. Smith, *A Defence of the System of Solitary Confinement of Prisoners Adopted by the State of Pennsylvania* (Philadelphia, 1833), 6. On Dutch prisons, see above, note 40.

156. The repealing statute of 1718 retained hard labor as punishment for clergied felons, and for third convictions of all larcenies not made felony. *Pa. Stats. at Large,* 3:207, 212–13 [1718]. For subsequent extensions of hard labor, see also id., 4:282 [1735], 315 [1738], 388 [1743], 401 [1744], 6:452 [1765].

157. New Jersey: *The Acts of the General Assembly of the Province of New Jersey,* ed. Samuel Nevill (Philadelphia and Woodbridge, N.J., 1752–61), 1703–52:236–37 [1738], 272–73 [1741], 415–17 [1748], 1753–61:28–30 [1754]; Harry Elmer Barnes, *A History of the Penal Reformatory and Correctional Institutions of the State of New Jersey* (Trenton, 1918), 34–35, 38–40 (acts of 1681, 1700). Rhode Island: *Acts and Laws of His Majesty's Colony of Rhode Island* (Newport, 1745), 260 [1743]. Connecticut: Richard Gaskins, "Changes in the Criminal Law in Eighteenth-Century Connecticut," *Am. J. Legal Hist.* 25 (1981):335 (acts of 1752, 1773). Delaware: *The First Laws of the State of Delaware,* ed. John D. Cushing (Wilmington, 1981), 1, pt. 1:72–73 [1719].

158. *Mass. Rec.,* 4, pt. 1:257; *Mass. Col. Laws,* § 2:127 [1672]. Another statute refers to the list as encompassing "misdemeanors and evil practices," *Mass. Rec.,* 4, pt. 1:222; see also id., 4, pt. 2:394–95; *Mass. Col Laws,* § 2, 208, 236 [1672]; Powers, *Crime and Punishment,* 225–27. The criminal orientation of the workhouse in Massachusetts, as in England, was often emphasized by its physical proximity or attachment to the jail. Id., 224–25; "Records of the Courts of General Sessions of the Peace for the County of Worcester, Massachusetts, from 1731 to 1737," in *Collections of the Worcester Soc'y of Antiquity* 18 (1882):58; *Plymouth Court Records,* 1:199. In New York, suggestively, the workhouse was overseen by the criminal court of general sessions. *Minutes of the Common Council,* 4:309 [1736].

159. *Mass. Prov. Laws,* 1:67 [1692], 378–81 [1699].

160. *Mass. Rec.,* 1:177, 193; *Records of the Court of Assistants of the Colony of the Massachusetts Bay, 1630–1692* (Boston, 1901–28), 2:118, 126 [hereinafter *Ct. of Assistants*].

161. Mather's plea, contained within a sermon in 1713, was not unequivocally aimed at the province: "No doubt, a *Workhouse* would be a juster or wiser Punishment than the gallows, for some *Felonies,* which yet in several Nations are Capitally Prosecuted." Mather, *Flying Roll,* 6 (emphasis in original).

162. *Mass. Prov. Laws,* 3:479 [1749] (this statute's striking severity probably owed to the fact that the governor and his councilmen were the complaining victims [3:504–5]); *Journal of the House of Representatives of Massachusetts,* ed. Mass. Hist. Soc'y (Boston, 1919–80), 15:10, 18 [1737], 25:244 [1749], 26:8 [1749] [hereinafter *Mass. House J.*]); *Mass. Prov. Laws,* 3:498–99 [1750]. These acts resulted in actual criminal sentences to hard labor, see, e.g., id., 19:86; King v. How, Mass. Super. Ct., Jan. 1762, fols. 285–86; King v. Wheeler, Mass. Super. Ct., Sept. 1763, fol. 172; Commonwealth v. Gubtail, Mass. Sup. Jud. Ct., June 1784, fol. 197 (unpublished court records,

Mass. Archives); Hull, *Female Felons,* 112. Cf. Michael S. Hindus, *Prison and Planta-tion: Crime, Justice, and Authority in Massachusetts and South Carolina, 1767–1878* (Chapel Hill, 1980), 163 (erroneously tracing the first "authorization" of criminal incarceration at hard labor in Massachusetts to 1767).

163. One act combining ten to twenty years' hard labor in a workhouse with whipping, pillory, and mutilation for burglary was passed by the house but rejected by the council in 1762. Another act mandating whipping and seven years' hard labor in a workhouse for assault with intent to commit robbery was approved by both the house and council in 1765, but Governor Bernard declined to sign it. "Mass. Ar-chives," 47:498–99, 503–4. On the comprehensive initiative of 1765, see chapter 4, text at notes 69–79.

164. This assertion appears in Rothman, *Discovery of the Asylum,* 53. See also Kai Erik-son, *Wayward Puritans* (New York, 1966), 196–98.

165. In Massachusetts, the Body of Liberties of 1641 was drafted by Nathaniel Ward, a minister (and attorney). (A code prepared by the Reverend John Cotton was re-jected by the General Court.) Subsequently, "five of . . . the most distinguished ministers in Massachusetts served on one or more of the committees that drafted the provisions of the Code of 1648," known as the Laws and Liberties. Haskins, *Law and Authority,* 106. Likewise in Pennsylvania, the Great Law of 1682 was drafted by William Penn, author of some forty religious tracts. "The ideas and customs of the Quakers furnish the best explanation of the nature and content of their criminal code." Barnes, *Evolution of Penology,* 31–32.

166. *John Bellers,* 15–16.

167. John Calvin, *Institute of the Christian Religion,* trans. John Allen (Philadelphia, 1932), 1:263. This had also been a common theme in England; see Faller, *Turned to Account,* 54.

168. See generally Perry Miller, *The New England Mind: The Seventeenth Century* (Cam-bridge, Mass., 1939), ch. 16.

169. The social covenant, in contrast to the national covenant, bound the people not to God, but to one another. Once the people had agreed to abide by the will of God, this additional joint compact granted *government* the authority to enforce God's will.

170. Miller, *New England Mind,* 400, 411.

171. Haskins, *Law and Authority,* 210; Edmund S. Morgan, *The Puritan Dilemma: The Story of John Winthrop* (Boston, 1958), 136–37. E.g., Samuel Danforth, *The Duty of Believers to Oppose the Growth of the Kingdom of Sin* (Boston, 1708).

172. [Samuel Danforth], *The Cry of Sodom* (Cambridge, Mass., 1674), 18–23; Cotton Mather, *Pillars of Salt* (Boston, 1699), 52–58; Cotton Mather, *A True Survey and Re-port of the Road* (Boston, 1712), 42–43; Moodey, *Summary Account,* 3; Hugh Hender-son, *The Confessions and Dying Words of Hugh Henderson* [1737] (Boston, n.d.); Arthur Browne, *Religious Education of Children Recommended* (Boston, 1739), 7. As early as the seventeenth century, proposals were made, and actual legislation passed, in Massachusetts to reduce crime by influencing the environment; see Wadsworth, *Vicious Courses,* 18, 21; Faber, "Evil That Men Do," 153–54 and ch. 4. David Rothman claims that the Jacksonians, as the original environmentalists, were first to investigate the background of individual criminals, in order to discover the environmental roots of crime. Rothman, *Discovery of the Asylum,* 62–69. In fact, criminal biographies tracing the descent of offenders into crime (though often following a formulaic typology) were common in eighteenth-century Massachu-setts, e.g., *The American Bloody Register* (Boston, 1784); Tufts, *Autobiography;* John

Stewart, *The Confession, Last Words, and Dying Speech of John Stewart* [1797] (n.p., n.d.); Mather, *Pillars of Salt,* 59–111; Moodey, *Summary Account;* Henderson, *Confessions; The Last Speech and Dying Words of William Welch,* [1754] (n.p., n.d.); Masur, *Rites of Execution,* 33–39. A similar body of literature also coexisted in England; see generally Faller, *Turned to Account.*

173. "God, often presents unto the Sinner, those *Objects,* which are the *Occasions* and *Incentives* of his falling into Sin. . . . And now, what needed any more to Captivate the *Forsaken of the Lord.*" Mather, *Pillars of Salt,* 19 (emphasis in original); similarly, Browne, *Religious Education,* 7; Ezra Ripley, *Love to Our Neighbour Explained and Urged* (Boston, 1800), 24. For environmentalist rhetoric in other colonies, see Joseph J. Kelley, *Pennsylvania: The Colonial Years, 1681–1776* (Garden City, N.Y., 1980), 266, 462; John K. Alexander, *Render Them Submissive: Responses to Poverty in Philadelphia, 1760–1800* (Amherst, Mass., 1980), 62; Mohl, *Poverty in New York,* 210–11.

174. For example [Eddy], *Account,* 58–61 (making the same environmental connections in 1801, and proposing environmental legislation).

175. Haskins, *Law and Authority,* 204–6. For an eighteenth-century discussion of this theory of rehabilitation, see Solomon Stoddard, *The Duty of Gospel-Ministers to Preserve People from Corruption* (Boston, 1718), 9, 24–25.

176. Innes, "Prisons for the Poor," 72.

177. On the New Divinity, see Perry Miller, *Jonathan Edwards* (New York, 1949).

178. [Cotton Mather], *A Faithful Monitor* (Boston, 1704), 46. See also, e.g., Cotton Mather, *Methods and Motives for Societies to Suppress Disorders* [Boston, 1703] (n.p., n.d.), 7. See generally Daniel A. Cohen, "In Defense of the Gallows: Justifications of Capital Punishment in New England Execution Sermons, 1674–1825," *Am. Q.* 40 (1988):147.

179. Offenders are "Poisoned by the Contagion of Bad Examples." [Mather], *Faithful Monitor,* 54. "See whither lesser sins will lead you ever unto *greater* till at last you come to the great Transgression. . . . *Custom* of sin will take away *Conscience* of sin; & when Conscience of sin is gone, what sin is there that you are not ready for?" Mather, *Call of the Gospel* [1686] (Boston, n.d.), 87 (emphasis in original); similarly, Mather, *True Survey,* 26–28, 42–43; Henderson, *Confessions;* Aaron Hutchinson, *Iniquity Purged by Mercy and Truth* (Boston, 1769), 28; Andrew Eliot, *Christ's Promise to the Penitent Thief* (Boston, 1773), 28–29; Danforth, *Duty of Believers,* 16; Nathaniel Fisher, *A Sermon Delivered at Salem, January 14, 1796* (Boston, 1796), 17–18; Ripley, *Love to Our Neighbour,* 31. In Maryland, see *Am. Musium* 7 (1790):137. The analogy of crime to a disease fit neatly into rationalist criminology, and remained current in the Jacksonian period, e.g., *Report [on the State Prison],* 1822:6–7 (legislative document, Harvard Law Library) (also printed in "Mass. Legislative Documents," 1817–22, no. 52:1, State Library Annex); [Austin], "Book Review," 238, 246–47; [William Tudor], "Book Review," *North Am. Rev.* 13(1821):439; [Bradford], *State Prisons,* 61; Edward Livingston, *The Complete Works of Edward Livingston on Criminal Jurisprudence* (New York, 1873), 1:72. For English examples, see above, note 2.

180. *Mass. Rec.,* 1:393, 2:241; *Mass. Col. Laws,* § 2:13 [1642], 59–60 [1651]; *Ct. of Assistants,* 1:189 [1680], 2:60 [1635]; *Mass. Prov. Laws,* 1:5 (§ 4) [1692] (third conviction of burglary to be punished with death, the burglar thereby "being incorrigible"). This was a common theme in theological literature: "Sometimes in the beginning of a distemper it is easily cured, but when it is grown inveterate it rejects all means. . . . When men are habituated to do evil, it is an hard lesson to learn to do well."

Solomon Stoddard, *The Danger of Degeneracy* (Boston, 1705), 26; "*Experience* commonly discovers a *Sinner of years old* to be *hardened* beyond all recovery." "Last Speech of Hugh Stone," in Cotton Mather, *Speedy Repentance Urged* (Boston, 1690), app. 7 (emphasis in original; Mather's commentary); similarly, Browne, *Religious Instruction*, 7; Peres Fobes, *The Paradise of God Opened to a Penitent Thief* [1784] (Providence, n.d.), app. 9.

181. For example, *Mass. Rec.*, 4, pt. 1:59–60, pt. 2:449; *Winthrop Papers*, ed. Mass. Hist. Soc'y (Boston, 1929–47), 4:474; Resolve of Nov. 17, 1786, ch. 134, *Mass. Acts & Resolves*, 1786–87:413; Browne, *Religious Instruction*, 7; Faber, "Evil That Men Do," 144–54, 172–73; Masur, *Rites of Execution*, 33–37; Edmund S. Morgan, *The Puritan Family: Religion and Domestic Relations in Seventeenth-Century New England*, rev. ed. (New York, 1966), 66–78, 87–108, 139, 148, 169–73. For an English Puritan theologian's accordant view, see William Perkins, "ΕΠΙΕΚΕΙΑ, or a Treatise of Christian Equity and Moderation," excerpted in *Puritan Political Ideas, 1558–1794*, ed. Edmund S. Morgan (Indianapolis, 1965), 63.

182. On the coincidence of terminology, notice the term *overseer* in *Mass. Prov. Laws*, 3:108 [1743], and Act of Mar. 14, 1785, ch. 63, *Mass. Acts & Resolves*, 1784–85:165 (a term still current in the 1820s and 1830s, "Rules and Orders of 1823," in *Rules and Regulations*, 53–54; *Laws of the Commonwealth for the Government of the State Prison* [Boston, 1839], 38–40).

183. "Mass. Archives," 44:526, 526a, 538–39 [1765]; *Mass. House J.*, 41:186, 230 [1765]. The report of 1765 called for criminal incarceration but was independent of the subsequent move to open Castle Island. On the workhouse analogy, see also Alden Bradford, *History of Massachusetts* (Boston, 1822–29), 2:251–52.

184. Brissot de Warville, *New Travels*, 370. Likewise in Connecticut, the institution was described as a "public Gaol or Work-House." Act of 1773, *Acts and Laws of His Majesty's Colony of Connecticut in New England* (New London, 1774), 384. The analogy was also drawn in England, where similar legislation was floated in the eighteenth century. Jeremy Bentham, "A View of the Hard-Labour Bill" [1778], in *Works*, 4:7; Hanway, *Solitude in Imprisonment*, 117; Howard, *State of the Prisons*, 262–63, 265n; Radzinowicz, *History*, 1:263 n.11.

185. "[T]his mode of punishment was suggested by Sir *Thomas Moor* . . . above two centuries ago." E. Gillespy, *A Disquisition upon the Criminal Laws* [c.1793] (Northampton, Eng., n.d.), 16; similarly, [Denne], *Letter to Lord Ladbroke*, 76–77n (More, among other writers); Emlyn, "Preface," xxxiii n.*f* (More, among others). "Nor is the idea of reforming criminals, by a system of discipline, new to this country. The establishment of Bridewells and Houses of Correction, at different periods, demonstrates that such plans have been considered by our ancestors as neither visionary nor impractical." William Roscoe, *Observations on Penal Jurisprudence* (London, 1819), 129. For references to continental institutions, see *Thoughts on Capital Punishment*, 19–20, 28, 31, 38; *Means of Effectually Preventing Theft and Robbery*, 78–79.

186. Brewster, *On the Religious Improvement of Prisons*, 4–5.

187. For example, *Mass. Centinel*, Oct. 16, 1784, at 1, Jan. 5, 1785, at 3; Thomas Eddy to William Roscoe (Dec. 15, 1825), in Samuel L. Knapp, *The Life of Thomas Eddy* (New York, 1834), 321; Society for the Prevention of Pauperism, *Report on the Penitentiary System in the United States* (New York, 1822), 11–14; Smith, *Defence*, 5–9; *Letter from Edward Livingston, Esq., to Roberts Vaux on the Advantages of the Pennsylvania System of Prison Discipline* (Philadelphia, 1828), 5–6 (originally published in the *Nat'l*

Gazette). David Rothman is aware of Pennsylvania's Great Law but fails to connect it ideologically to the penitentiary. Rothman, *Discovery of the Asylum,* 59.

188. When the Englishman William Crawford toured American prisons in 1834, he encountered claims that the penitentiary was an American invention; Crawford responded with an analysis to prove that both "the suggestion" and "the example" came from England. Crawford's analysis was then answered in "Book Review," *Am. Q. Rev.* 18 (1835):459–68 (quoting Crawford at 462), reasserting the American roots of the penitentiary. This analysis, while correcting a number of Crawford's errors, ignored early English proposals for criminal hard labor and solitary confinement, as well as evidence of conscious borrowing by American advocates; see chapter 4, notes 27–28 and accompanying text, and chapter 5, note 24.

189. William Roscoe to Thomas Eddy (Feb. 20, 1819), in Knapp, *Life,* 291. Similarly, *Letter from Edward Livingston, Esq., to Roberts Vaux,* 5–6.

Chapter 3

1. David Rothman speaks of the nineteenth-century penitentiary as a "discovery." Philip Rawlings calls it a "rediscovery." David J. Rothman, *The Discovery of the Asylum: Social Order and Disorder in the New Republic* (Boston, 1971); Christopher Harding, Bill Hines, Richard Ireland, and Philip Rawlings, *Imprisonment in England and Wales: A Concise History* (London, 1985), ch. 5.

2. Evarts B. Greene and Virginia D. Harrington, *American Population before the Federal Census of 1790* (New York, 1932), 19–21; Kenneth A. Lockridge, *A New England Town: The First Hundred Years, Dedham, Massachusetts* (New York, 1970), 63–66 (quotation at 64); Darrett B. Rutman, *Winthrop's Boston: Portrait of a Puritan Town, 1630–1649* (New York, 1965), 178–80; Kenneth A. Lockridge, "The Population of Dedham, Massachusetts, 1636–1736," *Econ. Hist. Rev.,* 2d ser., 19 (1966):318. The story of Andover was similar: see Philip J. Greven, *Four Generations: Population, Land, and Family in Colonial Andover, Massachusetts* (Ithaca, 1970), 22–28, 39–40, 268–71.

3. For a similar analysis of communal criminal justice in seventeenth-century England, from which colonial punishments were derived, see Cynthia B. Herrup, *The Common Peace: Participation and the Criminal Law in Seventeenth-Century England* (Cambridge, 1987), ch. 7.

4. John Winthrop, *Winthrop's Journal "History of New England," 1630–1649,* ed. James K. Hosmer (New York, 1908), 1:310–14. The offender subject to admonition was to "be reclaimed by gentle correccion." *Records of the Governor and Company of the Massachusetts Bay,* ed. Nathaniel Shurtleff (Boston, 1853–54), 1:393 [hereinafter *Mass. Rec.*].

5. See chapter 2, text at note 175.

6. Rosemary Zagarri, "Public Confession in Seventeenth-Century Massachusetts," (unpublished paper, Yale University, 1978, on file with the author), 12–13; David H. Flaherty, *Privacy in Colonial New England* (Charlottesville, 1972), 158–59.

7. "The Effects of such a chastisement may be that the Rebuked and Censured Sinners will be reclaimed from their Sins." Cotton Mather, *Methods and Motives for Societies to Suppress Disorders* [Boston, 1703] (n.p., n.d.), 7; "[B]y the penalty of the Law inflicted on [sinners], their healing and reformation may be endeavored." Samuel Danforth, *The Duty of Believers to Oppose the Growth of the Kingdom of Sin* (Boston, 1708), 16. Additional early references to the goal of rehabilitation via public punishment are found in the text and notes following.

8. Danforth, *Duty of Believers*, 15, 23. "When a Person has thus received an *Admonition* for a Scandal, the *Private Christians* who dwell near him, reckon it their Duty, by *Visiting* of him, and by Discoursing with him, to prosecute the *good Effects* thereof upon him." Cotton Mather, *Ratio Disciplinae Fratrum Nov-Anglorum* (Boston, 1726), 148 (emphasis in original); [Cotton Mather], *A Faithful Monitor* (Boston, 1704), 23–37.

9. Commentators distinguished the physical and psychic elements of punishment. Thus a seventeenth-century writer remarked that fornication was punished "either by some public shame or smart or both as the Judges shall see the sin aggravated." "Discourse on Fornication and Theft," in "Miscellaneous, 1657–1774," 87:267 (unpublished MS, Mass. Archives).

10. Under Puritan doctrine, being disgraced might literally indicate a lack of saving grace. On the Puritan theory of manifest predestination, see Edmund S. Morgan, *Visible Saints: The History of a Puritan Idea* (New York, 1963).

11. For example, *Records of the Court of Assistants of the Colony of the Massachusetts Bay, 1630–1692* (Boston, 1901–28), 2:62, 89, 90 [hereinafter *Ct. of Assistants*]; Powers, *Crime and Punishment*, 198–201.

12. *Records and Files of the Quarterly Courts of Essex County, Massachusetts, 1636–1683*, ed. George Dow (Salem, 1911–21), 1:138 [1647]. Likewise in New York, see Julius Goebel, Jr., and T. Raymond Naughton, *Law Enforcement in Colonial New York: A Study in Criminal Procedure, 1664–1776* (New York, 1944), 515.

13. If the aggrieved recovered any portion of the goods stolen, the award was mitigated accordingly. E.g., Commonwealth v. Lisk, Mass. Sup. Jud. Ct., Feb. 1785, fols. 72–73 (two indictments) (unpublished court records, Mass. Archives); Lawrence Towner, "A Good Master Well Served: A Social History of Servitude in Massachusetts, 1620–1750" (Ph.D. diss., Northwestern University, 1954), 397–409.

14. Compare William E. Nelson, *Americanization of the Common Law* (Cambridge, Mass., 1975), 40; Towner, "Good Master Well Served," 118–19.

15. *Ct. of Assistants*, 2:126; *Records of the Suffolk County Court, 1671–1680*, ed. Zechariah Chaffee (Boston, 1933), 89, 125, 185. This policy persisted into the provincial period. *Acts and Resolves of the Province of the Massachusetts Bay* (Boston, 1869–1922), 3:926–28 [1756] [hereinafter *Mass. Prov. Laws*]. Cf. Act of Mar. 16, 1784, ch. 53, *Mass. Acts & Resolves*, 1782–83:633.

16. In England, Jeremy Bentham noted the rehabilitative potential of service to a "private master" but considered institutional hard labor superior, because then the rehabilitative objective would be "express." Jeremy Bentham, "A View of the Hard-Labour Bill" [1778], in *The Works of Jeremy Bentham*, ed. John Bowring (Edinburgh, 1843), 4:7.

17. John Winthrop described the case of a woman hanged at Boston in 1638: "After much patience, and diverse admonitions not prevailing, the church cast her out. Whereupon she grew worse; so as the magistrate caused her to be whipped. Whereupon she was reformed for a time . . . but soon after she was . . . possessed with Satan." Winthrop, *Journal*, 1:282–83. On branding practices, see Edwin Powers, *Crime and Punishment in Early Massachusetts, 1620–1692* (Boston, 1966), 180–81.

18. The earliest acts against theft, passed in the mid-seventeenth century, did however advert to the rising incidence of crime as a justification for imposing statutory penalties. *Mass. Rec.*, 3:244 [1651], 4 pt. 1:82 [1652]; *The Colonial Laws of Massachusetts*, ed. William Whitmore (Boston, 1890), § 2:12–14 [1642–52] [hereinafter *Mass. Col. Laws*]. On moral declension, see generally Perry Miller, *The New England Mind: From Colony to Province* (Cambridge, Mass., 1953).

19. [Mather], *Faithful Monitor,* 46.

20. Samuel Checkley, *Murder a Great and Crying Sin* (Boston, 1733), 15.

21. Eli Faber, "The Evil That Men Do: Crime and Transgression in Colonial Massachusetts" (Ph.D. diss., Columbia University, 1974), 369–82; Eli Faber, "Puritan Criminals: The Economic, Social, and Intellectual Background to Crime in Seventeenth-Century Massachusetts," *Persp. Am. Hist.* 11 (1977–78):83.

22. See generally George Lee Haskins, *Law and Authority in Early Massachusetts: A Study in Tradition and Design* (New York, 1960), 25–47; Carol Lee, "Discretionary Justice in Early Massachusetts," *Essex Inst. Hist. Coll.* 112 (1976):120; Faber, "Evil That Men Do," 10–30.

23. On the Child affair, see Samuel Eliot Morison, *Builders of the Bay Colony* (Boston, 1930), ch. 8.

24. Though punishment in colonial Massachusetts was in some respects more moderate than in England, that was not Child's concern. Rather, he desired "that *no greater* punishments be inflicted upon offenders than are allowed and sett by the laws of our native country." Quoted in Faber, "Evil That Men Do," 26 (emphasis added).

25. Greene and Harrington, *American Population,* 21–30; Allan Kulikoff, "The Progress of Inequality in Revolutionary Boston," *Wm. & Mary Q.,* 3d ser., 28 (1971): 393. For figures from a typical community, see Greven, *Four Generations,* 103–24, 175–79. Modern estimates of the population of early Massachusetts have relied on literary evidence, not the statistical methods that have been applied to individual townships, and are therefore extremely rough. The Census Bureau estimates that Massachusetts contained 56,000 inhabitants in 1700 and 188,000 inhabitants in 1750; according to the first federal census taken in 1790 the state then contained some 379,000 inhabitants. These figures suggest that the population of the province was doubling every thirty to forty years. U.S. Bureau of the Census, *Historical Statistics of the United States, Colonial Times to 1970* (Washington, D.C., 1976), 29, 1153, 1168. Cf. Greene and Harrington, *American Population,* 14–19.

26. Greene and Harrington, *American Population,* 123, 211–14; Lockridge, *New England Town,* 139–40 and n.2, 146–47; Kulikoff, "Progress of Inequality," 399.

27. Lockridge, *New England Town,* 400–401; Edward M. Cook, Jr., "Social Behavior and Changing Values in Dedham, Massachusetts, 1700–1775," *Wm. & Mary Q.,* 3d ser., 27 (1970):565–73; Douglas L. Jones, "The Strolling Poor: Transiency in Eighteenth-Century Massachusetts," *J. Soc. Hist.* 8 (1975):39–41; Kenneth A. Lockridge, "The Evolution of New England Society, 1630–1790," *Past & Present* 39 (Apr. 1968):62–80; Douglas L. Jones, *Village and Seaport: Migration and Society in Eighteenth-Century Massachusetts* (Hanover, 1981).

28. Jones, "Strolling Poor," 28–54; Kulikoff, "Progress of Inequality," 403 (quotation); Lockridge, "Evolution of New England Society," 73. See generally James A. Henretta, "Economic Development and Social Structure in Colonial Boston," *Wm. & Mary Q.,* 3d ser., 22 (1965):75–92; Gregory H. Nobles, *Divisions throughout the Whole: Politics and Society in Hampshire County, Massachusetts, 1740–1775* (Cambridge, 1983), 111–12; *A Report of the Record Commissioners of the City of Boston, Containing the Boston Town Records* (Boston, 1876–1909), 1700–1728:93, 97 [hereinafter *Boston Town Records*]; *A Report of the Record Commissioners of the City of Boston, Containing the Records of the Boston Selectmen,* 1716–36: 66, 108, 275 [hereinafter *Boston Selectmen Records*]; *Mass. Prov. Laws,* 4:911 [1767].

29. For impressionistic statements of the growth of crime, see *Mass. Prov. Laws,* 1:673–74 [1711], 2:5 [1715], 838 [1736], 4:488–89 [1761], 5:43 [1770]; "Mass. Archives,"

47:555 [1773] (unpublished MS, Mass. Archives); *Journals of the House of Representatives of Massachusetts,* ed. Mass. Hist. Soc'y (Boston, 1919–80), 46:108 [1770] [hereinafter *Mass. House J.*]; Grand Jury Charge, Mass. Super. Ct., 1766, 1786, in Josiah Quincy, *Reports of Cases Argued and Adjudged in the Superior Court of Judicature of the Province of Massachusetts Bay, between 1761 and 1772* (Boston, 1865), 223, 260–61; Ephraim Clark, *Sovereign Grace Displayed in the Conversion and Salvation of a Penitent Sinner* (Boston, 1773), 19; Cotton Mather, *A Flying Roll Brought Forth, To Enter into the House and Hand of the Thief* (Boston, 1713), 4, 25–29; Peres Fobes, *The Paradise of God Opened to a Penitent Thief* [1784] (Providence, n.d.), app. 7–8; *Boston Gazette,* Sept. 27, 1764, at 3, Nov. 12, 1764, at 3; *Mass. Centinel,* Oct. 16, 1784, at 1, Sept. 12, 1784, at 1. (Newspapers of the period are strewn with advertisements offering rewards for the return of stolen goods, e.g., *Independent Chron.,* July 21, 1785, at 1.) On crime in cities, see Carl Bridenbaugh, *Cities in the Wilderness: The First Century of Urban Life in America, 1625–1742* (New York, 1938), 68–73; Carl Bridenbaugh, *Cities in Revolt: Urban Life in America, 1743–1776* (New York, 1955), 110–12, 299–302 (notes available in the Oxford University Press edition only, 1971); Christine L. Heyrman, *Commerce and Culture: The Maritime Communities of Colonial Massachusetts, 1690–1750* (New York, 1984), 68 and n.28, 245–53, 337–38. Noting the concentration of offenses "in the Capital and on the sea coast," see "Report Respecting Convicts" appended to "Resolves," 1802, ch. 54 (passed) (unpublished MS, Mass. Archives); similarly, John Lathrop, *God Our Protector and Refuge in Danger and Trouble* (Boston, 1797), 8.

30. *Mass. House J.,* 46:108 [1770]; Nathaniel Sargeant, "Court Minutes" [n.d.], quoted in Linda Kealey, "Crimes and Society in Massachusetts in the Second Half of the Eighteenth Century" (Ph.D. diss., University of Toronto, 1981), 306–7. For similar examples, see Fobes, *Paradise of God,* app. 7–8; *Independent Gazetteer,* Dec. 4, 1784, at 2; "Report Respecting Convicts"; *Boston Town Records,* 1700–1728:93, 97; *Boston Selectmen Records,* 1701–15:178; Heyrman, *Commerce and Culture,* 252 (petition of 1731); Lathrop, *God Our Protector,* 8–9, 28, 30.

31. [Samuel Denne], *A Letter to Sir Robert Ladbroke . . . With an Attempt to Shew the Good Effects Which May Reasonably Be Expected from the Confinement of Criminals in Separate Apartments* (London, 1771), 3–4.

32. The following data indicate the number of convictions for property crime in the Massachusetts Superior Court, 1750–1794: *1750–54,* 14; *1755–59,* 15; *1760–64,* 35; *1765–69,* 38; *1770–74,* 58; *1775–79,* 16 [wartime]; *1780–84,* 84; *1785–89,* 259; *1790–94,* 217 (Kealey, "Crime and Society in Massachusetts," 330 [see also 326–37]; Linda Kealey, "Patterns of Punishment: Massachusetts in the Eighteenth Century," *Am. J. Legal Hist.* 30 [1986]:163). Additional statistics are compiled in David H. Flaherty, "Crime and Social Control in Provincial Massachusetts," *Hist. J.* 24 (1981):357–60; and on the statistically disproportionate crime rate in Boston, see N. E. H. Hull, *Female Felons: Women and Serious Crime in Colonial Massachusetts* (Urbana, 1987), 155–64 (see also 146–54). But note that prosecution and conviction rates are influenced by many variables besides the crime rate, such as popular sensitivity to crime. While these data indicate low absolute numbers of convictions, they also indicate dramatic proportional growth. The low absolute numbers may speak to problems of law enforcement; see below, text at note 59.

33. The statistical significance of these life histories is problematic, however. Because juries may have been less hesitant to sentence outsiders to capital punishment, transient persons may be represented disproportionately. For examples of life his-

tories, see chapter 2, note 172. See generally Daniel A. Cohen, "A Fellowship of Thieves: Property Criminals in Eighteenth-Century Massachusetts," *J. Soc. Hist.* 22 (1988):65.

34. The point is made in Bruce H. Mann, *Neighbors and Strangers: Law and Community in Early Connecticut* (Chapel Hill, 1987), 2–5. For tension among quarters in Boston, see Edmund S. Morgan and Helen M. Morgan, *The Stamp Act Crisis: Prologue to Revolution,* rev. ed. (New York, 1962), 159–60.

35. William Bradford, *An Enquiry How Far the Punishment of Death Is Necessary in Pennsylvania* (Philadelphia, 1793), 22; Francis Lieber, "Translator's Preface," in Gustave de Beaumont and Alexis de Tocqueville, *On the Penitentiary System in the United States and Its Application in France* (Philadelphia, 1833), xxii; Franklin Bache, *Observations and Reflections on the Penitentiary System* (Philadelphia, 1829), 6–7; cf. Benjamin Rush, *An Enquiry into the Effects of Public Punishments upon Criminals and upon Society* (Philadelphia, 1787), 35–36; Samuel Howe, *Report of the Minority of a Special Committee of the Boston Prison Discipline Society* (Boston, 1846), 40–41. The tendency in colonial times to view servants and slaves as classes prone to criminality may be seen as an antecedent to such notions; see Faber, "Evil That Men Do," 150–72. On the development of the concept of a criminal class in England, see Leon Radzinowicz and Roger Hood, "Incapacitating the Habitual Criminal: The English Experience," *Mich. L. Rev.* 78 (1980):1305; John Tobias, *Crime and Industrial Society in the Nineteenth Century* (London, 1967), 52–59; J. M. Beattie, *Crime and the Courts in England, 1660–1800* (Princeton, 1986), 251–52, 629, 632, 637; Clive Emsley, *Crime and Society in England, 1750–1900* (London, 1987), ch. 6.

36. Fobes, *Paradise of God,* app. 7–8; "Report Respecting Convicts"; in New York, see [Thomas Eddy], *An Account of the State Prison or Penitentiary House in the City of New-York* (New York, 1801), 58–61. Cf. chapter 2, notes 172–74 and accompanying text.

37. *Mass. Centinel,* Oct. 16, 1784, at 1 (quotation), Sept. 22, 1784, at 1; *Columbian Centinel,* June 8, 1796, at 1–2; Samuel Dexter to William Cushing (Jan. 15, 1785), in "Robert Treat Paine Papers" (unpublished MS, Mass. Hist. Soc'y); Grand Jury Charge, Mass. Super. Ct., 1768, in Quincy, *Reports,* 261. For subsequent assessments of the ineffectiveness of the old sanctions, see, e.g., Soc'y for the Prevention of Pauperism, *Report on the Penitentiary System in the United States* (New York, 1822), 48; [Gamaliel Bradford], *State Prisons and the Penitentiary System Vindicated* (Charlestown, 1821), 11–12.

38. Compare the sources cited above in note 37, Mather, *Flying Roll,* 4–6, 25–29, and the writings of English advocates of hard labor earlier in the eighteenth century. Although several of these posited the superiority of hard labor over existing punishments to control crime effectively, they lacked the alarmism of later Massachusetts tracts—a distinction of tone and emphasis, but a discernible one. See, e.g. R[ichard] H[aines], *Proposals for Building in Every County a Working-Alms-House or Hospital* (London, 1677), 7–8; Timothy Nourse, *Campania Foelix; or, A Discourse of the Benefits and Improvements of Husbandry* (London, 1700), 229; [William Hay], *Remarks on the Laws Relating to the Poor with Proposals for Their Better Relief and Employment* (London, 1735), 41; Joseph Massie, *A Plan for Establishing Charity-Houses* (London, 1758), 119.

39. *Mass. Centinel,* Sept. 22, 1784, at 1.

40. Emphasizing the low absolute numbers of convictions, David Flaherty argues that crime control remained effective throughout the provincial period in Massachu-

setts; see Flaherty, "Crime and Social Control," 339–60. I would agree that dissatisfaction did not peak until the 1780s, but Flaherty's analysis ignores earlier literary expressions of alarm and legislative reactions beginning as early as 1711; see below, notes 68ff.

41. *Mass. Prov. Laws,* 1:504. Similar provisions occasionally appeared in court records dating back to the seventeenth century. *Ct. of Assistants,* 1:189 [1680]. For an early English reference to the potential difficulty of selling convicts, see Samuel Chidley, *A Cry against a Crying Sinne* (London, 1652), 16. Cf. William E. Nelson, "Emerging Notions of Modern Criminal Law in the Revolutionary Era: An Historical Perspective," *N.Y.U. L. Rev.* 42 (1967):460.

42. *Mass. Centinel,* Oct. 16, 1784, at 1.

43. For example, Governor's Message, June 13, 1799, *Mass. Acts & Resolves,* 1798–99:639.

44. It is suggestive that the first expression of doubt about the salability of convicts in the records of the Court of Assistants involved a pair of "Incorrigible Theeves" who had threatened "if loose to burne the Town." *Ct. of Assistants,* 1:189 [1680]. A late eighteenth-century itinerant criminal related that authorities failed to sell him because "no man in his senses would purchase such kind of trumpery." Henry Tufts, *The Autobiography of a Criminal* [1807], ed. Edmund Pearson (New York, 1930), 155.

45. Lawrence Towner, "'A Fondness for Freedom': Servant Protest in Puritan Society," *Wm. & Mary Q.,* 3d ser., 19 (1962):201–19.

46. A commentator in 1818 could only ridicule the possibility of diverting young convicts from the state penitentiary: "But you say send them to some other place. Then let them be sentenced to your family." *Columbian Centinel,* Mar. 18, 1818, at 1.

47. *Winthrop Papers,* ed. Mass. Hist. Soc'y (Boston, 1929–47), 4:476.

48. Zagarri, "Public Confession," 17–18; Flaherty, *Privacy,* esp. 160–61. Likewise, the practice of "holy watching," whereby neighbors were to watch one another for signs of deviance, declined with time. Id., 151–52, 161, 169.

49. *Mass. Centinel,* Oct. 16, 1784, at 1; similarly, id., Sept. 22, 1784, at 1.

50. *Mass. House J.,* 46:108 [1770].

51. Danforth, *Duty of Believers,* 23. "Such a *Bitter Pill* as a *Reproof,* must be rolled up in the *Sugar* of *Love*. . . . When we *Reprove,* we must not let the Reproved have cause to think, that we purpose rather to *Disgrace* him, or *Deride* him, than to *Amend* him." [Mather], *Faithful Monitor,* 29–30 (emphasis in original).

52. *Mass. Centinel,* Sept. 22, 1784, at 1 (emphasis added).

53. *Mass. Centinel,* Oct. 16, 1784, at 1. For similar discussions, see Governor's Message, Jan. 30, 1793, *Mass. Acts & Resolves,* 1792–93:694; *Columbian Centinel,* June 8, 1796, at 1–2. The frequent repetition of offenses is again confirmed by life histories. See chapter 2, note 172.

54. The Jacksonian publicist Francis Lieber later connected the effectiveness of public punishment to the intimacy of the community involved: "If used with great caution and so that it does not embitter, ridicule may be advantageously used . . . everywhere where the individuals form a close community. . . . I have seen good effects of it in the army. It is not, however, to be used in civil punition, for it would assume at once the character of public dishonor." Lieber, *Popular Essays on Subjects of Penal Law* (Philadelphia, 1838), 46.

55. Recognizing the limited effectiveness of fining, see *Mass. Prov. Laws,* 1:122 [1693], 287 [1695], 3:711–12 [1754].

56. For example, *Ct. of Assistants,* 2:59.
57. See generally Josiah H. Benton, *Warning Out in New England* (Boston, 1911); Douglas L. Jones, "The Transformation of the Law of Poverty in Eighteenth-Century Massachusetts," in *Law in Colonial Massachusetts, 1630–1800,* ed. Colonial Soc'y of Mass. (Boston, 1984), 171–90. Given the demographic trends of the eighteenth century, the incidence of warning out initially rose sharply. Bridenbaugh, *Cities in the Wilderness,* 231; Cook, "Social Behavior," 569; Kulikoff, "Progress of Inequality," 399–400; Lockridge, "Evolution of New England Society," 72–73.
58. *Boston Town Records,* 1700–1728:93, 97; Lathrop, *God Our Protector,* 8; Bridenbaugh, *Cities in the Wilderness,* 231; Robert W. Kelso, *The History of Public Poor Relief in Massachusetts, 1620–1920* (Boston, 1922), 54–55; Jones, "Transformation," 174; Flaherty, *Privacy,* 173–75. For a similar observation in Pennsylvania, see John K. Alexander, *Render Them Submissive: Responses to Poverty in Pennsylvania, 1760–1800* (Amherst, 1980), 73; and in England, see William Paley, *The Principles of Moral and Political Philosophy,* 7th ed. (London, 1790), 2:289; Frank McLynn, *Crime and Punishment in Eighteenth-Century England* (London, 1989), 3–4.
59. On law enforcement in early Massachusetts, see Flaherty, *Privacy,* ch. 7. On the rise of the police in the nineteenth century, see Roger Lane, *Policing the City: Boston, 1822–1885* (Cambridge, Mass., 1967). In England, William Paley opposed the creation of a police force for political reasons, but he recognized how it would diminish the social significance of punishment: "These expedients [a police], although arbitrary and vigorous, are many of them effectual; and in proportion as they render the omission or concealment of crimes more difficult, they subtract from the necessity of severe punishment." Paley, *Principles,* 2:288–89.
60. Zagarri, "Public Confession," 18. Public confession did, however, remain a part of church discipline into the nineteenth century.
61. Kelso, *History of Public Poor Relief,* 53–60. Even after penitentiaries were erected, convicts were occasionally pardoned on condition that they leave the state. *Annual Report of the Board of Managers of the Prison Discipline Society* 2 (1827):24 [hereinafter *Prison Discipline Soc'y*]; Soc'y for the Prevention of Pauperism, *Report,* 40.
62. For an example of informal action to display an offender, see *Salem Gazette,* Dec. 28, 1784, at 3. For a later reference to this purpose of public punishment, see *Boston Daily Examiner,* Feb. 18, 1818, at 2. And in England, see Sollom Emlyn, "Preface," in *Collections of State Trials* (London, 1730), xxxvi.
63. The practice was codified in the last Massachusetts code incorporating public punishments. *Mass. Acts & Resolves,* 1784–85:134, 157, 169–70, 175, 1786–87:89.
64. *Letters and Diary of John Rowe, Boston Merchant, 1759–1762, 1764–1779* (Boston, 1903), 65 [1764]; *Recollections of Samuel Breck,* ed. H. E. Scudder (Philadelphia, 1877), 36–37. In England, see Emsley, *Crime and Society,* 214–15; Beattie, *Crime and the Courts,* 466–68, 614–16; McLynn, *Crime and Punishment,* 282–85.
65. These statutes are collected in Powers, *Crime and Punishment,* 239–40. Imprisonment was also used to facilitate the process of multiple public punishments, serving as a way-station between separate acts of punishment.
66. See chapter 2, note 162.
67. *Mass. Prov. Laws,* 1:52. This provision traces back to 1642. *Mass. Col. Laws,* § 2, at 12–13.
68. *Mass. Prov. Laws,* 1:673–74.
69. *Mass. Prov. Laws,* 2:5.
70. *Mass. Prov. Laws,* 2:838 (without benefit of clergy) ("whereas the punishments

already provided by law against stealing have proved ineffectual").

71. *Mass. Prov. Laws,* 4:488–89 (without benefit of clergy) (the previous act being "insufficient to restrain ill-minded and wicked ruffians").

72. *Mass. Prov. Laws,* 5:43 (without benefit of clergy). Several sorts of counterfeiting were also made capital offenses. Powers, *Crime and Punishment,* 307–8.

73. Douglas Greenberg has argued that a similar increase in the harshness of punishment that occurred in New York during the eighteenth century was prompted in part by a desire to imitate English solutions to the problem of crime and thus can be viewed as an aspect of the general phenomenon of "Anglicization," postulated by John Murrin to have occurred in all colonies in the eighteenth century. Greenberg, *Crime and Law Enforcement in the Colony of New York, 1691–1776* (Ithaca, 1976), 222–25; Murrin, "Anglicizing an American Colony: The Transformation of Provincial Massachusetts" (Ph.D. diss., Yale University, 1966). Nonetheless, the Massachusetts statutes made no mention of English law, and they never truly resembled the English bloody code, with its vast array of capital statutes, each directed at a specific item of property. For a recent criticism of Murrin's thesis as it applies to the law, see Daniel R. Coquillette, "Introduction: The 'Countenance of Authority,'" in *Law in Colonial Massachusetts,* xxxix–xlv.

74. On jury power in colonial America, cf. William E. Nelson, "The Eighteenth-Century Background of John Marshall's Constitutional Jurisprudence," *Mich. L. Rev.* 76 (1978):904–17; David H. Flaherty, "Chief Justice Samuel Sewall, 1692–1728," in *The Law in America, 1607–1861,* ed. William Pencak and Wythe W. Holt, Jr. (New York, 1989), 131–35. On jury nullification of capital indictments in seventeenth-century Massachusetts, see chapter 1, notes 27–29 and accompanying text.

75. For example, Mass. Sup. Jud. Ct.: Commonwealth v. Cook, Sept. 1785, fol. 180, and Commonwealth v. Baker, Feb. 1786, fol. 75. It remains possible, however, that factual matters distinguished such cases.

76. For example, King v. Robinson, Mass. Super. Ct., Aug. 1765, fols. 126–27; Commonwealth v. Mount, Mass. Sup. Jud. Ct., Aug. 1785, fols. 81–83; Commonwealth v. Coldbroth, id., Aug. 1797, fol. 240. Again, factual distinctions may have been made: on other occasions, the death penalty *was* meted out for property crime, e.g., Mass. Sup. Jud. Ct.: Commonwealth v. Grout, Aug. 1784, fol. 230; Commonwealth v. Covin, Aug. 1784, fol. 232; Commonwealth v. Dixon, Oct. 1784, fol. 316; Commonwealth v. Campbell, Feb. 1785, fols. 70–71. For a newspaper account of a case in which an alleged burglar was found guilty of housebreaking in the daytime, see *Salem Gazette,* Nov. 18, 1794, at 3.

77. See Mass. Sup. Jud. Ct.: Commonwealth v. Powers, Apr. 1785, fols. 177–78, and Commonwealth v. Titcom, Aug. 1785, fol. 80, for examples of burglary convictions punished according to the provisions of the overridden 1692 act, instead of the 1715 and 1770 acts. The 1715 act established the death penalty for burglary "any former law, usage or custom to the contrary notwithstanding." Another string of burglary cases also reached this outcome, though they appear to have involved a sort of incipient plea bargaining: defendants pleaded innocent, and subsequently entered amended guilty pleas. (On the historical origins of plea bargaining, see John H. Langbein, "Understanding the Short History of Plea Bargaining," *Law & Soc. Rev.* 13 [1979]:261.) In any event, the sentences pronounced in these cases had no statutory mandate. For example, Mass. Sup. Jud. Ct.: Commonwealth v. Joyce, Aug. 1784, fol. 231; Commonwealth v. Smith, Sept. 1784, fols. 263–64; Commonwealth v. Fanueil, Feb. 1785, fols. 75–76; Commonwealth v. Daken, Feb. 1785, fols. 67–68. For a capital

statute against counterfeiting that was not enforced, see Faber, "Evil That Men Do," 362 (see also 364). Benefit of clergy was also permitted in some cases, where not denied by statute. David H. Flaherty, "Criminal Practice in Provincial Massachusetts," in *Law in Colonial Massachusetts,* 236–39; Powers, *Crime and Punishment,* 607 n.151.

78. Leon Radzinowicz, *A History of English Criminal Law and Its Administration from 1750* (London, 1948), 1:241–43 and n.41, 256–57. Historians have debated Parliament's intent when it passed the bloody code, cf. id., 1:158–64; Douglas Hay, "Property, Authority, and the Criminal Law," in *Albion's Fatal Tree: Crime and Society in Eighteenth-Century England,* ed. Douglas Hay et al. (New York, 1975), 22–23, 56 and n.1.

79. There is some evidence of legislative dissatisfaction with the evasion of capital statutes. In 1762, two years *before* Beccaria published his denunciation of capital punishment, legislators in Massachusetts passed a bill (rejected by the council) to downgrade burglary to a noncapital offense. As the preamble complained, "[T]he Law of this Province against Burglary . . . is so severe that many Offenders escape Punishment." "Mass. Archives," 47:498–99 [1762].

80. See chapter 2, text at notes 82–85. Expansion of the capital list also violated the theoretical principle of proportionality; see *Mass. Centinel,* Oct. 20, 1784, at 1.

81. The observation that pickpockets did their briskest business at the hangings of their comrades was already current. *Independent Chron.,* Feb. 14, 1793, at 2; in England, A. G. L. Shaw, *Convicts and the Colonies* (Victoria, Australia, 1966), 41.

82. "Mass. Archives," 47:507–8 [1766], 555–58 [1773]; [William Tudor], "Book Review," *N. Am. Rev.* 13 (1821):430; Grand Jury Charge, Mass. Super. Ct., 1768, in Quincy, *Reports,* 261; *Report [on the Mass. State Prison],* 1822:1–2 (legislative document, Harvard Law Library) (also in "Mass. Legislative Documents," 1817–22, no. 52, State Library Annex).

83. *Mass. Centinel,* Oct. 16, 1784, at 1.

84. Alexander, *Render Them Submissive,* 73–76 (quotation at 73); Negley K. Teeters, *The Cradle of the Penitentiary: The Walnut Street Jail at Philadelphia, 1773–1835* (n.p., 1955), 15; Michael Meranze, "The Penitential Ideal in Late Eighteenth-Century Philadelphia," *Pa. Mag. Hist. & Biog.* 108 (1984):426–27; Bradford, *Enquiry,* 22 (noting the concentration of crime in urban areas).

85. Alexander, *Render Them Submissive,* 73–74, 180–81; Meranze, "The Penitential Ideal," 425–27; Jacques Brissot de Warville, *New Travels in the United States of America, Performed in 1788* (London, 1792), 369–70; noting generally the ineffectiveness of public punishment, see Rush, *Enquiry; Am. Musium* 6 (1789):223.

86. Act of Sept. 15, 1786, ch. 1241, *Statutes at Large of Pennsylvania from 1682 to 1801* (Harrisburg, 1908), 12:280 (preamble) [hereinafter *Pa. Stats. at Large*]. As in Massachusetts, this act was preceded by a number of new capital statutes: between 1767 and 1780, the death penalty was added to counterfeiting, arson, stealing when disguised and armed, and robbery. Lawrence H. Gipson, "Crime and Its Punishment in Provincial Pennsylvania," *Lehigh University Publications* 9 (1935):8–9. Noting a tendency toward harsher penalties throughout the century, see also Herbert W. K. Fitzroy, "The Punishment of Crime in Provincial Pennsylvania," *Pa. Mag. Hist. & Biog.* 60 (1936):268–69.

87. W. David Lewis, *From Newgate to Dannemora* (Ithaca, 1965), 3–5; Arthur A. Ekirch, Jr., "Thomas Eddy and the Beginnings of Prison Reform in New York," *Proc. N.Y. State Hist. Assoc.* 61 (1943):376; Philip E. Mackey, *Hanging in the Balance: The Anti-*

Capital Punishment Movement in New York State, 1776–1861 (New York, 1982), 63–65 (see 48–78 on the legislative history of the act).

88. Act of Mar. 18, 1785, ch. 40, *Laws of the State of New York,* 8th sess.:31. As applied, hard labor was conducted "at the public works of this city." *Independent Gazetteer,* Aug. 26, 1786, at 2. This act has often been overlooked by historians; cf. above, note 87.

89. Act of Mar. 24, 1787, ch. 65, *Laws of the State of New York,* 10th sess.:124 (quotation); Act of Feb. 6, 1789, ch. 18, id., 12th sess.:21. On the attribution of crime to strangers, see also *Independent Gazetteer,* Aug. 26, 1786, at 2; [Eddy], *Account,* 58–59 (outsiders *and* urbanization).

90. *Independent Gazetteer,* Jan. 1, 1784, at 2; Sidney I. Pomerantz, *New York: An American City, 1783–1803* (New York, 1938), 297–307; Robert E. Cray, *Paupers and Poor Relief in New York City and Its Rural Environs, 1700–1830* (Philadelphia, 1988), 78. Once again, crime rates had begun to climb in New York as early as the 1750s, and authorities had first responded by increasing resort to capital punishment. Greenberg, *Crime and Law Enforcement,* 222–23.

91. Beattie, *Crime and the Courts,* 493–94. On this act, see chapter 2, notes 41–42.

92. Jonas Hanway, *Solitude in Imprisonment* (London, 1776), 12; Paley, *Principles,* 2:287–90; Beattie, *Crime and the Courts,* 540–48; A. Roger Ekirch, *Bound for America: The Transportation of British Convicts to the Colonies, 1718–1775* (Oxford, 1987), 225–26. One English author proposed that transportees be diverted to Hudson's Bay, which he hoped would be more terrifying. But another suggested that insolvent debtors be henceforth banished to America, where they would stand a better chance of satisfying their creditors! Michael Kraus, *The Atlantic Civilization: Eighteenth-Century Origins* (Ithaca, 1949), 130, 137. Again, the new capital statutes of the bloody code can be seen as an initial, reflexive reaction to the perception of rampant crime; see Beattie, *Crime and the Courts,* 524–25.

93. The American colonies had long resented the practice of transportation; see Beattie, *Crime and the Courts,* 479–80, 505; Ekirch, *Bound for America,* 134–40.

94. 16 Geo. 3 c.43 (1776); likewise, 19 Geo 3 c.74 (1779) ("Whereas the Punishment of Felons . . . by Transportation to . . . America, is attended with many Difficulties . . . .") See also Bentham, "A View of the Hard-Labour Bill," in *Works,* 4:5.

95. Hanway, *Solitude in Imprisonment,* 12; Beattie, *Crime and the Courts,* 543–46, 554–59, 627–32. Englishmen had begun the search for punishments more potent than death long before Beccaria; see, e.g., *Hanging Not Punishment Enough* [1701] (London, 1812), and [Daniel Defoe], *Street-Robberies Consider'd* (London, 1728), 53–54. See also chapter 2, note 26. On English alarmism, see Michael Ignatieff, *A Just Measure of Pain: The Penitentiary in the Industrial Revolution, 1750–1850* (London, 1978), 82–93; Harding et al., *Imprisonment in England and Wales,* 111, 120–21; Beattie, *Crime and the Courts,* 213–35. By the same token, reform of the administration of local jails in England appears to have been spurred less by the force of John Howard's writings than by a crisis engendered by "gaol fever" epidemics in the 1780s; see Margaret DeLacy, *Prison Reform in Lancashire, 1700–1850: A Study in Local Administration* (Stanford, 1986), 70–94, 112–13. Cf. chapter 2, note 51.

96. Some early advocates endeavored consciously to export their local carceral programs to other states; see, e.g., Thomas Eddy to Patrick Colquhoun (June 5, 1802), in Samuel L. Knapp, *The Life of Thomas Eddy* (New York, 1834), 179.

97. Meranze, "Penitential Ideal," 426–27; *Independent Gazetteer,* Aug. 26, 1786, at 2; Alexander, *Render Them Submissive,* 73–74. A Massachusetts commentary urging

hard labor was also reprinted in Philadelphia. *Independent Gazetteer,* Nov. 27, 1784, at 2.

98. Both programs initially featured public hard labor, and convicts in both programs were referred to as "wheelbarrow men" (because they were chained to their wheelbarrows). Later, Thomas Eddy cited back to Pennsylvania to support a full-fledged program in New York. [Eddy], *Account,* 11–12.

99. George Taylor, *Substance of a Speech Delivered in the House of Delegates of Virginia* (Richmond, 1796), 31–32; *The Writings of Thomas Jefferson,* ed. Paul L. Ford (New York, 1892), 65.

100. Edward L. Ayers, *Vengeance and Justice: Crime and Punishment in the Nineteenth-Century American South* (New York, 1984), ch. 2.

101. The deterrence of transportation was also debated. For early discussions, see Rush, *Enquiry,* 33–34; *Boston Gazette,* Nov. 29, 1784, at 3. For subsequent debates, see James Mease, *Observations on the Penitentiary System* (Philadelphia, 1828); Soc'y for the Prevention of Pauperism, *Report,* app. 24–26; [Bradford], *State Prisons,* 61–63; "Mass. Legislative Documents," 1817–22, no. 1: 21–22 and n. (State Library Annex); *Report [on the Mass. State Prison],* 1822:5, 14–15, May 1830:15 (also in "Mass. Legislative Documents," 1830–31:67); [Tudor], "Book Review," 421–23; *Remarks on Prisons and Prison Discipline* (Boston, 1826), 26–27, 35–36 (reprinted from the *Christian Examiner,* vol. 3, no. 3); Mathew Carey, *Thoughts on Penitentiaries and Prison Discipline* (Philadelphia, 1831), 72–73; Charles Shaler, Edward King, and Thomas Wharton, "Report on Punishment and Prison Discipline," in *Journal of the Senate of the Commonwealth of Pennsylvania, 1827–1828* (Harrisburg, 1828), 2 app.:312–15 (noting that the punishment of transportation "of late years [c. 1827] has occupied a large share of public attention"); Beaumont and Tocqueville, *On the Penitentiary System,* 131–50; Soc'y for the Prevention of Pauperism, *Report,* 76–80, 96, app. 10, and answers following; "Book Review," *Am. Q. Rev.* 14 (1833):251–53; Edward Livingston, *The Complete Works of Edward Livingston on Criminal Jurisprudence* (New York, 1873), 1:33 and n. For an English criticism, see Jeremy Bentham, "Panopticon vs. New South Wales" [1802], in *Works,* 4:173. Another idea floated in Connecticut was to aggravate the harshness of traditional public punishments. Richard Gaskins, "Changes in the Criminal Law in Eighteenth-Century Connecticut," *Am. J. Legal Hist.* 25 (1981):340. Cf. Rothman, *Discovery of the Asylum,* 88 (suggesting that no alternatives were considered).

102. Governor's Message, Jan. 15, 1802, *Mass. Acts & Resolves,* 1800–1801:583.

103. It is no coincidence that the first active criminal offenses made punishable by service and hard labor in provincial Massachusetts were property-related. See chapter 2, text at notes 157–63.

104. For example, Caleb Lownes, "An Account of the Alteration and Present State of the Penal Laws of Pennsylvania," in Bradford, *Enquiry,* 92–93 (combining severity and certainty). See chapter 2, notes 105–6 and accompanying text.

105. *Mass. Centinel,* Sept. 22, 1784, at 1; Oct. 16, 1784, at 1; Governor's Message, Jan. 15, 1802, *Mass. Acts & Resolves,* 1800–1801:583–84; Answer of the House, Jan. 19, 1802, id., 479–80; Kealey, "Crime and Society in Massachusetts," 306–7. In Pennsylvania, see Soc'y for Alleviating the Miseries of Public Prisons, *Extracts & Remarks on the Subject of Punishment and Reformation of Criminals* (Philadelphia, 1790), 4 [hereinafter *Extracts & Remarks*]; and in England, see, e.g., Jeremy Bentham, "Principles of Penal Law" [MSS 1775–1802], in *Works,* 1:424, 500–501.

106. *Mass. Centinel,* Sept. 22, 1784, at 1; Oct. 16, 1784, at 1; Oct. 20, 1784, at 1. The

economic goals of penitentiaries are discussed at greater length in chapter 7.

107. For example, *Extracts & Remarks,* 3–4; Thomas Eddy to Patrick Colquhoun (June 5, 1802), in Knapp, *Life,* 179.

108. For example, Gamaliel Bradford to William Roscoe (Sept. 10, 1823), in William Roscoe, *A Brief Statement of the Causes That Have Led to the Abandonment of the Celebrated System of Penitentiary Discipline in Some of the United States of America* (Liverpool, 1827), 51; *Remarks on Prisons and Prison Discipline,* 4–5.

109. *Mass. Centinel,* Sept. 22, 1784, at 1 (quotation); id., Jan. 5, 1785, at 3 (quotation); *Am. Musium* 6 (1789):223; *Extracts & Remarks,* 4; Governor's Message, Jan. 3, 1795, *Journal of the Assembly of the State of New York,* 18th sess.:5; Taylor, *Substance of a Speech,* 7; and in the Jacksonian period, e.g., George W. Smith, *A Defence of the System of Solitary Confinement of Prisoners Adopted by the State of Pennsylvania* (Philadelphia, 1833), 5; Soc'y for the Prevention of Pauperism, *Report,* 80–83; John Reynolds, *Recollections from Windsor Prison* (Boston, 1834), 5–6; *Letters on the Pennsylvania System of Solitary Imprisonment,* 2d ed. (Philadelphia, 1837), 30; "Book Review," *N. Am. Rev.* 43 (1836):315. Cf. chapter 2, note 50.

110. In England this same duality of perspective often appeared in the writings of philanthropists, which may help to account for their compatibility with the more strictly secular-minded rationalists, e.g., Hanway, *Solitude in Imprisonment,* 4 ("humane and effectual"); *Gentleman's Mag.,* quoted in Beattie, *Crime and the Courts,* 630. The duality also appeared occasionally in the writings of early workhouse advocates, e.g., H[aines], *Proposals,* 7 ("Christian and effectual"). Cf. Beattie, *Crime and the Courts,* 614–16, 630–31, and Ignatieff, *A Just Measure of Pain,* 91, suggesting the rise of an independent moral scruple against physical abuse. But in America the movement to abandon corporal punishment in other settings, such as schools and the military, did not appear until later in the nineteenth century. See generally Myra C. Glenn, *Campaigns against Corporal Punishment* (Albany, 1984).

111. *Mass. Prov. Laws,* 2:756 (quotation) [1735], 3:108 [1734]; *N.Y. Gazette,* no. 434, Feb. 11–18, 1734, at 3; Gary B. Nash, "Poverty and Poor Relief in Pre-Revolutionary Philadelphia," *Wm. & Mary Q.* 3d ser., 33 (1976):3.

112. Michel Foucault, *Discipline and Punish: The Birth of the Prison* (New York, 1977), 57–65, 126–31; Ignatieff, *A Just Measure of Pain,* 21–24, 88–90, 105; Paul Takagi, "The Walnut Street Jail: A Penal Reform to Centralize the Power of the State," *Fed. Probation* 39, pt. 4 (1975):18.

113. The penitentiary in Massachusetts did not isolate "political" offenders, as had on occasion the traditional jails; see chapter 1, note 41 and accompanying text. Though the Castle Island Act was passed during the political tensions that foreshadowed Shays's Rebellion, the penitentiary played no role in its suppression. The rebels in Shays's Rebellion (known as Regulators) were again imprisoned in county jails. Not one sentence to Castle Island appeared in the court minutes. Mass. Sup. Jud. Ct., 1786, fols. 204–6; 1787, fols. 59–66, 76–81, 101–2, 122–26, 241–42, 259–61; Robert J. Taylor, *Western Massachusetts in the Revolution* (Providence, 1954), 164–65. During the political crisis of 1798, the Federalists who controlled Massachusetts saw fit to close the Castle Island prison, even as they began to hand down indictments for sedition. Amid the American Reign of Terror, Massachusetts made do with no penitentiary at all. See generally John C. Miller, *The Federalist Era, 1798–1801* (New York, 1960), 102, 126–28, 228–50. Cf. Ignatieff, *A Just Measure of Pain,* 119–23, 160–62, 174 (political prisoners in English penitentiaries).

114. "Mass. Archives," 44:538–39 [1765]; "Report Respecting Convicts"; Governor's Message, Jan. 13, 1804, *Mass. Acts & Resolves,* 1802–3:980–81; Answer of the House,

Jan. 18, 1804, id., 875; "Mass. Legislative Documents," 1817–22, no. 2:1–2; discussing the advantages of centralization in other states, see Bradford, *Enquiry,* 45; *A View of the New-York State Prison in the City of New-York* (New York, 1815), 50. Centralization on these grounds had likewise been urged by prior workhouse advocates. Josiah Child, *A New Discourse of Trade* (London, 1693), 77–78; Massie, *Plan,* 112–14; H[aines], *Proposals,* 8. Nonetheless, decentralized incarceration was tried briefly in Massachusetts in the late 1790s and revived for petty offenders in 1819; the idea remained under advisement as late as the 1820s. See chapter 5, notes 12, 83 and accompanying text; *Columbian Centinel,* Nov. 22, 1823, at 1; for proposals elsewhere, see "Memorial," Jan. 12, 1818, in Negley K. Teeters, *They Were in Prison: A History of the Pennsylvania Prison Society, 1787–1937* (Philadelphia, 1937), 456; Henry Zouch, *Observation upon a Bill Now Depending in Parliament* (London, 1779), 13–14.

115. Stephen Burroughs, *Memoirs of the Notorious Stephen Burroughs* [1798] (New York, 1924), 135.

116. The penitentiary operated "to seclude the criminals from their former associates," so that they would subsequently evade "the community of convicts." *Prison Discipline Soc'y* 3 (1828):66 (quotation); id. 6 (1831):70 (quotation); "Remarks on the Massachusetts State Prison," in *Rules and Regulations for the Government of the Massachusetts State Prison Adopted by the Board of Directors* (Boston, 1823), 21; Howe, *Report of a Minority,* 40–41; Bache, *Observations and Reflections,* 6–7. For similar rhetoric in England, see chapter 2, note 93. Such ideas emerged naturally out of environmental theories of crime but also out of a changing social and demographic landscape.

117. Mather, *Ratio Disciplinae,* 141 (emphasis omitted; see also 148). This theme traces to the outset of settlement. For additional examples, see *Mass. Rec.,* 1:406–7; Faber, "Evil That Men Do," 217–18; Charles Chauncy, *The Horrid Nature and Enormous Guilt of Murder* (Boston, 1754), 21–22; Nathan Strong, *The Reasons and Design of Public Punishment* (Hartford, 1777), 9; Powers, *Crime and Punishment,* 199. In Pennsylvania, see Joseph J. Kelley, *Pennsylvania: The Colonial Years, 1681–1776* (Garden City, 1980), 83.

118. Bentham, "Principles of Penal Law," in *Works,* 1:404.

119. William Eden, *Principles of Penal Law* (London, 1771), 50. Criticizing transportation on the same ground, see Paley, *Principles,* 2:289–90, and Bentham, "Panopticon vs. New South Wales," in *Works,* 4:174.

120. For commentary expressly rejecting hard labor in prison in favor of public hard labor, see *Thoughts on Capital Punishment* (London, 1770), 2; David Brion Davis, *The Problem of Slavery in the Age of Revolution, 1770–1783* (Ithaca, 1975), 252–53; "Observations on Capital Punishment," *Am. Musium* 4 (1788):445; Beattie, *Crime and the Courts,* 524n; Eden, *Principles,* 33–34, 50 (Eden nonetheless helped to draft England's Penitentiary Act of 1779); William Smith, *Mild Punishments Sound Policy* (London, 1777), 19–20, 29–32, 36, 39 (public hard labor contrasted with incarceration in jail). This idea remained under consideration as late as the 1820s; see Soc'y for the Prevention of Pauperism, *Report,* app. 10; [Tudor], "Book Review," 423; Eugene E. Doll, "Trial and Error at Allegheny: The Western State Penitentiary, 1818–1838," *Pa. Mag. Hist. & Biog.* 81 (1957):3, 12.

121. The original draft of the bill establishing public hard labor in Pennsylvania in 1786 had called for carceral labor. It was changed at the urging of the chief justice. On the legislative history, see Mease, *Observations,* 61n. The final bill cited explicitly the aim of general deterrence. Act of Sept. 15, 1786, ch. 1241, *Pa. Stats. at Large,* 12:280 (preamble). A bill calling for public hard labor was narrowly defeated by the

Virginia legislature in 1787, see *The Papers of Thomas Jefferson,* ed. Julian P. Boyd (Princeton, 1950), 2:492–507, 11:152.

122. A Student of Politics, *Proposals to the Legislature for Preventing the Frequent Executions and Exportations of Convicts* (London, 1754), 26. This theme traces back to Thomas More and was adopted by Beccaria; see Thomas More, *Utopia* [1516], trans. Paul Turner (London, 1972), 105; Cesare Beccaria, *On Crimes and Punishments,* ed. Henry Paolucci (Indianapolis, 1963), 47–50. For additional examples, see William Webster, *A Casuistical Essay on Anger and Forgiveness* (London, 1750); 64; Shaw, *Convicts and the Colonies,* 42; Beattie, *Crime and the Courts,* 523; Radzinowicz, *History,* 1:475; *Papers of Thomas Jefferson,* 2:493; *Independent Gazetteer,* Aug. 26, 1786, at 2; *Mass. Centinel,* Oct. 20, 1784, at 1; *Independent Chron.,* Feb. 14, 1793, at 2; Meranze, "Penitential Ideal," 425; also suggesting public hard labor, see *Mass. Centinel,* Oct. 16, 1784, at 1.

123. Rush, *Enquiry,* 4–5 (quotation); Soc'y for the Prevention of Pauperism, *Report,* app. 21, 71, 73; Robert Turnbull, *A Visit to the Philadelphia Prison* (London, 1797), 6–7 (first published in the *Charleston Gazette*); Act of April 5, 1790, ch. 1516, *Pa. Stats. at Large,* 13:511 (preamble) (notice the rapid evolution of legislative views; cf. above, note 121); Bentham, "Principles of Penal Law," in *Works,* 1:441. For another aspect of this debate, see chapter 6, text at notes 123–31.

124. [Bradford], *State Prisons,* 7. Cf. *Boston Daily Examiner,* Feb. 18, 1818, at 2; Josiah Quincy, *A Municipal History of the Town and City of Boston* (Boston, 1852), 29.

125. *Pa. Const.* (1776), § 30. Also noting the utility of visitors for this purpose, see Shaler, King, and Wharton, "Report," 325. Cf. advocates who opposed this practice on the ground that it would counteract rehabilitation. Thomas Eddy, *Communication to Stephen Allen* (New York, 1823), 4; Howe, *Report of the Minority,* 46–48 (expressly comparing this practice to the pillory).

126. The passage continued: "Buildings employed for this purpose ought therefore to have a character of seclusion and restraint, which should take away all hope of escape, and should say, 'this is the dwelling place of crime.'" Bentham, "Principles of Penal Law," in *Works,* 1:424, 498–99; see also Bentham, "Panopticon vs. New South Wales," in *Works,* 4:174; Bentham, "A View of the Hard-Labour Bill," in *Works,* 4:32. Jonas Hanway was first to suggest this theme; see Hanway, *The Defect of Police the Cause of Immorality* (London, 1775), 223 (reissued in 1780 under the title *The Citizen's Monitor*). For later references to the exemplarity of prison architecture, see Livingston, *Complete Works,* 1:60, 548–49, 568; *A View and Description of the Eastern Penitentiary of Pennsylvania* (Philadelphia, 1830), 2–3. An ideological antecedent of dramatic prison architecture was the practice of posting cautionary inscriptions over workhouse doors, e.g., in England, Sidney Webb and Beatrice Webb, *English Prisons under Local Government* (London, 1922), 13n, and in colonial Massachusetts, *Boston Town Records,* 1729–42:234. On continuing interest in inscriptions, see Bentham, "View of the Hard-Labour Bill," in *Works,* 4:32; Ignatieff, *A Just Measure of Pain,* 102; and Shaler, King, and Wharton, "Report," 325. The New Jersey penitentiary bore such an inscription. Harry Elmer Barnes, *A History of the Penal Reformatory and Correctional Institutions of the State of New Jersey* (Trenton, 1918), 59–60.

127. Simultaneously, advocates developed theoretical means of instilling general deterrence alternative to limited visual spectacles. One advocate suggested that convicts could be counted on to spread tales of the hardship of incarceration after their release. Proposals were also made to disseminate printed accounts of the routine of incarceration (and to publish the names of convicts, for specific deterrence) in

newspapers. Shaler, King, and Wharton, "Report," 325; Soc'y for the Prevention of Pauperism, *Report,* app. 48; "Observations on Capital Punishment," *Am. Musium* 4 (1788):445 (denying the utility of newspaper accounts because not enough people read them). A more fundamental challenge to the primacy of visual spectacles was made by Benjamin Rush, who, without denying their utility, asserted that secret punishment would inspire even *greater* fear, because "the human mind is disposed to exaggerate every thing that is removed at a distance from it . . . and to magnify such things as are *secret.*" Rush, *Enquiry,* 18 (emphasis in original).

128. [Bradford], *State Prisons,* 8–9, 46; Josiah Quincy, *Remarks on Some of the Provisions of the Laws of Massachusetts Affecting Poverty, Vice, and Crime* (Cambridge, Mass., 1822), 26–28; "Mass. Legislative Documents," Senate 1831:527–29; Howe, *Report of a Minority,* 47–48. More fundamentally, William Roscoe challenged the justice of taking general deterrence into consideration when establishing punishments. This, he said, was tantamount to punishing the criminal "for unperpetrated, or, in other works, *imaginery crimes.*" Roscoe, *Observation on Penal Jurisprudence, Part III* (London, 1825), 44 (emphasis in original); also on this subject, see Roscoe, *Observations on Penal Jurisprudence* (London, 1819), 13–20; Roscoe, *Additional Observations on Penal Jurisprudence* (London, 1823), 7–9; cf. [James Austin], "Book Review," *N. Am. Rev.* 10 (1829):240–41.

129. Rothman, *Discovery of the Asylum,* 79, 89–90, 107.

130. Gideon Haynes, *Pictures from Prison Life: An Historical Sketch of the Massachusetts State Prison* (Boston, 1870), 24–25, 37; Act of Mar. 14, 1806, ch. 113, *Mass. Acts & Resolves,* 1804–5:549; "Minutes of the Meetings of the Board of Visitors/Directors/ Inspectors, 1805–1879," 1:n.p. (Dec. 4, 1811), 2:142–43 (June 30, 1821) (unpublished MS, Mass. Archives). Similar punishments had been authorized within the Boston workhouse. *Boston Town Records,* 1729–42:239. In New York, see Lewis, *From Newgate to Dannemora,* 63.

131. Shaler, King, and Wharton, "Report," 327 (quotation).

Chapter 4

1. Such a connection has been posited by David Rothman, who argues that "independence in this new world made the time and place right for reform," by bringing Americans a repugnance for old English institutions, the political freedom to replace them, and a newfound adherence to "revolutionary ideals." "Even at the close of the colonial period," he asserts, "there was no reason to think that the prison would soon become central to criminal punishment." Rothman, *The Discovery of the Asylum: Social Order and Disorder in the New Republic* (Boston, 1971), 56, 59–61. Edward Ayers argues more narrowly that republicanism was "the core of the ideology that made the penitentiary seem logical, even essential," and he contends that debate over the merits of the carceral institution was "in effect a debate over the meaning of republican government." Edward L. Ayers, *Vengeance and Justice: Crime and Punishment in the Nineteenth-Century American South* (New York, 1984), 35–36, 40 (see generally 34–49). See also Louis P. Masur, *Rites of Execution: Capital Punishment and the Transformation of American Culture* (New York, 1989), ch. 3, and Louis P. Masur, "The Revision of the Criminal Law in Post-Revolutionary America," *Crim. Just. Hist.* 8 (1987):2, emphasizing the impact of the Revolution on the movement against capital punishment. Tracing the rise of the prison to the process of "state formation" rather than to republicanism per se, see Pieter Spierenburg, "From Amsterdam to Auburn: An Explanation for the Rise of the Prison

in Seventeenth-Century Holland and Nineteenth-Century America," *J. Soc. Hist.* 20 (1987):439.

2. For a general introduction to the problem, see Jackson Turner Main, "The Results of the American Revolution Reconsidered," *Historian* 31 (1969):539. For discussions of the problem focusing on legal development, see Daniel R. Coquillette, "Introduction: The 'Countenance of Authoritie,' " in *Law in Colonial Massachusetts, 1630–1800,* ed. Colonial Soc'y of Mass. (Boston, 1984), xlv–lvi; David H. Flaherty, "The Enlightenment and the Reform of American Criminal Law," *Illuminismo e dottrine penali* 10 (1990):501.

3. Donald Veall, *The Popular Movement for Law Reform, 1640–1660* (Oxford, 1970), 78–96. Similarly in France, "The four major spurts in penal reforms directly followed the four revolutions in the period under consideration—1798, 1830, 1848, and 1871." Patricia O'Brien, *The Promise of Punishment: Prisons in Nineteenth-Century France* (Princeton, 1982), 20.

4. Mark De Wolf Howe, "The Process of Outlawry in New York: A Study of the Selective Reception of English Law," in *Essays in the History of Early American Law,* ed. David H. Flaherty (Chapel Hill, 1969), 435–38; *The Papers of Thomas Jefferson,* ed. Julian P. Boyd (Princeton, 1950), 2:305–24; *The Writings of Thomas Jefferson,* ed. Paul L. Ford (New York, 1892), 1:57–66.

5. Draft of Resolve, Nov. 29, 1780, in "Cushing Papers," pt. 2 (unpublished MS, Mass. Hist. Soc'y). For a later reference to the commission's work, see Governor's Communication to Senate & House, June 4, 1807, in "James Sullivan Papers," pt. 2 (unpublished MS, Mass. Hist. Soc'y). The original members of the commission were James Bowdoin, William Cushing, Robert Treat Paine, John Pickering, Nathaniel Sargeant, David Sewell, and James Sullivan. Subsequently, Samuel Dexter joined the commission. Samuel Dexter to William Cushing (Jan. 15, 1785), in "Robert Treat Paine Papers" (unpublished MS, Mass. Hist. Soc'y.).

6. James Bowdoin to William Cushing (Dec. 22, 1780), in "Cushing Papers," pt. 2; Commission papers in "Robert Treat Paine Papers."

7. Order of Nov. 1, 1784, in "Robert Treat Paine Papers." For additional references to the commission's activities in 1785, see William Cushing to David Sewell (Dec. 1, 1785), and David Sewell to William Cushing (Dec. 22, 1785), in "Cushing Papers," pt. 2.

8. For example, *Columbian Centinel,* June 4, 1796, at 1; "Report of the Board of Inspectors of the Prison for the City and County of Philadelphia in the Year 1791," in William Roscoe, *Observations on Penal Jurisprudence* (London, 1819), app. 2; Robert Turnbull, *A Visit to the Philadelphia Prison* (London, 1797), 10; [Thomas Eddy], *An Account of the State Prison or Penitentiary House, in the City of New-York* (New York, 1801), 15, 56. Such descriptions remained current as late as the 1830s, e.g. [Gamaliel Bradford], *State Prisons, and the Penitentiary System Vindicated* (Charlestown, 1821), 4–5; *Mass. Resolves,* Jan. 1822:396; id., 1828–31:23, 222; id., 1832–34:277, 280. Not everyone was enchanted with the prospect of social experiments, however. One opponent of the new punishment in Pennsylvania complained that "Experiments in philosophy are very proper. . . . But I never before heard of an *experimental* law." *Independent Gazetteer,* Nov. 11, 1786, at 2 (emphasis in original).

9. On the notion of the Republic as a political experiment, see Gordon S. Wood, *The Creation of the American Republic, 1776–1787* (New York, 1969), 226–27. On postrevolutionary experimentalism generally, see Edmund S. Morgan, "Challenge and Response: Reflections on the Bicentennial," in *The Challenge of the American Revo-*

lution (New York, 1976), 196. The mood of general experimentalism was noticed contemporaneously; see, e.g., Soc'y for the Prevention of Pauperism, *Report on the Penitentiary System in the United States* (New York, 1822), 12.

10. *Mass. Centinel,* Jan. 5, 1785, at 3 (quotation); *Columbian Centinel,* June 1, 1796, at 1; Governor's Message, Jan. 3, 1795, *Journal of the Assembly of the State of New-York,* 18th sess.:5; Soc'y for the Prevention of Pauperism, *Report,* 12. On the evolution of American attitudes toward England, see Edmund S. Morgan, "The Puritan Ethic and the American Revolution," in *Challenge of the American Revolution,* 103–8.

11. Francis Aumann, "The Influence of English and Civil Law Principles upon the American Legal System during the Critical Post-Revolutionary Period," *U. Cin. L. Rev.* 12 (1938):289; see also Peter Stein, "The Attraction of the Civil Law in Post-Revolutionary America," *U. Va. L. Rev.* 52 (1966):403. Interest in other legal systems preceded the Revolution, however. Daniel R. Coquillette, "Justinian in Braintree: John Adams, Civilian Learning, and Legal Elitism, 1758–1775," in *Law in Colonial Massachusetts, 1630–1800,* 359.

12. One may also speculate that the process of political union encouraged the *spread* of the penitentiary, once the movement began. By confederating, American states gained a greater awareness of, and interest in, innovations in other states. It seems doubtful that the penitentiary would have advanced so rapidly from code to code had the Eastern seaboard remained a patchwork of quarrelsome colonies. On the problem of legal borrowing, see generally George L. Haskins and Samuel E. Ewing, "The Spread of Massachusetts Law in the Seventeenth Century," in *Essays,* ed. Flaherty, 186; George L. Haskins, "Influences of New England Law on the Middle Colonies," *Law & Hist. Rev.* 1 (1983):238.

13. Soc'y for the Prevention or Pauperism, *Report,* 11–14 (quotation at 14); [Eddy], *Account,* 8–9; Turnbull, *Visit,* 5–6; William Bradford, *An Enquiry How Far the Punishment of Death Is Necessary in Pennsylvania* (Philadelphia, 1793), 14–20.

14. On this power, see generally Joseph H. Smith, *Appeals to the Privy Council from the American Plantations* (New York, 1950), ch. 9; Elmer B. Russell, *The Review of American Colonial Legislation by the King in Council* (New York, 1915).

15. These were issued to various colonies between 1682 and 1728. *Royal Instructions to British Colonial Governors, 1670–1776,* ed. Leonard W. Labaree (New York, 1930), 342–43.

16. Edwin Powers, *Crime and Punishment in Early Massachusetts, 1620–1692* (Boston, 1966), 303–5. The Privy Council affirmatively approved both acts. *Acts and Resolves of the Province of Massachusetts Bay* (Boston, 1869–1922), 3:504 [hereinafter *Mass. Prov. Laws*].

17. Fifty-three of the 104 acts that comprised the Great Law were disallowed. Lawrence H. Gipson, "Crime and Its Punishment in Provincial Pennsylvania," *Lehigh U. Publications* 9 (1935):7.

18. See the references above in note 13. David Rothman repeats this myth; see Rothman, *Discovery of the Asylum,* 59.

19. Gipson, "Crime and Its Punishment," 6–7; Herbert Fitzroy, "The Punishment of Crime in Provincial Pennsylvania," *Pa. Mag. Hist. & Biog.* 60 (1936):247–50 and n.24.

20. The attorney general's report is preserved in the statutory record. *Statutes at Large of Pennsylvania from 1692 to 1801* (Harrisburg, 1808), 2:479–97.

21. Gipson, "Crime and Its Punishment," 7–9; Fitzroy, "Punishment of Crime," 250–52; Harry Elmer Barnes, *The Evolution of Penology in Pennsylvania* (Indianapolis, 1927), 37–39.

22. See, e.g., the Declaration of Independence, which lists many other "legal" griev-
    ances. John Reid contrasts colonial American contentment with their criminal law
    with Irish discontent. John Phillip Reid, *In a Defiant Stance: The Conditions of Law
    in Massachusetts Bay, the Irish Comparison, and the Coming of the American Revo-
    lution* (University Park, Pa., 1977), 25, 65.

23. In Massachusetts, fewer than 1 percent of the province's acts were disallowed during
    the eighteenth century. Powers, *Crime and Punishment,* 607 n.141.

24. See generally chapter 1, notes 1–32 and accompanying text.

25. See chapter 2, notes 2–48 and accompanying text.

26. See the references above, note 10.

27. On communication with John Howard and references to his ideas, see *Letters of
    Benjamin Rush,* ed. Lyman H. Butterfield (Princeton, 1951), 1:417, 441, 515, 517, 526–
    28; Benjamin Rush, *An Enquiry into the Effects of Public Punishments upon Criminals
    and upon Society* (Philadelphia, 1787), 26; Bradford, *Enquiry,* 70–71 n.13; Roberts
    Vaux, *Notices of the Original and Successive Efforts to Improve the Discipline of the
    Prison of Pennsylvania* (Philadelphia, 1826), 24–25; Negley K. Teeters, *They Were In
    Prison: A History of the Pennsylvania Prison Society, 1787–1937* (Philadelphia, 1937),
    34–41. See also Michael Meranze, "The Penitential Ideal in Late Eighteenth-Century
    Philadelphia," *Pa. Mag. Hist. & Biog.* 108 (1984):434 and nn.

28. For early reprints of English tracts on prisons, see, e.g., Soc'y for Alleviating the
    Miseries of Public Prisons, *Extracts & Remarks on the Subject of Punishment and
    Reformation of Criminals* (Philadelphia, 1790), 5–23; *Am. Musium* 6 (1789):223–
    26, 456–58. New York's first penitentiary, Newgate, was named after the prison in
    London. W. David Lewis, *From Newgate to Dannemora: The Rise of the Peniten-
    tiary in New York, 1796–1848* (Ithaca, 1965), 5. On the use of English pamphlets
    and transatlantic correspondence generally, see Teeters, *They Were in Prison,* 30–
    41, 487–506; Samuel L. Knapp, *The Life of Thomas Eddy* (New York, 1834), 274–93,
    310–20. Among English administrative proposals, Bentham's Panopticon scheme
    (embodying the "inspection principle") was widely considered in America and to
    some extent adopted in New York and Pennsylvania. Teeters, *They Were in Prison,*
    496; Barnes, *Evolution of Penology,* 139; *Letter from Gershom Powers in Answer to
    a Letter of the Honorable Edward Livingston, in Relation to the Auburn State Prison*
    (Albany, 1829), 14–15 and n; in Massachusetts, see *Columbian Centinel,* Jan. 19, 1822;
    [Bradford], *State Prisons,* 20. See also chapter 5, note 24, and J. Thorsten Sellin,
    "The Origins of the 'Pennsylvania System of Prison Discipline,' " in *Penology: The
    Evolution of Corrections in America,* ed. George G. Killinger and Paul F. Cromwell
    (St. Paul, 1973), 12.

29. Elizabeth G. Brown, *British Statutes in American Law, 1776–1836* (Ann Arbor, 1964),
    38; Lawrence M. Friedman, *A History of American Law,* rev. ed. (New York, 1985),
    107–15; *Writings of Thomas Jefferson,* ed. Ford, 1:64–65.

30. William E. Nelson, *Americanization of the Common Law: The Impact of Legal
    Change on Massachusetts Society, 1760–1830* (Cambridge, Mass., 1975), 67; James
    Ely, "American Independence and the Law: A Study of Post-Revolutionary South
    Carolina Legislation," *Vanderbilt L. Rev.* 26 (1973):950–51; *The Law Practice of Alex-
    ander Hamilton,* ed. Julius Goebel, Jr. (New York, 1964), 1:8–9.

31. The continuity of colonial law was achieved in most states by express statute or by
    constitutional provision. Brown, *British Statutes.* See, e.g., *Mass. Const.* (1780), pt. 2,
    ch. 6, art. 6.

32. On the transformation of American political ideology, see generally Wood, *Creation*

of the American Republic; Bernard Bailyn, *The Ideological Origins of the American Revolution* (Cambridge, Mass., 1967); J. G. A. Pocock, *The Machiavellian Moment: Florentine Political Thought and the Atlantic Republican Tradition* (Princeton, 1975).

33. For example, Governor's Message, Jan. 30, 1793, *Mass. Acts & Resolves,* 1792–93:694 (quotation); Answer of the House, Feb. 15, 1793, id., 1792–93:242; *Mass. Centinel,* Jan. 5, 1785, at 3; Eddy, *Account,* 9.

34. For example [Benjamin Austin], "Observations on the Pernicious Practice of the Law" [1786], reprinted in *Am. J. Legal Hist.* 13 (1969):241, 257.

35. Quoted in Wood, *Creation of the American Republic,* 55–56.

36. Quoted in Wood, *Creation of the American Republic,* 60–61 (see also 23, 64).

37. In Thomas Jefferson's view, American law had to be "corrected, in all its parts, with a single eye to reason, & the good of those for whose government it was framed," if it was to be "adapted to our republican form of government." The notion that criminal justice should be contoured to the common good was also a cardinal principle of rationalism; see Cesare Beccaria, *On Crimes and Punishments,* ed. Henry Paolucci (Indianapolis, 1963), 8–13; Jeremy Bentham, "An Introduction to the Principles of Morals and Legislation" [1780], in *The Works of Jeremy Bentham,* ed. John Bowring (Edinburgh, 1843), 1:1–4, 81–83, 96–98. The Reverend Henry Cumings illustrated the idea with a Copernican flourish: "The public good is the attracting point, the common centre of gravity, which should confine, regulate and govern the motions of all members of society. When any fly off from this point and take an eccentric course, the coercion of the law should be used, to check their irregular motions, and reduce them back to their proper centre." Henry Cumings, *A Sermon Preached before His Honor Thomas Cushing . . . May 28, 1783* (Boston, 1783), 15.

38. For example [Eddy], *Account,* 56; *Columbian Centinel,* June 1, 1790, at 1. See also chapter 7, note 79 and accompanying text. For a more extended discussion, see Adam J. Hirsch, "From Pillory to Penitentiary: The Rise of Criminal Incarceration in the New Republic" (Ph.D. diss., Yale University, 1987), 264–69.

39. Quoted in Wood, *Creation of the American Republic,* 66. See also Meranze, "Penitential Ideal," 426.

40. For example, Benjamin Rush, *Considerations on the Injustice and Impolicy of Punishing Murder by Death* (Philadelphia, 1792), 18–19; Bradford, *Enquiry,* 5; Masur, *Rites of Execution,* 61–66.

41. Thomas Jefferson dismissed the suggestion: "The fantastical idea of virtue and the public good being a sufficient security to the state against the commission of crimes, which you say you have heard insisted on by some, I assure you was never mine. It is only the sanguinary hue of our penal laws which I meant to object to." Thomas Jefferson to Edmund Pendleton (Aug. 26, 1776), in *Papers of Thomas Jefferson,* ed. Boyd, 1:505; see also Pendleton to Jefferson (Aug. 19, 1776), in id., 1:490.

42. *Independent Chron.,* Feb. 22, 1787, at 4. Similarly, e.g., Beccaria, *On Crimes and Punishment,* 12.

43. William Symmes, *A Sermon Preached before His Honor Thomas Cushing . . . May 25, 1785* (Boston, 1785), 19–21; Moses Hemmenway, *A Sermon Preached before His Excellency John Hancock . . . May 26, 1784* (Boston, 1784), 31–33 (emphasis omitted); Samuel West, *A Sermon Preached before His Excellency James Bowdoin . . . May 31, 1786* (Boston, n.d.), 21. These themes were pervasive and were repeated by legal commentators, e.g., William Cushing, "Draft of Grand Jury Charge in York County, June, 1780," at 5–7 (unpublished MS, Mass. Hist. Soc'y); William Cushing, "Draft of Grand Jury Charge, 1783," in "Cushing Papers," 2:19–20 (unpublished MS, Mass.

Hist. Soc'y). See also Wood, *Creation of the American Republic*, 61 n.30, 66–70, 413–18. Similar lines of reasoning appeared in some rational tracts, though they were not emphasized. Cf. Bentham, "Introduction to the Principles," in *Works*, 1:21.

44. John Brooks, *An Oration Delivered to the Society of the Cincinnati in the Commonwealth of Massachusetts, July 4, 1787* (Boston, 1787), 7.

45. For example, Joseph Lyman, *A Sermon Preached before His Excellency James Bowdoin . . . May 30, 1787* (Boston, n.d.), 41–42; West, *Sermon*, 22–23; Jonas Clark, *A Sermon Preached before His Excellency John Hancock . . . May 30, 1781* (Boston, n.d.), 33; see generally Wood, *Creation of the American Republic*, 413–18.

46. *Independent Chron.*, June 21, 1787, at 1; Clark, *Sermon*, 28; Cumings, *Sermon*, 42–43; Wood, *Creation of the American Republic*, 414, 415, 417 (quotation at 414). Other manifestations, more frequently cited, were luxury, intemperance, idleness, indebtedness, and immorality—all of which were ideologically linked to propensities for crime.

47. Governor's Message, Jan. 30, 1793, *Mass. Acts & Resolves*, 1792–93:694 (quotation); William Cushing, "Draft of Grand Jury Change, 1783," in "Cushing Papers," 2:19–20.

48. For example, Cushing, "Draft of Grand Jury Charge in York County," 20.

49. Lyman, *Sermon*, 29–30, 43 (emphasis omitted); West, *Sermon*, 7; James Bowdoin, *A Proclamation for the Encouragement of Piety, Virtue, Education, and Manners, and for the Suppression of Vice* [1785] (Boston, n.d.); Cumings, *Sermon*, 11–12, 15, 43. The political threat posed by crime, and the accordant importance of effectual criminal laws, continued to weigh on Jacksonian criminologists, e.g., Gershom Powers, *A Brief Account of the Construction, Management, & Discipline &c. &c. of the New-York State Prison at Auburn* (Auburn, 1826), 33; "Extract from the Inspector's Report of January, 1824," in id., 51; [James Austin], "Book Review," *N. Am. Rev.* 10 (1820):239; [Francis Wayland], "Book Review," id. 49 (1839):18–19.

50. In Massachusetts, see, e.g., *Mass. Centinel*, Jan. 5, 1785, at 3; id., Sept. 22, 1784, at 1; id., Oct. 16, 1784, at 1; id., Oct. 20, 1784, at 1. The preamble of the Castle Island Act refers only to "the safety of the industrious inhabitants of the Commonwealth." Act of Mar. 14, 1785, ch. 63, *Mass. Acts & Resolves*, 1784–85:163. For similar legislative references, see Answer of the Legislature, Feb. 15, 1793, id., 1792–93:242; "Report Respecting Convicts" [1799] appended to "Resolves," 1802, ch.54 (passed) (unpublished MS, Mass. Archives).

51. Grand Jury Charges by Hutchinson, C.J., Mass. Super. Ct., 1765, 1766, 1768, in Josiah Quincy, *Report of Cases Argued and Adjudged in the Superior Court of Judicature of the Province of Massachusetts Bay, between 1761 and 1772* (Boston, 1865), 110, 175, 221–22, 261, 305 (quotations at 221–22).

52. For example, Charles Chauncy, *The Horrid Nature, and Enormous Guilt of Murder* (Boston, 1754), 8; Samuel Danforth, *The Duty of Believers to Oppose the Growth of the Kingdom of Sin* (Boston, 1708), 10; Noah Hobart, *Excessive Wickedness, the Way to an Untimely Death* [1768] (New Haven, n.d.), 13–14; Eli Faber, "The Evil That Men Do: Crime and Transgression in Colonial Massachusetts" (Ph.D. diss., Columbia University, 1974), 313–16.

53. William Perkins, "ΕΡΙΕΚΕΙΑ, or a Treatise of Christian Equity and Moderation," excerpted in *Puritan Political Ideas, 1558–1794*, ed. Edmund S. Morgan (Indianapolis, 1965), 60.

54. Thus a criminal was admonished in 1681 "that he do no more so offend, and become an occasion of bringing down Gods Judgmente upon the Land." *Colonial Justice in Western Massachusetts, 1639–1702: The Pynchon Court Record*, ed. Joseph H. Smith

(Cambridge, Mass., 1961), 122–23. For an example of eighteenth-century legislation espousing this notion, see *Mass. Prov. Laws,* 3:318 [1746]. Ministers continued to invoke the threat of divine wrath after the Revolution, though such admonitions were probably taken less seriously in the secular atmosphere of the late eighteenth century. Cf. Wood, *Creation of the American Republic,* 417; Edmund S. Morgan, "The Revolution Considered as an Intellectual Movement," in *Challenge of the American Revolution,* esp. 66–67, 74–75. Property crime as a means of livelihood also violated the Puritan theological doctrine of "calling," which also persisted into the postrevolutionary period; see Morgan, "The Puritan Ethic and the American Revolution," in id., 90–91, 93–94.

55. Compare Rothman, *Discovery of the Asylum,* 69, arguing that the *Jacksonian* period was one of special sensitivity to criminal activity.

56. Benjamin Rush put the case in terms any patriot could appreciate: "Personal liberty is so dear to all men, that the loss of it, for an indefinite time, is a punishment so severe, that death has often been preferred to it." Rush, *Enquiry,* 19.

57. For English, and additional American, examples of the theme, see chapter 6, note 120.

58. The issue is explored in chapter 6.

59. Wood, *Creation of the American Republic,* 70–75, cf. 418–19, 476–83. See, e.g., Aaron Bancroft, *The Importance of a Religious Education Illustrated and Enforced* (Worcester, 1793), 9–10.

60. See chapter 7, text at note 112.

61. Louis B. Wright, *The Dream of Prosperity in Colonial America* (New York, 1965); Irvin G. Wyllie, *The Self-Made Man in America* (New Brunswick, 1954), 10–13; Gary Nash, *The Urban Crucible: Social Change, Political Consciousness, and the Origins of the American Revolution* (Cambridge, Mass., 1979), 7–13, 24–25, 326.

62. The theme also had religious roots; see Eric Foner, *Free Soil, Free Labor, Free Men* (New York, 1970), 12–13.

63. John Shy, "The Legacy of the American Revolutionary War," in *Legacies of the American Revolution,* ed. Larry R. Gerlach, James A. Dolph, and Michael L. Nicholls (Logan, 1978) (citing to unpublished mobility studies).

64. J. M. Beattie, *Crime and the Courts in England, 1660–1800* (Princeton, 1986), 226–34; Douglas Hay, "War, Dearth, and Theft in the Eighteenth Century: The Record of the English Courts," *Past & Present* 95 (May 1982):esp. 135–46.

65. Masur, *Rites of Execution,* 59–60.

66. On the postwar depression, see Curtis P. Nettles, *The Emergence of a National Economy, 1775–1815* (New York, 1962), chs. 3–4.

67. James Henretta, *The Evolution of American Society, 1700–1815* (Lexington, Mass., 1973), 169.

68. See chapter 3, notes 68–72 and accompanying text.

69. *Journal of the House of Representatives of Massachusetts,* ed. Mass. Hist. Soc'y (Boston, 1919–80), 41:186 [hereinafter *Mass. House J.*].

70. Also drafted to serve on the committee were Oxenbridge Thacher, a respected lawyer and Otis ally, and Joseph Lee, who sat on the Inferior Court of Common Pleas. William T. Davis, *History of the Judiciary of Massachusetts* (Boston, 1900), 141, 155; Emory Washburn, *Sketches of the Judicial History of Massachusetts* (Boston, 1840), 221–24, 300–311.

71. "Mass. Archives," 44:526, 538–39 (the report was signed by Hutchinson) (unpublished MS, Mass. Archives).

72. *Mass. House J.*, 41:230.
73. "Mass. Archives," 44:538–39 (the concurrence is signed by A. Oliver, Secretary).
74. Samuel Dexter to William Cushing (Jan. 15, 1785), in "Robert Treat Paine Papers" (unpublished MS, Mass. Hist. Soc'y).
75. "Mass. Archives," 44:538–39.
76. *Boston Gazette,* Sept. 27, 1764, at 3; Nov. 12, 1764, at 3; Grand Jury Charge by Hutchinson, C.J., Mass. Super. Ct., 1766, in Quincy, *Reports,* 223.
77. Samuel Dexter to William Cushing (Jan. 15, 1785), in "Robert Treat Paine Papers."
78. See generally Edmund S. Morgan and Helen M. Morgan, *The Stamp Act Crisis,* rev. ed. (New York, 1963).
79. Nor did the combination of Thomas Hutchinson and James Otis bode well for the effective operation of the committee. On the gulf of animosity that separated these two politicians, see Morgan and Morgan, *Stamp Act Crisis,* 266.
80. Act of Oct. 1773, *Acts and Laws of His Majesty's Colony of Connecticut in New England* (New London, 1774), 385–9.
81. Richard H. Phelps, *Newgate of Connecticut* (Hartford, 1844), 5–9; Noah A. Phelps, *A History of the Copper Mines and Newgate Prison* (Hartford, 1845), 11–18.
82. George W. Smith, *A Defence of the System of Solitary Confinement of Prisoners Adopted by the State of Pennsylvania* (Philadelphia, 1833), 6–7 (quotation); Barnes, *Evolution of Penology,* 80–81.
83. Perversely, the Revolution may have done more to stimulate the rise of criminal incarceration in England than it did in the Republic. See chapter 3, text at notes 91–95.

Chapter 5

1. Castle Island had received special prisoners on occasion since colonial times. Edwin Powers, *Crime and Punishment in Early Massachusetts, 1620–1692* (Boston, 1966), 220–21. The initial flow of inmates after 1785 was accommodated in the existing building, but an additional "gaol" was soon constructed on the island. Governor's Message, Nov. 5, 1785, ch. 39, *Mass. Acts & Resolves,* 1784–85:756; Governor's Message, Nov. 7, 1786, ch. 78, id., 1786–87:950.
2. These were: attempted robbery; fraud; buying or receiving a convict's clothing; assisting or harboring an escapee; accessory after the fact to rape, sodomy, robbery, arson, or burglary; accessory before or after the fact to larceny; three grades of forgery; three crimes against the Massachusetts Bank; three grades of arson; and five grades of larceny. Act of Mar. 11, 1785, ch. 58, *Mass. Acts & Resolves,* 1784–85:157–58; Act of Mar. 9, 1785, ch. 52, id., 135; Act of Mar. 14, 1785, ch. 63, id., 167; Act of Mar. 15, 1785, ch. 65, id., 169–70; Act of Mar. 15, 1785, ch. 66, id., 171–74; Act of Nov. 1, 1785, ch. 21, id., 473–74.
3. Prescriptions of hard labor for buying or receiving a convict's clothing, and for assisting or harboring an escapee, were alternative to a fine only. Act of Mar. 14, 1785, ch. 63, *Mass. Acts & Resolves,* 1784–85:167.
4. Act of Mar. 15, 1785, ch. 66, *Mass. Acts & Resolves,* 1784–85:171. This act underscores the sanctional purpose of the sale into servitude, which was made *interchangeable* with hard labor on Castle Island. Convicts sent to Castle Island were required to make no restitution to the aggrieved out of prison earnings; the provision of Castle Island as an alternative to service ensured that convicts performed hard labor under one aegis or the other, not that they made satisfaction one way or another. (See the draft of the act, "Acts," 1785, ch. 66 [passed] [unpublished MS, Mass. Archives],

which expressly excused satisfaction for Castle Island inmates, a clause omitted from the printed version of the act, presumably by mistake, for no deletion was authorized in the bill of amendments.) Interpreting the provision as penal in nature, see Commonwealth v. Cleaves, Mass. Sup. Jud. Ct., Nov. 1785, fols. 324–26 (2 indictments) (unpublished court records, Mass. Archives); Commonwealth v. Andrews, *Mass. Reports* 2 (1806):13; Smith v. Drew, id. 5 (1809):513.

5. In some (usually aggravated) cases, the court ordered treble damages *and* hard labor on Castle Island, e.g., Commonwealth v. Cook, Mass. Sup. Jud. Ct., Sept. 1785, fol. 180; Commonwealth v. Baker, Mass. Sup. Jud. Ct., Feb. 1786, fol. 75 ("felonious" theft). In other cases, the court ordered hard labor without making it alternative to service, though in such instances victims may have informed the court before sentencing that they would not attempt to dispose of the convict; see, e.g., Commonwealth v. Ferrell, Mass. Sup. Jud. Ct., Feb. 1792, fol. 30. Sentences to hard labor on Castle Island also emerged out of county courts, e.g., *Plymouth Court Records, 1686–1859,* ed. David T. Konig (Wilmington, 1978–81), 4:77, 82 [1790].

6. Act of Mar. 11, 1785, ch. 58, *Mass. Acts & Resolves,* 1784–85:157.

7. The rational program espoused by Beccaria is hardly reflected in the structure of the Massachusetts code of 1785. On the contrary, Beccaria had urged an inflexible, certain scheme of penalties, which Massachusetts legislators never accepted. For a further discussion, see Adam J. Hirsch, "From Pillory to Penitentiary: The Rise of Criminal Incarceration in the New Republic" (Ph.D. diss., Yale University, 1987), 45–51.

8. For example, Mass. Sup. Jud. Ct.: Commonwealth v. Ewers, Aug. 1785, fols. 83–84 (two indictments); Commonwealth v. Cleaves, Nov. 1785, fols. 324–26 (two indictments); Commonwealth v. Tack, May 1785, fol. 222.

9. Governor's Message, Nov. 5, 1785, ch. 39, *Mass. Acts & Resolves,* 1784–85:755.

10. "The punishment of the man of *ninety-three* for a *rape,* it seems, is imprisonment for two years, and to be kept at *hard labor!* This proceeds upon a very nice calculation, a *rape* at *ninety-three* equal to *two years hard labor!*" *Mass. Mercury,* Mar. 28, 1797, reprinted in "Trivia," *Wm. & Mary Q.,* 3d ser., 36 (1979):460 (emphasis in original).

11. Governor's Message, Jan. 11, 1799, *Mass. Acts & Resolves,* 1798–99:636. Governor Samuel Adams added his endorsement in 1794. Powers, *Crime and Punishment,* 242.

12. Resolve of June 26, 1798, ch. 47, *Mass. Acts & Resolves,* 1798–99:196–97; Governor's Message, Jan. 15, 1802, id., 1800–1801:583; Governor's Message, Jan. 13, 1804, id., 1802–3:980; "Petition of a number of Prisoners confined in Concord Jail," appended to "Resolves," 1802, ch. 54 (passed) (unpublished MS, Mass. Archives); "Report Respecting Convicts" [1799], appended to "Resolves," 1802. The minute books of the Massachusetts Supreme Judicial Court reveal an abrupt cessation of sentences to incarceration beginning in the February 1799 term; such sentences did not resume until the new state prison opened in 1805.

13. For legislative documents pertinent to the construction, see chapter 1, note 84.

14. Resolve of Feb. 23, 1804, ch. 108, *Mass. Acts. & Resolves,* 1802–3:906–7. For the duo's report, see Nathan Dane and Samuel Sewall, "Report of the Comm[ittee] app[ointed] to revise penal laws and on the subject of the state prison," Feb. 16, 1805, "Senate Documents," no. 3232 (1805) (unpassed) (unpublished MS, Mass. Archives) (also printed in "Mass. Legislative Documents," 1798–1809, no. 3, State Library Annex).

15. Act of Mar. 16, 1805, ch. 143, *Mass. Acts & Resolves,* 1804–5:246 (§ 16) (servitude restricted to three years). I have found no subsequent reference to the use of servitude, despite this provision.

16. *Mass. Acts & Resolves,* 1804–5:172, 179, 202, 209, 240, 504, 517, 522, 546.
17. "Senate Documents," no. 333 (1785) (unpassed).
18. Act of Feb. 27, 1813, ch. 134, *Mass. Acts,* 1807–16:427.
19. "Senate Documents," no. 3283 (1805) (unpassed); Dane and Sewall, "Report."
20. Act of Feb. 28, 1826, ch. 105, *Mass. Acts,* 1826–28:174; *Mass. Rev. Stat.,* pt. 4, tit. 1, ch. 126, §§ 21, 23 (1836).
21. See chapter 3, notes 88–90. The act of 1796 abolished corporal punishment. Act of Mar. 26, 1796, in *Laws of the State of New-York* (New York, 1797), 3:292. Eddy commented on the decision to retain the death penalty under the act of 1796: "Great changes . . . in matters so deeply interesting to the community, should not be too suddenly made. . . . It was prudent to listen to the voice of those who advised a forbearance of further change till experience had fully ascertained the advantages and defects of the new system." [Thomas Eddy], *An Account of the State Prison or Penitentiary House in the City of New-York* (New York, 1801), 15.
22. Act of Oct. 1773, *Acts and Laws of His Majesty's Colony of Connecticut in New England* (New London, 1774), 387–88; Richard Gaskins, "Changes in the Criminal Law in Eighteenth-Century Connecticut," *Am. J. Legal Hist.* 25 (1981):334–41. As in Massachusetts, offenders subject to hard labor under the Connecticut statutes of 1783 were additionally or alternatively punishable by whipping; see *Acts and Laws of the State of Connecticut in America* (New London, 1784), 18, 24, 244–45. (Despite these acts, centralized hard labor did not get underway in Connecticut until 1790; see chapter 4, notes 80–81 and accompanying text.)
23. Act of Sept. 15, 1786, ch. 1241, *Statutes at Large of Pennsylvania from 1682 to 1801* (Harrisburg, 1908), 283–84 (§§ 4, 7) [hereinafter *Pa. Stats. at Large*].
24. In Massachusetts, see the extracts from John Howard in *Mass. Magazine* 1 (1789): 639–40; id. 2 (1790):476–78, 685–88; an edition of William Dodd's *Thoughts in Prison* (London, 1777), recommending solitary confinement, was printed in Boston in 1783. In Virginia, see *The Writings of Thomas Jefferson,* ed. Paul L. Ford (New York, 1892), 1:64–65 (taking the idea from "a benevolent society in England"). In Pennsylvania, see Thomas Beevor's account of the Norfolk "Bridewell, or Penitentiary House," expounding the rehabilitative powers of solitary confinement, in *Am. Musium* 6 (1789):223–26, 456–58, and Soc'y for Alleviating the Miseries of Public Prisons, *Extracts & Remarks on the Subject of Punishment and Reformation of Criminals* (Philadelphia, 1790), 5. The earliest American proponent of solitary confinement appears to have been Benjamin Rush: his writings on the subject date from 1787. Benjamin Rush to John Lettsom (Sept. 28, 1787) and Rush to Enos Hitchcock (Apr. 24, 1789), in *Letters of Benjamin Rush,* ed. Lyman Butterfield (Princeton, 1951), 1:443, 512. Like Jonas Hanway in England, Rush believed that a prison could "suppl[y] the place of a church and out-preaches the preacher in conveying useful instruction to the heart." Rush to Lettsom (Sept. 28, 1787), in id., 1:441. By 1788, according to Rush, "Private punishments by means of solitude and labor are now generally talked of." Rush to Jeremy Belknap (Nov. 5, 1788), in id., 1:496. A proposal for solitary confinement appeared in the earliest memorials from the Philadelphia Society for Alleviating the Miseries of Public Prisons to the Pennsylvania legislature in 1788. Negley K. Teeters, *They Were in Prison: A History of the Pennsylvania Prison Society, 1787–1937* (Philadelphia, 1937), 447, 451.
25. On the wheelbarrowmen, see Teeters, *They Were in Prison,* 22–24; James Mease, *The Picture of Philadelphia* (Philadelphia, 1811), 160–61; Caleb Lownes, "An Account of the Alteration and Present State of the Penal Laws of Pennsylvania," in William Bradford, *An Enquiry How Far the Punishment of Death Is Necessary in Pennsylvania*

(Philadelphia, 1793), 76–79; "Extract from the Diary of Ann Warder," *Pa. Mag.* 18 (1894):61; *Pa. J.,* Oct. 21, 1786, at 3; id., Jan. 27, 1787, at 3; id., Feb. 3, 1787, at 3; id., Mar. 3, 1787, at 3; Louis P. Masur, *Rites of Execution: Capital Punishment and the Transformation of American Culture, 1776–1865* (New York, 1989), 80 and n.25. This system was borrowed from the pilot project in New York; see chapter 3, notes 88, 97–98. The sobriquet referred to the wheelbarrows to which the convicts were chained.

26. Act of Apr. 5, 1790, ch. 1516, *Pa. Stats. at Large,* 13:515 (§ 7). (The wheelbarrow law of 1786 contained a hint of this idea; see act of Sept. 15, 1786, ch. 1241; id., 12:285 [§ 8].) The provision of 1790 was clarified under a subsequent statute mandating that all persons convicted of crimes previously capital but now punishable by imprisonment serve between a twelfth and half of their terms in solitary confinement. Act of Apr. 22, 1794, ch. 1777, id., 15:178 (§§ 10–11). But sentences to solitary confinement appear to have been few in the 1790s. Negley K. Teeters, *The Cradle of the Penitentiary: The Walnut Street Jail at Philadelphia, 1773–1835* (n.p., 1955), 41.

27. Lownes, "Account." This pamphlet was by and large descriptive and did not contain an elaboration of the underlying ideology of reclamation. Solitary confinement at Walnut Street was intended to be rehabilitative; see act of Apr. 5, 1790, ch. 1516, *Pa. Stats. at Large,* 13:511 (§ 1). Those who toured the facility came away with an understanding of the ideological principles of solitary reclamation; see, e.g., Duke de la Rochefoucault-Liancourt, *Travels Through the United States of North America . . . in the Years 1795, 1796, and 1797* (London, 1799), 2:337–39; [Duke de la Rochefoucault-Liancourt], *On the Prisons of Philadelphia* (Philadelphia, 1796), 10–11 (also published in London under the title *A Comparative View of Mild and Sanguinary Laws*).

28. Act of Mar. 26, 1796, ch. 30, *Laws of the State of New-York,* 3:291–92.

29. [Eddy], *Account,* 11–13; W. David Lewis, *From Newgate to Dannemora: The Rise of the Penitentiary in New York, 1796–1848* (Ithaca, 1965), 4–5, 30–32. The practice of subjecting inmates to solitary confinement as a part of their sentences was rapidly abandoned in New York, but solitary cells continued to be used as a punishment. [Eddy], *Account,* 32–33. New York experimented again with solitary confinement in 1821; see Lewis, *From Newgate to Dannemora,* 68–70.

30. *Columbian Centinel,* June 4, 1796, at 1. The attorney general, James Sullivan, was also involved in the debate. As one visitor reported, "[H]e is a zealous partizan, it seems, of the criminal law of Pennsylvania, and is now engaged in endeavors to get it adopted by the legislature of Massachusetts." It is unclear whether Sullivan's advocacy was restricted to the structure of the Pennsylvania code, which had radically restricted capital punishment, or also included solitary confinement. Rochefoucault-Liancourt, *Travels,* 2:405–6. See also Governor's Message, Jan. 11, 1799, *Mass. Acts & Resolves,* 1798–99:636 (carceral punishment should afford "time for reflection").

31. "Senate Documents," no. 2445 (1799) (unpassed). (This narrative corrects Powers, *Crime and Punishment,* 242.) Thomas Eddy also offered unsolicited information on Newgate prison to Massachusetts officials involved in constructing the state prison at Charlestown. Thomas Eddy to Charles Bulfinch (Mar. 28, 1800), appended to "Resolves," 1802, ch. 54 (passed). On the influence of Walnut Street in other states, see George Taylor, *Substance of a Speech Delivered in the House of Delegates of Virginia* (Richmond, 1796), 31–32; Robert Turnbull, *A Visit to the Philadelphia Prison* (London, 1797) (first published in the *Charleston Gazette*).

32. "Report Respecting Convicts."

33. Resolve of Feb. 19, 1799, ch. 135, *Mass. Acts & Resolves,* 1798–99:273.
34. See above, note 16.
35. In Pennsylvania, Benjamin Rush suggested that hard labor and solitude "may be used separately, or more or less combined, according to the nature of the crimes, or according to the variations of the constitution and temper of the criminal." Rush, *Enquiry,* 25. In New York, Thomas Eddy accepted the therapeutic value of solitary reflection but considered hard labor the primary means of rehabilitation. [Eddy], *Account,* 31–35, 53–54. In Massachusetts, no surviving legislative history speaks to this matter, nor did the drafters' report to the legislature offer any explanation for the dual sentencing structure. Oddly, the drafters' report never mentioned solitary confinement, only "imprisonment and confinement to hard labor." See Dane & Sewall, "Report." But years later, Dane complained that "[w]hen Judge Sewall & myself drew the bills enacted for governing the State prison[,] we fully expected that adequate means would be provided for giving full effect to solitary confinement." Nathan Dane to Josiah Quincy (May 6, 1822), in "Quincy Papers," reel 40 (unpublished MS, Mass. Hist. Soc'y). For an early English proposal along the same lines, see Henry Fielding, *A Proposal for Making an Effectual Provision for the Poor* (London, 1753), 75–76 (suggesting one day of solitude followed by hard labor).
36. On internal conflicts in New York and Pennsylvania, which were fueled by political and religious differences as well as ideological concerns, see Lewis, *From Newgate to Dannemora,* 34–37, 146–49; below, note 88.
37. "Remarks on the Massachusetts State Prison," in *Rules and Regulations for the Government of the State Prison Adopted by the Board of Directors* (Boston, 1823), 4, 21–22.
38. "Remarks on the Mass. State Prison," 4–5.
39. "Remarks on the Mass. State Prison," 4–10, 27 (quotation at 9). For other expositions of this philosophy in Massachusetts, see Josiah Quincy, *Remarks on Some of the Provisions of the Laws of Massachusetts Affecting Poverty, Vice, and Crime,* (Cambridge, Mass., 1822), 20–26; "Mass. Legislative Documents," 1817–22, no. 2:3 (State Library Annex); [James Austin], "Book Review," *N. Am. Rev.* 10 (1820):249–50, 259.
40. [Gamaliel Bradford], *State Prisons and the Penitentiary System Vindicated* (Charlestown, 1821), 13, 20, 24, 45 (quotation at 24). See also the report of a committee investigating alternative American prison systems, "Mass. Legislative Documents," 1817–22, no. 1:8–13.
41. [Bradford], *State Prisons,* 19, 24, 38–39; "Mass. Legislative Documents," 1817–22, no. 1:17–18; *Annual Report of the Board of Managers of the Prison Discipline Society* 3 (1828):14–15 [hereinafter *Prison Discipline Soc'y*], 8 (1833):22.
42. Edmund S. Morgan has argued that the revolutionary generation perpetuated, and often pursued policies directly shaped by, Puritan religious values. Edmund S. Morgan, "The Puritan Ethic and the American Revolution," in *The Challenge of the American Revolution* (New York, 1976), 88.
43. This theme is treated extensively in Edmund S. Morgan, *The Puritan Dilemma: The Story of John Winthrop* (Boston, 1958).
44. [Bradford], *State Prisons,* 19. But Bradford's philosophical premise was no longer shared universally in Massachusetts, e.g., "Ode to Solitude," *Mass. Mag.* 4 (1792):517. For English commentary similar to Bradford's, see William Godwin, *An Enquiry Concerning Political Justice* (London, 1793), 2:754–55; William Roscoe to Roberts Vaux (July 24, 1827), in *Liverpool Chron.,* July 28, 1827, at 3 (also in *Nat'l Gazette,* Sept. 11, 1827, at 2). For a subsequent American recitation, see "Book Review," *Christian Examiner* 20 (July 1836):392.

45. "[W]hat faith may be placed in resolutions (let them, when made, be perfectly sincere,) formed in the bosom of solitude, against the temptations of the world when that solitude is at an end? It requires but a slight knowledge of the human heart to answer this question. St. Paul has answered it—'when I would do good evil is present with me.'" [Bradford], *State Prisons,* 19. By comparison, early Puritans had sought to enlighten the consciences of offenders, but only those of community members whose histories and characters were well known and whose subsequent progress could be scrutinized; see chapter 3, text at notes 47–48.

46. A term of reclamatory solitary confinement would "leave the men enfeebled, and unable to work, when they left the Prison; and as ignorant of any useful business, as when they were committed." *Prison Discipline Soc'y* 2 (1827):66 (quotation); [Bradford], *State Prisons,* 19–20.

47. [Bradford], *State Prisons,* 18–19, 47–51; Gamaliel Bradford to William Roscoe (Sept. 10, 1823), in Roscoe, *A Brief Statement of the Causes Which Have Led to the Abandonment of the Celebrated System of Penitentiary Discipline in Some of the United States of America* (Liverpool, 1827), 52–53 (quotation); [Bradford], "Observations on Prisons and Punishment," in *Columbian Centinel,* Dec. 26, 1821, at 1 (authorship revealed in Roscoe, *Brief Statement,* 52) (continued in *Columbian Centinel,* Dec. 29, 1821, at 1); Bradford to Governor and Visitors (Oct. 16, 1823), in Governor and Council, "Reports and Papers of the State Prison at Charlestown, 1807, 1822–1823," in Misc. Box no. 3, pt. 1 (unpublished MS, Mass. Archives); Bradford to the Legislature, Jan. 27, 1824, "Senate Documents," no. 7029 (1824) (unpassed). Bradford was not averse to the possibility of setting up a *second* facility for solitary confinement and then testing the two institutions against each other for several years. [Bradford], "Observations on Prisons and Punishment," in *Columbian Centinel,* Dec. 29, 1821, at 1.

48. Introduction of extended solitary confinement would have required structural changes, for the solitary cells at Charlestown proved unfit for long terms of confinement. As a consequence, judges generally restricted the solitary confinement stage of prison sentences in Massachusetts to a fraction of the period permitted by law, often fewer than ten days. Quincy, *Remarks,* 20–22, 25; "Remarks on the Mass. State Prison," 20–21; "Mass Legislative Documents," 1817–22, nos. 2:3, 1:20. Bradford's priorities are set out in his *State Prisons,* 49–51. An early plea of his to expand the workshops was turned down by the directors as "inexpedient," though they later relented and agreed to forward the request to the governor. "Minutes of the Meetings of the Board of Visitors/Directors/Inspectors," 1:n.p. (Feb. 1, 1815), 2:2 (Feb. 7, 1816) (unpublished MS, Mass. Archives) [hereinafter "Visitors Minutes"].

49. Both parties complained of this persistent problem. [Bradford], *State Prisons,* 33–34, 49; "Remarks on the Mass. State Prisons," 18–19; *Prison Discipline Soc'y* 1 (1826):29–31; 3 (1828):37–39; Governor's Message, Jan. 3, 1827, *Mass. Resolves,* 1824–28:449–50; Thomas Harris to Governor Lincoln (Dec. 18, 1826), in State Prison, "Reports and Papers of the Officers, 1809–1828," in Misc. Box no. 84, pt. 1 (unpublished MS, Mass. Archives).

50. On the conflict, which rapidly degenerated into an exercise in reciprocal character assassination, see "Remarks on the Mass. State Prison," 18–19 (claiming to be on good terms with Bradford); [Gamaliel Bradford], "Review," in *Columbian Centinel,* Jan. 21, 1824, at 1, continued Jan. 25, 1824, at 1, and Jan. 31, 1824, at 1 (deriding the directors as "three learned men with the classics at their fingers end"); id., Jan. 28, 1824, at 2, separately published as [James Austin], *Reply to the Centinel Review* (Boston, 1824) (describing Bradford as "a nuisance" prone to "ebullitions of un-

governable passion"); Gamaliel Bradford to Governor and Visitors (Oct. 16, 1823), in Governor and Council, "Reports and Papers," pt. 1; "Visitors Minutes," 2:291–92 (Jan. 28, 1824). A subsequent warden speculated that Bradford's state of "indisposition" may have caused the conflict; he had sickened, and died later in 1824. Gideon Haynes, *Pictures from Prison Life: An Historical Sketch of the Massachusetts State Prison* (Boston, 1869), 45–46. For references to other internal administrative conflicts in Massachusetts, see Memorial and Petition of John Pelham to Governor and Council (May 18, 1810), in "General Correspondence with Governor Regarding State Prison at Charlestown, 1807–10, 1815, 1817–18, 1823–24" (unpublished MS, Mass. Archives); Visitors to Governor Gore (May 1, 1810), in id.; "Visitors Minutes," 1:42 (Apr. 14, 1807), 112–14 (Apr. 9, 1810), 115–16 (May 1, 1810), 140 (Sept. 13, 1810), 2:148 (Sept. 25, 1821).

51. Governor's Message, Jan. 2, 1828, *Mass. Resolves,* 1824–28:632. It was a common observation during this period; see, e.g., "Mass. Legislative Documents," 1817–22, no. 2:3; Society for the Prevention of Pauperism, *Report on the Penitentiary System in the United States* (New York, 1822), app. 96.

52. Administrative safeguards at Charlestown matched or refined those undertaken at Castle Island. The object, once again, was to avoid the shortcomings of the local jails; Answer of the House, Jan. 18, 1804, *Mass. Acts & Resolves,* 1802–3:875; Governor's Message, Jan. 13, 1804, id., 980–81. Accordingly, a physician and chaplain were appointed to the state prison staff, and a board of directors was established to furnish the facility, appoint its officers, write the bylaws, and inspect the prison monthly. In addition, the governor, council, and justices of the Supreme Judicial Court were all to inspect the prison annually. Act of June 15, 1805, ch. 23, *Mass. Acts & Resolves,* 1804–5:427; Act of Mar. 14, 1806, ch. 113, id., 546; Haynes, *Pictures,* 25–27. Sketchy at first, the bylaws of the state prison were ultimately elaborated in detail and periodically updated. "Visitors Minutes," 1:14–22 (Apr. 5, 1806); Haynes, *Pictures,* 233; [Gamaliel Bradford], *Description and Historical Sketch of the Massachusetts State Prison* (Charlestown, 1816), 27–37; *Rules and Regulations,* 44–62; *Laws of the Commonwealth for the Government of the State Prison* (Boston, 1839). The importance of hiring competent officers was noted, e.g., in Austin, "Book Review," 259; Mass. Legislative Documents, 1817–22, no. 1:19–20; *Report [on the Mass. State Prison],* 1827:4–6 (legislative document, Harvard Law Library) (also in "Mass. Legislative Documents," Senate & House, 1826–27, no. 23); *Prison Discipline Soc'y* 1 (1826):29; id., 2 (1827):11–13, 49–52. Those officers who were found to be incompetent or corrupt were discharged, e.g., "Daily Reports," 1:n.p. (Mar. 20, Apr. 14, June 28, July 29, Sept. 1, 1806) (warden's record, unpublished MS, Mass. Archives); "Visitors Minutes," 1:27 (Apr. 14, 1806), 42 (Apr. 14, 1807), 2:101 (Sept. 1, 1819).

53. Haynes, *Pictures,* 20–38; Governor's Message, Jan. 25, 1811, *Mass. Resolves,* Jan. 1811:66; Governor's Message, June 7, 1811, *Mass. Resolves,* May 1811:189; Answer of the Senate, June 15, 1811, *Mass. Resolves,* 193; Governor's Message, Jan. 8, 1812, *Mass. Resolves,* Jan. 1812:282; "Mass. Legislative Documents," 1817–22, no. 1:4; id., no. 2:1–2; [Bradford], *State Prisons,* 9–12; *Report [on the Mass. State Prison],* 1827:1. The warden's record book is filled with accounts of violence and escape attempts; the first successful escape occurred in 1806 (the convict was soon recaptured). "Daily Reports," 1:n.p. (Feb. 24, 1806). In 1825 it was discovered that counterfeiters had been carrying on their trade *within* prison walls. *Prison Discipline Soc'y* 2 (1827):11–12, 21–23; "Visitors Minutes," 3:n.p. (Oct. 22, 1825). In the area of prison hygiene, however, the state prison achieved a record of sustained success—prison

mortality was consistently low. E.g., *Mass. Resolves,* May 1811:189; *Prison Discipline Soc'y* 2 (1827):35.

54. *Columbian Centinel,* Mar. 11, 1818, at 1 (quotation), Dec. 4, 1816, at 1, Aug. 21, 1816, at 1, Apr. 12, 1817, at 1; *Boston Daily Examiner,* Feb. 18, 1818, at 2.

55. Answer of the Senate, n.d., *Mass. Resolves,* May 1818:587 (quotation); Governor's Message, June 2, 1818, id., 578–79; "Mass. Legislative Documents," 1817–22, no. 2:2.

56. For example, *Report [on the Mass. State Prison],* 1827:1; *Boston Daily Examiner,* Feb. 18, 1818, at 2; cf. *Columbian Centinel,* Dec. 4, 1816, at 1 (proposing sentences to corporal punishment *within* prisons).

57. "Mass. Legislative Documents," 1817–22, no. 1:8–11 (weighing whether the penitentiary should "be abandoned as useless or bad in its tendency").

58. On administrative problems in other postrevolutionary prisons, see, e.g., Lewis, *From Newgate to Dannemora,* ch. 2; Teeters, *Cradle of the Penitentiary,* ch. 5; Soc'y for the Prevention of Pauperism, *Report,* 19–47, app. 90–95; William Roscoe, *Observations on Penal Jurisprudence* (London, 1819), 93–99; William Roscoe, *Additional Observations on Penal Jurisprudence* (London, 1823), 44–58, 106–7, 125–26. On widespread dissatisfaction with the penitentiary and contemplation of its abandonment and a return to traditional sanctions or some alternative, see Roscoe, *Brief Statement,* 18–21, 52; Soc'y for the Prevention of Pauperism, *Report,* 4, 76–96, app. 9–10, 46–47, 67; *Remarks on Prisons and Prison Discipline* (Boston, 1826), 5–6 (reprinted from the *Christian Examiner,* 3, no. 3); [Bradford], *State Prisons,* 61–63; Lewis, *From Newgate to Dannemora,* 61–63; [William Tudor], "Book Review," *N. Am. Rev.* 13 (1821):418–27; [Austin], "Book Review," 238; William Tudor to William Roscoe (Apr. 24, 1819), in Roscoe, *Additional Observations,* app. 78–83; William Tudor to William Roscoe (Sept. 10, 1819), in "Roscoe Papers: Materials Relating to the United States," no. 4878 (unpublished MS, Picton Library, Liverpool); for dissatisfaction in England, see William Roscoe to William Tudor [c. 1823], in id., no. 4881. Cf. Austin, "Book Review," 245 (suggesting that proponents of traditional punishment were few). In Pennsylvania, dissatisfaction with carceral punishment and proposals to return to corporal sanctions began much earlier, with the failure of the public hard labor program of 1786. Soc'y for Alleviating the Miseries of Public Prisons, *Extracts and Remarks,* 4; Turnbull, *Visit to the Philadelphia Prison,* 7; Benjamin Rush to Thomas Eddy (Oct. 19, 1803), in *Letters of Benjamin Rush,* 1:874–75; for an early reference in New York, see [Eddy], *Account,* 16.

59. [Bradford], *State Prisons,* 17–18; "Remarks on the Mass. State Prison," 22; *Columbian Centinel,* Mar. 18, 1818, at 1; Warden and Directors' report to the Senate, in "Visitors Minutes," 2:60–61 (Jan. 26, 1818).

60. [Bradford], *State Prisons,* 11–12, 15–16; [Bradford], *Description,* 15; "Remarks on the Mass. State Prison," 3–4; *Columbian Centinel,* May 18, 1822, at 1; Gamaliel Bradford to William Roscoe (Oct. 20, 1823), in "Roscoe Papers," no. 420 ("one great advantage . . . if not the principal one"). Critics shrewdly pointed out the limitations of incapacitation, however: crime would continue unabated if an inmate's *confederates* remained free. *Remarks on Prisons and Prison Discipline,* 10; see also *The Complete Works of Edward Livingston on Criminal Jurisprudence* (New York, 1873), 1:47.

61. Whereas Bradford demonstrated the inadequacy of deterrence on the basis of rational notions of sensational psychology, the directors did so on the basis of the philanthropic theme of estrangement from God. Cf. [Bradford], *State Prisons,* 15–16; "Remarks on the Mass. State Prison," 25–26. See also William Roscoe to William

Tudor (July 18, 1819), in Roscoe, *Additional Observations,* app. 83–94. Cf. chapter 2, text at notes 57, 88.

62. "Remarks on the Mass. State Prison," 24.

63. It was suggested that persons committed crimes "in order to be well fed" in the state prison. *Columbian Centinel,* Mar. 18, 1818, at 1; the claim appeared widely, e.g., [Tudor], "Book Review," 434–35; Gershom Powers, *A Brief Account of the Construction, Management, & Discipline &c. &c. of the New-York State Prison at Auburn* (Auburn, 1826), 66–67; Soc'y for the Prevention of Pauperism, *Report,* app. 28, 40; Lewis, *From Newgate to Dannemora,* 62; in England, see chapter 2, note 16.

64. Some tempers were lost: "Another error which it might be presumed a moment's reflection would destroy, has been propagated with thoughtless alacrity. . . ." *Report [on the Mass. State Prison],* 1822:8 (also in "Mass. Legislative Documents," 1817–22, no. 52).

65. "Remarks on the Mass. State Prison," 24–25; [Bradford], *State Prisons,* 14–15, 31–33; *Report [on the Mass. State Prison],* 1822:8–9; *Columbian Centinel,* May 18, 1822, at 1; [Tudor], "Book Review," 434–35. In common with English advocates, Bradford hoped to stabilize the balance by convincing criminals that their punishment was just and inflicted "with a view to [their] own improvement." [Bradford], *State Prisons,* 47. See also chapter 2, note 72 and accompanying text.

66. "Remarks on the Mass. State Prison," 9–11; Quincy, *Remarks,* 12, 23–26; [Bradford], *Description,* 15; [Austin], "Book Review," 250–51, 257, 259.

67. [Bradford], *State Prisons,* 12–13, 16–17; "Remarks on the Mass. State Prison," 3 and n.; [Austin], "Book Review," 252, 259. Cf. "Mass. Legislative Documents," 1817–22, no. 1:7, 15. William Tudor spiced the argument with a dash of ridicule: "To that class of economists, and unfortunately they are not few in number, who are apt to look at this branch of legislation exclusively in reference to expense, and to calculate every thing only in dollars and cents, it may be suggested, that the hanging of one culprit costs the community in the loss of labor of the thousands who flock to behold it, a thousand times as much as it would to keep him in prison a century" ([Tudor], "Book Review," 431–34). The economic argument noted in the text (which was heard widely, e.g., Soc'y for the Prevention of Pauperism, *Report,* 45, app. 59, 62) echoed arguments propagated by early defenders of loss-making workhouses, both in England and colonial North America; see T[homas] F[irmin], *Some Proposals for the Imployment of the Poor* (London, 1681), 15; Matthew Hale, *A Discourse Touching Provisions for the Poor* (London, 1683), 17–20, 22–23; *A Report of the Record Commissioners of the Town of Boston, Containing the Boston Town Records,* 1742–57:198.

68. "Remarks on the Mass. State Prison," 13, 26–27; [Bradford], *State Prisons,* 45; *Report [on the Mass. State Prison],* 1822:13–14. Labor opposition to the penitentiary is further discussed in chapter 7, notes 73–79 and accompanying text.

69. [Bradford], *State Prisons,* 16, 29–30; *Boston Daily Examiner,* Feb. 18, 1818, at 2; *Columbian Centinel,* Mar. 7, 1818, at 1; "Mass. Legislative Documents," 1817–22, no. 1:2–4, 6–8; the problem was noted widely, e.g., Soc'y for the Prevention of Pauperism, *Report,* 19–32, app. 14.

70. *Columbian Centinel,* June 4, 1796, at 1; "Report Respecting Convicts." Thomas Eddy also made this criticism early; [Eddy], *Account,* 38, 54, 61–63; Thomas Eddy to Patrick Colquhoun (June 5, 1802), in Samuel L. Knapp, *The Life of Thomas Eddy* (New York, 1834), 180; the same criticism had been made in England of the prison hulks and of the Penitentiary Act. Jonas Hanway, *Distributive Justice and Mercy*

(London, 1781), 111–16; Henry Zouch, *Observations upon a Bill Now Depending in Parliament* (London, 1779), 12. The need to separate inmates to prevent mutual contamination had been a principal tenet of English philanthropic ideology since the eighteenth century, although references to this idea appeared as early as the sixteenth century; e.g., Roger North, *A Discourse of the Poor* (London, 1753), 26 (jail was a "College of Thieves"); see chapter 2, note 53. The earliest American legislation directed to the problem of communication between convicts dated to 1786; see Act of Sept. 15, 1786, ch. 1241, *Pa. Stats. at Large,* 286–87 (§ 11). Cf. David J. Rothman, *The Discovery of the Asylum: Social Order and Disorder in the New Republic* (Boston, 1971), 83 (dating the perception of the deleterious consequences of inmate congregation to the 1830s).

71. Governor's Message, Jan. 4, 1826, *Mass. Resolves,* 1824–28:252; *Prison Discipline Soc'y* 1 (1826):38. Even the workshops had become crowded by 1818. "Mass. Legislative Documents," 1817–22, no. 2:1–2. The solitary cells were so insufficient that the arrival of convicts had to be delayed on occasion until vacant solitary cells became available. Id., 3; "Visitors Minutes," 2:80–81 (June 3, 1818). See also above, note 48.

72. Against this analysis, Michel Foucault argues that the penitentiary served the political interests of the upper class by *creating* a convict subculture, thereby fracturing the lower orders into weaker subgroups that could be played against one another. In Foucault's view, the penitentiary was actually "called upon to participate in the fabrication of a delinquency that it is supposed to combat." Michel Foucault, *Discipline and Punish: The Birth of the Prison* (London, 1977), 264–92 (quotation at 278). But to reach this critical thesis, Foucault must wink not only at every pronouncement by penitentiary advocates that they sought precisely the opposite (e.g., [John Gallison], "Book Review," *N. Am. Rev.* 9 [1819]:291; Franklin Bache, *Observations and Reflections on the Penitentiary System* [Philadelphia, 1829], 6–7), but also at their *actual undertakings,* discussed below, to combat the administrative flaws that had allowed the convict subculture to flourish. Did the ultimate failure of their efforts betray a lack of good intentions? Contemporary commentators were less cynical: "It is just to observe that if the present system has failed in its object, that failure has not been for want of zeal and effort in the administration of it." Soc'y for the Prevention of Pauperism, *Report,* app. 95–96.

73. Some defenders also argued that the corrupting influence of the penitentiary was exaggerated; see *Columbian Centinel,* Mar. 14, 1818, at 1, and May 18, 1822, at 1.

74. Solitary confinement, of course, represented the *ne plus ultra* of separation. Quincy, *Remarks,* 20–21; "Remarks on the Mass. State Prison," 4–5, 8; "Report Respecting Convicts."

75. "We have it from the highest authority, that 'evil communications corrupt good manners' [1 Cor. 15:33]—but the communication even between convicts is not always evil—they have been known to pray in their rooms with each other, and to form associations for religious purposes—and it is not altogether unreasonable to suppose, that examples and practices of this kind should have their influence, as well as wicked ones." [Bradford], *State Prisons,* 18–19; similarly, [Tudor], "Book Review," 438.

76. "[A] man works much more cheerfully when in company than when alone; when he sees all around him at work, it encourages him to be active from example, and a sort of feeling of sympathy: he becomes industrious." [Bradford], *State Prisons,* 18–20. On the incompatibility of solitude and instruction in trades, see also *Letter of*

Gershom Powers in Answer to a Letter of the Hon. Edward Livingston, in Relation to the Auburn State Prison (Albany, 1829), 16; Charles Shaler, Edward King, and T. J. Wharton, "Report on Punishment and Prison Discipline," in *Journal of the Senate and the Commonwealth of Pennsylvania, 1827–1828* (Harrisburg, 1828), 2 app.:357.

77. [Bradford], *State Prisons,* 49, 51; Communication from Gamaliel Bradford, Jan. 27, 1824, in "Senate Documents," no. 7029 (1824) (unpassed); "Mass. Legislative Documents," 1817–22, no. 1; Roscoe, *Brief Statement,* 7–8, 53–58; Knapp, *Life,* 244, 285, 299, 310–11, 320–21 (Eddy letters, 1816–25); Thomas Eddy, *Communication to Stephen Allen* (New York, 1823), 4–7. Eddy was already leaning in this direction by 1801; see above, citations in note 70.

78. According to one advocate, defenders of the penitentiary system at this time had "to contend against fearful odds." *Columbian Centinel,* Mar. 11, 1818, at 1. The penitentiary in New York also survived an early challenge; see Lewis, *From Newgate to Dannemora,* 44, 56–57. Only in Georgia, where complaints about the penitentiary culminated in a fire that gutted the facility, was the penitentiary system briefly abandoned in 1831; see *Prison Discipline Soc'y* 2 (1827):83; id., 7 (1832):54–55; id., 9 (1834):66–68; James C. Bonner, "The Georgia Penitentiary at Milledgeville, 1817–1874," *Ga. Hist. Q.* 55 (1971):308–10.

79. Advocates in Massachusetts played on these concerns, insisting that the institution had not yet been "fairly and fully tried" and that "with some small improvements" it could be salvaged. "Mass. Legislative Documents," 1817–22, no. 1:21–23; [Bradford], *State Prisons,* 4–5; "Mass. Legislative Report," 1819, in Roscoe, *Additional Observations,* app. 66 (emphasizing expense of initial investment); *Columbian Centinel,* Mar. 18, 1818, at 1 (emphasizing the want of alternatives); [Tudor], "Book Review," 421–27 (same).

80. Act of Feb. 23, 1818, ch. 176, *Mass. Acts,* 1815–18:602–5. For the first time, guards were given explicit authority to use deadly force to compel obedience (a right previously ambiguous). On this controversy, see Haynes, *Pictures,* 20–22, 38–39; Visitors to Governor Gore (June 12, 1809), in "General Correspondence with Governor Regarding State Prison at Charlestown"; "Visitors Minutes," 1:89 (June 12, 1809), n.p. (July 18, 1812); id., 2:73 (Apr. 1, 1818).

81. A commission established in 1817 to inquire into problems with the penitentiary had proposed to construct a new building that would permit separate confinement of all convicts at night; this proposal was shelved by the legislative committee entrusted with the commission's report, against the wishes of the governor. As a subsequent committee noted dryly, "The legislature . . . adopted every [proposal] which involved no expenditure, and rejected or postponed every [proposal], that required an appropriation." *Report [on the Mass. State Prison],* 1822:3 (quotation); "Mass. Legislative Documents," 1817–22, nos. 1:20, 2:4; William Tudor to William Roscoe (Sept. 10, 1819), in "Roscoe Papers," no. 4878. A subsequent request by Governor Brooks in 1822 was also ignored; Governor's Message, Jan. 9, 1822, *Mass. Resolves,* Jan. 1822:391–97.

82. See above, note 80; "Visitors Minutes," 2:72 (Apr. 1, 1818), 79–80 (May 14, 1818). On the notion that classification substituted for separate confinement, see [Bradford], *State Prisons,* 48; *Prison Discipline Soc'y* 1 (1826):15. Once again, this idea sprang from England. 19 Geo. 3 c.74 § 38 (1779); U. R. Q. Henriques, "The Rise and Decline of the Separate System of Prison Discipline," *Past & Present* 54 (Feb. 1972):66–67.

83. Act of Feb. 19, 1819, ch. 123, *Mass. Acts,* 1818–22:196. This provision had been strongly pressed by the penitentiary commission established in 1817, which also

recommended the construction of new district bridewells to hold the diverted inmates. Once again, the commission's proposal for new construction was vetoed by the legislature. "Mass. Legislative Documents," 1817–22, nos. 1, 2:1–2, 4. This was not an entirely new effort: ad hoc measures to isolate young convicts had been made as early as 1813. "Visitors Minutes," 1:n.p. (Dec. 15, 1813).

84. Compare *Mass. Resolves,* May 1819:29–30, 33; May 1818:578–79, 587.

85. Advocates disappointed by the legislature's failure to open the public purse had anticipated the sequel: "By avoiding any disbursements," William Tudor predicted in 1819, "the evil was only put off to accumulate, until it will at no distant period force the State into a heavy expenditure to pay for this piece of pretended economy." William Tudor to William Roscoe (Sept. 10, 1819), in "Roscoe Papers," no. 4878.

86. Haynes, *Pictures,* 40–46, 131–37; *Report [on the Mass. State Prison],* 1822:6; *Remarks on Prisons and Prison Discipline,* 10; Governor's Message, Jan. 9, 1822, *Mass. Resolves,* Jan. 1822:392–95; Governor's Message, Jan. 1, 1823, id., Jan. 1823:564; Governor's Message, id., 1824–28:24; Governor's Message, Jan. 6, 1830, id., 1828–31:223–24; "Visitors Minutes," 2:299 (Mar. 12, 1824) (reporting another prisonwide mutiny). The directors argued that the criteria of the classification scheme had, in any event, been misconceived; see "Remarks on the Mass. State Prison," 20–21. As for the diversion program for low-level offenders, the legislature had neglected to ensure the serviceability of *local* jails. The result was another fiasco. [Bradford], *State Prisons,* 22–23; Quincy, *Remarks; Report [on the Mass. State Prison],* 1822:3–5; [Austin], "Book Review," 255–59.

87. Governor Lincoln sweetened the pill by proposing that prison profits accrued up to that time be allocated to the new construction project, that convict labor be used to reduce the project's cost, and that future prison profits be pledged to make up the difference. All of these suggestions were followed. Governor's Message, Jan. 31, 1825, Jan. 4, 1826, Jan. 3, 1827, *Mass. Resolves,* 1824–28:105, 251–54, 447–48; Governor's Message, Jan. 6, 1830, id., 1828–31:224–25.

88. On these carceral developments in Pennsylvania, see Negley K. Teeters and John D. Shearer, *The Prison at Philadelphia: Cherry Hill* (New York, 1957), ch. 1; Eugene E. Doll, "Trial and Error at Allegheny: The Western State Penitentiary, 1818–1838," *Pa. Mag. Hist. & Biog.* 81 (1957):3; Harry Elmer Barnes, *The Evolution of Penology in Pennsylvania* (Indianapolis, 1927), ch. 3; LeRoy B. DePuy, "The Triumph of the 'Pennsylvania System' at the State's Penitentiaries," *Pa. Hist.* 21 (1954):128. Solitary confinement without labor retained a following at least through the 1820s; see, e.g., James Mease to William Roscoe (Oct. 11, 1821), in Roscoe, *Additional Observations,* app. 28–32; Mease to Roscoe (May 18, 1827), in *U.S. Gazette,* June 2, 1827, at 1; Shaler, King, and Wharton, "Report," 323; George W. Smith, *A Defence of the System of Solitary Confinement of Prisoners Adopted by the State of Pennsylvania* (Philadelphia, 1833), 4, 57n; Samuel Gridley Howe, *Report of the Minority of a Special Committee of the Boston Prison Discipline Society* (Boston, 1846), 16–17.

89. See chapter 2, text at notes 60–64.

90. On the development of the Auburn system, see Lewis, *From Newgate to Dannemora,* ch. 4. The Auburn administrative measures were homegrown, not borrowed from abroad. Michael Ignatieff, *A Just Measure of Pain: The Penitentiary in the Industrial Revolution, 1750–1850* (London, 1978), 178; "Book Review," *Am. Q. Rev.* 18 (1835):459–60. Cf. conclusion, note 9. Nevertheless, the *ideals* of silence, strict discipline, and constant oversight, even if not scrupulously enforced, can all be found in Massachusetts prison regulations long before the Auburn reforms. Regulations

of 1815 in Haynes, *Pictures,* 232–35; Rules and Orders of 1816 in [Bradford], *Description,* 35–36; Rules and Orders of 1823 in "Remarks on the Mass. State Prison," 53–54, 56–59. (Tocqueville doubted whether silence could realistically be copied by French prisons, since "it would be infinitely more painful to Frenchmen than to Americans." Gustave de Beaumont and Alexis de Tocqueville, *On the Penitentiary System in the United States and Its Application in France* [Philadelphia, 1833], 92n.)

91. Powers, *Brief Account,* 55 (quotation); S[tephen] A[llen], *An Examination of the Remarks on the Report of the Commissioners* (New York, 1826), 11; Stephen Allen, Samuel Hopkins, and George Tibbits, "Report," in *Journal of the Assembly of the State of New York* (New York, 1825), 108.

92. Act of Feb. 15, 1826, ch. 84, *Mass. Acts,* 1825–28:144; Governor's Message, Jan. 3, 1827, *Mass. Resolves,* 1824–28:447; *Report [on the Mass. State Prison],* 1827:1.

93. Governor's Message, Jan. 4, 1826, *Mass. Resolves,* 1824–28:253–54.

94. Founded in 1825, the Prison Discipline Society propagandized relentlessly for the Auburn plan, e.g., *Prison Discipline Soc'y* 1 (1826):57–60, and subsequent annual reports. These reports were widely circulated; the first report (1826) went through four editions in a year, and five hundred copies went to the Massachusetts legislature. The society also conducted a lobbying campaign, which, so it claimed, was instrumental in securing the renovation legislation. Id. 2 (1827):60–61; *Remarks on Prisons and Prison Discipline,* 10–12, 17. On Dwight's personal efforts, see Lewis Dwight to Governor Lincoln (Jan. 16, May 3, 1826), in State Prison, "Reports and Papers of the Officers, 1809–1828," in Misc. Box no. 84, pt. 1 (unpublished MS, Mass. Archives). The Prison Discipline Society was so closely associated with the Auburn plan that it became known in Europe as the Auburn System Society. Howe, *Report of the Minority,* 7, 87–88, 90. Advocates of the Pennsylvania plan resented the society's partiality; see, e.g., *A Vindication of the Separate System of Prison Discipline* (Philadelphia, 1839), 43–48.

95. The New Prison, later known as the North Wing, was built within the original Charlestown prison compound. For a description, see *Report [on the Mass. State Prison],* 1829:1–8 (also in "Mass. Legislative Documents," 1829–30:135). The rule of silence, orderly marching, inspection at labor, and solitary sleeping and dining were all introduced in accordance with the Auburn plan. Id., 8–9; Act of Mar. 11, 1828, *Mass. Acts,* 1825–28:825; Governor's Message, Jan. 6, 1830, *Mass. Resolves,* 1828–31:22–24. At Louis Dwight's urging, Massachusetts sought to recruit the celebrated warden of Connecticut's prison at Wethersfield, Amos Pillsbury, to run the new facility, but Connecticut refused to let him go. Louis Dwight to Governor Lincoln (Nov. 17, 30, 1828), Martin Wells to Louis Dwight (Nov. 17, 1828), Amos Pillsbury to Directors of the Connecticut State Prison (Nov. 26, 1828), in "Correspondence with Governor Relating to Appointment at State Prison, Charlestown, 1828, 1830" (unpublished MS, Mass. Archives).

96. *Report [on the Mass. State Prison],* May 1830:10–14 (also in "Mass. Legislative Documents," 1830–31:67).

97. *Report [on the Mass. State Prison],* May 1830:10. Under the Massachusetts code of 1836, the old format of two successive sentences, the first to solitary confinement and the second to hard labor, standard since 1805, was terminated. Thereafter, the statutes specified single terms of hard labor, the judge retaining discretion to set a preliminary term of solitary confinement of up to twenty days in all cases (far shorter than under previous statutes). *Mass. Rev. Stat.,* 1836:pt. 4, tit. 2, ch. 139, § 8.

98. Act of Mar. 11, 1828, ch. 118, *Mass. Acts,* 1825–28:819; Haynes, *Pictures,* 47.

99. On the Jacksonian penitentiary debates, which are only adumbrated here, see gen-

erally Barnes, *Evolution of Penology,* 176–79 (citing to some of the copious primary literature); Harry Elmer Barnes, *New Horizons in Criminology,* 2d ed. (New York, 1951), ch. 21. The debate also had a transatlantic dimension in the shape of William Roscoe, the English theorist, who took on both sides of the Auburn-Pennsylvania system controversy and maintained a spirited public dialogue with advocates of both models (including Stephen Allen and Roberts Vaux). A defender of the Auburn system, Samuel Hopkins, counted Roscoe (rather than one of his American critics) as "our most formidable opponent." Samuel Hopkins, *Sketch of the Public and Private Life of Samuel Miles Hopkins* (Rochester, 1898), 40. The issues in the debate were thoroughly aired: "so frequently and so completely investigated, by powerful minds, as to be worn threadbare." Matthew Carey, *Thoughts on Penitentiaries and Prison Discipline* (Philadelphia, 1831), 3; "we come now to the beaten ground of penitentiary discipline. . . ." Livingston, *Complete Works,* 1:547.

100. William Roscoe mischievously cross-cited the advocates' reciprocal denunciations to discredit *both* systems: "whilst . . . each of you stigmatized the system advocated by the other, as *in the highest degree cruel and severe,* and as totally unfit for . . . adoption . . . I trust I may venture to express my hopes that the legislative bodies of the different states will pause before they give effect to plans . . . liable to such well founded and unanswerable objections." William Roscoe to Roberts Vaux (Aug. 2, 1827), in *Liverpool Chron.,* Aug. 4, 1827, at 3 (emphasis in original) (also in *Nat'l Gazette,* Sept. 20, 1827, at 2). The temperature of the debate may have stemmed in part from the religiosity of the advocates. The English philanthropist Jonas Hanway had urged his readers that "[e]very plan, which affords a prospect of success, should be attended to with a religious anxiety, and with the same zeal as we would worship God." Hanway, *Distributive Justice,* 72–73. Such zeal certainly infected the Reverend Louis Dwight, "a born missionary, with the militant spirit strongly developed in what he believed to be a righteous cause." Orlando F. Lewis, *The Development of American Prisons and Prison Customs, 1776–1845* (Albany, 1922), 226–28. Furthermore, the advocates were, to some degree, religiously divided. Many (though not all) of the Pennsylvania advocates were Quakers, whose religious tenets supported the efficacy of solitude. [George Ticknor], "Book Review," *N. Am. Rev.* 18 (1824):183; Teeters, *They Were in Prison,* 122, 152–53; cf. "Book Review," *Am. Q. Rev.* 14 (1833):232. (In England, a reviewer asserted that "the silence of solitude is an inherent principle of Quakerism," *Gentleman's Mag.* 69 [1799]:504, although early English philanthropists had also belonged to other Nonconformist sects, see Ignatieff, *A Just Measure of Pain,* 58–59, 146–53.) By contrast, the officers of the Prison Discipline Society, centered in Boston, were all Hopkinsian Calvinists; see *Remarks on Prisons and Prison Discipline,* 17; Lewis, *From Newgate to Dannemora,* 107, for whom solitude held less appeal (see above, notes 42–43 and accompanying text). The Louisiana criminologist Edward Livingston criticized both camps for urging their respective models with a "spirit that belongs to sectarian controversy." *Letter from Edward Livingston, Esq., to Roberts Vaux on the Advantages of the Pennsylvania System of Prison Discipline* (Philadelphia, 1828), 13 (originally published in the *Nat'l Gazette*). Whether religiously motivated or not, many advocates were at odds over their ideological approach to rehabilitation (see below, notes 105–6), and they recognized that, given the costs involved, each state's decision, once taken, would be difficult to reverse. "The consequences of error must be endured for half a century, perhaps." *Prison Discipline: The Auburn and Pennsylvania Systems Compared* (New York, 1839), 4. Cf. Rothman, *Discovery of the Asylum,* 81–82, 85 (tracing Jacksonian zeal to exaggerated goals and expectations).

101. Among American states, only New Jersey and Rhode Island briefly joined Penn-sylvania in adopting the Pennsylvania system. Lewis, *Development of American Prisons,* 326.

102. For example, *Prison Discipline Soc'y* 8 (1833):6–8. Pennsylvania advocates gamely responded by citing to numerous *European* adoptions of their system; see Howe, *Report of a Minority,* 78, 82–87.

103. The evolution of prison architecture in England is explored in depth in Robin Evans, *The Fabrication of Virtue: English Prison Architecture, 1750–1840* (Cambridge, 1982).

104. One of the criticisms emphasized by Pennsylvania advocates was that the Auburn system failed to isolate prisoners sufficiently to prevent their mutual corruption. See, e.g., Roberts Vaux to William Roscoe (Sept. 21, 1827), in *Nat'l Gazette,* Sept. 25, 1827, at 4; Smith, *Defence,* 49–50, 103; Howe, *Report of a Minority,* 31–37, 48–52; *Prison Discipline . . . Compared,* 6–8; *Vindication of the Separate System,* 6–31. On the cost-efficiency of carceral punishment, see chapter 7, notes 18–19, 36 and ac-companying text. The relative deterrence of the two systems was also debated (cf., e.g., Beaumont and Tocqueville, *On the Penitentiary System,* 68n [Francis Lieber's commentary]; Howe, *Report of the Minority,* 24–25; *Columbian Centinel,* Dec. 29, 1821, at 1, and Jan. 15, 1823, at 1–2), as was the proclivity (hotly denied by Penn-sylvania advocates) of solitude to cause madness and infirmity (cf., e.g., Shaler, King, and Wharton, "Report," 346–53; Powers, *Brief Account,* 36–37; Franklin Bache to Roberts Vaux [Oct. 16, 1830], in *J. Law* 1 [1830]:122–27; James Mease, *Observa-tions on the Penitentiary System* [Philadelphia, 1828], 45–48; Smith, *Defence,* 64–74, 99–100; *Vindication of the Separate System,* 46–47).

105. Whereas the Massachusetts State Prison had from 1805 combined elements of soli-tude and hard labor sequentially, under both the Auburn and Pennsylvania sys-tems they were combined simultaneously. Gershom Powers of New York described Auburn as "the best possible middle ground between the two extremes of peniten-tiary punishment," and he wished convicts to undergo both training and reflection. Powers, *Brief Account,* 16, 34–35, 37–38 (quotation at 37). Others asserted the ideo-logical equivalence of the two systems, but branded Auburn a "partial and imper-fect" rendering of the Pennsylvania model. Howe, *Report of a Minority,* 7–8, 18–19 (quotation at 18); "Book Review," *Am. Q. Rev.* 18 (1835):470. For other assertions of ideological synthesis, see [Francis Wayland], "Book Review," *N. Am. Rev.* 49 (July 1839):29–43; Francis Lieber to Charles Penrose (Jan. 22, 1835), in Thomas McElwee, *A Concise History of the Eastern Penitentiary of Philadelphia* (Philadelphia, 1835), 60–61 ("Solitude is as necessary as labor; labor is as indispensable as solitude").

106. Like earlier criminologists, many Jacksonian advocates granted the utility of both labor and reflection but viewed the issue as one of *priority:* Auburn gave priority to labor, while Pennsylvania gave it to reflection. Cf., e.g., Bache, *Observations and Reflections,* 10; Shaler, King, and Wharton, "Report," 353–62; *Prison Discipline Soc'y* 1 (1826):8; id., 2 (1827):55–56; id., 8 (1833):21–22. For earlier amalgamations of these therapies, see above, notes 35, 47–48, and chapter 2, note 67. Other advocates took more extreme positions, focusing either on hard labor (at Auburn) or solitude (at Pennsylvania) as the single active ingredient of rehabilitation. Cf., e.g., Beau-mont and Tocqueville, *On the Penitentiary System,* 156 n.*p* (quoting Elam Lynds); Smith, *Defence,* 75, 89–93. See also chapter 6, notes 171–78 and accompanying text. European visitors also recognized (or exhibited) these philosophical differences. Tocqueville acknowledged a duality of rehabilitative objectives and remarked the different emphasis of the two systems: "Now, to what point is this reformation actu-ally effected by the different systems which we have examined? Before we answer

this question, it will be necessary to settle the meaning attached to the word '*refor-mation.*' . . . The [Pennsylvania] system being also that which produces the deepest impressions on the soul of the convict, must effect more reformation than that of Auburn. The latter, however, is perhaps more conformable to the habits of men in society, and on this account effects a greater number of reformations, which might be called 'legal,' inasmuch as they produce the external fulfillment of social obliga-tion. If it be so, the [Pennsylvania] system produces more honest men, and that of New York more obedient citizens." Beaumont and Tocqueville, *On the Penitentiary System,* 48–60 (quotations at 55, 59–60). By contrast, English inspectors of Auburn Prison viewed its discipline through alternative ideological lenses, either as "moral machinery" or as a "mere manufactur[y]." Ignatieff, *A Just Measure of Pain,* 194–95. Cf. Rothman, *Discovery of the Asylum,* 79–88 (asserting the philosophical identity of the two systems).

107. [Austin], "Book Review," 235–37, 246–49, 259 (quotation at 247); Carey, *Thoughts,* 25; [Bradford], *State Prisons,* 4–5, 10–11, 16–18, 29–30, 48, 61; S[tephen] A[llen], *Observations on Penitentiary Discipline Addressed to William Roscoe* (New York, 1827), 33, 65; Livingston, *Complete Writings,* 1:563–64; Smith, *Defence,* 77–80, 97, 101; *Fourth Annual Report of the Inspectors of the Eastern State Penitentiary of Philadelphia* (Philadelphia, 1833), 9; *Prison Discipline Soc'y* 1 (1826):33–35; id., 8 (1833):29–30; *Report [on the Mass. State Prison],* May 1830:7; id., Sept. 1830:25–26 (also in "Mass. Legislative Documents," 1830–31:151); id., 1831:24 (also in "Mass. Legislative Documents," Senate & House 1832:218); "Mass. Legislative Documents," Senate 1831:523; "Book Review," *Christian Examiner* 20 (1836):379–90; *Letters on the Pennsylvania System of Solitary Imprisonment,* 1st ed. (Charleston, 1835), 4; Allen, Hopkins, and Tibbits, "Report," 103–4, 108, 119, 121, 125. William Roscoe was so struck by Jacksonian ideological retrenchment that he published an extended response, provocatively entitled *A Brief Statement of the Causes That Have Led to the Abandonment of the Celebrated System of Penitentiary Discipline in Some of the United States of America* (Liverpool, 1827) (for prior salvos, see William Roscoe, *Remarks on the Report of the Commissioners Appointed by the Legislature of New York* [Liverpool, 1825]; A[llen], *Examination;* see also William Roscoe to Thomas Eddy (Mar. 31, 1825), in Knapp, *Life of Thomas Eddy,* 313–14). Americans, however, pled innocent to Roscoe's exaggerated charge. *Prison Discipline Soc'y* 3 (1828):48–55 ("What abandonment?"); James Mease to William Roscoe (May 18, 1827), in *U.S. Gazette,* June 2, 1827, at 1, continued June 6, 1827, at 1; Roberts Vaux, *Letter on the Penitentiary System of Pennsylvania* (Philadelphia, 1827), 5; Roberts Vaux, *Reply to Two Letters of William Roscoe, Esquire* (Philadelphia, 1827), 3–4, 7; A[llen], *Obser-vations,* 3 (answered, in turn, in William Roscoe to Stephen Allen [Nov. 1, 1827], in *Liverpool Chron.,* Jan. 5, 1828, at 3, continued Jan. 12, 1828, at 3, Jan. 19, 1828, at 2–3, and Jan. 26, 1828, at 2).

108. For commentaries opposing the transition, see *Independent Gazetteer,* Nov. 11, 1786, at 2; [Robert Annon], "Observations on Capital Punishment," *Am. Musium* 4 (1788):444 (defending the death penalty and all public punishments).

109. *Am. Musium* 7 (1790):193–95 (quotation at 194).

110. David Rothman argues that this ideological theme was both central and unique to penitentiary advocacy in Jacksonian America. Rothman, *Discovery of the Asylum,* xix, 71, 79, 83–85, 107–9. For a more direct response to Rothman's analysis, see Adam J. Hirsch, "From Pillory to Penitentiary: The Rise of Criminal Incarceration in the New Republic" (Ph.D. diss., Yale University, 1987), ch. 5.

111. Jeremy Bentham, "Panopticon; or the Inspection-House" [1791], in *The Works of*

Jeremy Bentham, ed. John Bowring (Edinburgh, 1843), 4:40, 58–66 (quotation at 40) (emphasis omitted). Bentham, too, promised his readers the world: "Morals reformed—health preserved—industry invigorated—instruction diffused ... the gordian knot of the Poor-Laws not cut, but untied—all by a simple idea in Architecture!" (39; emphasis omitted). In another essay, Bentham offered an elaborate plan for a network of panopticons for paupers, see "Pauper Management Improved" [1798], in *Works,* 8:369, 375.

112. *Prison Discipline Soc'y* 4 (1829):54–69 (quotation at 54–55). Dwight hoped to further the overall purpose of crime control via such preventive measures. Bentham, by contrast, viewed the "inspection principle" of his architectural plan as reinforcing the effectiveness of each institution "no matter how different, or even opposite the purpose." Bentham, "Panopticon," in *Works,* 4:40.

113. *Prison Discipline Soc'y* 4 (1829):55.

114. Commentators both early and late occasionally suggested that *all* persons could benefit from a carceral regimen, but these were mere figurative asides, spinning off the traditional theme of the universality of sin, not literal suggestions; see Hanway, *Distributive Justice,* 42–43; James Finley, *Memorials of Prison Life* (Cincinnati, 1850), 41–42, cf. 16–20 (setting out orthodox objectives for the penitentiary). Cf. Rothman, *Discovery of the Asylum,* 84–85 (reading Finley literally).

115. Beaumont and Tocqueville, *On the Penitentiary System,* 48.

116. For example, Beaumont and Tocqueville, *On the Penitentiary System,* xviii, 48, 80, 160n.3 ("imaginary effects"); Smith, *Defence,* 77 ("visionary"); Livingston, *Complete Writings,* 1:563–64 ("the visionary belief of a moral panacea"); [Bradford], *State Prisons,* 61 ("altogether an utopian idea"). Cf. Rothman, *Discovery of the Asylum,* 62, 69, 78 (identifying faith in the ability to eradicate crime as Jacksonian gospel).

117. "Remarks on the Mass. State Prison," 4; [Gamaliel Bradford], *Columbian Centinel,* Jan. 21, 1824, at 1. The sting in Bradford's prose doubtless reflected in part his conflict with the directors, see above, notes 48–50 and accompanying text. The directors here may simply have meant that by rehabilitating criminals, the level of criminality in society would be reduced. Cf. the phrasing in Bache, *Observations and Reflections,* 6–7.

118. "Book Review," *Am. Q. Rev.* 14 (1833):237 (answering Tocqueville's suggestion that the penitentiary effected the "expiation" of the offender).

119. [Bradford], *State Prisons,* 20.

120. Of Bentham's plan to extend the Panopticon model to poor relief "there is no record of any response ... except Bentham's own bitter tirades against the king for preventing its adoption." Gertrude Himmelfarb, *The Idea of Poverty: England in the Early Industrial Age* (New York, 1984), 83.

121. For example, Smith, *Defence,* 96; Livingston, *Complete Works,* 1:547–48; A[llen], *Observations,* 62; *Letters on the Pennsylvania System of Solitary Imprisonment,* 2d ed. (Philadelphia, 1837), 16–17; Howe, *Report of a Minority,* 20. There are literally scores of such examples.

122. Stephen Allen thus scolded William Roscoe: "[A]lthough you have thought and wrote much on penal jurisprudence, . . . still . . . there is a want of experimental and practical knowledge, without which, no man can form a correct judgement." A[llen], *Examination,* 4; see also Lewis, *From Newgate to Dannemora,* 79.

123. The admission of visitors and the looming architecture of the penitentiary were intended to inspire general deterrence; see chapter 3, notes 125–26 and accompanying text.

124. As a Jacksonian advocate wrote of the Walnut Street prison: "[A] penitential and reforming system was actually in operation, possessing all the characteristics of the
present plans excepting only the means and machinery subsequently obtained by
the persevering labours of the reformers." "Book Review," *Am. Q. Rev.* 14 (1833):232.
Similarly, see, e.g., Allen, Hopkins, and Tibbits, "Report," 103; Governor's Message,
Mass. Resolves, Jan. 1822:395–97; *Report [on the Mass. State Prison],* 1829:8. In
Massachusetts, the renovations of 1829 were the culmination of a gradual process of
administrative trial and error; see Gamaliel Bradford to Governor and Board of Visitors (Nov. 2, 1820), in Governor and Council, "Reports and Papers," pt. 1; "Visitors
Minutes," 1:108 (Feb. 12, 1810), 110 (Mar. 8, 1810), 117–18 (May 21, 1810), n.p. (Jan. 1,
1812), n.p. (June 22, 1813), and many other entries on administrative tinkering.

125. For a sampling of plaudits, see, e.g., *Report [on the Mass. State Prison],* Sept.
1830:3–4, 18–27; id., 1831:4–7; *Mass. Resolves,* 1828–31:222–24, 451–54; id., 1832–
34:32–34, 277–80, 596; id., 1835–38:35–36; *Prison Discipline Soc'y* 5 (1830):6–8; id.,
7 (1832):10–19.

126. Francis Lieber, "Translator's Preface," in Beaumont and Tocqueville, *On the Penitentiary System,* xviii–xix. In the South, opposition to criminal incarceration was more
prolonged; see Edward L. Ayers, *Vengeance and Justice: Crime and Punishment in
the Nineteenth-Century American South* (New York, 1984), ch. 2.

Chapter 6

1. On the development of slavery in Virginia, see Edmund S. Morgan, *American
Slavery, American Freedom: The Ordeal of Colonial Virginia* (New York, 1975).
Slavery played a smaller, but not insignificant, role in the economies of the middle
Atlantic colonies and of New England. David Brion Davis, *The Problem of Slavery in
Western Culture* (Ithaca, 1966), 135 and n.18.

2. A functional connection between the two institutions was first postulated by Michael
Hindus in his comparative study of the criminal justice systems of Massachusetts
and South Carolina; see Michael S. Hindus, *Prison and Plantation: Crime, Justice,
and Authority in Massachusetts and South Carolina, 1767–1878* (Chapel Hill, 1980),
esp. 125–27.

3. "[T]he labor assigned to [the inmates] must be performed with faithfulness, and
the slightest disposition to neglect it noticed and corrected." Regulations of 1815,
in Gideon Haynes, *Pictures from Prison Life: An Historical Sketch of the Massachusetts State Prison* (Boston, 1870), 233. For examples of punishment administered
for "neglecting" work, see, e.g., "Daily Reports, 1805–29," 1:n.p. (Apr. 24, July 4,
Sept. 11, Nov. 10, Feb. 26, Mar. 26, June 12, July 29, Aug. 26, 1806), 4:n.p. (Feb. 12,
Feb. 25, 1819, Oct. 16, 1823) (warden's record, unpublished MS, Mass. Archives). On
prison working hours, see Stephen Burroughs, *Memoirs of the Notorious Stephen
Burroughs* (New York, 1924), 137–38 (Castle Island); "Minutes of the Meetings of the
Board of Visitors/Directors/Inspectors," 1:28 (June 2, 1806) (unpublished MS, Mass.
Archives) [hereinafter "Visitors Minutes"] (Mass. State Prison). James Mease stated
that at the Walnut Street prison, "the labour [is] constant, and the working hours
greater than among mechanics." James Mease, *The Picture of Philadelphia* (Philadelphia, 1811), 166. But subsequently, when recommending that penitentiaries be
built on the solitary plan, he suggested that hard labor was no deterrent: "Even
when labor is performed in society [within the prison], it is neither so hard, nor so
long continued, as to amount to a punishment. The hours of work are fewer, than
those prescribed by custom to honest mechanics." James Mease to William Roscoe

(May 18, 1827), in *U.S. Gazette,* June 6, 1827, at 1; likewise, James Mease, *Observations on the Penitentiary System* (Philadelphia, 1828), 20–21. See also Gustave de Beaumont and Alexis de Tocqueville, *On the Penitentiary System in the United States and Its Application in France* (Philadelphia, 1833), 103n; *Annual Report of the Board of Managers of the Prison Discipline Society,* 8:14–15 (Boston, 1833) [hereinafter *Prison Discipline Soc'y*]; W. David Lewis, *From Newgate to Dannemora: The Rise of the Penitentiary in New York, 1796–1848* (Ithaca, 1965), 134–35, 153–54.

4. On the "overseer" of the prison, see chapter 2, note 182. On "hard labor" by slaves, see, e.g., Thomas Jefferson, *Notes on the State of Virginia* [1787], ed. William Peden (Williamsburg, 1955), 139.

5. On prison garb, see chapter 2, note 118. For the regulation of slave garb, see, e.g., Act of May 10, 1740, no. 670, *Statutes at Large of South Carolina, 1682–1838,* ed. Thomas Cooper and David J. McCord (Columbia, 1836–41), 7:408 (§ 40). Inmates in some workhouses had also worn special garb, see chapter 2, note 21.

6. Chains were used at the Massachusetts State Prison as a disciplinary device. See, e.g., "Daily Reports," 1:n.p. (July 20, Feb. 8, Apr. 24, Sept. 8, Dec. 11, 1806).

7. John Locke, *Two Treatises of Government* [1698], ed. Peter Laslett (Cambridge, 1964), 302 (emphasis omitted).

8. Burroughs, *Memoirs,* 153, 169–70 (quotation at 153); *Boston Daily Examiner,* Feb. 18, 1818, at 2.

9. On slaveholders' fears, see Morgan, *American Slavery, American Freedom,* 308–9. On slave rebellions, see, e.g., Gerald W. Mullin, *Flight and Rebellion: Slave Resistance in Eighteenth-Century Virginia* (New York, 1972), 59, 140–63. The Massachusetts State Prison regulations of 1815 admonished officers to "consider the prison as a volcano, containing lava, which, if not kept in subjection, will destroy friends and foes; and therefore they should ever be on their guard against an eruption." Regulations of 1815, in Haynes, *Pictures,* 234. In New York, see Beaumont and Tocqueville, *On the Penitentiary System,* 156 n.Q.

10. On slave escapes, see, e.g., Mullin, *Flight and Rebellion,* 34–35, 39–47, 55–58, 105–23. On prison escapes in Massachusetts, see chapter 5, notes 53, 86. The directors of the Massachusetts State Prison were convinced that the plotting was "daily . . . [d]aring and desperate." "Remarks on the Massachusetts State Prison," in *Rules and Regulations for the Government of the Massachusetts State Prison Adopted by the Board of Directors* (Boston, 1823), 24.

11. Burroughs, *Memoirs,* 152–54, 156.

12. There are scores of such entries. For examples, see above, note 3.

13. On slave sabotage, see, e.g., Mullin, *Flight and Rebellion,* 33–35, 53–54. On inmate sabotage in Massachusetts, see [Gamaliel Bradford], *Description and Historical Sketch of the Massachusetts State Prison* (Charlestown, 1816), 10; "Daily Reports," e.g., 4:n.p. (Oct. 14, 1823); "Visitors Minutes," 2:206–9 (Sept. 26, 1822) (destruction of brush storehouse, "probably an act of revenge in some one or more of them"), 315 (Apr. 6, 1824) (destruction of finished cabinet work); id. 1:n.p. (June 22, 1813) (measures to prevent convict "waste or plunder"); in New York, see S[tephen] A[llen], *An Examination of the Remarks on the Report of the Commissioners* (New York, 1826) 8; Stephen Allen, Samuel Hopkins, and George Tibbits, "Report," in *Journal of the Assembly of the State of New York* (New York, 1825), 107; Gershom Powers, *A Brief Account of the Construction, Management, and Discipline, &c., &c., of the New York State Prison at Auburn* (Auburn, 1826), 55, 61 (measures taken to prevent sabotage); in Pennsylvania, sabotage was anticipated under the carceral legislation of 1790,

Act of Apr. 5, 1790, ch. 1516, *The Statutes at Large of Pennsylvania from 1682 to 1801* (Harrisburg, 1908), 13:517 (§ 13) [hereinafter *Pa. Stats. at Large*]. One observer opposed the English Dock-Yards Bill of 1750 because convicts might destroy vital naval stores in time of war. Charles Jones, *Some Methods Proposed toward Putting a Stop to the Frequent Crimes of Murder, Robbery, and Perjury* (London, 1752), 11–12. The English Penitentiary Act of 1779 called for the selection of prison industries least susceptible to sabotage. 19 Geo. 3 c.74, § 32 (1779).

14. Haynes, *Pictures,* 29–30; "Visitors Minutes," 1:n.p. (Jan. 6, Jan. 7, 1813), 2:299 (Mar. 12, 1824); *Report [on the Mass. State Prison],* 1831:9 (unpublished document, Harvard Law Library) (also in "Mass. Legislative Documents," Senate and House, 1832:218, State Library Annex); Governor's Message, Jan. 1, 1823, *Mass. Resolves,* Jan. 1823:564. On at least one occasion, the convicts engaged in a peaceful labor protest; "Visitors Minutes," 2:262–63 (Apr. 12, 1823).

15. On slaves feigning illness and slave suicides, see Mullin, *Flight and Rebellion,* 34, 53, 55, 60. On convicts feigning illness, self-induced illness, and self-mutilation at the Massachusetts State Prison, see *Report [on the Mass. State Prison],* Sept. 1830:16–17, 22 (also in "Mass. Legislative Documents," 1830–31:151); Warden Bradford to Governor and Visitors (Oct. 16, 1823), in Governor and Council, "Reports and Papers of the State Prison at Charlestown, 1807, 1822–23," Misc. Box no. 3, pt. 1 (unpublished MS, Mass. Archives). On a case of suicide, see Haynes, *Pictures,* 137–38 (quotation).

16. "The prisoner, in bondage, who toils for others, works with a dejected mind, and spares himself so much as he can." James Mease to William Roscoe (May 18, 1827), in *U.S. Gazette,* June 6, 1827, at 1; likewise, e.g., Bentham, "Principles of Penal Law" [MSS 1775–1802], in *The Works of Jeremy Bentham,* ed. John Bowring (Edinburgh, 1843), 1:441; "Remarks on the Mass. State Prison," 8–9; "Mass. Legislative Documents," 1817–22, no. 1:15.

17. "Visitors Minutes," 1:n.p. (June 3, 1812) (quotation); Beaumont and Tocqueville, *On the Penitentiary System,* 36–37.

18. On slave punishment, see, e.g., Morgan, *American Slavery, American Freedom,* 310–13.

19. Corporal punishment was permitted in many penitentiaries at various times. When not permitted, solitary confinement ordinarily served as the substitute. On inmate punishment, see Beaumont and Tocqueville, *On the Penitentiary System,* 39–47. In Massachusetts, loss of rations and solitary confinement were the usual punishment for ordinary offenses, such as refusal to work, but corporal punishment was inflicted for serious offenses. All punishment was carefully regulated, however. Act of Mar. 15, 1785, ch. 63, *Mass. Acts & Resolves,* 1784–85:164–65; "Rules and Orders of 1823," in *Rules and Regulations,* 46, 58–59; Act of Mar. 11, 1828, ch. 118, *Mass. Acts,* 1825–28:829 (§ 21); in practice, see, e.g., "Daily Reports," 1:n.p. (Dec. 19, 1805, July 20, Feb. 8, Feb. 10, Feb. 26, Mar. 18, Mar. 19, Mar. 20, Apr. 11, Apr. 23, Apr. 24, May 16, July 4, Aug. 26, Sept. 8, Sept. 11, Oct. 3, Nov. 10, Dec. 3, 1806). Later entries are similar. For an example of extraordinary punishment, see "Visitors Minutes," 2:142–43 (June 30, 1821). In Pennsylvania in the 1820s, where convicts were subjected to solitary confinement as a matter of course, "Our Commissioners believe that no inducement will exist to ensure their industry; for they suppose that no further or additional punishment can be inflicted." George W. Smith, *A Defence of the System of Solitary Confinement of Prisoners Adopted by The State of Pennsylvania* (Philadelphia, 1833), 89.

20. Powers, *Brief Account,* 3. The connection to prison discipline is emphasized in [Gamaliel Bradford], *State Prisons and the Penitentiary System Vindicated* (Charlestown, 1821), 43.

21. See below, notes 133–43 and accompanying text.

22. "The man must be a prodigy who can retain his manners and morals undepraved by such circumstances." Jefferson, *Notes on the State of Virginia,* 162.

23. Jacques Brissot de Warville, *New Travels in the United States of America Performed in 1788* (London, 1792), 372–73 (emphasis added). See also [Francis Wayland], "Book Review," *N. Am. Rev.* 49 (1839):10–11 ("can anyone doubt whether . . . there is one out of a thousand who would not, under such circumstances, become a tyrant?").

24. See, e.g., Winthrop D. Jordan, *White Over Black: American Attitudes toward the Negro, 1550–1812* (Chapel Hill, 1968), 128–31, 406. Craftworkers in the North had made the same protest before abolition in the northern states. Richard B. Morris, *Government and Labor in Early America* (New York, 1946), 182–88.

25. See chapter 7, text at notes 73–79.

26. Quoted in Donald L. Robinson, *Slavery in the Structure of American Politics, 1765–1820* (New York, 1971), 72. This ultimately became a major theme of antislavery ideology; Eric Foner, *Free Soil, Free Labor, Free Men: The Ideology of the Republican Party before the Civil War* (New York, 1970), 46–47, 60–61.

27. Walter E. Hugins, *Jacksonian Democracy and the Working Class: A Study of the New York Workingmen's Movement, 1829–1837* (Stanford, 1960), 157; Lewis, *From Newgate to Dannemora,* 189–90; Bentham, "Principles of Penal Law," in *Works,* 1:441. One observer believed that the English Dock-Yards Bill of 1750 was defeated, among other reasons, because "it would be a great discouragement to the ship-wrights and other artificers, who would think it scandalous to be fellow-labourers with men of such infamous characters." [Samuel Denne], *A Letter to Sir Robert Ladbroke . . . With an Attempt to Shew the Good Effects Which May Reasonably Be Expected from the Confinement of Criminals in Separate Apartments* (London, 1771), 77. Francis Lieber ridiculed this contention: "As if honesty itself were degraded, because the convicts are taught to be honest; or is the Bible of the honest part of the community insulted, because the same Bible is given into the hands of convicts? The convicts breathe, eat, sleep; are all these actions henceforth degraded?" Francis Lieber to Charles Penrose, (Jan. 22, 1835), in Thomas McElwee, *A Concise History of the Eastern Penitentiary of Pennsylvania* (Philadelphia, 1835), 62.

28. See below, note 119.

29. See chapter 3, note 35.

30. The first such theory to make a noticeable impact in the criminological literature of America was "phrenology"; see Charles Caldwell, *New Views of Penitentiary Discipline* (Philadelphia, 1829); Lewis, *From Newgate to Dannemora,* 231–37.

31. On incapacitation as an aim of carceral punishment, see chapter 3, note 105.

32. *Report [on the Mass. State Prison],* 1822:14 (also in "Mass. Legislation Documents," 1817–22, no. 52); *Prison Discipline Soc'y* 1 (1826):35–36; id., 2 (1827):43–46, 79–80; Mease, *Observations,* 34–36; [Thomas Eddy], *An Account of the State Prison or Penitentiary House in the City of New-York* (New York, 1801), 86. This phenomenon did not escape the notice of southern advocates of slavery. *The Pro-Slavery Argument as Maintained by the Most Distinguished Writers of the Southern States* (Charleston, 1852), 434–35.

33. Gershom Powers, "Communication to the Assembly, Jan. 7, 1828," in *Journal of the*

Assembly of the State of New York (New York, 1828), 30–31 (quotation); John Sergeant and Samuel Miller, *Observations and Reflections on the Design and Effects of Punishment in Letters Addressed to Roberts Vaux* (n.p., 1828), 4; Orlando F. Lewis, *The Development of American Prisons and Prison Customs, 1776–1845* (Albany, 1922), 62–63.

34. See chapter 7, text at notes 42–51.

35. Convicts sold into servitude had been disposed of in this manner as late as 1787. *Pa. J.,* Jan. 3, 1787, at 3.

36. *Columbian Centinel,* Jan. 7, 1824, at 3, Jan. 21, 1824, at 1.

37. Lewis, *Development of American Prisons,* 152, 256–59; Edward L. Ayers, *Vengeance and Justice: Crime and Punishment in the Nineteenth-Century American South* (New York, 1984), 68.

38. This was especially true in the penitentiaries of New York. See below, notes 135–37 and accompanying text.

39. Oliver Wolcott to Committee (Jan. 11, 1822), in Society for the Prevention of Pauperism, *Report on the Penitentiary System in the United States* (New York, 1922), app. 28; for additional examples of analogical reasoning, see below, text at notes 126, 166.

40. Burroughs, *Memoirs,* 98, 117–18, 128, 139, 156, 162, 175, 179, 183, 190 (quotation at 118). For additional examples of inmate self-characterization, see Haynes, *Pictures,* 137–38; [W. A. Coffey], *Inside Out* (New York, 1823), 147; Levi Burr, *A Voice from Sing-Sing* (Albany, 1833), 32 ("Slaves at Tripoli"); John Reynolds, *Recollections of Windsor Prison* (Boston, 1834), 136. Allusions to slavery are still made by convicts. Barbara Esposito and Lee Wood, *Prison Slavery* (Washington, D.C., 1982), 1–2.

41. Burroughs, *Memoirs,* 161, 164; see also Lewis, *Development of American Prisons,* 155–56; Lewis, *From Newgate to Dannemora,* 274.

42. Analogy of the workhouse to slavery: T[homas] F[irmin], *Some Proposals for the Imployment of the Poor* (London, 1681), 11. Analogy of proposed criminal hard labor programs to slavery: Thomas More, *Utopia* [1516], trans. Paul Turner (London, 1972), 50–53, 105; Samuel Chidley, *A Cry against a Crying Sinne* (London, 1652), 16–17; William Petty, "A Treatise of Taxes and Contributions" [1662], in *The Economic Writings of Sir William Petty,* ed. Charles Hull (New York, 1899), 1:68–69; Gerrard Winstanley, "The Law of Freedom in a Platform" [1652], in *The Works of Gerrard Winstanley,* ed. G. H. Sabine (Ithaca, 1941); A Student of Politics, *Proposals to the Legislature for Preventing the Frequent Execution and Exportation of Convicts* (London, 1754), 26–27; *Hanging Not Punishment Enough* [1701], (London, 1812), 20; Francis Hutcheson, *A System of Moral Philosophy* (London, 1755), 201–2; Cesare Beccaria, *On Crimes and Punishments* [1764], ed. Henry Paolucci (Indianapolis, 1963), 47–50; [Denne], *Letter,* 76–77; Manasseh Dawes, *An Essay on Crimes and Punishments* (London, 1782), 67–68; *Thoughts on Capital Punishment* (London, 1770), 19–20, 34; Bernard Mandeville, *An Enquiry into the Causes of the Frequent Executions at Tyburn* (London, 1725), 53–54. (Mandeville also suggested that convicted criminals be exchanged for captured English seamen enslaved on the Barbary Coast [48–53]. Subsequent advocates returned to this idea, Sollom Emlyn, "Preface," in *Collection of State Trials* [London, 1730], xxxiii; [Thomas Robe], "Some Consideration for Rendering the Punishment of Criminals More Effectual," in *A Collection of Political Tracts* [London, 1735], 46–47 [cf. Robe's proposal cited in chapter 7, note 157]; William Eden, *Principles of Penal Law* [London, 1771], 34.) Analogy on the Continent of hard labor to slavery: Max Grunhut, *Penal Reform: A Comparative Study*

(Oxford, 1948), 26. Analogies of the penitentiary to slavery: [Bradford], *State Prisons*, 14, 43; "Remarks on the Mass. State Prison," 24; Powers, *Brief Account*, 68; *Letters on the Pennsylvania System of Solitary Imprisonment*, 1st ed. (Charleston, 1835), 4; and in England, Jeremy Bentham, "Panopticon, or the Inspection-House" [1791], in *Works*, 4:32; Bentham, "Principles of Penal Law," in id., 1:441; William Smith, *Mild Punishments Sound Policy* (London, 1777), 29–30, 40. Again, this analogy is occasionally made by modern scholars; Charles E. Reasons and Russell L. Kaplan, "Tear Down the Walls? Some Functions of Prisons," *Crime & Delinquency* 21 (1975):368.

43. Thomas Jefferson to Edmund Pendleton (Aug. 26, 1776), in *The Papers of Thomas Jefferson*, ed. Julian P. Boyd (Princeton, 1950), 1:505.

44. For example [Benjamin Rush], *An Address to the Inhabitants of the British Settlements in America upon Slavekeeping* (New York, 1773), 29; Benjamin Rush to Nathaniel Greene (Sept. 16, 1782), in *Letters of Benjamin Rush*, ed. L. H. Butterfield (Princeton, 1951), 1:547.

45. Beaumont and Tocqueville, *On the Penitentiary System*, 47. Tocqueville developed his political theory of despotism by using the prison as his prototype. Roger Boesche, "The Prison: Tocqueville's Model for Despotism," *Western Pol. Q.* 33 (1980): 550. For similar observations of this incongruity, see Burroughs, *Memoirs*, 98; Burr, *Voice from Sing-Sing*, 16; *Remarks on Prisons and Prison Discipline* (Boston, 1826), 12–13; "Declaration of Samuel Hopkins, 1830," reprinted in Lewis, *Development of American Prisons*, 114.

46. Mandeville, *Enquiry*, 53 (emphasis in original). For seventeenth-century references to this objection, which was leveled against workhouses as well as hard labor programs for criminals, see Richard Haines, *A Breviat of Some Proposals* (London, 1679), 6 (objection to workhouses); Chidley, *Cry against a Crying Sinne*, 16–17.

47. Bentham, "Principles of Penal law," in *Works*, 1:411, 441 (quotation at 411). The English Dock-Yards Bill of 1750 had been similarly castigated by Jonas Hanway, an advocate of solitary confinement; see Leon Radzinowicz, *A History of English Criminal Law and Its Administration from 1750* (London, 1948), 1:422–23 n.58. For other eighteenth-century references to this objection, see Dawes, *Essay*, 68; [Denne], *Letter*, 76–77; *Thoughts on Capital Punishment*, 19–20, 34; Smith, *Mild Punishments Sound Policy*, 40–41; Henry Fielding, *A Proposal for Making an Effectual Provision for the Poor* (London, 1753), 73; A. Roger Ekirch, *Bound for America: The Transportation of British Convicts to the Colonies, 1718–1775* (Oxford, 1987), 20–21, 226–27, 230. For eighteenth-century objections to workhouses on this ground, see Gertrude Himmelfarb, *The Idea of Poverty: England in the Early Industrial Age* (New York, 1984), 81, 84.

48. Bentham, "Principles of Penal Law," in *Works*, 1:441.

49. *Mass. Centinel*, Oct. 16, 1784, at 1.

50. See chapter 4, text at note 33.

51. *Remarks on Prisons and Prison Discipline*, 12.

52. On opposition to the penitentiary in the South, see note 60, below.

53. *Prison Discipline Soc'y* 2 (1827):56–57. The report states: "This is sufficiently apparent; because it has been introduced in all the United States where Penitentiaries have been established."

54. English antagonism to the idea of slavery as a punishment does not appear to have impeded enactment of hard labor sanctions in colonial North America, since such statutes, passed on occasion, were not disallowed. See chapter 4, text at notes 16–21. But in one instance, a Pennsylvania statute against housebreaking, mandating

fourfold restitution "and [the offender] to be sold for the forfeiture if not able to pay," was disallowed because "selling a man is not a punishment allowed by the law of England." *Pa. Stats. at Large*, 2:491 [1700].

55. He preferred to call the punishment "short or long labor" (as of course it did come, more or less, to be called). Student of Politics, *Proposals*, 36.

56. Robe responded by noting that the Dutch had already instituted hard labor without having "occasioned the least Infringement upon the Liberties of their honest Subjects: Wherefore should we fear any worse Consequences from confining Felons to hard Labour at Home, in respect to our Liberties, than we find at present from Transporting them Abroad to our Plantations." [Robe], *Some Considerations*, 48.

57. Bentham, "Principles of Penal Law," in *Works*, 1:411; see also Ekirch, *Bound for America*, 230.

58. Morgan, *American Slavery, American Freedom*, 324–25. Slavery had been briefly mandated as a punishment for vagrancy in the sixteenth century. C. S. L. Davies, "Slavery and Protector Somerset: The Vagrancy Act of 1547," *Econ. Hist. Rev.*, 2d ser., 19 (1966):533.

59. See Morgan, *American Slavery, American Freedom*, esp. ch. 18.

60. At the same time, the existence of chattel slavery on a large scale in parts of North America, and the racism with which it was associated, could have evoked other sentiments. When proposed in the South in the 1820, penitentiaries were highly controversial and sometimes denounced as slavery—a controversy fed perhaps by the fear of ever equating white convicts with black slaves. On southern anti-penitentiary rhetoric, see Ayers, *Vengeance and Justice*, esp. 46–49, 68–69.

61. Blackstone modified slightly his treatment of chattel slavery in subsequent editions of the *Commentaries*. But at the same time, Blackstone enumerated slavery without comment as one of many possible punishments. William Blackstone, *Commentaries on the Laws of England* (London, 1765–69), 4:*12; David Brion Davis, *The Problem of Slavery in the Age of Revolution, 1770–1823* (Ithaca, 1975), 273, 485–86 and n.28 (quotation at 273).

62. William Roscoe, *Observations on Penal Jurisprudence and the Reformation of Criminals, Part III* (London, 1825), 57; Davis, *Problem of Slavery in the Age of Revolution*, 355.

63. On Roscoe's antislavery activities, see Henry Roscoe, *The Life of William Roscoe, by His Son* (London, 1833), 1:75–97, 2:305–9.

64. Among other English penitentiary advocates who actively worked for the abolition of slavery were William Allen, Thomas Buxton, Samuel Romilly, and William Wilberforce. As in the movement for criminal incarceration, rationalists and philanthropists made common cause in the fight for abolition. Michael Ignatieff, *A Just Measure of Pain: The Penitentiary in the Industrial Revolution, 1750–1850* (London, 1978), 143–73; Davis, *Problem of Slavery in the Age of Revolution*, 242–43, 248, 355–56, 446; Radzinowicz, *History*, 1:344–45, 349–50.

65. Not without exceptions. James T. Austin, a director of the Massachusetts State Prison, took a proslavery stance, though hardly an ardent one; see [James Austin], *Remarks on Dr. Channing's Slavery* (Boston, 1835); James S. Loring, *The Hundred Boston Orators* (Boston, 1852), 476.

66. [Duke de la Rochefouchault-Liancourt], *On the Prisons of Philadelphia* (Philadelphia, 1776), 40 (also published under the author's name in London under the title *A Comparative View of Mild and Sanguinary Laws*).

67. Negley K. Teeters, *They Were in Prison: A History of the Pennsylvania Prison Society,*

1787–1937 (Philadelphia, 1937), 4; Davis, *Problem of Slavery in the Age of Revolution,* 216, 533–35. Likewise, the leaders of Pennsylvania's second generation of penitentiary advocates, Roberts Vaux and James Mease, see Roberts Vaux, *Memoirs of The Lives of Benjamin Lay and Ralph Sandiford* (Philadelphia, 1815); Mease, *Observations,* 23–24.

68. Samuel L. Knapp, *The Life of Thomas Eddy* (New York, 1834), 20–21, 172–73.

69. William Jenks, *A Memoir of the Rev. Louis Dwight* (Boston, 1856), 40; Haynes, *Pictures,* 236–37.

70. On Jefferson's criminological activities, see Lewis, *Development of American Prisons,* 210–11.

71. Robert Turnbull, *A Visit to the Philadelphia Prison* (London, 1797), 28–30; see also Soc'y for the Prevention of Pauperism, *Report,* 91–92; and in England, Jonas Hanway, *Distributive Justice and Mercy* (London, 1781), 133–34; William Roscoe, *Observations on Penal Jurisprudence* (London, 1819), 174. Likewise private letters, see Davis, *Problem of Slavery in the Age of Revolution,* 252–53; Benjamin Rush to John Lettsom (May 18, Sept. 28, 1787) in *Letters of Benjamin Rush,* 1:417, 441–43; Thomas Eddy to William Roscoe (Dec. 15, 1825), in Knapp, *Life,* 316; Roscoe to General Lafayette (Aug. 29, 1830), in "Roscoe Papers: Materials Relating to the United States," no. 2297 (unpublished MS, Picton Library, Liverpool).

72. S[tephen] A[llen], *Observations on Penitentiary Discipline Addressed to William Roscoe* (New York, 1827), 54–55.

73. *Pennsylvania Mercury,* Oct. 2, 1788, at 2 (under the pseudonym "Philochorus"). For the complete Annon-Rush debate, focusing principally on the propriety of capital punishment, see id., Sept. 30, Oct. 2, Oct. 4, Oct. 21, Oct. 23, 1788; *Am. Musium* 4 (1788):444–54, 547–53; id. 5 (1789):63–65, 121–23.

74. Dawes, *Essay,* 68.

75. Locke, *Two Treatises of Government,* 290–93, 302–3, 340–41, 400–406 (quotations at 291–92). Perhaps to answer those who rated slavery worse than death, Locke added that if the slave ever found that to be so, he could commit suicide (302). But for criminologists who sought a deterrent more potent than death, the possibility of suicide was a *drawback* of penal slavery! *Hanging Not Punishment Enough,* 21.

76. The concept of *felony* initially covered violations of the feudal contract. The felon became an "outlaw." Frederick Pollock and Frederic W. Maitland, *The History of English Law before the Time of Edward I,* ed. S.F.C. Milsom (Cambridge, 1968), 1:303–5.

77. *The Colonial Laws of Massachusetts,* ed. William H. Whitmore (Boston, 1890), § 1:53, 55. *Records of the Governor and Company of the Massachusetts Bay in New England,* ed. Nathaniel Shurtleff (Boston, 1853–54), 2:168 [1646] [hereinafter *Mass. Rec.*]. On the Puritan political theorists who addressed slavery, see Davis, *Problem of Slavery in Western Culture,* 197–203.

78. *Mass. Rec.,* 2:168 [1646]. In the eighteenth century, however, chattel slavery gained a foothold in Massachusetts; see the references in Davis, *Problem of Slavery in Western Culture,* 135 n.18.

79. The implications of such a sentence in early Massachusetts are unclear: sentences to slavery were either for life or for indefinite terms, but were frequently commuted after several months. On the enslavement of Indian captives, see Alden T. Vaughan, *New England Frontier: Puritans and Indians, 1620–1675,* rev. ed. (New York, 1979), 207–8, 319; *Mass. Rec.,* 1:181 [1636] (life sentence). On the enslavement of criminals, see Edwin Powers, *Crime and Punishment in Early Massachusetts, 1620–1692*

(Boston, 1966), 208–9; *Mass. Rec.,* 1:246 [1638], 269 [1639], 297 [1640], 2:21 [1642]; *Records of the Court of Assistants of the Colony of the Massachusetts Bay, 1630–1692* (Boston, 1901–28), 2:90 [1639], 97 [1640], 118 [1642] [hereinafter *Ct. of Assistants*]. The only statutory prescription of slavery as a punishment for particular crimes (as opposed to the general authorization contained in the Body of Liberties) appeared in the unenacted code composed by John Cotton, "Moses His Judicials"; see "An Abstract of the Laws of New England" [1641], in Mass. Hist. Soc'y, *Collections,* 1st ser., 5 (1798):184. Cases condemning persons to slavery expressly distinguished this condition from servitude: thus, in several cases, convicts committed to slavery subsequently had their sentences *commuted* to servitude. *Mass. Rec.,* 1:269 [1639]; *Ct. of Assistants,* 2:97 [1640]. As under Lockean theory, the distinction between captives and criminals was blurry: captives were "adjudged" to suffer slavery. *Mass. Rec.,* 1:181 [1636].

80. See chapter 1, notes 11–12 and accompanying text.

81. Samuel Willard, *A Compleat Body of Divinity* [1726], quoted in Lawrence Towner, "A Fondness for Freedom: Servant Protest in Puritan Society," *Wm. & Mary Q.,* 3d ser., 19 (1962):202.

82. Student of Politics, *Proposals,* 32–33, 39. Likewise, Dawes, *Essay,* 68; Emlyn, "Preface," xxxiii; and in Massachusetts, "The liberty of the offender is forfeited by his having abused the privilege." *Mass. Centinel,* Sept. 22, 1784, at 1.

83. "Dr. Nugent's Travels through Germany," quoted in *Thoughts on Capital Punishment,* 19–20 (emphasis in original). To the same effect, see Chidley, *Cry against a Crying Sinne,* 17; Dawes, *Essay,* 68.

84. Transportation was also sometimes equated with slavery and cited as a precedent for carceral hard labor. *The Poor Unhappy Transported Felon's Sorrowful Account of His Fourteen Years Transportation at Virginia in America* (London, n.d.), 5, 8; George Ollyffe, *An Essay Humbly Offer'd for an Act of Parliament to Prevent Capital Crimes* (London, 1731), 14; Henry Zouch, *Observations upon a Bill Now Depending in Parliament* (London, 1779), 11–12; Student of Politics, *Proposals,* 35; Ekirch, *Bound for America,* 223–24, 227.

85. 31 Car. 2 c.2 § 14 (1679); 4 Geo. 1 c.11 (1717); 16 Geo. 3 c.43 (1776); Radzinowicz, *History,* 1:108–10; John H. Langbein, "The Historical Origins of the Sanction of Imprisonment for Serious Crime," *J. Legal Stud.* 5 (1976):53–58.

86. Dawes, *Essay,* 68; "Dr. Nugent's Travels through Germany," quoted in *Thoughts on Capital Punishment,* 20 ("[I]f we live in a *free* Country, grant the poor Wretches the *Liberty* to chuse whether to *die* at the *Hands* of the Executioner, or to *live* and work with *their own*").

87. J.P.M. to the editor of the Universal Magazine (London) (Mar. 25, 1789), in *They Were in Prison,* 487; *Letter of Gershom Powers to the Hon. Edward Livingston, in Relation to the Auburn State Prison* (Albany, 1829), 13 (argument directed to convicts). One American defender of capital punishment reversed the equation: convicts who merited imprisonment for life could with equal justice be executed! James Dana, *The Intent of Capital Punishment* [1790] (New Haven, n.d.), 9.

88. *U.S. Const.* amend. XIII § 1 (1864); for other legislative references, see Esposito and Wood, *Prison Slavery,* 94, 207–22, and for a judicial statement see the jury charge by William Cushing, C.J., in the *Quok Walker* case (Mass., 1783), in Mass. Hist. Soc'y, *Proceedings,* 1st ser., 13 (1875):294.

89. Student of Politics, *Proposal,* 27; A Citizen, *The Gaol of the City of Bristol Compared with What a Gaol Ought to Be* (London, 1815), 20.

90. *Documents Illustrative of the History of the Slave Trade to America,* ed. Elizabeth Donnan (New York, 1969), 2:352n, 355, 395–96, 569, 571, 634, 659; Davis, *Problem of Slavery in Western Culture,* 181–86. The Virginia legislature in 1823 passed an act under which free blacks could be reenslaved as punishment for crime. Startlingly, the act was repealed after four years as "incompatible with every principle of morality and justice." Ayers, *Vengeance and Justice,* 62.

91. Locke, *Two Treatises of Government,* 302–3n.

92. Some commentators explicitly contrasted unjustly enslaved Africans with justly condemned transportees and other offenders sentenced to hard labor; see Emlyn, "Preface," xxxiii; Bernard Bailyn, *The Ideological Origins of the American Revolution* (Cambridge, Mass., 1967), 239–45; generally on the assertion of fraud, see Davis, *Problem of Slavery in the Age of Revolution,* 267–71, 283; Jordan, *White Over Black,* 297–301, 432–33.

93. Hutcheson, *System of Moral Philosophy,* 2:201–12 (quotation at 202).

94. Locke, *Two Treatises of Government,* 289.

95. *Independent Chron.,* Feb. 7, 1793, at 1, continued Feb. 14, 1793, at 1–2; *Am. Musium* 7 (1790):135; [Roberts Vaux], *An Appendix to the Essays on Capital Punishments* (Philadelphia, 1812), 23–24; in England, *Thoughts of Capital Punishment,* 37; Henry Dagge, *Considerations on Criminal Law* (London, 1772), 185–86. For Beccaria's analysis, conceding also a utilitarian justification for capital punishment omitted by his subsequent restators, see Beccaria, *On Crimes and Punishment,* 45–46. One proponent of capital punishment replied that the argument was "ingenious indeed, but too refined, and even sophistic." *Nat'l Gazette,* Dec. 23, 1828, at 2. For reasoned responses, see Dawes, *Essay,* 64 (inalienable right trumped by biblical sanction); "Observations on Capital Punishment," *Am. Musium* 4 (1788):449–54, 547–48 (same); "Mass. Legislative Documents," Senate 1831:520–21 (inalienable right trumped by utility); "Book Review," *N. Am. Rev.* 17 (1823): 265–66 (same, citing to Beccaria's dualism); William Turner, "Essay on Crimes and Punishments" [1785], excerpted in Basil Montague, *The Opinions of Different Authors upon the Punishment of Death* (London, 1809), 295n (rights over oneself qualitatively different from rights over others).

96. Locke, *Two Treatises of Government,* 302–3. Other political theorists were split on this question; see William S. Jenkins, *Pro-Slavery Thought in the Old South* (Chapel Hill, 1935), 117–18. Some southern advocates justified chattel slavery as an implied contract for service; id., 112–13.

97. James Otis, "The Rights of the British Colonists Asserted and Proved" [1764], reprinted in *Pamphlets of the American Revolution, 1750–1776,* ed. Bernard Bailyn (Cambridge, Mass., 1965), 1:477. The Declaration of Independence also characterized liberty as an "inalienable" right.

98. Quoted in Ayers, *Vengeance and Justice,* 48.

99. Benjamin Rush, *Considerations on the Injustice and Impolicy of Punishing Murder by Death* (Philadelphia, 1792), 3. Beccaria appears to have been of like mind, although he did not face the issue directly; see Beccaria, *On Crimes and Punishments,* 48–49.

100. Locke explicitly rejected the alternative view that "lesser breaches" of law could be punished with death. Locke, *Two Treatises of Government,* 292–93 (emphasis in original). Cf. Blackstone: "Whenever any *laws* direct [capital punishment] for light and trivial causes, such laws are . . . tyrannical, though in an inferior degree; because here the subject is aware of the danger he is exposed to, and may, by prudent caution, provide against it." Blackstone, *Commentaries,* 1:*133.

101. Beccaria, *On Crimes and Punishments,* 43 and n.

102. Student of Politics, *Proposals,* 26–27; A[llen], *Examination,* 4.

103. See generally Louis P. Masur, *Rites of Execution: Capital Punishment and the Trans-formation of American Culture, 1776–1865* (New York, 1989), ch. 3.

104. Burroughs, *Memoirs,* 98. This argument also appeared in the South; Ayers, *Vengeance and Justice,* 47. See also Charles de Secondat Montesquieu, *The Spirit of Laws* (London, 1752), 337.

105. William Roscoe, *Remarks on the Report of the Commissioners* (Liverpool, 1825), 8–9. Roscoe made the same point with regard to solitary confinement without labor; Roscoe to James Mease (Apr. 21, July 17, 1821), in William Roscoe, *Additional Observations on Penal Jurisprudence* (London, 1823), app. 24, 36.

106. A[llen], *Examination,* 4. Similarly, Gamaliel Bradford: "[B]y their vices and violations of law, they have no rights . . . they have forfeited their liberty, and all privileges of freemen . . . they are slaves and outlaws." [Bradford], *State Prisons,* 43. In a case challenging the power of keepers to whip convicts in New York, the presiding judge charged the jury that "by their willful misconduct and depravity, [convicts] had forfeited all rights [of freemen] while there, but the rights of humanity." Powers, *Brief Account,* 68. Nonetheless, Allen conceded the desirability of proportionality respecting the duration of hard labor; see above, note 102.

107. Roscoe, *Observations,* 38–50; William Roscoe, *A Brief Statement of the Causes Which Have Led to the Abandonment of the Celebrated System of Penitentiary Discipline in Some of the United States of America* (Liverpool, 1827), esp. 4–5; Roscoe, *Remarks,* esp. 9–10 (quotation at 9). Among American advocates, Roberts Vaux agreed that "a criminal retains all his natural rights, except so far as he is legally divested of them," and he asserted that such divestment occurred in *quantum meruit:* "In return for the benefit of protection [the citizen] is considered as . . . covenanting to yield due obedience to all . . . laws and regulations. . . . By small transgressions he forfeits a proportionate share of the protection, confidence, and hospitality due to him from the community. By the greatest, he may forfeit all the blessings peculiar to the social state." On this analysis, the discipline imposed at Auburn Prison was "utterly unjustifiable." Roberts Vaux, *Letter on the Penitentiary System of Pennsylvania Addressed to William Roscoe* (Philadelphia, 1827), 5; [Vaux], *Appendix,* 23–24.

108. Roscoe, *Brief Statement,* 6–7. Likewise, see Vaux, *Letter,* 5–7.

109. "[H]owever *effectual* the remedy may be, it ought not to be obtained by any sacrifice of *principle.*" Roscoe, *Remarks,* 7–9 (quotation at 8) (emphasis in original).

110. Bentham, "Principles of Penal Law," in *Works,* 1:441. For similar expressions of utilitarian justification, see, e.g., Student of Politics, *Proposals,* 29; [James Austin], "Book Review," *N. Am. Rev.* 10 (1820):239.

111. Davis, *Problem of Slavery in the Age of Revolution,* 351–53.

112. For example, Chidley, *Cry against a Crying Sinne,* 17; Dawes, *Essay,* 67; "Dr. Nugent's Travels through Germany," quoted in *Thoughts on Capital Punishment,* 19; Student of Politics, *Proposals,* 26.

113. Bailyn, *Ideological Origins,* 232–35.

114. Henry Fielding, "An Enquiry into the Causes of the Late Increase of Robbers" [1751], in *The Works of Henry Fielding, Esq.* (London, 1806), 10:348. Likewise, Jonas Hanway: "We enjoy the pleasure of calling ourselves a *free people;* but this violence of *Immorality* (London, 1775), 224–25 (emphasis in original) (reissued in 1780 under the title *The Citizen's Monitor*).

115. For example, Samuel West, *A Sermon Preached before the Honorable Council and*

206 Notes to Pages 83–85

the Honorable House of Representatives . . . May 29, 1776 (Boston, 1776), 13 ("where licentiousness begins, liberty ends"); William Symmes, *A Sermon Preached before His Honor Thomas Cushing . . . May 25, 1785* (Boston, 1785), 20 ("excess of wickedness has usually been attended with the loss of liberty"); Moses Hemmenway, *A Sermon Preached before His Excellency John Hancock . . . May 26, 1784* (Boston, 1784), 32 ("the abuse of liberty . . . is an inlet to tyranny and slavery"). See chapter 4, text at notes 42–43.

116. West, *Sermon,* 13. Cotton Mather added with unintended irony: "tis an *Hard Slavery* which [the transgressor] is in his way confin'd unto . . . . *Africa* knows nothing harder." Cotton Mather, *A True Survey and Report of the Road* (Boston, 1712), 10 (emphasis in original). See also, e.g., Phillips Payson, *A Sermon Preached before the Honorable Council . . . May 27, 1778* (Boston, 1778), 16; Nathaniel Fisher, *A Sermon Delivered at Salem, January 14, 1796, Occasioned by the Execution of Henry Blackburn* (Boston, 1796), 16; in England, Dawes, *Essay,* 253.

117. Smith, *Mild Punishments Sound Policy,* 40. Similarly, Henry Fielding: "Some Persons . . . represent the Restraint here laid on the lower People as derogatory from their Liberty. Such Notions are indeed of the enthusiastical Kind, and . . . are the natural Parents of that Licentiousness which . . . is sure at last to end in the Destruction of Liberty itself. . . . [Crimes] cannot be effectually abolished but by some such Law as this." Henry Fielding, *A Proposal for Making an Effectual Provision for the Poor* (London, 1753), 73; and the philanthropist Jonas Hanway: "To say we cannot have a *strict police* because we are a *free people,* is in effect to say, that it is in the nature of freedom to *destroy* itself." Hanway, *Distributive Justice and Mercy,* 6 (emphasis in original).

118. Jenkins, *Pro-Slavery Thought,* 44–46, 65–81; Davis, *Problem of Slavery in the Age of Revolution,* 353–54 and n.13.

119. Quoted in Morgan, *American Slavery, American Freedom,* 385; Jordan, *White Over Black,* 326, 407–8, 555–59, 577; *Pro-Slavery Argument,* 422–23, 433–35 (noting the tendency of freed slaves to land in penitentiaries); Larry E. Tise, *Proslavery: A History of the Defense of Slavery in America, 1701–1840* (Athens, Ga., 1987), 60–61.

120. Student of Politics, *Proposals,* 37 (emphasis in original). This was a common observation in both England and America; see, e.g., Smith, *Mild Punishments Sound Policy,* 29–30; Benjamin Rush, *An Enquiry into the Effects of Public Punishments upon Criminals and upon Society* (Philadelphia, 1787), 19; Edward Livingston, *The Complete Works of Edward Livingston on Criminal Jurisprudence,* ed. Salmon P. Chase (New York, 1873), 1:241; Bradford, *State Prisons,* 14; Bentham, "Panopticon," in *Works,* 4:144; *Am. Musium* 7 (1790):137.

121. For an express statement of the hope that carceral rehabilitation would serve to end the "state of war" between criminals and society, see *Report [on the Mass. State Prison],* Sept. 1830:8.

122. [Rush], *Address,* 4–5 (quotation); Benjamin Rush to Nathaniel Greene (Sept. 16, 1782), in *Letters of Benjamin Rush,* 1:286. This was a standard theme of antislavery advocacy, see Jordan, *White Over Black,* 281–83, and it was often repeated by penitentiary advocates who opposed slavery, e.g., [Eddy], *Account,* 86 (explaining the large number of black inmates in northern penitentiaries on this basis); Thomas Buxton, *The African Slave Trade and Its Remedy* (London, 1840), 460–86.

123. Act of Sept. 15, 1786, *Pa. Stats. at Large,* 12:280–81.

124. See chapter 3, note 120.

125. See chapter 3, notes 122–23 and accompanying text.

126. Rush, *Enquiry,* 16. One English proposal for public hard labor, the Dock-Yards Bill of 1750, was allegedly rejected on this basis; see note 28, above.
127. Rush, *Enquiry,* 22–29.
128. [William Tudor], "Book Review," *N. Am. Rev.* 13 (1821):418, 423 (quotation at 423). This distinction was also drawn by Edward Livingston: "There is a line of demarcation, which it would be rash in the extreme to destroy even in punishments; and the sight of the freeman performing . . . forced labour . . . must give rise to ideas of the most insubordinate nature." Livingston, *Complete Works,* 1:242. In England, see Roscoe, *Additional Observations,* 61. Not all advocates accepted the contention that even concealment of hard labor would suffice to protect free labor from stigmatization. See above, note 27 and accompanying text.
129. George Fitzhugh, *Cannibals All! or, Slaves without Masters* [1857], ed. C. Vann Woodward (Cambridge, Mass., 1960), 220–21; *Pro-Slavery Argument,* 461–62; *Slavery Defended: The Views of the Old South,* ed. Eric L. McKitrick (Englewood Cliffs, 1963), 169, 174.
130. Student of Politics, *Proposals,* 39; Smith, *Mild Punishments Sound Policy,* 41. For another counterargument, see above, note 27.
131. Davis, *Problem of Slavery in the Age of Revolution,* 252–53.
132. Student of Politics, *Proposals,* 27n.
133. Basil Hall, *Travels in North America* (Edinburgh, 1829), 3:226–29 (quotation at 228–29); Noah Webster, *Effects of Slavery on Morals and Industry* (Hartford, 1793), 18–22; Jordan, *White Over Black,* 281–82.
134. See chapter 2, notes 119, 125; chapter 5, note 52.
135. On abuses in New York, see Lewis, *From Newgate to Dannemora,* 93–99; Burr, *Voice from Sing-Sing,* 14–16.
136. William Roscoe to Stephen Allen (Nov. 1, 1827), in *Liverpool Chron.,* Jan. 19, 1828, at 2–3. See also Roscoe, *Remarks,* 11–13.
137. "Declaration of Samuel Hopkins, 1830," reprinted in Lewis, *Development of American Prisons,* 114. Also criticizing such administrative discretion, see, e.g., Livingston, *Complete Works,* 1:518–21, 552–55; *Letter from Edward Livingston, Esq., to Roberts Vaux on the Advantages of the Pennsylvania System of Prison Discipline* (Philadelphia, 1828), 9–10 (originally published in the *Nat'l Gazette*).
138. Quoted in Ayers, *Vengeance and Justice,* 68–69.
139. Scottish proslavery advocate Andrew Fletcher, quoted in Morgan, *American Slavery, American Freedom,* 325. This logic was applied in Virginia to rebut the imputation of malice aforethought in cases where masters killed their slaves. Id., 312. For other examples of this theme, see, e.g., Davis, *Problem of Slavery in Western Culture,* 186; [Austin], *Remarks,* 44; *Documents Illustrative of the History of the Slave Trade,* 2:352n.
140. A[llen], *Examination,* 7–8; Allen, Hopkins, and Tibbits, "Report," 103. Selection of good officers was an important element of penitentiary ideology; see chapter 2, note 125.
141. Some contractors in New York were prohibited from ever entering the penitentiary. Knapp, *Life,* 88–89; Powers, *Brief Account,* 25–26. Tocqueville argued that so long as convict leasing and prison service contracts were divided among a number of contractors, none could obtain more than a limited influence. Beaumont and Tocqueville, *On the Penitentiary System,* 35–36 (also 202–3).
142. Bentham, "Panopticon," in *Works,* 4:48, 52–54 (quotation at 54). Bentham recognized that this would be untrue of inmates incapable of work, and so he built some

basic limitations on contractors' powers into his system. For other proposals to give officers an interest in convict labor, but without administrative latitude, see Smith, *Mild Punishments Sound Policy,* 22–23; Livingston, *Complete Works,* 1:583–84.

143. Bentham, "Principles of Penal Law," in *Works,* 1:441.

144. Thomas Jefferson to Edward Bancroft (Jan. 26, 1788), in *Papers of Thomas Jefferson,* 1:492 (quotation); Jefferson, *Notes on the State of Virginia,* 142; Webster, *Effects of Slavery,* 6, 8.

145. Webster, *Effects of Slavery,* 38 (quotation). Jefferson spoke of the need for slaves to acquire "habits of property." *Papers of Thomas Jefferson,* 492–93. Likewise, English antislavery advocates, e.g., William Roscoe and Isaac Hodgson, *An Address from the Liverpool Society for the Abolition of Slavery on the Safest and Most Efficacious Means of Promoting the Gradual Improvement of the Negro Slaves in the British West India Islands* (Liverpool, 1824), 9–13, 17–18.

146. Bentham, "Panopticon," in *Works,* 4:144; cf. Bentham, "Principles of Penal Law," in *Works,* 1:440. Similarly, William Godwin, the English theorist, denounced coercive hard labor as "inexpressibly ill conceived." Godwin imagined the thought processes of a convict: "Do you desire that I should work? Do not drive me to it with the whip; for, if before I thought it better to be idle, this will but increase my alienation. Persuade my understanding, and render it the subject of my choice." Concluded Godwin, "It can only be by the most deplorable perversion of reason that we can be induced to believe any species of slavery, from the slavery of the schoolboy to that of the most unfortunate negro in our West India plantations, favorable to virtue." William Godwin, *An Enquiry Concerning Political Justice* (London, 1793), 708, 755–56.

147. Bentham, "Panopticon," in *Works,* 4:54–56.

148. Bentham was not concerned about the *size* of the reward, so long as there was *some* reward: "The workman [convict] lives in a poor country where wages are low; but in a poor country, a man who is paid according to his work will exert himself at least as much as in a rich one." Bentham, "Panopticon," in *Works,* 4:54. Bentham was thus able to reconcile effective rehabilitation with profitable administration. Cf. Thomas Buxton, also concerned about the effectiveness of hard labor as a rehabilitative therapy, who spoke of "making employment agreeable, by allowing [the convict] to share *largely* in its profits." Thomas Buxton, *An Inquiry Whether Crime and Misery Are Produced or Prevented by Our Present System of Prison Discipline* (London, 1818), 23, 115–16, 123–25 (quotation at 23) (emphasis added).

149. Austin Van der Slice, "Elizabethan Houses of Correction," *J. Am. Inst. Crim. L. & Criminology* 27 (1936):51, 60–63; J. Thorsten Sellin, *Pioneering in Penology: The Amsterdam Houses of Correction in the Sixteenth and Seventeenth Centuries* (London, 1944), 58; Sidney Webb and Beatrice Webb, *English Prisons under Local Government* (London, 1922), 13–14.

150. Matthew Hale, *A Discourse Touching Provisions for the Poor* (London, 1683), 4–5.

151. Overstint was established in the Massachusetts State Prison in 1806. "Visitors Minutes," 1:35 (Oct. 6, 1806). On inmate punishment, see above, note 19.

152. Roscoe, *Observations,* 142–43, 167. Bentham, who emphasized the therapeutic aims of inmate compensation, also recognized that "[t]his encouragement is necessary to his doing his utmost." Bentham, "Panopticon," in *Works,* 4:54.

153. Morgan, *American Slavery, American Freedom,* 311–13; Robert S. Starobin, *Industrial Slavery in the Old South* (New York, 1970), 98–104. On such occasions, masters spoke of the slave's "steint" and "overwork," another terminological intersection; id., 99, 103.

154. Act of Apr. 5, 1790, ch. 1516, *Pa. Stats. at Large*, 13:519 (§17). And in Massachusetts, see "Remarks on the Mass. State Prison," 21; *Remarks on Prisons and Prison
Discipline*, 35. Francis Lieber likewise characterized overstint as a "moral stimu-
lus." Beaumont and Tocqueville, *On the Penitentiary System*, 38n. Cf. Reynolds,
Recollections, 130–32 (charging that prison revenue was the sole consideration).

155. Samuel Gridley Howe, *Report of a Minority of the Special Committee of the Boston
Prison Discipline Society* (Boston, 1846), 45, 52–53 (quotations) (emphasis in original); Livingston, *Complete Works*, 1:521–23, 556–62; Caldwell, *New Views of Penitentiary Discipline*, 6–7, 34–35. William Roscoe took this position without embracing
the Pennsylvania plan. Roscoe, *Remarks*, 10–11, 15–16; Roscoe, *Additional Observations*, 25–26. For a convict's eye-view, see *Prison Discipline Soc'y* 8 (1833):142.

156. Roscoe, *Observations*, 130, 142–43, 154, 162–73 (quotations at 162–64) (emphasis in
original). Similarly, James Mease to William Roscoe (May 18, 1827), in *U.S. Gazette*,
June 6, 1827, at 1 ("despotism"); Livingston, *Complete Works*, 1:242.

157. *Remarks on Prisons and Prison Discipline*, 12–13; Livingston, *Complete Works*, 1:242.
Tocqueville flagged, but then begged, the question; see Beaumont and Tocqueville,
On the Penitentiary System, 44. Apparently stung by this criticism, some Auburn
advocates responded by accusing Pennsylvania of establishing a "tyrannical" prison
discipline. Francis Lieber, *Popular Essay on the Subject of Penal Law* (Philadelphia,
1838), 69–70; Teeters, *They Were in Prison*, 461. William Roscoe leveled the same
criticism against both systems; Roscoe, *Additional Observations*, 61–62; Beaumont
and Tocqueville, *On the Penitentiary System*, 294–96.

158. Charles Shaler, Edward King, and T. J. Wharton, "Report on Punishment and Prison
Discipline," in *Journal of the Senate of the Commonwealth of Pennsylvania, 1827–
1828* (Harrisburg, 1828), 2 app.:331, 361–62; "Fourth Annual Report of the Committee
of the London Society for the Improvement of Prison Discipline" [1822], reprinted
in Thomas Eddy, *Communication to Stephen Allen* (New York, 1823), 15–16; Thomas
Eddy to George Tibbits, Stephen Allen, and Samuel Hopkins (Jan. 7, 1825), in Knapp,
Life, 90. To this argument, proponents of overstint responded that other aspects
of prison life provided deterrence good and sufficient. Bentham, "Panopticon," in
Works, 4:144. Opponents of overstint also complained of the abuses associated with
it; see chapter 7, text at notes 63–74. These abuses undermined prison discipline
and thereby rehabilitation. *Report [on the Mass. State Prison]*, 1827:10 (also in
"Mass. Legislative Documents," Senate and House, 1826–27, no. 23); *Prison Discipline Soc'y* 1 (1826):47–50; id. 2 (1827):37. Proponents countered that abuses which
had plagued overstint were susceptible to cure; *Remarks on Prisons and Prison
Discipline*, 34–35; Matthew Carey, *Thoughts on Penitentiaries and Prison Discipline*
(Philadelphia, 1831), 52.

159. Jordan, *White Over Black*, 326, 556.

160. A[llen], *Examination*, 6–7; *Prison Discipline Soc'y* 1 (1826):47–50; *Report [on the
Mass. State Prison]*, 1827:9–11. This analysis conformed to the traditional vision
of the criminal as idler but ignored the possibility of a gradual change in the offender's propensities. Proponents of overstint countered that convicts, if deprived
of all alternative activities such as reading, would eventually try their hands at labor
and ultimately become accustomed to it. Alternatively, for convicts not yet accustomed, labor could be compelled *and* compensated. Howe, *Report of a Minority*,
53; *Remarks on Prisons and Prison Discipline*, 34–35; Livingston, *Complete Works*,
1:556–57.

161. For example [Austin], *Remarks on Dr. Channing's Slavery*, 41; Davis, *Problem of
Slavery in the Age of Revolution*, 462–63.

162. A[llen], *Examination,* 6. Roscoe responded to this argument by turning it around: If hunger was equivalent to other sorts of coercion, then the threat of hunger should prompt convicts to labor! William Roscoe to Stephen Allen (Nov. 1, 1827), in *Liverpool Chron.,* Jan. 12, 1828, at 3.

163. "Memoir of Stephen Allen," 4 (unpublished typescript, New-York Historical Society, 1927).

164. Thomas Jefferson to Edward Bancroft (Jan. 26, 1788), in *Papers of Thomas Jefferson,* 1:492.

165. Beaumont and Tocqueville, *On the Penitentiary System,* 62, 161 n.*cc.* For similar discussions, see Webster, *Effects of Slavery,* 6; Hall, *Travels,* 3:160–61.

166. Soc'y for the Prevention of Pauperism, *Report,* app. 43–45; similarly, id., app. 65–66; Brissot de Warville, *New Travels,* 372–73.

167. Howe, *Report of a Minority,* 41–42, 54–56, 61–63 (quotations at 61). William Roscoe denounced Bentham's Panopticon, which featured surveillance of convicts, on the same ground; Roscoe, *Observations . . . Part III,* 56–58; Roscoe, *Observations,* 172–73 (general analysis). Daniel Raymond, an advocate of solitary confinement without labor, suggested that such therapy could effect the convict's rehabilitation rapidly, before the offender had forgotten how to live independently. Soc'y for the Prevention of Pauperism, *Report,* app. 49.

168. Bentham, "Principles of Penal Law," in *Works,* 1:411. See also *Mass. Centinel,* Sept. 22, 1784, at 1 (chaining escapees "is not more so [an infringement of liberty] than any other punishment").

169. Quoted in Jenkins, *Pro-Slavery Thought,* 116.

170. Thus Fitzhugh's famous aphorism that citizens in the North were "too little governed." Fitzhugh, *Cannibals All,* 65. On this theme, see Jenkins, *Pro-Slavery Thought,* 299–308.

171. Beaumont and Tocqueville, *On the Penitentiary System,* 156 n.*p* (quoting Auburn's warden, Elam Lynds), 58–59; *Letter of Gershom Powers in Answer to a Letter of the Hon. Edward Livingston,* 13.

172. Hall, *Travels,* 1:68–69.

173. For example, Shaler, King, and Wharton, "Report," 331 ("appeals to the reason or consciences of such persons must, from the nature of things, be utterly ineffectual"), 339–40, 353–54. See also Beaumont and Tocqueville, *On the Penitentiary System,* 58–59. Workhouse advocates had likewise sought to make inmates "useful, if not honest." [Robe], *Some Considerations,* 47.

174. Lewis, *From Newgate to Dannemora,* 87; A[llen], *Examinations,* 8–9.

175. Hall, *Travels,* 3:160.

176. For example, Livingston, *Complete Works,* 1:521–23, 557, 559; "Book Review," *Am. Q. Rev.* 14 (1833):238–39; [Wayland], "Book Review," 21, 23, 31. In remarking the inherent noncoerciveness of attempts to reform the convict's conscience, Francis Lieber echoed the early English philanthropist Jonas Hanway: "To attribute a moral character to a submission which is produced only by the threat of . . . punishment . . . seems to me a solecism." Beaumont and Tocqueville, *On the Penitentiary System,* 40n (Lieber's commentary); see also *Letters on the Comparative Merits of the Pennsylvania and New York Systems of Penitentiary Discipline* (Boston, 1836), 25; cf. chapter 2, text at note 66.

177. The "strict discipline" and "instantaneous obedience" at Auburn "rather improve[s] the character of the prison than the character of the prisoner. . . . Such a course may break down the proud spirit, subdue the stubborn will, and enforce obedience," but

it did so "by crushing much that is good, and by withholding what is of more consequence than any thing else to the prisoner, the advantage of voluntary exercises and culture of self-government and self-elevation." Howe, *Report of a Minority*, 55–56; see also *Prison Discipline: The Auburn and Pennsylvania Systems Compared* (New York, 1839), 17.

178. Powers, *Brief Account*, 68; see also [Bradford], *State Prisons*, 43–44; *Prison Discipline . . . Compared*, 14.

179. Edmund S. Morgan, "The Puritan Ethic and the American Revolution," in *The Challenge of the American Revolution* (New York, 1976), 112–15.

Chapter 7

Note to epigraph: Jeremy Bentham, *Bentham's Theory of Legislation* [MSS 1775–1802], ed. Etienne Dumont (London, 1914), 1:269; cf. Jeremy Bentham, "Principles of the Civil Code" [same MSS], in *The Works of Jeremy Bentham,* ed. John Bowring (Edinburgh, 1843), 1:344.

1. A number of critical scholars have posited the preeminence of economic motives for the construction of penitentiaries; see Martin Miller, "At Hard Labor: Rediscovering the Nineteenth-Century Prison," *Issues in Criminology* 9 (1974):91; Martin Miller, "Sinking Gradually into the Proletariat: The Emergence of the Penitentiary in the United States," *Crime & Soc. Just.* 14 (1980):37; Georg Rusche and Otto Kirchheimer, *Punishment and Social Structure* (New York, 1939); Dario Melossi and Massimo Pavarini, *The Prison and the Factory: Origins of the Penitentiary System,* trans. Glynic Cousins (London, 1981); Ivan Jankovic, "Labor Market and Imprisonment," *Crime & Soc. Just.* 8 (1977):17; Russell Hogg, "Imprisonment and Society under Early British Capitalism," id. 12 (1979):4.

2. Many penitentiaries took on some of the trappings of a business. In Massachusetts, accountants kept the books of the state prison "in the Mercantile style." "Minutes of the Meetings of the Board of Visitors/Directors/Inspectors," 1:n.p. (June 3, 1812) (unpublished MS, Mass. Archives) [hereinafter "Visitors Minutes"]; authorities could come under criticism if they demonstrated incompetence at business, see id. 1:63–64 (June 27, 1808), 139 (Sept. 13, 1810).

3. Comparing overstint with free market wages, see Robert Turnbull, *A Visit to the Philadelphia Prison* (London, 1797), 16–19; "Remarks on the Massachusetts State Prison," in *Rules and Regulations for the Government of the Massachusetts State Prison Adopted by the Board of Directors* (Boston, 1823), 25. See also below, note 23.

4. "Visitors Minutes," 1:139 (Sept. 13, 1810) (remarking a search for employment that "requires more labor and less stock"); William Roscoe, *Additional Observations on Penal Jurisprudence, and the Reformation of Criminals* (London, 1823), 136 ("Those occupations are to be preferred, where the cost of the raw materials is small, and the value chiefly arises from the labour"). On the labor-intensiveness of chattel slave industries, see Edmund S. Morgan, *American Slavery, American Freedom: The Ordeal of Colonial Virginia* (New York, 1975), 114–15, 141–42, 298–303.

5. "Remarks on the Mass. State Prison," 9 (emphasis in original) (the reference is to the Emperor Vespasian's apocryphal tax on the public toilets of Rome, a suggestive analogy). James Mease of Pennsylvania: "The idea of deriving revenue from the labor of criminals . . . is unworthy of a moment's reflection." James Mease to William Roscoe (May 18, 1827), in *U.S. Gazette,* June 6, 1827, at 1. Society for the Prevention of Pauperism of New York: "We put convicts in the State Prisons to be punished and reclaimed, not to earn money for the people." Soc'y for the Prevention of Pau-

perism, *Report on the Penitentiary System in the United States* (New York, 1822), 75. Similar statements were common, e.g. [Gamaliel Bradford], *State Prisons and the Penitentiary System Vindicated* (Charlestown, 1821), at 39; *Columbian Centinel,* Aug. 21, 1816, at 1; [Thomas Eddy], *An Account of the State Prison or Penitentiary House, in the City of New-York* (New York, 1801), 55–58; *Letters on the Pennsylvania System of Solitary Imprisonment,* 1st ed. (Charleston, 1835), 13; cf. Act of Sept. 15, 1786, ch. 1241, in *Statutes at Large of Pennsylvania from 1682 to 1801* (Harrisburg, 1908), 12:288 (§ 14) (contemplating the possibility of profits) [hereinafter *Pa. Stats. at Large*]; Roberts Vaux, *Notices of the Original and Successive Efforts to Improve the Discipline of the Prison at Philadelphia* (Philadelphia, 1826), 51–55 (complaining of intermittent efforts to promote a profit). For government records in Massachusetts confirming the goal of a balanced budget, see Adam J. Hirsch, "From Pillory to Penitentiary: The Rise of Criminal Incarceration in the New Republic" (Ph.D. diss., Yale University, 1987), pt. 2, n. 473. This was also the financial goal of the ancient workhouse; see Matthew Hale, *A Discourse Touching Provisions for the Poor* (London, 1683), 18–23; "Ordinances and Rules Drawn Out for the Good Government of the House of Bridewell" [1557], in *Parliamentary Papers,* 19:406 (§ 50) (pt. 1) (1840) (British Library); Sidney Webb and Beatrice Webb, *English Prisons under Local Government* (London, 1922), 13–14 and n.3; see also chapter 2, note 22. Cf. W. David Lewis, *From Newgate to Dannemora: The Rise of the Penitentiary in New York, 1796–1848* (Ithaca, 1965), ch. 8.

6. Stephen Allen, Samuel Hopkins, and George Tibbits, "Report," in *Journal of the Assembly of the State of New York* (New York, 1825), 119 (quotation); Soc'y for the Prevention of Pauperism, *Report,* app. 55; Gustave de Beaumont and Alexis de Tocqueville, *On the Penitentiary System in the United States and Its Application in France* (Philadelphia, 1833), 37; S[tephen] A[llen], *An Examination of the Remarks on the Report of the Commissioners* (New York, 1826), 4; S[tephen] A[llen], *Observations on Penitentiary Discipline Addressed to William Roscoe* (New York, 1827), 62; Charles Shaler, Edward King, and T. J. Wharton, "Report on Punishment and Prison Discipline," in *Journal of the Senate of the Commonwealth of Pennsylvania, 1827– 1828* (Harrisburg, 1828), 2 app.:341–42; *A View of the New-York State Prison in the City of New-York* (New York, 1815), 43; [Bradford], *State Prisons,* 42. In 1808, James Sullivan suggested that fines for costs of conviction be abolished in Massachusetts, and that "where there is a sentence to hard labor, the courts may increase the term of the sentences, in consideration that the cost . . . is omitted." James Sullivan to Senate and House (Jan. 13, 1808), in James Sullivan Papers, vol. 2 (unpublished MS, Mass. Hist. Soc'y). In England, see, e.g., Henry Fielding, *A Proposal for Making an Effectual Provision for the Poor* (London, 1753), 84.

7. For example, *Plymouth Court Records, 1686–1859,* ed. David T. Konig (Wilmington, 1978–81), 1:194 [1688]. But see the counterarguments to this moral position in Jeremy Bentham, "Principles of Penal Law" [MSS 1775–1802] in *Works,* 1:423.

8. Beaumont and Tocqueville, *On the Penitentiary System,* 37n (Francis Lieber's commentary).

9. For moral condemnation of chattel slave exploitation, see chapter 6, note 179. For an estimate of the southern masters' "debt" to their slaves by an antislavery advocate, see [Benjamin Rush], *An Address to the Inhabitants of the British Settlements in America upon Slavekeeping* (New York, 1773), 20 and n.

10. Thus William Smith: "Society have a right, for a certain time, in proportion to the degree of criminality, to be absolute masters of the person and labour of a criminal,

who robs another of his property, in order to oblige him to repair by his labour and slavery the depredations he has made upon others, and thereby atone for his breach of the laws of society." William Smith, *Mild Punishments Sound Policy* (London, 1777), 20–23, 40–41 (quotation at 40–41); Francis Hutcheson, *A System of Moral Philosophy* (London, 1755), 201; Menasseh Dawes, *An Essay on Crimes and Punishments* (London, 1782), 131–33; William Petty, "A Treatise of Taxes and Contributions" [1662], in *The Economic Writings of Sir William Petty*, ed. Charles Hull (Cambridge, 1899), 1:68–69 (§§ 12–13); Cesare Beccaria, *On Crimes and Punishments*, ed. Henry Paolucci (Indianapolis, 1963), 47; *Am. Musium* 6 (1789):223; id. 7 (1790):137; *Mass. Centinel*, Oct. 16, 1784, at 1, Oct. 20, 1784, at 1. Cf. Robert Turnbull, *Visit*, 14–15 (right enforced sporadically).

11. *Annual Report of the Board of Managers of the Prison Discipline Society* 9 (1834):279 [hereinafter *Prison Discipline Soc'y*].

12. Lewis, *From Newgate to Dannemora*, 99–100; Orlando F. Lewis, *The Development of American Prisons and Prison Customs* (Albany, 1922), 133; Beaumont and Tocqueville, *On the Penitentiary System*, 37n (Francis Lieber's commentary); *Prison Discipline Soc'y* 9 (1834):279; *Prison Discipline: The Auburn and Pennsylvania Systems Compared* (New York, 1839), 17–20; Dorothea Dix, *Remarks on Prisons and Prison Discipline in the United States* (Boston, 1845), 10.

13. Governor's Message, Jan. 4, 1826, *Mass. Resolves, 1824–28*:251–54 (quotation at 252); Governor's Message, Jan. 2, 1828, id., 632–33; *Prison Discipline Soc'y* 2 (1827): 52–53.

14. Samuel Gridley Howe, *Report of a Minority of the Special Committee of the Boston Prison Discipline Society* (Boston, 1846), 79–80 (quotations); William Roscoe, *Observations on Penal Jurisprudence* (London, 1819), 163–72. Howe suggested that part of the profit could be used for additional means of convict improvement, instead of direct compensation. Roscoe believed that each convict should compensate the victim as well as pay all maintenance costs. At the Walnut Street prison in Philadelphia, convict earnings were held by the treasury of the county rather than the prison administration "to prevent the suspicions that would arise if the jailor held the money in his hands." Duke de la Rochefoucault-Liancourt, *Travels through the United States of North America* (London, 1799), 2:341; cf. George Smith, *A Defence of the System of Solitary Confinement of Prisoners Adopted in the State of Pennsylvania* (Philadelphia, 1833), 50 ("remuneration to society" should not be sought because it is impossible).

15. This conclusion followed from the observations that (1) rationalist doctrine called only for the minimum punishment necessary to control crime, (2) only a fraction of those responsible for the costs of criminal justice were apprehended, and (3) remuneration went to the state rather than the victim. *Prison Discipline . . . Compared*, 9–11, 14–15, 17, 20 (quotation at 10).

16. Thomas Eddy to Samuel Hoare (Nov. 15, 1819), in Samuel Knapp, *The Life of Thomas Eddy* (New York, 1834), 298. Also referring to the secondary status of this goal, see, e.g., William Bradford, *An Enquiry How Far the Punishment of Death Is Necessary in Pennsylvania* (Philadelphia, 1793), 70–71 (n.13); [Bradford], *State Prisons*, 39; Soc'y for the Prevention of Pauperism, *Report*, 43–46, 75–76, app. 36–37; *Letter of Gershom Powers in Answer to a Letter of the Hon. Edward Livingston, in Relation to the Auburn State Prison* (Albany, 1829), 27 (Auburn advocate) [hereinafter *Powers to Livingston*]; "Book Review," *Christian Examiner* 20 (1836):386 (same); *Prison Discipline . . . Compared*, 16–17 and n. (Pennsylvania advocate); Josiah Quincy, *Remarks*

on Some of the Provisions of the Laws of Massachusetts, Affecting Poverty, Vice, and Crime (Cambridge, Mass., 1822), 23 (same). And in England, e.g., William Roscoe to James Mease (Oct. 13, 1827), in *Liverpool Chron.,* Oct. 20, 1827, at 3. When, after touring American prisons, the Englishman William Crawford reported that "the great desire which exists, to rid the community of the burthen of supporting criminals, has occasioned in most of the states the establishment of penitentiaries," his suggestion drew a sharp rebuke from the *American Quarterly Review,* although the *Review* admitted to the existence of "mixed motives." William Crawford, *Report on the Penitentiaries of the United States* (n.p., 1835), 24; "Book Review," *Am. Q. Rev.* 18 (1835):457–58; cf. Vaux, *Notices,* 51–53 (complaining of increasing emphasis on pecuniary concerns).

17. *Remarks on Prisons and Prison Discipline* (Boston, 1826), 5 (reprinted from the *Christian Examiner,* 3, no. 3. For similar comments, see Board of Visitors to Governor Gore (Dec. 19, 1809), in "Reports of the Officers: Reports of Physician, Chaplain and Board of Visitors, 1807–1810, 1819–1823" (unpublished MS, Mass. Archives) [hereinafter "Officers Reports"]; [Bradford], *State Prisons,* 32; "Remarks on the Mass. State Prison," 8; Roscoe, *Additional Observations,* app. 104.

18. *Prison Discipline Soc'y* 1 (1826):23; *Report [on the Mass. State Prison],* 1827:6–9 (Harvard Law Library) (also in Mass. Legislative Documents, Senate and House 1826–27, no. 23).

19. Beaumont and Tocqueville, *On the Penitentiary System,* 53n; Howe, *Report of a Minority,* 79; *National Gazette,* Dec. 30, 1828, at 2; Smith, *Defence,* 91; Francis Lieber, *Popular Essays on the Subject of Penal Law* (Philadelphia, 1838), 68; *Prison Discipline . . . Compared,* 15; *Letters on the Comparative Merits of the Pennsylvania and New York Systems of Penitentiary Discipline* (Boston, 1836), 31–34; [James Austin], "Book Review," *N. Am. Rev.* 10 (1820):249–50, 259.

20. "Book Review," *Christian Examiner* 20 (1836):388; *Prison Discipline . . . Compared,* 10; Howe, *Report of a Minority,* 78, 80; Crawford, *Report,* 24. For a study suggesting a correspondence between preferences for hard labor and growth cycles of the economy (when hard labor was most profitable), see Christopher Adams, "Hard Labor and Solitary Confinement: Effects of the Business Cycle and Labor Supply on Prison Discipline in the United States, 1790–1835," *Research in Law, Deviance, & Soc. Control* 6 (1984):19.

21. Jeremy Bentham underwent such a mercenary conversion; see chapter 2, note 73. See also [Thomas Eddy], *An Account of the State Prison or Penitentiary House in the City of New-York* (New York, 1801), 32–33.

22. For example, Francis Lieber: "Many profitable species of labor cannot be pursued with us, because . . . they require joint labor. Be it so; penitentiaries are not erected to make money, but to punish, and, if possible, to reform by punishment." Lieber, *Popular Essay,* 68. Likewise, Howe, *Report of a Minority,* 79.

23. According to one of its inspectors, the Walnut Street prison granted inmates all profits above costs of their prosecution and maintenance; see Caleb Lownes, "An Account of the Alterations and Present State of the Penal Laws of Pennsylvania," in Bradford, *Enquiry,* 90. The statute, however, called only for *half* the profits above maintenance to be returned to inmates. Act of Apr. 5, 1790, ch. 1516, *Pa. Stats. at Large,* 13:519 (§ 17). But cf. chapter 6, notes 152–54 and accompanying text.

24. Soc'y for the Prevention of Pauperism, *Report,* 75; Lieber, *Popular Essays,* 68. On postbellum convict leasing in the South, which proved far more remunerative than the penitentiary, see Edward L. Ayers, *Vengeance and Justice: Crime and Punish-*

ment in the Nineteenth-Century American South (New York, 1984), ch. 6. In New York, contractors who had established a record of abiding by prison rules were preferred over others who might have offered to pay higher labor fees. Lewis, *From Newgate to Dannemora,* 188–89.

25. "Remarks on the Mass. State Prison," 11–12 ("the expense does not depend on the number of the convicts").

26. *Documents Illustrative of the History of the Slave Trade to America,* ed. Elizabeth Donnan (New York, 1969), 2:395–96. Commentators on the penitentiary recognized this danger, see *Letters on the Pennsylvania System,* 13; *Letters on the Comparative Merits,* 31, 34; James Mease to William Roscoe (May 18, 1827), in *U.S. Gazette,* June 6, 1827, at 1; *Prison Discipline . . . Compared,* 10–11; Ayers, *Vengeance and Justice,* 69.

27. For example, *Prison Discipline Soc'y* 7 (1832):11–12 (quotation); id. 2 (1827):79; Gamaliel Bradford to Governor and Board of Visitors (Nov. 2, 1820), in Governor and Council, "Reports and Papers of the State Prison at Charlestown, 1807, 1822–23," Misc. Box no. 3, pt. 2 (unpublished MS, Mass. Archives) [hereinafter "Reports and Papers"]; Governor's Message, Jan. 10, 1821, in *Mass. Resolves,* Jan. 1821:274; Governor's Message, Jan. 9, 1832, in id., 1832–34:33. Likewise, in the ancient workhouse, "the intent [is] that the house of Bridewell be not ever pestered, but may be able to receive such as shall need." "Ordinances and Rules Drawn Out for the Good Government of the House of Bridewell," 405 (§ 49).

28. Pardons were controversial on criminological grounds, in that they reduced the "certainty" of punishment; see Hirsch, "From Pillory to Penitentiary," pt. 1, notes 120–24 and accompanying text. One inmate charged that pardons in Windsor Prison, Vermont, were denied to productive prisoners; see John Reynolds, *Recollections of Windsor Prison* (Boston, 1834), 133–34. Unpublished correspondence confirms that such considerations influenced some prison authorities in other states. Authorities in Massachusetts and Pennsylvania issued complaints when productive inmates received pardons, though they were quick to add that "when mercy becomes an act of justice," which they denied in these instances, "pecuniary interests are not to be consulted." "Visitors Minutes," 1:n.p. (Nov. 18, 1811) (quotation); Samuel Wood to Governor Wolf (Aug. 31, 1833), reprinted in Leroy B. De Puy, "The Triumph of the 'Pennsylvania System' at the State's Penitentiaries," *Pa. Hist.* 21 (1954):140–41. In a published tract in New York, one advocate urged that pardons be spaced out over time so as to minimize the disruption of prison workshops. *View of the New-York State Prison,* 67, 72. On sentencing policy, cf. *Report [on the Mass. State Prison],* Sept. 1830:9 (also in "Mass. Legislative Documents," 1830–31:151); id., 1831:10–11 (also in "Mass. Legislative Documents," Senate and House 1832:218); "Mass. Legislative Documents," 1817–22, no. 1:17–19 (State Library Annex). In order to "make the interest of the officer and of the public to coincide," Edward Livingston proposed to grant prison officials a percentage of the proceeds from convict labor *and* a premium for reductions in the rate of inmate reconviction. Edward Livingston, *The Complete Works of Edward Livingston on Criminal Jurisprudence,* ed. Salmon Chase (New York, 1873), 1:583–84.

29. On the extent of inmate infirmity in the Massachusetts State Prison, see, e.g., *Report [on the Mass. State Prison],* 1829:21 (also in "Mass. Legislative Documents," 1829–30:135). Infirm and feeble inmates were not driven to work as hard as the able-bodied, see, e.g., "Visitors Minutes," 2:261–62 (Mar. 29, 1823).

30. William S. Jenkins, *Pro-Slavery Thought in the Old South* (Chapel Hill, 1935), 65–81;

Larry E. Tise, *Proslavery: A History of the Defense of Slavery in America, 1701–1840* (Athens, Ga., 1987), ch. 5.

31. See chapter 5, note 63.
32. Compare Bentham: "It is idle to try to prove, by elaborate calculation, that a man ought to be happy when he is, in fact, miserable; or that a state into which no one is willing to enter, and from which everyone is anxious to escape, is in itself a pleasant condition and one agreeable to human nature . . . . [A]ll reasoning from probabilities as to the happiness of slaves is quite superfluous; for we have the most ample proof that, in point of fact, slavery is never embraced by choice, but, on the contrary, is ever an object of aversion." Bentham, *Theory of Legislation,* 1:268–69.
33. For a statement of the principle, see Jeremy Bentham, "Panopticon, or the Inspection-House" [1791], in *Works,* 4:122–23. The doctrine was not expressly followed in the United States, but all advocates were alert to the concern. See chapter 5, notes 62–65 and accompanying text.
34. Allen, Hopkins, and Tibbits, "Report," 109–10.
35. State returns are compiled in Orlando F. Lewis, *The Development of American Prisons and Prison Customs, 1776–1845* (Albany, 1922), 55, 74–75, 104, 131–33, 149–52, 173–76, 181–83, 190, 236–39, 256–59. For a contemporary assessment, see Gamaliel Bradford to Governor and Board of Visitors (Oct. 16, 1823), in "Reports and Papers," pt. 1.
36. More forthrightly from the standpoint of their ideology, these advocates simultaneously emphasized that the issue of economic efficiency was marginal in comparison with the relative effectiveness of their carceral program in controlling crime. Francis Bache, *Observations and Reflections on the Penitentiary System* (Philadelphia, 1829), 10–11; Roberts Vaux, *Letter on the Penitentiary System of Pennsylvania* (Philadelphia, 1827), 10–11; Howe, *Report of a Minority,* 78–79; Smith, *Defence,* 85–93; *Nat'l Gazette,* Jan. 6, 1829, at 2; *Letters on the Comparative Merits,* 33–34. This combination of arguments was also offered in favor of solitary confinement without labor; see, e.g., James Mease, *Observations on the Penitentiary System* (Philadelphia, 1828), 45; Soc'y for the Prevention of Pauperism, *Report,* app. 100–104. These arguments had been anticipated by English reclamation advocates, see chapter 2, note 73.
37. Gamaliel Bradford to Governor and Board of Visitors (Oct. 16, 1823), in "Reports and Papers," pt. 1; similarly, *Prison Discipline Soc'y* 8 (1833):20–21. Nonetheless, Bradford strove to put the best possible face on his financial reports; see Gamaliel Bradford to Governor and Board of Visitors (Nov. 2, 1820), in "Reports and Papers," pt. 1; [Austin], "Book Review," 251 and n (questioning the accuracy of Bradford's accounts). Reports from the Eastern State Penitentiary in Pennsylvania carried no clear financial statistics at all, possibly in an effort—as rival advocates charged— to suppress the information. *Prison Discipline Soc'y* 10 (1835):20–21; "Book Review," *Christian Examiner* 20 (1836):387–88; responding to this charge, see *Letters on the Comparative Merits,* 35–36.
38. The classic economic analysis of slavery is Robert W. Fogel and Stanley L. Engerman, *Time on the Cross: The Economics of American Negro Slavery* (Boston, 1974).
39. This phenomenon was recognized contemporaneously. As Stephen Allen put it, convicts "always believe [their sentence] to be severe, if not unjust, and view the whole court as their enemies." A[llen], *Observations,* 19.
40. Stephen Burroughs, *Memoirs of the Notorious Stephen Burroughs of New Hampshire* [1798] (New York, 1924), 153.

41. The suggestion is drawn from David Brion Davis's famous thesis that antislavery advocacy isolated slavery as a singularly unacceptable mode of labor discipline, and thereby "clear[ed] an ideological path" to alternative disciplines, such as the factory. See generally David Brion Davis, *The Problem of Slavery in the Age of Revolution* (Ithaca, 1975), 251–54, 264–66, 303–6, 346–50, 433–39, 455–58, 466–68, 472, 481; cf. 266n.15, 468 (quotation at 467). The marriage of carceral and antislavery advocacy could be fitted into this thesis, though I ultimately reject this explanation for the marriage, as discussed below.

42. On the alternative convict labor systems, see Harry Elmer Barnes, "The Economics of American Penology as Illustrated by the Experience of the State of Pennsylvania," *J. Pol. Econ.* 29 (1921):624–32. The contract system employed in penitentiaries originated in the ancient workhouse. Michael Ignatieff, *A Just Measure of Pain: The Penitentiary in the Industrial Revolution, 1750–1850* (London, 1978), 110–11.

43. Beaumont and Tocqueville, *On the Penitentiary System,* 80–81, 163–64n.*kk* (noting, however, the existence of some unfavorable contracts); Gershom Powers, *A Brief Account of the Construction, Management, and Discipline &c &c of the New York State Prison at Auburn* (Auburn, 1826), 25–29. Other considerations, such as a contractor's record of observing prison regulations, also influenced the selection process. Lewis, *From Newgate to Dannemora,* 188–89. In Massachusetts, individual convicts were sometimes leased at different prices; see "Visitors Minutes," 2:181–83 (Mar. 25, 1822). In England, Jeremy Bentham's Panopticon scheme was rejected because of its emphasis on profit for the contractor. Gertrude Himmelfarb, "The Haunted House of Jeremy Bentham," in *Victorian Minds* (New York, 1968), 68. Compare Miller, "At Hard Labor," 296–97, 347 (suggesting state allegiance to the interests of contractors).

44. Gideon Haynes, *Pictures of Prison Life: An Historical Sketch of the Massachusetts State Prison* (Boston, 1870), 18; Board of Visitors to Governor Sullivan (Dec. 14, 1807), in "Officers Reports." The possibility of leasing convict labor in exchange for prison supplies was considered earlier at Castle Island, but there is no evidence that the proposal was put into effect. Joseph Ruggles and Ralph Smith, "Proposals for supplying the Garrison and Convicts on Castle Island" [1794], in Colonial Division, "Letters of Treasurers, 1794–1797," Letters, folder 8 (unpublished MS, Mass. Archives). One commentator in Massachusetts suggested the possibility of convict leasing in a proposal for carceral punishment that predated Castle Island. *Mass. Centinel,* Oct. 16, 1784, at 1.

45. Board of Visitors to Governor Sullivan (Dec. 14, 1807), in "Officers Reports"; [Gamaliel Bradford], *Description and Historical Sketch of the Massachusetts State Prison* (Charlestown, 1816), 12–14. Contractors were widely perceived to be better managers than state bureaucrats, and in Massachusetts production for the state's account was also hampered by shortages of raw material. Thomas Eddy to George Tibbits, Stephen Allen, and Samuel Hopkins (Jan. 7, 1825), in Knapp, *Life,* 88; Board of Visitors to Governor Gore (Dec. 19, 1809), in "Officers Reports"; Robert Dawes, "A Statemen[t] of Facts," n.d., in "General Correspondence with Governor Regarding State Prison at Charlestown, 1807–10, 1815, 1817–18, 1823–24" (unpublished MS, Mass. Archives); "Visitors Minutes," 1:108 (Feb. 12, 1810). One exception to the trend in Massachusetts was stone-cutting, an industry originally begun on contract and later taken over by the state. [Bradford], *Description,* 13; "Visitors Minutes," 1:n.p. (May 6, 1815), 2:82 (June 3, 1818). (Convicts were also employed on behalf of the state for internal construction work; see Board of Visitors to Lieutenant Governor Lincoln [Dec. 30, 1808], in "Officers Reports"; "Visitors Minutes," 1:29 [June 2,

1806], 65 [July 13, 1808]; chapter 5, note 87.) In Pennsylvania, a contract system was initiated virtually immediately in 1790 but was watered down when the Eastern State Prison opened in 1829; see Harry Elmer Barnes, *The Evolution of Penology in Pennsylvania* (Indianapolis, 1927), 164–69. In New York, the first contract dated to 1802, for shoemaking, after an unsuccessful effort by the prison to conduct the business. Thomas Eddy to Patrick Colquhoun (June 5, 1802), in Knapp, *Life,* 180–81. In 1817, virtually all prison industries were switched over to the contract system. Lewis, *From Newgate to Dannemora,* 44.

46. According to Tocqueville, convict labor cost contractors approximately half of what they would have had to pay free laborers. Beaumont and Tocqueville, *On the Penitentiary System,* 81. In Massachusetts, Warden Bradford assured a businessman: "I think there is no doubt but you could have the mechanical part of your work done cheaper here than at any other place, but I should decline your friendly offer of becoming personally interested in any work established here, from motives of propriety." Gamaliel Bradford to Francis Rotch (July 2, Aug. 18, 1815), in "Rotch Family Papers" (unpublished MS, Mass. Hist. Soc'y). The price offered for convict labor remained low in 1830; see *Report [on the Mass. State Prison],* Sept. 1830:7. Likewise, in New York, see [W. A. Coffey], *Inside Out* (New York, 1823), 140. In Pennsylvania in the 1790s, however, the price received for convict labor equaled the free market wage, according to one visitor. Rochefoucault-Liancourt, *Travels,* 2:341.

47. "Visitors Minutes," 2:206–9 (Sept. 26, 1822). Similar incidents occurred in New York; see Allen, Hopkins, and Tibbits, "Report," 107. In Pennsylvania, the prison compensated contractors for spoiled work. James Mease to William Roscoe (May 18, 1827), in *U.S. Gazette,* June 6, 1827, at 1.

48. Tocqueville explained the low price of convict labor by the fact that many convicts were unskilled. Beaumont and Tocqueville, *On the Penitentiary System,* 163 n.*kk.* The prison administration in Massachusetts sought to allay such fears by inviting potential contractors to inspect specimens of prison products. *Columbian Centinel,* Jan. 7, 1824, at 3, Jan. 21, 1824, at 1.

49. [Bradford], *Description,* 13–14.

50. Gamaliel Bradford to Governor and Council (Oct. 31, 1817), in "Reports & Papers," pt. 1; "Visitors Minutes," 2:53–54 (July 1, 1817), 54–55 (Aug. 6, 1817), 55 (Sept. 3, 1817), 190 (May 24, 1822).

51. "Remarks on the State Prison," 13 (quotation); "Visitors Minutes," 2:82 (June 3, 1818). Following disciplinary reforms in 1829, demand for convict labor increased, though contractors continued to offer "very low prices." *Report [on the Mass. State Prison],* Sept. 1830:7; id., 1831:9.

52. In addition to prison contractors, wholesale suppliers sold raw materials and other provisions to the institutions, though on a relatively small scale. In Massachusetts it was at first customary to barter prison-made goods for supplies, a practice ended by legislative decree, to the consternation of the directors. "Remarks on the Mass. State Prison," 12–13.

53. Thomas Eddy to Patrick Colquhoun (June 6, 1802), in Knapp, *Life,* 179; Beaumont and Tocqueville, *On the Penitentiary System,* 28–29. Cf. below, note 70. In Pennsylvania, inspectors of the state penitentiary received no compensation (as reported in 1818) "because these persons not well qualified might get the office for the sake of the Salary—now it is filled by persons acting from principles." Caleb Cresson to William Allen (May 26, 1818), in Negley K. Teeters, *They Were in Prison: A History of the Pennsylvania Prison Society, 1787–1937* (Philadelphia, 1937), 496.

54. "Visitors Minutes," 2:48 (May 11, 1817) (quotation); "Mass. Legislative Documents," 1817–22, no. 1:19–20. When the directors suggested that the warden's office be abolished, Warden Bradford responded that this was a "*hocus pocus trick* to conjure money into their own pockets. We believe their real design . . . is not in the end to save the salary to the State, but to share the spoil among themselves." *Columbian Centinel,* Jan. 25, 1824, at 1 (emphasis in original). This charge the directors denied. [James Austin], *Reply to the Centinel Review* (Boston, 1824), 2–3.

55. "Remarks on the Mass. State Prison," 16–17 (quotation); Beaumont and Tocqueville, *On the Penitentiary System,* 29 n. In 1823, the Massachusetts State Prison employed some thirty-four persons, amounting to an annual payroll of approximately $13,000. The directors commented: "It is presumed the emoluments allowed by law are not extravagant." "Remarks on the Mass. State Prison," 17.

56. "Remarks on the Mass. State Prison," 17.

57. See chapter 1, notes 66–80 and accompanying text, and chapter 2, notes 114–25 and accompanying text.

58. "Visitors Minutes," 1:n.p. (Feb. 6, 1815).

59. "Visitors Minutes," 1:n.p. (Jan. 1, 1812). On the commissary's duties, see *Rules and Regulations,* 49 (art. 6).

60. "Visitors Minutes," 1:n.p. (Dec. 17, 1814). A prison contractor made a similar offer to Warden Bradford, which he rejected, see note 46, above. But Bradford did supplement his income by selling molasses to the prison. "Visitors Minutes," 2:185 (March 28, 1822), 197 (June 29, 1822).

61. "Visitors Minutes," 1:35 (Oct. 6, 1806). The prison bylaws of 1823 included a provision permitting certain prisoners (members of the first and second classes, under the system of classification established in 1818) to spend a portion of their overstint moneys, not exceeding twenty-five cents per week, on specified items for immediate consumption. This provision was immediately repealed by the governor in council, over the objections of the directors, and prison officers were "specially enjoined to conform to the foregoing direction, any custom or usage to the contrary notwithstanding." *Rules and Regulations,* 58 (art. 13, § 9), 63–64; "Visitors Minutes," 2:273–74 (July 7, 1823); *Report [on the Mass. State Prison],* 1828:12 (also in "Mass. Legislative Documents," House and Senate, 1827–28:734).

62. *Prison Discipline Soc'y* 1 (1826):47–50; "Visitors Minutes," 1:41 (Mar. 2, 1807), 45 (June 20, 1807), 56–57 (Mar. 7, 1808). In 1827, total overstint earnings amounted to more than $5,000. Investigators found no evidence that "any considerable part," of these funds were paid to outsiders or accumulated, as required by law. *Prison Discipline Soc'y* 3 (1828):33, 36; *Report [on the Mass. State Prison],* 1828:12–15.

63. "Visitors Minutes," 2:101 (Sept. 1, 1819).

64. *Prison Discipline Soc'y* 3 (1828):33, 36; *Report [on the Mass. State Prison],* 1828:15. The problem had been noted more generally in *Prison Discipline Soc'y* 1 (1826):47–50.

65. The commissary's salary in 1823 was set at $950 per annum. In 1828 he admitted to earning between $400–$500 per annum by trafficking with convicts, "and stated that he had no book, or documents, by which the extent of his dealings or the profits could be shown." *Prison Discipline Soc'y* 3 (1828):36; *Report [on the Mass. State Prison],* 1828:14; "Remarks on the Mass. State Prison," 16. It was alleged that one prisoner used overstint money to bribe a guard to aid his escape. *Prison Discipline Soc'y* 3 (1828):33. For a reference to other abuses, see id. 2 (1827):11–12.

66. "Visitors Minutes," 2:46 (May 8, 1817), 244 (Feb. 25, 1823); id., 3:n.p. (Mar. 27, Mar. 28,

1826); Warden Harris to Governor Lincoln (Dec. 18, 1826), in State Prison, "Reports and Papers of the Officers, 1809–1828," in Misc. Box 84, pt. 1 (unpublished MS, Mass. Archives) [hereinafter "Officers Papers"]; *Prison Discipline Soc'y* 3 (1828):32; "Mass. Legislative Documents," 1825–26, no. 40:2–3.

67. "Visitors Minutes," 2:264–65 (Apr. 22, 1823).

68. "Visitors Minutes," 3:n.p. (Nov. 6, Dec. 4, Dec. 18, Dec. 20, Dec. 28, 1826, Jan. 8, Jan. 10, 1827); *Prison Discipline Soc'y* 3 (1828):32.

69. "Mass. Legislative Documents," 1825–26, no. 40:2–3; *Prison Discipline Soc'y* 3 (1828): 32–33 (quotations) (emphasis in original). Although conversion of prison property was a plain violation of prison bylaws, officers did gain permission to employ convicts by order of the directors in 1825; cf. *Rules and Regulations,* 56 (art. 12, § 6); "Visitors Minutes," 3:n.p. (Dec. 4, 1825). Johnson was also charged generally with "transactions of a very questionable character." *Report [on the Mass. State Prison],* 1828:15–16. The stint in Johnson's shop had been even shorter before 1823. "Visitors Minutes," 2:278 (July 30, 1823).

70. For example, New York: [Coffey], *Inside Out,* 138–40, 154–55; Lewis, *From Newgate to Dannemora,* 147–49. Even Thomas Eddy borrowed money from his prison, though when called upon for payment, he was able to demonstrate a balance in his favor. *View of the New-York State Prison,* 74–75. Pennsylvania: *Prison Discipline Soc'y* 5 (1830):21–32; Teeters, *They Were in Prison,* 211–16. At Walnut Street, "it was generally believed, but never fully ascertained, that some of the most expert of the convicts were let out at night to depredate on the public, and that some of the officers of the prison participated in the spoils." Matthew Carey, *Thoughts on Penitentiaries and Prison Discipline* (Philadelphia, 1831), 16.

71. *Report [on the Mass. State Prison],* 1828:15–16; *Prison Discipline Soc'y* 3 (1828):36–38. The first committee to discover Johnson's exorbitant commissions in 1826 urged that he be kept on because of his skill but that he be restricted to a fixed salary. In response, the directors limited his commissions to $2,000 per annum. Only in 1828 were Johnson's other abuses revealed. "Mass. Legislative Documents," 1825–26, no. 40:1–2; "Visitors Minutes," 3:n.p. (Mar. 27, Mar. 28, 1826). On the directors' toleration and misreporting of overstint, see *Prison Discipline Soc'y* 3 (1828):33, 37. The extent of the directors' conspiracy with Johnson is unclear; plainly they were allies in an administrative struggle against the warden, but no allegation that the directors benefited financially from Johnson's activities appeared. See Warden Harris to Governor Lincoln (Dec. 18, 1826), in "Officers Papers"; *Report [on the Mass. State Prison],* 1828:15–16; *Prison Discipline Soc'y* 3 (1828):30–32, 34.

72. Act of Feb. 23, 1822, ch. 108, *Mass. Acts,* 1818–22:727 (§ 5); *Prison Discipline Soc'y* 2 (1827):11–12.

73. For example, "Remarks on the Mass. State Prison," 13; *A Collection of the Political Writings of William Leggett,* ed. Theodore Sedgwick (New York, 1840), 1:263–71 [hereinafter *Writings of Leggett*]; Walter E. Hugins, *Jacksonian Democracy and the Working Class* (Stanford, 1960), 156–58. The term may have originated with Bentham, for whom it was no pejorative. See Bentham, "Panopticon," in *Works,* 4:54–56.

74. "Order Appointed to Be Executed in the City of London, by Act of Common Council" [1579], in *Parliamentary Papers,* 19 (1840) pt. 1:405 (§ 50) (British Library). Workhouse advocates frequently urged that inmates be placed in competition with *foreign* manufactures. E.g., R[ichard] H[aines], *Proposals for Building in Every County a Working-Alms-House or Hospital* (London, 1677), 3; Hale, *Discourse,* 23; see also Rice Bush, *The Poor Mans Friend* (London, 1649), 18–19; S[amuel] H[artlib], *London Charitie, Stilling the Poore Orphans Cry* (London, 1649), 8; and [Daniel Defoe],

Giving Alms No Charity, and Employing the Poor a Grievance to the Nation (London, 1704), 16–17 (noting the danger of domestic competition).

75. See chapter 5, note 68. Such lobbying efforts were often crowned with success. An act passed in Massachusetts in 1822 restricted the terms of all prison contracts to one year, which the directors of the state prison complained would be "a discouragement to contractors." The directors added that "the act probably grew out of a petition presented to the Legislature by sundry persons, complaining that the labour of the convicts was monopolized, and their work undersold in the market." Act of Feb. 23, 1822, ch. 108, *Mass. Acts,* 1818–22:727 (§ 5); "Remarks on the Mass. State Prison," 13. In 1826, the maximum term of contracts was raised to three years, Act of Feb. 15, 1826, ch. 84, *Mass. Acts,* 1825–28:146 (§ 5).

76. Hugins, *Jacksonian Democracy,* 155–61; Lewis, *From Newgate to Dannemora,* 187–200. As in Massachusetts, the legislature in New York was responsive to free labor interests; see id., 193–200. Free labor opposition to convict labor surfaced in other states, as well as in England. Francis Lieber to Charles Penrose (Jan. 22, 1835), in Thomas McElwee, *A Concise History of the Eastern Penitentiary of Pennsylvania* (Philadelphia, 1835), 61; Ayers, *Vengeance and Justice,* 65–66; Webb and Webb, *English Prisons,* 196. For examples of violence (threats against masons using prison-cut stone, and defacement of finished buildings), see Lewis, *From Newgate to Dannemora,* 191; *Writings of Leggett,* 1:63.

77. "The support of [convicts] . . . ought to be borne in the ratio of the benefit conferred—that is, equally." *Writings of Leggett,* 1:265. Free laborers had no moral quarrel with coercive labor in prisons; labor advocates favored the introduction of prison industries, such as iron making, that did not compete with the industries of local artisans. Lewis, *From Newgate to Dannemora,* 198–99; *Writings of Leggett,* 1:264.

78. "We are as decidedly opposed to the *principle* of state prison labour as any person can be; yet we believe that the *practical evil* of the present system, on any branch of productive industry, is exceedingly trifling." *Writings of Leggett,* 1:263, 266 (emphasis in original); see also chapter 5, note 68 and accompanying text. Prison products may not have even underbid free-made goods. The discount offered for convict wares may have reflected differentials in product quality; see "Visitors Minutes," 2:205–6 (Sept. 26, 1822); Lewis, *Development of American Prisons,* 130; James Mease to William Roscoe (May 18, 1827), in *U.S. Gazette,* June 6, 1827, at 1; Soc'y for the Prevention of Pauperism, *Report,* 74. Some students have speculated that the outcry over prison labor by free workers in the Jacksonian period traced to frustration over the very real competitive pressures caused by the emergence of factories, for which the prison became a convenient scapegoat; see Lewis, *From Newgate to Dannemora,* 187; Hugins, *Jacksonian Democracy,* 161.

79. Thomas Eddy, *Communication to Stephen Allen* (New York, 1823), 14–15 (quoting the London Society for the Improvement of Prison Discipline) (quotation); [Eddy], *Account,* 56; Lieber to Penrose, in McElwee, *Concise History,* 61–62; [Bradford], *State Prisons,* 45; Lewis, *From Newgate to Dannemora,* 192. Tocqueville argued that the "free working classes" would even *benefit* from prison competition, because it would translate into lower consumer prices; see Beaumont and Tocqueville, *On the Penitentiary System,* 156 n.s. By contrast, one early workhouse advocate argued that the workhouse would *lift* wages, by offering workers a base wage (although this analysis ran counter to the subsequent doctrine of less eligibility); see Hale, *Discourse,* 18–19, 24.

80. In England, Samuel Romilly reported with approval the case of a reformed thief who

"applied himself to his new trade with such indefatigable assiduity . . . that he had not stirred out of his room for eight months altogether." Samuel Romilly, *Observations on a Late Publication, Intitled Thoughts on Executive Justice* (London, 1786), 54–55.

81. For example, Thomas Eddy to Patrick Colquhoun (June 5, 1802), in Knapp, *Life,* 179; William Roscoe, *Remarks on the Report of the Commissioners* (Liverpool, 1825), 15. Similar phrases appeared in virtually every carceral proposal, beginning with the workhouse advocates, e.g., Hale, *Discourse,* 12. Some phrasings were more overtly mercenary in tone: against the background of the bloody code, Hanway allowed that his carceral plan would "preserve men's lives, and certainly render them more valuable, in a pecuniary view." Hanway, *Distributive Justice and Mercy,* 92. Haines aimed specifically at "the more speedy and profitable promoting [of] the Linnen Manufactury." R[ichard] Haines, *Provision for the Poor* (London, 1678), 3. Child considered "not much material" whether the workhouse "turns to *present* profit or not," so long as it transformed the poor into "useful Members of the Kingdom." Josiah Child, *A New Discourse of Trade* (London, 1693), 75 (emphasis added). Other advocates combined the theme with philanthropic rhetoric: "Render them useful members of Society here, and joyful Expectants of Happiness hereafter." John Brewster, *Sermons for Prisoners* (Stockton, 1790), vi–vii.

82. The thesis that penitentiaries were intended to grind unruly and unwilling subjects into a modern industrial proletariat is central to several critical studies of the carceral institution; see Melossi and Pavarini, *Prison and Factory,* esp. 21, 137–38, 143–45, 156–63; Michel Foucault, *Discipline and Punish: The Birth of the Prison* (London, 1977), 239–44; Miller, "Sinking Gradually into the Proletariat."

83. American penitentiaries produced far more deficits than dividends; see above, note 35.

84. See above, note 79 and accompanying text; chapter 4, notes 35–38 and accompanying text.

85. Adam Smith, *An Inquiry into the Nature and Causes of the Wealth of Nations* [1776], ed. Encyclopaedia Britannica (Chicago, 1952), 21, 27–62.

86. George Fitzhugh, *Sociology for the South, or The Failure of Free Society* (Richmond, 1854), 67–68. On the theme of "wage slavery," see Marcus Cunliffe, *Chattel Slavery and Wage Slavery: The Anglo-American Context, 1830–1860* (Athens, Ga., 1979); Wilfred Carsel, "The Slaveholders' Indictment of Northern Wage Slavery," *J. S. Hist.* 6 (1940):504; Jenkins, *Pro-Slavery Thought,* 296–99; Jonathan A. Glickstein, " 'Poverty Is Not Slavery': American Abolitionists and the Competitive Labor Market," in *Antislavery Reconsidered: New Perspectives on the Abolitionists,* ed. Lewis Perry and Michael Fellman (Baton Rouge, 1979), 202–18; Bernard Mandel, *Labor: Free and Slave* (New York, 1955), 76–110.

87. George Fitzhugh, *Cannibals All! or, Slavery without Masters,* ed. C. Vann Woodward (Cambridge, Mass., 1960), 5, 15–16.

88. See chapter 6, note 162.

89. At least one example dates to 1789: "all Europe evinces, that where there are no *black slaves,* there must be *white slaves.*" *Gazette of the United States,* May 2, 1789, quoted in Drew R. McCoy, *The Elusive Republic: Political Economy in Jeffersonian America* (Williamsburg, 1980), 119 n.38. For other early examples, see Cunliffe, *Chattel Slavery and Wage Slavery,* 5–6; *The Ideology of Slavery,* ed. Drew G. Faust (Baton Rouge, 1981), 18. See also David Brion Davis, *The Problem of Slavery in Western Culture* (Ithaca, 1966), 186 n. 48, 202 (parallel arguments by English and French

writers). In another variation, some early apologists argued that slaves in America lived better than their brethren in Africa. Id., 186; *Documents Illustrative . . . of the Slave Trade,* 2:352n.

90. Fitzhugh, *Sociology for the South*; Fitzhugh, *Cannibals All.*

91. Diary of Cotton Mather, quoted in Lawrence W. Towner, " 'A Fondness for Freedom': Servant Protest in Puritan Society," *Wm. & Mary Q.,* 3d ser., 19 (1962):202 (emphasis in original); see also Cotton Mather, *A Good Master Well Served* (Boston, 1696), 53; Davis, *Problem of Slavery in Western Culture,* 202 and n.11; Davis, *Problem of Slavery in the Age of Revolution,* 208.

92. *The Pro-Slavery Argument as Maintained by the Most Distinguished Writers of the Southern States* (Charleston, 1852), 259, 323; Jenkins, *Pro-Slavery Thought,* 116.

93. Quoted in Davis, *Problem of Slavery in the Age of Revolution,* 494. Half a century earlier, Bernard Mandeville cited to Dutch workhouses to justify his proposal to sell convicts into servitude on the Barbary Coast: "These [workhouse inmates] are not called Slaves; but such is their Abode, their Diet, and their Discipline, that of those who were confined there for any considerable Number of Years, I don't believe there ever was one who would not have thought it a glorious Preferment, if, instead of it, he might have taken his Chance, and been sold for a Slave in *Turky.*" Bernard Mandeville, *An Enquiry into the Causes of the Frequent Executions at Tyburn* (London, 1725), 53–54.

94. See chapter 6, note 40 and accompanying text.

95. Cunliffe, *Chattel Slavery and Wage Slavery,* 7–31; Davis, *Problem of Slavery in the Age of Revolution,* 244, 275; Mandel, *Labor: Free and Slave,* 76–89; Eric Foner, "Abolitionism and the Labor Movement in Antebellum America," in *Antislavery, Religion, and Reform,* ed. Christine Bolt and Seymour Drescher (Hampden, 1980), 254–71; Patricia Hollis, "Anti-Slavery and British Working-Class Radicalism in the Years of Reform," in id., 294–311.

96. *A Candid Enquiry Why the Natives of Ireland, Which Are in London, Are More Addicted to Vice Than the People of Any Other Nation* (London 1754), 4. For examples from sixteenth- and seventeenth-century England, see [Peter Chamberlen], *The Poore Mans Advocate* [1649] (London, n.d.), 12–13; Buchanan Sharp, *In Contempt of All Authority: Rural Artisans and Riot in the West of England, 1586–1660* (Berkeley, 1980), 41; and Karen O. Kupperman, *Settling with the Indians* (Totowa, 1980), 107.

97. Cunliffe, *Chattel Slavery and Wage Slavery,* 13; E. J. Hobsbawm, "The Machine Breakers," in *Laboring Men: Studies in the History of Labor* (London, 1964), 5.

98. Hollis, "Antislavery and British Working-Class Radicalism," 296, 310; Sidney Pollard, *The Genesis of Modern Management* (Cambridge, Mass., 1965), 164.

99. See above, note 95; Kupperman, *Settling with the Indians,* 137–40.

100. The complex relation between abolitionism and northern labor advocacy is addressed in Foner, "Abolitionism and the Labor Movement."

101. See above, epigraph. Bentham continued: "The habitual endurance of evil and, in a still greater degree, ignorance of a more blissful state, serve to bridge over the chasm between two conditions which, at first sight, appear so far apart." Bentham, *Theory of Legislation,* 1:269.

102. Davis, *Problem of Slavery in the Age of Revolution,* 491–93.

103. Defenders of slavery denounced this distinction as absurd. *Pro-Slavery Argument,* 161–63.

104. Davis, *Problem of Slavery in the Age of Revolution,* 465–67; Glickstein, " 'Poverty Is

Not Slavery,'" 214; Foner, "Abolitionism and the Labor Movement," 264–65.

105. Glickstein, "'Poverty Is Not Slavery,'" 214.

106. Glickstein, "'Poverty Is Not Slavery,'" 214–15; Cunliffe, *Chattel Slavery and Wage Slavery*, 29–30; Mandel, *Labor: Free and Slave*, 89–93.

107. See above, notes 75–77.

108. Quoted in Gary Nash, *The Urban Crucible: Social Change, Political Consciousness, and the Origins of the American Revolution* (Cambridge, Mass., 1979), 326. See also chapter 4, note 61.

109. On this line of rhetoric, see Eric Foner, *Free Soil, Free Labor, Free Men* (New York, 1970), 11–39; Howard Temperley, "Capitalism, Slavery, and Ideology," *Past & Present* 75 (May 1977):94.

110. Foner, *Free Soil, Free Labor, Free Men*, 16, 40–72; Cunliffe, *Chattel Slavery and Wage Slavery*, chs. 1–2. Some English commentators had also asserted the upward mobility of the English poor, e.g., Bernard Mandeville, *The Fable of the Bees* [1714], ed. F. B. Kaye (Oxford, 1924), 2:351–52 (denying that the poor were "for ever pinn'd down, they, and all their Posterity, to that slavish condition"). But cf. below, note 144.

111. Quoted in Cunliffe, *Chattel Slavery and Wage Slavery*, 29–30; see also Glickstein, "'Poverty Is Not Slavery,'" 203–5; Jenkins, *Pro-Slavery Thought*, 297n; Mandel, *Labor: Free and Slave*, 89–93; and Foner, "Abolitionism and the Labor Movement," 258.

112. *Mass. Centinel*, June 1, 1796, at 1, continued June 4, 1796, at 1, and June 8, 1796, at 1–2. Philanthropos's portrait of public punishment well illustrates its functional deterioration in the eighteenth century; see chapter 3, text at notes 49–54.

113. Morgan, *American Slavery, American Freedom*, 326. Officials on one occasion looked to stereotypes of the depressed poor for suggestions for prison garb: a legislative report in New York proposed to outfit convicts with wooden shoes "in the manner of those in common use by the laboring people of France." Allen, Hopkins, and Tibbits, "Report," 114. Wooden shoes were a longstanding English symbol of the degradation of continental peasants; see Edmund S. Morgan, *Inventing the People: The Rise of Popular Sovereignty in England and America* (New York, 1988), 158 and n.7.

114. The practice appears to have originated in Pennsylvania; see Lewis, *Development of American Prisons*, 31. On American states generally, see *Prison Discipline Soc'y* 8 (1833):30–32. In Massachusetts, before the practice of clothing ex-convicts was institutionalized, prisoners sometimes sought to provide their own garments to comrades who were about to be discharged. "Visitors Minutes," 2:84 (Apr. 10, 1809).

115. For example, Aaron Bancroft, *The Importance of a Religious Education Illustrated and Enforced* (Worcester, 1793), 8–10.

116. Winthrop D. Jordan, *White Over Black: American Attitudes toward the Negro, 1550–1812* (Chapel Hill, 1968), 133–34, 354–56, 399.

117. Mandeville, *Fable of the Bees*, 1:287–90; Morgan, *American Slavery, American Freedom*, 322–23, 381–82.

118. Officials sometimes spoke of convicts as occupying the position of an "apprentice" or even a "scholar." Powers, *Brief Account*, 60–61; Soc'y for the Prevention of Pauperism, *Report*, 60; *View of the New-York State Prison*, 29–30; "Remarks on the Mass. State Prison," 13.

119. For example, *Powers to Livingston*, 18; *Report [on the Mass. State Prison]*, 1827:8–9; Beaumont and Tocqueville, *On the Penitentiary System*, 34; A[llen], *Observations*, 62; Allen, Hopkins, and Tibbits, "Report," 109 (quotation). The Prison Discipline

Society advocated training in "simple" rather than "curious" arts, whereby ex-convicts could more "easily find employment." *Prison Discipline Soc'y* 1 (1826):23. In England, see e.g., Roscoe, *Additional Observations*, 133–41. Once again, this goal appeared initially in earlier proposals for workhouses, e.g., Fielding, *Proposal*, 40, 85. Cf. Thomas Eddy, who, while not averse to tradesmanship, did not consider it vital in the United States, where there were sufficient opportunities for unskilled laborers. Thomas Eddy to George Tibbits, Stephen Allen, and Samuel Hopkins (Jan. 7, 1825), in Knapp, *Life,* 91; Eddy to William Roscoe (Dec. 15, 1825), in id., 319–20.

120. Lieber to Penrose, in McElwee, *Concise History,* 62.
121. William Roscoe, *Remarks on the Report of the Commissioners* (Liverpool, 1825), 10.
122. A[llen], *Examination,* 5. See also *Report [on the Mass. State Prison],* 1827:6–9 ("reasonably profitable").
123. A[llen], *Observations,* 76–87 (esp. 79). At least one Auburn graduate was reported to have become a "merchant." *Powers to Livingston,* 49 (see also 47–52).
124. A school was in operation in the Massachusetts State Prison by 1823; see Haynes, *Pictures,* 45; *Rules and Regulations,* 61. Noting the existence of prison schools in various states, see *Prison Discipline Soc'y* 8 (1833):12–14; Beaumont and Tocqueville, *On the Penitentiary System,* 49–55 and nn.
125. Carey, *Thoughts,* 6. Tocqueville conceived education to be the central feature of a convict's therapy: "the authors of the system . . . aspire at reforming him . . . . Moral and religious instruction forms, in this respect, the whole basis of the system." Beaumont and Tocqueville, *On the Penitentiary System,* 49–50.
126. Tocqueville characterized as "eutopian" Edward Livingston's plan to offer convicts "a system of instruction almost as complete as that established in any of the free academies." Beaumont and Tocqueville, *On the Penitentiary System,* 87.
127. "Remarks on the Mass. State Prison," 5 (noting the division of labor, "some [convicts] doing one part, and some doing others"); Lewis, *From Newgate to Dannemora,* 109, 135, 187; Michael S. Hindus, *Prison and Plantation: Crime, Justice, and Authority in Massachusetts and South Carolina, 1767–1878* (Chapel Hill, 1980), 165–66.
128. Foner, *Free Soil, Free Labor, Free Men,* 36–37. One English critic of the penitentiary sought to direct inmates *away* from factory industries because "when the general demand [for manufactures] is inadequate to the supply, I feel no particular desire to increase that surplus, by calling forth to productive industry those who in all probability added little to the competition before they were in prison." William Roscoe replied: "Is there then a privileged *caste* in this country, who monopolize even the *right to labor* for a subsistence? . . . The fact is, that whenever the necessities of life are abundantly produced, the *population,* and consequently the *consumption,* will increase also." Roscoe, *Additional Observations,* 135n (emphasis in original).
129. William Roscoe urged that penitentiaries develop factory industries for this reason. William Roscoe, *Observations on Penal Jurisprudence and the Reformation of Criminals, Part III* (London, 1825), 57–58.
130. Quoted in Robert S. Starobin, *Industrial Slavery and the Old South* (New York, 1970), 207–9.
131. Eugene D. Genovese and Elizabeth Fox-Genovese, "Slavery, Economic Development, and the Law: The Dilemma of the Southern Political Economists, 1800–1860," *Wash. & Lee L. Rev.* 41 (1984):10, 12.
132. Jenkins, *Pro-Slavery Thought,* 295–308; see also above, text at note 91.
133. Soc'y for the Prevention of Pauperism, *Report,* app. 68–69. (This statement was made by Samuel Parsons of Virginia, where constitutional objections to the penitentiary system had been raised; see chapter 6, note 60. I am unable to determine

Parson's views on slavery.) See also Thomas Eddy to George Tibbits, Stephen Allen, and Samuel Hopkins (Jan. 7, 1825), in Knapp, *Life,* 87 (object is to "raise a fellow-creature from degradation").

134. Henry Fielding, "An Enquiry into the Causes of the Late Increase of Robbers" [1751], in *The Works of Henry Fielding, Esq.* (London, 1806), 10:409; Fielding, *Proposal,* 90.

135. On republican theory in the South, see Morgan, *American Slavery, American Freedom,* ch. 18.

136. See chapter 6, notes 170–78 and accompanying text.

137. See chapter 6, text at notes 129–31, 139–43, 158–63, 168–69.

138. References to slavery in other contexts were often metaphorical. Benjamin Franklin referred to soldiers and impressed sailors as "slaves." *The Writings of Benjamin Franklin,* ed. Albert H. Smyth (London, 1906), 9:298. Early references to the "slavery" of the poor may have mixed notions of exploitation with mere notions of baseness on the social scale; see Kupperman, *Settling with the Indians,* 139–40. Many advocates of hard labor who spoke explicitly of penal "slavery" and convict "slaves" plainly contemplated rehabilitative therapy, e.g., "Slavery . . . make[s] [convicts] useful, until employment grows habitual to them [and] works their reformation." Dawes, *Essay,* 67.

139. Likewise, the ancient workhouse was conceived for their inmates' "reformation, and not for perpetual servitude." "Ordinances and Rules Drawn Out for the Good Government of the House of Bridewell," 405 (§ 49). Nevertheless, a few advocates, including Jeremy Bentham, found attractive the possibility of exercising continued control over ex-convicts; see Himmelfarb, "The Haunted House of Jeremy Bentham," 54–57; William Paley, *The Principles of Moral and Political Philosophy,* 7th ed. (London, 1790), 2:293–94. See also *Report [on the Mass. State Prison],* May 1830:9 (also in "Mass. Legislative Documents," 1830–31:67) (raising the possibility of inviting discharged convicts to stay on in the state prison).

140. See chapter 6, text at note 45.

141. Jordan, *White Over Black,* 281–83, 352–56; Edmund S. Morgan, "Slavery and Freedom: The American Paradox," in *The Challenge of the American Revolution* (New York, 1976), 150–51.

142. For example, *Pro-Slavery Argument,* 89, 422–35, 446–47 (noting the disproportionate numbers of freed slaves in northern penitentiaries).

143. Michael Hindus argues that the plantation system "prevented" South Carolina and other slave states from constructing penitentiaries on the northern rehabilitative model, because property crime was associated with slaves who were deemed unreformable and who were already controlled by private masters. Thus, he asserts, the two institutions were incompatible. Hindus, *Prison and Plantation,* 125–27, 242–49. This overstates the case, for, as Edward Ayers has since shown, many southern states did build penitentiaries expressly for rehabilitation, as a supplement to the crime control offered by the plantation system. Ayers, *Vengeance and Justice,* ch. 2. Southerners appear to have reconciled rehabilitative and proslavery ideology by distinguishing between reformable whites and incorrigible blacks; free and enslaved blacks were excluded from many southern penitentiaries; see id., 61; see also below, note 159.

144. For example, Mandeville: "Everybody knows that there is a vast number of Journeymen Weavers, Tailors, Clothworkers, and twenty other Handicrafts; who, if by four Days Labour in a Week they can maintain themselves, will hardly be persuaded

to work the fifth. . . . When Men shew such an extraordinary proclivity to Idleness and Pleasure, what reason have we to think that they would ever work, unless they were oblig'd to it by immediate Necessity?" Mandeville, *Fable of the Bees*, 1:181–98 (quotation at 192). The aspect of incorrigibility is illustrated by the quotation in chapter 2, note 11. On this line of ideology, see Morgan, *American Slavery, American Freedom*, 323–26.

145. Morgan, *American Slavery, American Freedom*, 324–25.
146. "Some persons, I am aware, are so far from admitting the possibility of a reformation of these abandoned wretchs, that they imagine them to be entirely ignorant of the fundamental principles of all religion, and incapable of any troublesome reflection." [Samuel Denne], *A Letter to Sir Robert Ladbroke . . . With an Attempt to Shew the Good Effects Which May Reasonably Be Expected from the Confinement of Criminals in Separate Apartments* (London, 1771), 52. See also [William Crawford and Whitworth Russell], *Extracts from the Second Report of the Inspectors of Prisons* (London, 1837), 26–27.
147. Among these was Mandeville, whose vision of the poor is quoted above, note 144. Mandeville sought to condemn criminals to hard labor only until such time as they could be traded for Englishmen *unjustly* enslaved by Barbary pirates. Mandeville, *Enquiry*, 48–55. For other hard labor proposals in Europe that failed to mention rehabilitation, see chapter 2, note 31.
148. In England, Jonas Hanway emphatically rejected the pessimistic vision: "To suppose any man so devoid of sentiment, as to be absolutely incorrigible by any effort, is a *false principle*." Jonas Hanway, *Distributive Justice and Mercy* (London, 1781), 137 (emphasis in original). Likewise, Edward Livingston in America: "The error, it appears to me, lies in considering [criminals] as beings of a nature so inferior as to be incapable of elevation, and so bad as to make any amelioration impossible." Livingston, *Complete Works*, 1:563. See also, e.g., Josiah Quincy, *Remarks on Some of the Provisions of the Laws of Massachusetts Affecting Poverty, Vice, and Crime* (Cambridge, Mass., 1822), 19–20. This was, *mutatis mutandis*, also a common criticism by opponents of slavery, e.g., Jordan, *White Over Black*, 281–82. Daniel Raymond, who favored penitentiaries that featured solitary confinement, interrupted his discussion of incarceration to add a word about slavery: "[Slaveholders] perpetually exclaim, 'see the effects of manumission! The blacks are not capable of being free, and providing for themselves. They are an inferior order of beings, and are fit only to be slaves!' And this they will maintain in opposition to reason and authority, although they see a multitude of instances, of blacks . . . educated with the expectation of being free, who make as industrious, sober, good citizens, as any in the country." Soc'y for the Prevention of Pauperism, *Report*, app. 45.
149. On seventeenth-century workhouse advocates who expressly rejected the pessimistic vision and encouraged raising the wages of the poor, see chapter 2, note 12; John Cary, *An Essay on the State of England in Relation to its Trade* (Bristol, 1695), 156–59; Joyce O. Appleby, *Economic Thought and Ideology in Seventeenth-Century England* (Princeton, 1978), 143–44, 147–48. The debate over this issue continued into the eighteenth century; see A. W. Coats, "Changing Attitudes to Labor in the Mid-Eighteenth Century," *Econ. Hist. Rev.*, 2d ser., 11 (1958):35. Eighteenth-century workhouse advocates again championed the notion of increasing productivity by offering higher wages, e.g., Fielding, *Proposal*, 82–83. At least one labor economist explicitly related the alternative of low wages to slavery: "In the one case [subsis-

tence wages], you must be satisfied with the drudgery of an enervated slave; in the other [higher wages], you may expect new efforts of ingenuity." Quoted in Coats, "Changing Attitudes," 62.

150. Quoted in Coats, "Changing Attitudes," 37 n.6. On Berkeley's criminological advocacy, see Leon Radzinowicz, *A History of English Criminal Law and Its Administration from 1750* (New York, 1948), 1:263 n.11.

151. For example, [Bradford], *State Prisons*, 61; Bradford, *Enquiry*, 44–45; Knapp, *Life*, 21; James T. Alexander, *Render Them Submissive: Responses to Poverty in Philadelphia, 1760–1800* (Amherst, 1980), 152 (Benjamin Rush); "Memoir of Stephen Allen," 111–13 (unpublished typescript, New-York Historical Society, 1927); *Prison Discipline Soc'y* 7 (1832):11; Mease, *Observations*, 69; Beaumont and Tocqueville, *On the Penitentiary System*, 288 (Roberts Vaux). Education for free blacks: *Prison Discipline Soc'y* 1 (1826):35–38; id., 2 (1827):79. Rush suggested that freed slaves be "instructed in some business whereby they may be able to maintain themselves," rhetoric analogous to proposals to train convicts. Rush, *Address*, 22–23. In England, see David Owen, *English Philanthropy, 1660–1960* (Cambridge, Mass., 1964), 113–21 (William Allen, Thomas Buxton, James Mackintosh, Samuel Romilly).

152. See chapter 2, notes 13, 69, 102, 113, and accompanying text; chapter 5, note 107 and accompanying text.

153. For example, Allen, Hopkins, and Tibbits, "Report," 103–4, 108, 119. See also chapter 5, note 103.

154. Lewis, *From Newgate to Dannemora*, 85, 101–2. Lynds nonetheless paid lip service to the goal of rehabilitation. On his rehabilitative philosophy, cf. Beaumont and Tocqueville, *On the Penitentiary System*, 202; *Letter from Edward Livingston, Esq., to Roberts Vaux on the Advantages of the Pennsylvania System of Prison Discipline* (Philadelphia, 1828), 7 (originally published in the *Nat'l Gazette*).

155. Compare chapter 6, note 160, and accompanying text with note 150, above, and accompanying text.

156. *Powers to Livingston*, 10 (quotation), 26–27. Powers expressed anger that other advocates relied on Lynds's statements to determine the Auburn philosophy. In fact, Powers asserted, Lynds did not "relish or understand its principles and philosophy." Id., 4–5, 9–10.

157. James Mease proposed to transport all second offenders: "To try again the reforming influences of confinement and labour would only perpetuate the evils we are striving to prevent. . . . The prisoners confined under the expectation of being reclaimed, finding themselves intermixed with abandoned profligates, who have gone through the process without effect, will despair of their own recovery." Mease, *Observations*, 19–20. William Roscoe agreed that offenders should never be sent to the penitentiary twice and that transportation was a reasonable punishment for second offenders. Roscoe, *Observations*, 99–104, 150; William Roscoe to James Mease (Apr. 21, 1821), in Roscoe, *Additional Observations*, app. 19–20. The early hard labor advocate Thomas Robe proposed to exchange for Englishmen enslaved "in Foreign Parts" convicts "found to be Incorrigible under such [workhouse] Discipline." [Thomas Robe], *A Method Whereby Criminals Liable to Transportation May Be Render'd Not only Useful but Honest Members of the Publick* [c. 1727] (n.p., n.d.). The early solitary advocate Jonas Hanway favored capital punishment for repeat offenders. Hanway, *Distributive Justice and Mercy*, 137. William Tudor considered the policy of sending repeat offenders to the penitentiary an "absurd contradiction in terms." [Tudor], "Book Review," 419.

158. "Soc'y for the Prevention of Pauperism," *Report,* app. 48–49 (quotation); Allen, Hopkins, and Tibbits, "Report," 125 (proposing a perpetual "criminal colony" at home for "all incorrigible offenders"). In many instances, female convicts were considered unredeemable and, though admitted to penitentiaries, received no therapy there. See generally Lewis, *From Newgate to Dannemora,* ch. 7; Nicole Hahn Rafter, *Partial Justice: Women, Prisons, and Social Control,* rev. ed. (New Brunswick, 1990), ch. 1.

159. Proposal to colonize former slaves who do not respond to education: *Prison Discipline Soc'y* 1 (1826):35–38. Proposal to subject former slaves who do not become "good citizens" to "government" and "oblige them to labour": Thomas Jefferson to Edward Bancroft (Jan. 26, 1788), in *The Papers of Thomas Jefferson,* ed. Julian P. Boyd (Princeton, 1950), 14:492–93; similarly, [Rush], *Address,* 22. Of course, some emancipationists favored the colonization of *all* black slaves, either because they considered them innately depraved or because they deemed the two races incompatible; see George M. Frederickson, *The Black Image in the White Mind* (New York, 1971), 11–18, 22, though other advocates challenged these views, 28–31. Proposals to transport repeat offenders tended to blend with proposals to colonize chattel slaves, on the assumption that few slaves would make the adjustment successfully. See Mease, *Observations,* 29, 34, 66; *Report [on the Mass. State Prison],* 1822:14 (proposing to transport only black convicts); Allen, Hopkins, and Tibbits, "Report," 117 (same). Francis Hutcheson completed the triangle by making a similar proposal for the idle poor: they should be subject to servitude for seven years and then granted their liberty if they had "acquired a habit of diligence"; if after this "trial" their habits remained unchanged, "they should be adjudged to slavery for life." Hutcheson, *System of Moral Philosophy,* 2:202. Such themes trace to the earliest workhouses. The Bridewell ordinances of 1557 specified that vagrants who had been sent once to the institution should not be recommitted but instead should be "used as rogues" under the old poor law. "Ordinances and Rules . . . of the House of Bridewell," 403. By act of Parliament in 1597, idlers unreformed by a term in the workhouse were to be transported or condemned to perpetual servitude in the "Gallyes of this Realme." 39 Eliz. c.4 (1597), long version of the act reprinted in *Tudor Economic Documents,* ed. R. H. Tawney and Eileen Powers (London, 1924), 2:357.

160. Beaumont and Tocqueville, *On the Penitentiary System,* 18. See also [Basil Montagu], *An Account of the Origin and Object of the Society for the Diffusion of Knowledge upon the Punishment of Death* (London, 1812), 6. Notice also the connection of jail reform to antislavery in *The Third Report of the Society for the Diffusion of Knowledge Respecting the Punishment of Death* (London, 1816), 4 (comparing jail conditions to the holds of slaveships). The connection between penitentiary advocacy and jail reform was also close, beginning with the dual efforts of English philanthropists such as John Howard and continuing with such American organizations as the Philadelphia Society for Alleviating the Miseries of Public Prisons and the Prison Discipline Society; see, e.g., Vaux, *Notices; Prison Discipline Soc'y* 1 (1826):7–33 (and subsequent reports). Education reform and carceral advocacy had a direct link, in that education was seen as forestalling criminal activity; see, e.g., [John Gallison], "Book Review," *N. Am. Rev.* 9 (1819):291–93; *Letters on the Pennsylvania System of Solitary Imprisonment,* 2d ed. (Philadelphia, 1827), 25; Knapp, *Life,* 92; M. J. Heale, "Humanitarianism in the Early Republic: The Moral Reformers of New York, 1776–1825," *J. Am. Stud.* 2 (1968):164–71. For a broad statement of the "career of improvement," connecting penitentiary advocacy with the movements for public education, protection of child labor, and the distribution of religious tracts, in

addition to jail reform and antislavery advocacy, see Roscoe, *Observations,* 35–37, 174–75.

161. Compare David Rothman, who associates the penitentiary movement with other *carceral* movements in the Jacksonian period: the almshouse for paupers, the hospital for the insane, the orphanage for homeless children, and the reformatory for delinquent juveniles. Jacksonian advocates had formed "a cult of asylum." David J. Rothman, *The Discovery of the Asylum: Social Order and Disorder in the New Republic* (Boston, 1971), esp. xiii, xv, 130, 187–90 (quotation at 130). In fact, the "cult" as such was far older than Rothman claims and had spawned a variety of institutions, including workhouses, in earlier centuries; it was also broader in scope than Rothman claims, expressing its central premise—the potential for uplifting individuals—in such diverse movements as wage reform, jail reform, public education, temperance, and antislavery advocacy. Penitentiary advocates in the Jacksonian era, as in earlier times, did not look exclusively to the carceral model for solutions to social problems.

162. Roscoe juxtaposed the philosophy of "moral improvement" against "that absurd and exploded doctrine, that the security of government is founded on the ignorance and debasement of the people." Roscoe, *Observations,* 36 (emphasis omitted).

163. Jordan, *White Over Black,* 281–82; Frederickson, *Black Image in the White Mind,* 34–35. Thomas Eddy remarked that the disproportionate number of freed slaves in New York's Newgate prison "afford[s] an instructive lesson on the influence of . . . Negro slavery." [Eddy], *Account,* 86. Cf. above, note 142 and accompanying text.

164. Coats, "Changing Attitudes," 38 and n.1, 41–42. In ascribing immutable characteristics to debased groups, pessimistic commentators sometimes hinted that slaves, paupers, and criminals were less than human, "a brutish sort of people." Morgan, *American Slavery, American Freedom,* 325–26 (quotation); Paul Slack, *Poverty and Policy in Tudor and Stuart England* (London, 1988), 25; Mandeville, *Enquiry,* 52. Antislavery, workhouse, and penitentiary advocates, in turn, protested the humanity of all three groups, e.g., Jordan, *White Over Black,* 505 ("the erroneous notion that the blacks are . . . a species different from the whites"); Hale, *Discourse,* 25 (workhouses for the poor were "[a] work of great Humanity, and such as we owe to those of our Nature, as we are men"); Hanway, *Distributive Justice and Mercy,* 135 ("Let us try the experiment [of solitary confinement], we shall find they are *men,* like ourselves," not "so many monsters in human shape"); *Letters on the Pennsylvania System,* 1st ed., 14 ("We look upon them [convicts] as men (not as brutes), as a part of the great human family with ourselves"); *Prison Discipline Soc'y* 8 (1833):35–38.

165. "Were a number of *Whites* treated just as they are . . . who will venture to assert that it would not occasion a like depression of Spirit, and consequent Depravity of Manners?" Quoted in Jordan, *White Over Black,* 282. See also Thomas Buxton, *The African Slave Trade and Its Remedy* (London, 1840), 460–86 (citing examples of whites enslaved by Africans and Arabs).

166. "Remarks on the Mass. State Prison," 10n.

167. Alexis de Tocqueville, *Democracy in America,* ed. J. P. Mayer and Max Lerner (New York, 1966), 552. On Jacksonian striving, see Marvin Meyers, *The Jacksonian Persuasion: Politics and Belief* (Stanford, 1957), ch. 6.

168. See above, note 95. Once again, southern commentators agreed; see Foner, *Free Soil, Free Labor, Free Men,* 66; *Pro-Slavery Argument,* 47–48.

169. [Coffey], *Inside Out,* 134–36 (emphasis in original). Advocates of the Pennsylva-

nia system sometimes leveled similar charges against Auburn system prisons; see *Prison Discipline . . . Compared,* 11–14.

170. Horace Lane, *Five Years in State's Prison,* 5th ed. (New York, 1835), 18–19; Reynolds, *Reflections,* 137–40, 209 (quotations at 138); Lewis, *From Newgate to Dannemora,* 128–29, 190; *Prison Discipline Soc'y* 8 (1833):144. Nor did the practice of tattooing convicts, begun in Massachusetts in 1818, improve the situation. Act of Feb. 23, 1818, ch. 176, *Mass. Acts,* 1815–18:602–5; Act of Mar. 11, 1828, ch. 118, id., 1825–28:830; Haynes, *Pictures,* 40–41; *Report [on the Mass. State Prison],* 1829:11. However, at least one early ex-convict wrote in praise of the Massachusetts State Prison; see John Southack, *The Life of John Southack* (n.p., 1809), 63.

171. [Bradford], *State Prisons,* 47 (quotation); *Powers to Livingston,* 13–14.

172. "Visitors Minutes," 2:29 (Oct. 6, 1816).

173. See above, note 91 and accompanying text. To complete the triangle once more, William Paley offered another version of this argument to the English poor, assuring poor laborers that they were happier than their *employers,* who were saddled with administrative responsibilities. This echoed planters who asserted that slaves were happier than *masters* for the same reason. Davis, *Problem of Slavery in the Age of Revolution,* 359. I have, however, found no statement to the effect that convicts ought to have considered themselves happier than their keepers.

174. Massachusetts abolished the practice of tattooing inmates in 1830. Act of Mar. 12, 1830, ch. 114, *Mass. Acts,* 1828–31:459. Affirmative efforts to aid ex-convicts varied from state to state. Absent overstint, inmates in most penitentiaries received clothing and small sums of money on their departure to help them return home and to tide them over until they could secure employment. The adequacy of these sums was questionable (in some prisons, including Massachusetts, they could be withheld at the warden's discretion). In Massachusetts, see Act of Feb. 23, 1818, ch. 176, *Mass. Acts,* 1815–18:602–05; Act of Mar. 11, 1828, ch. 118, id., 1825–28:825, 830; *Report [on the Mass. State Prison],* 1827:15–16; id., May 1830:11; id., 1831:21; Vouchers, 1807, no. 22 (2d ser.), in "Reports and Papers," pt. 2; "Visitors Minutes," 2:33 (Nov. 6, 1816), 60–61 (Jan. 26, 1818); elsewhere, see Lownes, *Account,* 90; *Powers to Livingston,* 18; Carey, *Thoughts,* 53. Ad hoc efforts were also made to secure employment for ex-convicts, and some former inmates received good conduct certificates to aid them in that effort. [Austin], "Book Review," 254; "Daily Reports, 1805–1829" 1:n.p. (May 26, 1806) (warden's record, unpublished MS, Mass. Archives). Government-sponsored programs to provide employment to ex-convicts, or to open a halfway house, were contemplated at various times, but nothing came of them. In Massachusetts, see "Mass. Legislative Documents," 1817–22, no. 1:20–21; Resolve of Mar. 3, 1826, ch. 93, *Mass. Resolves,* 1824–28:307; Resolve of Mar. 4, 1830, ch. 64, id., 1828–31:283; Governor's Message, May 31, 1830, ch. 2, id., 392; Beaumont and Tocqueville, *On the Penitentiary System,* 37–38n; *Report [on the Mass. State Prison],* 1827:15; and the delightfully reasoned id., May 1830; elsewhere, see Teeters, *They Were in Prison,* 361–62; Soc'y for the Prevention of Pauperism, *Report,* app. 20; Livingston, *Complete Works,* 1:565–66. Community groups were encouraged to participate. [Bradford], *State Prisons,* 51–52; *Prison Discipline Soc'y* 7 (1832):12. A state agent whose sole responsibilities were to "counsel and advise" discharged convicts was appointed in Massachusetts in 1845. Act of Mar. 22, 1845, ch. 176, *Mass. Acts,* 1845–46:504; Act of Mar. 24, 1848, ch. 82, id., 1847–49:647. Similar agents were employed by benevolent societies in New York and Pennsylvania at around the same time; see Dorothea Dix,

Remarks on Prisons and Prison Discipline in the United States (Boston, 1845), 11–
12; Teeters, *They Were in Prison,* 362–63. (For one ex-convict's efforts to found an
after-care society, see Lewis, *Development of American Prisons,* 156.) For a survey of state efforts on behalf of ex-convicts in 1833, see *Prison Discipline Soc'y* 8
(1833):30–32.
175. See chapter 2, text at note 1.

Conclusion

1. The Massachusetts State Prison entertained the duke of Saxe-Weimer Eisenack
in 1825, among other distinguished guests. Karl Bernhard, *Travels through North
America, during the Years 1825 and 1826* (Philadelphia, 1828), 1:38–40; Gamaliel
Bradford to Governor and Board of Visitors (Nov. 2, 1820), in Governor and Council,
"Reports and Papers of the State Prison at Charlestown, 1807, 1822–1823" in Misc.
Box no. 3, pt. 1 (unpublished MS, Mass. Archives). But the early postrevolution-
ary American penitentiaries had also attracted such European tourists as Joseph
Priestly, Jacques Brissot de Warville, and the duke de la Rochefoucault-Liancourt.
"Long before the Eastern [State] Penitentiary [of Pennsylvania] was completed [in
1829], [the Walnut Street prison] attracted the notice of intelligent foreigners, and
very high encomiums were pronounced upon its system and management." "Book
Review," *Am. Q. Rev.* 18 (1835):468. For further information on visitors, see Adam J.
Hirsch, "From Pillory to Penitentiary: The Rise of Criminal Incarceration in the New
Republic" (Ph.D. diss., Yale University, 1987), pt. 1, n. 216.
2. "It is an era in the progress of civilization, and a circumstance highly flattering to
our national pride, that the European governments should look to this side of the
Atlantic for lessons in moral judicature." "Book Review," *Am. Q. Rev.* 14 (1833):228;
similarly, "Book Review," id. 18 (1835):453; [Edward Everett], "Book Review," *N. Am.
Rev.* 37 (1833):135–38; [Francis Wayland], "Book Review," id. 49 (July 1839):2–3;
"Book Review," *Christian Examiner* 20 (1836):337.
3. See chapter 5, note 12 and accompanying text.
4. Compare David J. Rothman, *The Discovery of the Asylum: Social Order and Disorder
in the New Republic* (Boston, 1971), 94 ("Europeans traveled to the new world to
examine an American creation, not to see a minor variant on an old world theme").
5. Michael Ignatieff, *A Just Measure of Pain: The Penitentiary in the Industrial Revolution, 1750–1850* (London, 1978), 94. The word was first used in the English Penitentiary Act of 1779, although the term *penitential hospital* appeared in institutional
proposals as early as 1698. Robin Evans, *The Fabrication of Virtue: English Prison
Architecture, 1750–1840* (Cambridge, 1982), 63; Rod Morgan, "Divine Philanthropy:
John Howard Reconsidered," *History* 62 (1977):401; chapter 2, notes 46–48 and accompanying text. American sources had adopted the word by the 1790s. Act of
Apr. 22, 1794, ch. 1777, in *Statutes at Large of Pennsylvania from 1682 to 1801* (Harrisburg, 1908), 15:175; Resolve of June 23, 1802, ch. 54, *Mass. Acts & Resolves,* 1802–
3:380–81; [Thomas Eddy], *An Account of the State Prison or Penitentiary House,
in the City of New York* (New York, 1801). See also [Everett], "Book Review," 124
(American recognition of the English origin of the term).
6. Whereas early American penitentiary advocates cited to English institutions to
prove the administrative practicability of prisons, these roles were soon reversed.
Cf. Society for Alleviating the Miseries of Public Prisons, *Extracts and Remarks
on the Subject of Punishment and Reformation of Criminals* (Philadelphia, 1790),

4–5; Jeremy Bentham, "Principles of Penal Law" [MSS, 1775–1802], in *The Works of Jeremy Bentham,* ed. John Bowring (Edinburgh, 1843), 1:502–3.

7. Nonetheless, Jacksonians retained an interest in European developments; the intellectual flow continued in both directions. For continued references to English tracts, see, e.g., *Annual Report of the Board of Managers of the Prison Discipline Society* 3 (1828):205–26 [hereinafter *Prison Discipline Soc'y*]. In 1820, the American advocate George Smith made a pilgrimage to Europe to investigate *its* penitentiaries. George Smith, *A Defence of the System of Solitary Confinement of Prisoners Adopted by the State of Pennsylvania* (Philadelphia, 1833), 48, 57n. For correspondence between English and American advocates, see chapter 4, notes 27–28, and chapter 5, notes 24, 99–100, 107.

8. See generally Ignatieff, *A Just Measure of Pain,* 93–109.

9. Ignatieff, *A Just Measure of Pain,* 193–200 (quotation at 195). Crawford was plainly irked by Jacksonian pretensions. He stated in his report: "To the merits of this penitentiary [the Eastern State Prison] I have much pleasure in bearing favorable testimony. In doing so, however, it is but right to observe, that there is no peculiar novelty in the general features of the plan, nor any just ground for the claim to originality which some of its advocates have been induced to urge. The main principles of the system were in force in England at the Gloucester Penitentiary forty years ago." William Crawford, *Report on the Penitentiaries of the United States* (n.p., 1835), 14. For a Jacksonian reply to Crawford, see "Book Review," *Am. Q. Rev.* 18 (1835):461–68. Not all Jacksonians were impervious to Crawford's logic. As a member of the Prison Discipline Society stated in 1833: "[John Howard's English] publications suggested almost every thing that has since been attempted. The reform commenced in this country. Here it has been carried forward and perfected." *Prison Discipline Soc'y* 8 (1833):4 (statement by Edward Everett); similarly, Francis Gray, *Prison Discipline in America* (Boston, 1847), 59–61; Roberts Vaux, *Reply to Two Letters of William Roscoe, Esquire* (Philadelphia, 1828), 9–10. American arguments over originality became entangled with the debate between advocates of the Auburn and Pennsylvania systems of prison discipline. Some Pennsylvania advocates tied the Auburn plan to earlier Dutch prisons, leading one author to accuse New York of being a "servile imitator," whereas Pennsylvania preferred to "disdain an obsequious regard to transatlantic projects." *Nat'l Gazette,* Dec. 30, 1828, at 2. Cf. Charles Shaler, Edward King, and T. J. Wharton, "Report on Punishment and Prison Discipline," in *Journal of the Senate of the Commonwealth of Pennsylvania, 1827–1828* (Harrisburg, 1828), 2:363 (drawing the connection without pejorative connotation).

10. See chapter 1, notes 25–29, 32, and accompanying text; chapter 2, notes 137–42 and accompanying text; and chapter 3, notes 67–77 and accompanying text.

11. David Rothman makes repeated reference to Jacksonian utopianism. Rothman, *Discovery of the Asylum,* xix, 89, 129, 133.

12. "Book Review," *Am. Q. Rev.* 14 (1833):232; James Mease, *The Picture of Philadelphia* (Philadelphia, 1811), 161; [Gamaliel Bradford], *State Prisons and the Penitentiary System Vindicated* (Charlestown, 1821), 61; chapter 7, note 126. Nor had Thomas Eddy enjoyed being called "an enthusiast, a visionary." Thomas Eddy to Patrick Colquhoun (July 15, 1803), in Samuel L. Knapp, *The Life of Thomas Eddy* (New York, 1834), 203.

13. Tocqueville continued: "They were not left alone, but their zeal gave the impulse to

all, and thus excited in all minds the ardor that animated theirs." Gustave de Beaumont and Alexis de Tocqueville, *On The Penitentiary System in the United States and Its Application in France* (Philadelphia, 1833), 93.

14. The psychological dislocation was mitigated by the familiarity of the proposal and by experience with similar institutions for vagrants. Fears of the expense were likewise reduced by promises of inmate contributions through hard labor, although the penitentiary still required a substantial initial capital investment. See also chapter 4, text at notes 30–31.

15. Cesare Beccaria, *On Crimes and Punishment* [1764], ed. Henry Paolucci (Indianapolis, 1963), 52. The observation was repeated over and over again, e.g., George Smith, *Defence,* 12–13; [William Tudor], "Book Review," *N. Am. Rev.* 13 (1821): 427–28; Robert Turnbull, *A Visit to the Philadelphia Prison* (London, 1797), 83 (originally published in the *Charleston Gazette*); [Eddy], *Account,* 15. Complaints of inertia began with the workhouse advocates; see R[ichard] Haines, *Provision for the Poor* (London, 1678), 7.

16. Bentham continued: "It may not even be altogether extravagant to suppose, that at the end we may be found to have profited not much less than we have suffered by these misfortunes, when the benefits of this improvement [the penitentiary system] come to be taken into the account." Jeremy Bentham, "A View of the Hard-Labour Bill" [1778], in *Works,* 4:5.

17. The story of Bentham's crusade has been often told, e.g., Coleman Phillipson, *Three Criminal Law Reformers: Beccaria, Bentham, Romilly* (London, 1923), 127–31.

18. Jeremy Bentham, "Panopticon versus New South Wales" [1802], in *Works,* 4:194–95. For Bentham's copious correspondence on the Panopticon, see *Works,* 11:96–170.

19. *Mass. Centinel,* Oct. 16, 1784, at 1.

20. *Mass. Centinel,* Jan. 5, 1785, at 3.

21. The Great Law of Pennsylvania, substantially enacted at the first session of the Provincial Assembly in 1682, was an exception—a product not of social crisis, but of William Penn's enormous influence, and eased forward, no doubt, by the fact that (to recall Beccaria) laws here *were* for the first time being decreed for the province (see above, text at note 15).

22. For an account of Eddy's lobbying efforts, see Knapp, *Life,* 56–58. On the lobbying efforts of the Philadelphia Society for Alleviating the Miseries of Public Prisons, see Negley K. Teeters, *They Were in Prison* (Philadelphia, 1937), 26–30.

23. Though the early record of legislative lobbying in Massachusetts survives only in the form of anonymous essays appearing in newspapers, the state ultimately spawned the Prison Discipline Society, probably the most influential body of carceral advocates in Jacksonian America; see, e.g., Samuel Gridley Howe, *Report of a Minority of a Special Committee of the Boston Prison Discipline Society* (Boston, 1846), 81–82.

24. This was true even of such English philanthropists as Jonas Hanway: "It requires time to deliberate on change of customs: but every day's experience proves the punishments we now inflict have lost their effect: something *new* must be devised." Jonas Hanway, *The Defects of Police the Cause of Immorality* (London, 1775), xii (emphasis in original) (reissued in 1780 under the title *The Citizen's Monitor*). On the importance of individuals in the transition to the penitentiary, see generally Robert A. Cooper, "Ideas and Their Execution: English Prison Reform," *Eighteenth Cent. Stud.* 10 (1976):73.

25. See chapter 5, notes 81–87 and accompanying text.

26. Act of Feb. 19, 1819, ch. 123, *Mass. Acts,* 1818–22:196.

27. Act of June 18, 1819, ch. 158, *Mass. Acts,* 1818–22:246.

28. Quincy continued: "It is not pretended, that there is any thing new, in these suggestions. Would to heaven that there did not rest upon our state any deeper stain than
that of ignorance!" Josiah Quincy, *Remarks on Some of the Provisions of the Laws
of Massachusetts Affecting Poverty, Vice, and Crime* (Cambridge, Mass., 1822), 12–
19 (quotation at 12–13). Similarly, William Tudor: "But in this state [Massachusetts]
particularly the man who takes up against any expenditure almost always carries
his point. This word *expense* has a magic influence here, it annihilates at once the
past & the future." William Tudor to William Roscoe (Sept. 10, 1819), in "Roscoe
Papers: Materials Relating to the United States," no. 4878 (unpublished MS, Picton
Library, Liverpool).

29. Jacques Brissot de Warville, *New Travels in the United States of America Performed
in 1788* (London, 1792), 372. Similarly in England, William Paley anticipated the
difficulty of finding employment for ex-convicts. Paley opposed the incarceration
of petty offenders "until this inconvenience be remedied." William Paley, *The Principles of Moral and Political Philosophy,* 7th ed. (London, 1790), 2:293 and n. By
contrast, Benjamin Rush dismissed as misguided the fear that incarceration would
produce alienation; see his *Enquiry into the Effects of Public Punishment upon
Criminals and upon Society* (Philadelphia, 1787), 27–29.

30. "Remarks on The Massachusetts State Prison," in *Rules and Regulations for the Government of the Massachusetts State Prison Adopted by the Board of Directors* (Boston,
1823), 26. The observation was common, e.g., Society for the Prevention of Pauperism, *Report on the Penitentiary System in the United States* (New York, 1822), app.
20; Beaumont and Tocqueville, *On the Penitentiary System,* 38n (Francis Lieber's
commentary); "Mass. Legislative Documents," 1817–22, no. 1:20–21 (State Library
Annex); Edward Livingston, *The Complete Works of Edward Livingston on Criminal Jurisprudence* (New York, 1873), 1:73; [James Austin], "Book Review," *N. Am.
Rev.* 10 (1820):253–55; Roberts Vaux, *Notices of the Original and Successive Efforts
to Improve the Discipline of the Prison at Philadelphia* (Philadelphia, 1826), 42–43;
Prison Discipline Soc'y 1 (1826):68; id. 8 (1833):144. (For a similar indictment of
the early workhouse, see [Peter Chamberlen], *The Poore Mans Advocate* [1649]
[London, n.d.], 47.) Thomas Eddy knew of only *two* ex-convicts who had achieved
success and won the respect of their communities. Eddy added tellingly that their
status as former inmates had been kept secret from their neighbors. Thomas Eddy
to George Tibbits, Stephen Allen, and Samuel Hopkins (Jan. 7, 1825), in Knapp, *Life,*
78–79; cf. *Prison Discipline Soc'y* 8 (1833):22; Beaumont and Tocqueville, *On the
Penitentiary System,* 56–57.

31. *Acts and Resolves of the Province of the Massachusetts Bay* (Boston, 1869–1922),
1:287 [1695].

32. See chapter 7, note 174, on efforts to combat convict alienation. Warden Bradford
could be so callous as to identify loss of family support as part of the *deterrence* of
carceral punishment; see [Bradford], *State Prisons,* 14–15. But the custom of overstint was instituted in part to facilitate family support. E.g., Beaumont and Tocqueville, *On the Penitentiary System,* 38n (Francis Lieber's commentary); *Remarks on
Prisons and Prison Discipline* (Boston, 1826), 35 (reprinted from the *Christian Examiner, 3, no. 3).

33. Apathy was widespread by the 1850s, when organizations devoted to the study of
carceral theory, such as the Prison Discipline Society, disbanded. W. David Lewis,
From Newgate to Dannemora (Ithaca, 1965), ch. 11; Rothman, *Discovery of the Asy-*

lum, ch. 10; see generally Francis A. Allen, *The Decline of the Rehabilitative Ideal* (New Haven, 1981).

34. Answer of the Senate, n.d., *Mass. Resolves,* May 1818:587.
35. See generally Calvert P. Dodge, *A World without Prisons: Alternatives to Incarceration throughout the World* (Lexington, 1979); Douglas McDonald, *Punishment without Walls: Community Service Sentences in New York City* (New Brunswick, 1986).

Index